A
BROTHERHOOD
OF
VALOR

✛

The Common Soldiers of

the Stonewall Brigade, C.S.A.,

and the Iron Brigade, U.S.A.

JEFFRY D. WERT

SIMON & SCHUSTER

SIMON & SCHUSTER
Rockefeller Center
1230 Avenue of the Americas
New York, NY 10020

Designed by Karolina Harris
Manufactured in the United States of America
10 9 8 7 6 5 4 3 2 1
Library of Congress Cataloging-in-Publication Data
Wert, Jeffry D.
A brotherhood of valor : the common soldiers of the Stonewll Brigade, C.S.A., and the Iron
Brigade, U.S.A. / Jeffry D. Wert.
p.   cm.
Includes bibliographical references and index.
1. Confederate States of America. Army. Stonewall Brigade. 2. United States. Army. Iron
Brigade (1861–1865) 3. United States—History—Civil War, 1861–1865—Regimental histories.
4. United States—History—Civil War, 1861–1865—Personnal narratives. 5. United States—
History—Civil War, 1861–1865—Personnal narratives, Confederate. 6. United States—His-
tory—Civil War, 1861–1865—Campaigns. I. Title.
E581.4.S8W47   1999
973.7'4—dc21   98-27643
CIP
ISBN 0-684-82435-3
All illustrations except the sketch by Sullivan Green are from the U.S. Army and Military His-
tory Institute; the sketch by Sullivan Green is from Sullivan Green Papers, Bentley Historical Library, University of Michigan.

To the memory of
Ruth McCool Springer,
my grandmother, who told me
wonderful stories about the past,
and of Richard and Bernice Mann,
who gave me an opportunity.

CONTENTS

PREFACE

O N a July morning nearly seventeen months ago, I stood alone at the edge of the Cornfield on Antietam National Battlefield outside Sharpsburg, Maryland. I had arrived early, before the park opened and others shared the ground with me. Before me lay some of the most hallowed ground in the United States, where visitors, like myself, try to understand, to see what can no longer be seen, or to hear what time has silenced. It was a special place for me, however. I knew the names of men who had fought there on that terrible Wednesday in September 1862, and had read their letters and diaries. I remembered Edwin A. Brown, a Wisconsin captain who wanted only to go home and to rest, and a Virginia private whom I knew only as Robbie, whose poignant letter to his wife after the battle reminded me of war's price.

I had time to look at the Miller and Poffenberger farmsteads, to walk across Hagerstown Pike to a rock ledge and to West Woods. The white-washed Dunker Church was unmistakable as the morning sun touched its walls. There was a silence over the ground, a welcome companion. Monuments, with chiseled words, marked unit positions. It was an awful place once on a late summer's day.

A group of uncommon men had brought me back to Antietam. Where I stood, they had fought each other directly as enemies during the battle. They were more alike than different, believed in duty and honor, but had answered opposing summons when their nation had embraced a furious wind. Home to them meant Virginia or Wisconsin and Indiana. Where I stood, men of the Stonewall Brigade and men of the Iron Brigade bled together across a killing ground.

This book is their story. It is more a dual history than a comparative study. Recounted together, however, their separate stories allow for the integration of comparative analysis. All soldiers share a brotherhood, the common experience of warfare. By interweaving their journeys through four years of civil war, this book offers a different perspective upon two groups of common soldiers who comprised the most renowned infantry commands of the conflict. Much of the retelling of their story has been left to them.

I selected these two brigades for several reasons. First of all, their reputations as combat units enticed me. Secondly, members of both commands left behind a wealth of manuscript material from which an account could be fashioned. Thirdly, they fought in the same theater, participated in many of the same battles, and on three fields stood opposite each other in combat. Finally, as a historian, I wanted to share their journeys, to revisit with them Henry House Hill, Kernstown, Brawner's Farm, the Cornfield, McPherson's Ridge, and the Bloody Angle.

My journey has only been possible because of the collective efforts of others. For those individuals who offered their assistance, I extend my sincere gratitude. Their knowledge and insight have made this a better book, but all errors are solely the responsibility of the author.

First of all, I wish to thank the archivists and librarians at the institutions cited in the bibliography for their understanding, expertise, and patience with my requests for materials.

Other individuals deserve my particular recognition:

Michael Musick, archivist, National Archives; Dr. Richard Sommers and David Keough, archivists, and Michael Winey, photograph curator, United States Army Military History Institute; Ted Alexander and Paul Chiles, historians, Antietam National Battlefield; D. Scott Hartwig, historian, Gettysburg National Military Park; Donald Pfanz, historian, Fredericksburg-Spotsylvania National Military Park; David L. Poremba, librarian, Detroit Public Library; Diane B. Jacob, archivist, Virginia Military Institute; John M. Coski, historian, Museum of the Confederacy; Harold L. Miller, archivist, State Historical Society of Wisconsin; and C. Stanley Vaughan, librarian, Washington and Lee University.

Curtis R. Kemery, a Civil War reenactor, for sharing with me material on the Thirty-third Virginia.

Gary L. Ecelbarger, a fellow historian, for sharing with me material related to the Battle of Kernstown.

Brian Pohanka, Civil War historian and author, for sharing with me material on Charles S. Winder.

Catherine Boyers, a fellow Civil War buff, for assisting with the research.

Gary Kross, Licensed Battlefield Guide at Gettysburg and a fellow historian, for reading my chapter on that battle.

Allan Tischler, longtime friend and fellow historian, for his extraordinary research efforts on my behalf, and for his friendship.

Nick Picerno, Sr., dear family friend and fellow historian, for reading my chapters on Antietam and Gettysburg, and for his friendship and counsel.

William Miller, Civil War historian and editor, for reading several chapters of the manuscript.

Alan Nolan, a friend and a historian, whose study of the Iron Brigade remains the benchmark for all who follow, for reading most of the manuscript, offering much insight, and correcting errors.

Robert K. Krick, a friend, historian, and the authority on the Army of Northern Virginia, for reading the portions of the manuscript on the Stonewall Brigade, correcting my mistakes, challenging my conclusions, and improving the text.

Robert Gottlieb, my agent, for his counsel and support.

Bob Bender, my editor, for his acceptance of the idea, for his advice, kindness, and understanding, and for his friendship.

Jason and Natalie, our son and daughter, and Kathy, our daughter-in-law, for their love and for their understanding.

Gloria, my wife, for sharing my journey from beginning to end, for her countless hours of work on the manuscript, for her love, and for all that makes life meaningful and fulfilling.

Jeffry D. Wert
Centre Hall, Pennsylvania
December 3, 1997

Author's Note

Officers and enlisted men earned promotions throughout the course of the Civil War. Given the large number of names in this book, such promotions are seldom noted. Instead, when soldiers are mentioned in the text, they are given the rank they held at that point in the war.

1

GATHERINGS

CHURCH bells rang in Winchester, Virginia, on Thursday, April 18, 1861. More than ninety miles farther south, up the Shenandoah Valley, in Staunton, "a great state of excitement" prevailed as townsfolk jammed the streets. What had been speculated about for weeks and anticipated for days in both towns had become a reality. Telegrams had arrived from Richmond, announcing the secession of Virginia from the Union. The bells of Winchester tolled for a revolution.[1]

A second telegram followed from Governor John Letcher, ordering militia companies in the Valley, as the region was familiarly known, to seize the United States arsenal at Harper's Ferry and its valuable cache of weapons and arms-making machinery. Letcher's directive brought an immediate response, and by midnight of the 19th, units from Winchester and Charlestown entered Harper's Ferry, located at the northern end of the Valley at the confluence of the Potomac and Shenandoah rivers. The arsenal's contingent of troops had torched many buildings before it departed, but the militiamen and local residents saved the machinery and thousands of finished rifles and parts.[2]

In the days that ensued additional companies of Valley men arrived at Harper's Ferry. The units bore names such as the West Augusta Guards,

Augusta Rifles, Rockbridge Rifles, Staunton Artillery, Southern Guards, and Mountain Guards. Each company had its own "uniform"—the Mountain Guards wore red flannel shirts and gray trousers; the West Augusta Guards and Augusta Rifles, gray woolen jackets and trousers; and the Southern Guards, blue flannel shirts, gray trousers, and United States Navy caps. One company carried a flag given to it while en route from women in Harrisonburg.[3]

The colorful attire could not hide the rawness of the militiamen. Before these days, the companies had "played military," in the words of one member. But the seizure of the arsenal heralded a reckoning, an act of war against their national government. The novice soldiers, however, embraced the future. The men "are ready for a fight," a militia captain assured friends and relatives at home, adding that "if a fight occurs, we will be the first in it, and the last out of it." Another officer in a letter to a newspaper asserted that "we are in the midst of a great revolution; our people are united as one man, and are determined to maintain their rights at every sacrifice."[4]

During their trip northward, down the Valley, the militiamen had witnessed a flood of enthusiasm and support by neighbors and strangers. "I have never seen such an outpouring of popular feelings in behalf of the South," recounted an officer. "We were as well treated as if we were paying 3/per day," claimed a private. The civilians cheered and hugged the volunteers, shared food with them, and pledged devotion to the cause.[5]

This response to recent events had followed a winter of doubt and apprehension. Like their fellow Americans, Valley residents had watched closely the quickening of time since the election of Republican Abraham Lincoln to the presidency in November 1860. Many citizens in the region had voted for John Bell, the compromise candidate in the election. The secession of Lower South states and the formation of the Confederate States of America "weighed heavily on spirits" of those in the Valley. They opposed unsuccessfully a secessionist convention for Virginia, and when the time came to select delegates, they chose "conservative *Union* men" in many of the counties.[6]

In the Shenandoah Valley of Virginia, roots went deep into the rich soil. Pioneer settlers had entered the region between the Blue Ridge Mountains on the east and the Allegheny Mountains on the west decades before the American Revolution. They were Scotch-Irish, who wrenched it from the natives, whose name for the region meant "Daughter of the Stars," and built homes and mills and platted towns. Germans followed and made the fertile earth blossom and nourish. Craftsmen offered various products, and amid the natural beauty, the inhabitants prospered. The region sent forth its own as riflemen under Daniel Morgan to fight the British, and gave again during the War of 1812 and the conflict with Mexico. By the 1850s, a macadamized turnpike linked villages, and railroads breached the Blue Ridge. Within the valley's confines, night often settled in easily.[7]

The Valley seeped into bones, touched souls, and when the national crisis climaxed in April 1861, the Valley residents looked to their own. The bombardment and surrender of Fort Sumter in Charleston, South Carolina, harbor on April 12–14 caused Lincoln to call for volunteers to suppress the rebellion. With the proclamation, allegiance to the Union ended in much of the Shenandoah Valley. In Staunton, a newspaper publisher spoke for his readers, writing that the people "were united with a firm and universal determination to resist the scheme set on foot by Lincoln to subjugate the South."[8]

And so the Valley gave once again of its fathers, sons, and husbands. The response of the militia companies to Governor Letcher's summons was but small eddies that during April, May, and June turned into a river of volunteers. On April 20, the governor asked for recruits to "repel invasion and protect the citizens of the state in the present emergency." From the length and breadth of the Valley, men enlisted for twelve months. Farmers in Grayson County along the North Carolina border, mountain men from Highland and Allegheny counties, students from Washington College and cadets from Virginia Military Institute (VMI) in Lexington, merchants and clerks from Staunton, and Irish railroad workers from Shenandoah County enrolled. They walked, crowded into wagons, or boarded trains, with some detoured to Richmond before being ordered to their common destination at Harper's Ferry. Watching the passage from her home in Winchester, a woman likened it to a "gathering of the clans."[9]

At Harper's Ferry, the companies with such names as the Montgomery Highlanders, Tenth Legion Minute Men, Emerald Guard, Liberty Hall Volunteers, Virginia Hibernians, and Berkeley Border Guards would be organized in the weeks ahead into regiments. Companies of Valley men filled entirely, except for a handful of units from the western mountains, the ranks of the five infantry regiments and artillery battery that would become the Stonewall Brigade. The command "comprised the very pride and flower of the upper counties of Virginia," boasted a Winchester woman.[10]

Few, if any, Confederate brigades reflected such commonality of place, heritage, and kinship. "I never saw so many persons I knew in my life," remarked a member, "every third person speaks to me." Every company of the command contained descendants of the Scotch-Irish pioneers. Those of German, English, Irish, and Swedish ancestry stood beside the Scotch-Irish in the ranks. A surgeon of the brigade estimated later that only one man in thirty belonged to a slaveholding family. Little class distinction separated enlisted men from officers. Strong-armed farmers stood beside eloquent lawyers; unshaven college students beside bearded mountaineers.[11]

Blood ties bound many to each other. One volunteer thought that the brigade appeared to be a "cousinwealth." One regiment counted eighteen members of the Bell family of Augusta County, eleven of whom were destined to be either killed or mortally wounded in battle or to die of disease. Pairs of brothers, fathers and sons, uncles and nephews shared mess fires in the regiments.[12]

"America was young, and filled with younger sons," recalled a member. Approximately sixty percent of the volunteers were those "younger sons" between eighteen and twenty-five years old. The most common age was nineteen, with the majority of men in this age group in their early twenties. A few members had lived for sixty years, while a handful at fourteen and fifteen had barely passed childhood. Private David Scanlon was an unusual recruit, a fifty-one-year-old drummer boy.[13]

Characteristic of the Valley and of much of America, farmers and farm laborers comprised the largest segment of the command. There were dozens of professional men, clerks, and merchants, and scores of artisans, craftsmen, and mechanics that reflected the vibrancy and diversity of the economy in the region. Other occupations listed on enrollment papers included undertaker, jeweler, nailcutter, druggist, artist, distiller, confectioner, hatter, toymaker, and gentleman. One private listed himself as a "comedian," and another as a "Yankee school master." One company of roughly one hundred men had twenty-six different occupations noted on the rolls.[14]

"Probably no brigade in the Civil War contained more educated men," a historian of the command has asserted. Current students and alumni of Washington College and the Virginia Military Institute in Lexington, and the University of Virginia in Charlottesville were among the rank and file in each regiment. One company, the Liberty Hall Volunteers, was recruited on the campus of Washington College and included fifty-seven members of the seventy-three-man student body, with a quarter of the volunteers studying for the ministry. VMI cadets and graduates provided a core of drillmasters and officers for the brigade.[15]

The organization of the companies into regiments occurred throughout April, May, and June. Most of the volunteers entered the service under the authority of Virginia, but on June 8, Governor Letcher transferred the state units into the armies of the Confederacy, with the men's original twelve-month term of enlistment remaining in effect.[16]

Civil War infantry regiments consisted, as a rule, of ten companies, designated by the letters A–K, except for the letter J. United States Army regulations prescribed a company size of 3 officers and 98 enlisted men. With 15 field and staff officers, a regiment numbered 1,025 officers and men at authorized strength. Although the Confederacy would adopt a slightly higher figure for a regiment—1,389 officers and men—few regiments on either side ever had a full complement during the war. The recruitment of new volunteers and the infusion of conscripted or drafted men never restored a regiment to the numbers it possessed at its original mustering in. Both governments chose to create new units instead of filling old regiments to authorized strength.[17]

In turn, usually three or four regiments were organized into a brigade, which was, according to a historian, "the fundamental fighting unit of the army." Once again, Confederate brigades consisted generally of more regiments—five or six—than their Union counterparts. Because of the importance of localism in the South, most Confederate brigades contained regiments from the same state. Regulations in both armies designated a brigadier general as commander of a brigade. Casualties among officers of that rank resulted often, however, in the temporary appointment of a senior colonel to the command. Finally, three or four brigades comprised a division under a major general. In time, both governments created corps of three or four divisions within an army or department.[18]

Consequently, as the companies of Valley men gathered at Harper's Ferry, officers organized them into regiments. The effort consumed weeks, but eventually forty-eight companies were assigned to the five regiments—the Second, Fourth, Fifth, Twenty-seventh, and Thirty-third Virginia—that would constitute the future Stonewall Brigade. Each regiment had at its core companies from a particular section of the region—the Second Virginia consisted entirely of companies from four counties in the northern end or Lower Valley; the Fourth was formed with a majority of its companies from the Upper Valley; the Fifth originated from the militia companies of Staunton and Augusta County; the Twenty-seventh counted most of its members from the mountainous counties of southwestern Virginia, beyond the Valley proper; and, the Thirty-third contained volunteers from six counties, with Shenandoah County contributing one half of the number.[19]

The regimental field officers—colonel, lieutenant colonel, and major for each unit—were men who possessed either prior military education, militia training, or Mexican War experience, or had been leaders within their communities. Of the thirteen field officers—the Thirty-third had only a colonel initially—five were graduates of VMI, two had attended West Point, four had fought in the Mexican War, and/or four had served as militia officers. One of them, Lawson Botts, an attorney, had been a "decided and uncompromising opponent of secession doctrines" and had defended abolitionist John Brown, whose raid on Harper's Ferry, in October 1859, hastened the destruction of the Union. Like Botts, four others practiced law, while Kenton Harper, a native Pennsylvanian, was a distinguished newspaper publisher, politician, and farmer.[20]

The company commanders or captains in the five regiments reflected the diverse origins and composition of their units. Like the field officers, at least one third of them had either prior military training or experience. The remaining captains were usually men of local stature—mayors, attorneys, state legislators, businessmen, and well-to-do farmers. Among the group several were destined to attain higher rank and to play prominent roles in the brigade's history, including John Quincy Adams Nadenbousch, James A. Walker, Charles A. Ronald, John Henry Stover Funk, Hazael J. Williams, Frederick W. M. Holliday, and Abraham Spengler.[21]

Among the regimental captains none perhaps had sacrificed more for his loyalty to Virginia than Thompson McAllister. Born in Juniata County, Pennsylvania, in 1811, McAllister had prospered in his native state and had served in the legislature. In 1849, he moved with his family to Covington, Virginia, bought 2,200 acres of land, built a large brick home, Rose Dale, and made money in the milling business and in promoting railroads. McAllister remained in touch with his family, particularly his brother Robert. In January 1860, he returned to Pennsylvania for a family reunion during which he and Robert engaged in a heated argument over politics. The brothers departed enemies, and when the nation divided, Thompson joined the Twenty-seventh and Robert became lieutenant colonel of the First New Jersey. The wound between the brothers never healed.[22]

In May, an artillery battery from Lexington arrived in Harper's Ferry, and in time would be attached to the brigade of Shenandoah Valley regiments. Within a week of Virginia's secession, seventy recruits had enrolled, voted to be an artillery company, and adopted the name Rockbridge Artillery. On May 1, William Nelson Pendleton asked the company if he could serve as its captain, and the men accepted the offer. Pendleton was an 1830 graduate of West Point, but since 1838 had devoted his life to the ministry. He was serving as rector of the Grace Episcopal Church in Lexington when the war began.[23]

"Old Penn," as the young gunners dubbed Pendleton, drilled the company with borrowed small brass cannon from VMI. On May 11, the Rockbridge Artillery departed for Harper's Ferry with two cannon while Pendleton traveled to Richmond for additional guns. Pendleton obtained two, and rejoining the company at Harper's Ferry, resumed drilling the gunners with four cannon that were soon named Matthew, Mark, Luke, and John. By June 30, the battery consisted of Pendleton, three lieutenants, and eighty-one enlisted men.[24]

The formal organization of the forty-eight infantry companies and one artillery company lasted into July. Throughout the weeks, the Valley men labored with the rigors of military drill and discipline. But the volunteers maintained their morale and gave the reasons for their and their families' sacrifices. "The men work willingly," Captain William S. H. Baylor assured folks in Augusta County, "eat heartily, and sleep as soundly on the ground, as a prince in a palace. They are ready for a fight, and I believe are eager to show their courage in driving back any invading force."[25]

To the officers and men of the brigade, the stakes were evident. The actions of the Lincoln administration threatened the rights of Virginians and the beloved Valley itself. They understood the gravity of their choice, for as a member asked his wife, "Is not this Revolution?" A lieutenant stated to his wife that he and his men were engaged "in a glorious cause," one "of defending our good old dominion from the threatened invasion of northern hords."[26]

Lieutenant Samuel J. C. Moore, Second Virginia, worried whether his young sons would understand their father's absence and his reasons for entering the army. Most likely speaking for many other fathers he wrote home:

Do you know for what your Papa has left his family and his home and his office and his business? I will tell you. The State of Virginia called for all the men who are young and able to carry arms, to defend her against Lincoln's armies, and it is the duty, I think, of every man to answer her call, and be ready to keep the army of our enemies from ever setting their feet in the State.

War is a dreadful thing, and I would rather do anything in the world than kill a man or help to kill one, but then if we were to let Lincoln's army pass here, they might go into the State of Virginia, and burn our houses and kill the old men and the women and children, and do a great deal more harm, and I am sure I would rather see a thousand of them killed around me, than to know that they had done any harm to my wife and dear little boys.[27]

So Moore and his comrades prepared for the "dreadful thing" at the gateway to the Shenandoah Valley. With a swiftness they probably never expected, their lifelong allegiance to the old country had been severed. Now they were willing revolutionaries, defending home and family, bound to the cause by duty. In the Valley, as they learned to be warriors, the wheat crop "never was more promising." For it to ripen and to nourish those at home, the Valley men stood in ranks.[28]

Spring only beckoned across Wisconsin in mid-April 1861. Winter was a stubborn adversary, a season with an iron grip. During the months of the long nights, in farmhouses, villages, and lumbering camps, the residents had waited for news from the East. The state's voters had gone for Abraham Lincoln, and then watched as a succession of Southern states withdrew from the Union and created a new government. And now they waited more as the melting snows filled creeks.

Wisconsin had offered them a renewal, like the promise within spring's new grasses and flowers. During the previous two decades, they had flooded into the territory and brought it statehood in 1848. They were Americans come from New England, New York, Pennsylvania, and the states along the Ohio River, and German, Scandinavian, and Irish immigrants. In 1860, the census counted a population of over three quarters of a million residents in fifty-eight counties. They planted fertile fields in grains, milked cows, sheared sheep, cured cheese, hewed timber, and brewed beer. For many, if not most, Wisconsin had kept its word.[29]

But they saw beyond Wisconsin's promise to that of America's. To them, the country offered opportunity found nowhere else in the world, for if Wisconsin played out, a common man could begin again in another territory or state. As the crisis, brought by secession, deepened, they steeled themselves. A La Crosse newspaper in a typical editorial admonished its readers: "There is a grand old storm coming up—there will be such fighting as this country has never yet seen, and that right soon. This is no time for wavering."[30]

When the news of Fort Sumter, followed by Lincoln's summons for volunteers, reached Wisconsin, the citizenry did not waver. "Patriotism was effervescent," claimed one man. On April 18, as militiamen marched away to cheers in Staunton, Virginia, residents of Oshkosh met in what the local newspaper described as the "greatest and most enthusiastic gathering which ever assembled" in the community. Across the state townsfolk held similar "war meetings." "Every rugged backwoodsman, whether American, German or Norwegian, was full of patriotism," a citizen avowed. "Indignation at the firing on Fort Sumter was genuine and universal." An Irish farmhand and future recruit put it simply, "I want to do what I can for my country."[31]

Two days before the Oshkosh meeting, on April 16, Governor Alexander W. Randall issued a proclamation to the state's residents. "For the first time in the history of this Federal Government," Randall began, "organized treason has manifested itself with several States of the Union, and armed rebels are making war against it." He then noted the consequences of treason, affirming that the attack against a federal installation must be met "with a prompt response." He concluded with a call for unity: "It is a time when, against the civil and religious liberties of the people, and against the integrity of the Government of the United States, parties and politicians and platforms must be as dust in the balance. All good citizens, everywhere, must join in making common cause against a common enemy."[32]

Randall also stated in the proclamation that one regiment of militia "will be required for immediate service, and further service will be required as the exigencies of the Government may demand." Within days enough companies had volunteered for three months' service to organize the First Wisconsin Infantry. An additional nineteen companies had offered their services, so on April 23, the governor authorized the creation of the Second Wisconsin Infantry, the first regiment to be organized that would become a part of the Iron Brigade. Randall ordered the three-month volunteers of the Second Wisconsin to report to Madison, the state capital, by May 1.[33]

The ten companies of the Second Wisconsin came from nine counties across the breadth of the state. From Racine County came the Belle City Rifles, a unit composed entirely of unmarried men; from Winnebago County, the Oshkosh Volunteers, formed by members of a local fire company; from Rock County, the Beloit Cadet Rifles, whose ranks included a dozen students and graduates of Beloit College; and from Grant County, the Grant County Grays, one fifth of its members listing their place of birth as outside the United States. Four companies—the Portage Light Guard, La Crosse Light Guard, Citizens Guard, and Miners Guard—originated as prewar militia units. The Janesville Volunteers, like the Beloit Cadet Rifles, hailed from Rock County, while the Randall Guards filled its ranks in Madison and surrounding Dane County.[34]

The volunteers departed from their homes for the state capital amid an outpouring of support. The local heroes received meals, heard speeches, were presented with flags, and were accompanied to railroad stations by vociferous crowds. Like Virginians and other Americans, North and South, Wisconsinites gave of their own in a torrent of celebration. Over a year later, after the cheers had died long past, one of the recruits explained to his parents why he had boarded a train for Madison. "With thousands of others," he wrote, "I was so much excited at the thought of treason breaking out in our Old Union that I thought nothing but to be if possible the first to enroll my name amongst those of her defenders."[35]

The La Crosse Light Guard from La Crosse County and the Portage Light Guard from Columbia County arrived together on the same train in Madison, on May 1. Officials directed them to the State Agricultural Society's Fairgrounds, a forty-acre area located about a mile from the city that had been converted recently into a training camp for soldiers. Even as the two companies passed through the gate, scores of workers were changing cattle pens into barracks. During the next fortnight, the remaining companies of the Second Wisconsin joined the La Crosse and Portage volunteers at the fairgrounds, now designated as Camp Randall.[36]

Camp Randall served as home to the regiment for the next seven weeks. The installation offered few comforts. "We are cooped up in a 40 acre lot fenced in," Horace Emerson informed his brother on May 10, "and our Barracks are made up by the side of the fence and every time it rains the damn Shanties leak and wets our beds." They slept on beds of hay, had not enough blankets, drank "dish water coffee," and awoke each morning from the discharge of a large brass cannon. The regimental historian later described their stay at the camp as "the short woodshed life in Madison."[37]

The cannon's blast began the daily routine for the men at Camp Randall. The recruits drilled twice a day at first, four times a day by the end of the month. First sergeants of companies usually conducted the drills, with one or more officers present. At night, many of the men visited Madison, and if the opinion of one of them was shared by most of the men, the city had few inducements. Alured Larke grumbled that "there is scarcely a pretty woman here," adding that "as a town Madison is miserably dull, as a capital wretched." After some members of the Janesville Volunteers participated in a "great rumpus" in the city, no man was allowed to leave camp without a pass signed by his captain and the regimental colonel.[38]

Despite the assertion by one member that "our boys are all good hearted Noble fellowes we all love one another as Brothers," evidence indicates that an element in the regiment did not accept willingly the strictures of military discipline. In fact, one officer described them "on the whole" as "rough, vulgar blackguards." Even the Second's historian admitted that "the regiment had become a terror" to Madison's citizens by the time it departed.[39]

Responsibility for the discipline of and instruction of the rank and file belonged to the company commanders and field officers, the latter of whom had been selected by Governor Randall. For the colonelcy of the Second, Randall picked a prominent Milwaukee lawyer and former attorney general of the state, S. Park Coon. A forty-one-year-old native of New York, Coon had been a resident of Wisconsin for nearly two decades, and during the winter of 1861 had been outspoken in his support of the Union. He knew little, if anything, about commanding a regiment, drank too much whiskey, but counted among his friends the governor for whom Coon had named the camp. Within the regiment, it was believed that the subordinate officers would compensate for Coon's shortcomings.[40]

Randall appointed Henry W. Peck as lieutenant colonel and Duncan McDonald as major. Peck was an Ohioan by birth and had attended West Point but withdrew before being graduated. "A great deal was expected of Peck," stated a member of the Second. Like Peck, McDonald had some military experience, having served for two years as a colonel in the state militia. When the war began, McDonald was a prominent and respected Milwaukee businessman.[41]

The captains, elected by their respective companies, were men of local stature. Six of them had practiced law in their communities, while the other four owned and/or operated a business. Each captain had been involved in the recruitment of a company. George H. Stevens of the Citizens Guard, John Mansfield of the Portage Light Guard, and William E. Strong of the Belle City Rifles would be the best of the group.[42]

On May 9, the volunteers heard a rumor that their three-month term of enlistment was to be changed to three years. For several days, individual companies met and discussed the news, with some men from each company deciding to return home. But only one company, the Beloit Cadet Rifles, refused to enroll for three years. On May 15, officers read the order that authorized the change, and at 10:00 A.M., on the 16th the regiment formed, with 517 members sworn in for three years. A week later, the Wisconsin Rifles from Milwaukee County, led by Captain Andrew J. Langworthy, former county sheriff, marched into Camp Randall, replacing the departed Beloit Cadet Rifles.[43]

By the end of May, most of the company ranks had been refilled with unassigned recruits in the camp. June 11 was designated for the mustering in of the regiment into Federal service. To allow men to visit friends and relatives, Coon approved passes to upward of four hundred members on the night of the 10th. Uncounted others sneaked out of camp without passes, and by the early hours of the 11th, gangs of drunken soldiers roamed the streets. A large group of them gathered outside a brewery, demanding admittance. When someone broke a window and others grabbed whiskey bottles, the owner, from an upstairs window, fired a shotgun over the crowd. Several soldiers discharged pistols and threw stones at the gunman. The men fled, however, when neighbors ran into the street.[44]

The next morning, a sobered Second Wisconsin, dressed in state-issued gray uniforms, entered the service of the United States. Nine days later, on June 20, the regiment marched from Camp Randall after receiving a national flag, with "2ND REGT. WISCONSIN VOL." on each side, and after listening to a speech by Randall. The governor wanted to say farewell and to remind them of the cause for which they had volunteered. "This rebellion must be put down in blood," Randall averred, "and treason punished by blood. You go forth not on any holiday errand, not on any Fourth of July excursion, but as men to perform great and urgent duties." They go, he added, "because you will to aid with your own right arms in maintaining the integrity of your Government and my Government."[45]

The 1,048 officers and enlisted men of the Second Wisconsin boarded railroad freight cars for the nation's capital to a chorus of cheers. Many in attendance were undoubtedly glad to see the soldiers leave Madison. The town meetings, the sumptuous meals, and the boisterous support upon the men's enlistment had given away now to the reality of leaving families, friends, and Wisconsin. "It is safe to say," remembered Captain Thomas S. Allen, "that not a man in the regiment knew anything of actual warfare." But the recruits, Allen believed, were "actuated by a common motive and by similar patriotic impulses, yet differing as to policies and parties." Perhaps Corporal Horace Emerson, as he found a place in a car, recalled the words he had told his brother at the time of enlistment. "If I fall," Emerson stated as explanation, "I die in defence of the Flag I was born under and which I will die."[46]

The train carried the Wisconsin men east, through Chicago, Cleveland, Pittsburgh, and on to Harrisburg. At the Pennsylvania state capital, Colonel Coon refused to continue the trip until the regiment was issued arms. During the previous weeks, contingents of Union troops had encountered mobs in Baltimore, Maryland, the next stop for the Second Wisconsin. Authorities consented, issuing 780 Harper's Ferry muskets to the unit. The train proceeded to Baltimore, where the regiment marched from one station to another with loaded and capped muskets. On June 25, the Wisconsin soldiers reached Washington, D.C., and camped along Seventh Street, next to a regiment of New Hampshire troops.[47]

The Western men roamed through the capital as sightseers for about a week, visiting the stone edifices that marked the government they had volunteered to save. Horace Emerson and two fellow corporals arranged a meeting with President Lincoln and drank a glass of wine with the chief executive. After they left the White House Emerson wrote, "bulley for old Abe he is a Brick." "If ever I get a chance to draw sight on a Rebel," the corporal vowed, "down goes his shanty."[48]

The Second Wisconsin filed into column on the afternoon of July 2, and marched across a bridge over the Potomac River into Virginia, a land of "Devels," as one called the Southerners. They were halted at Fort Corcoran on the road to Fairfax Court House, and assigned to a brigade under Colonel William Tecumseh Sherman. "Many were confident," a soldier asserted about his comrades, "that the war would last but for a few months and none anticipated remaining more than a year" away from Wisconsin.[49]

2

✠

FURY ON A HILL

HARPER'S FERRY, Virginia, sat at the northern boundary of the Confederate States of America. The action taken by Virginia Governor John Letcher to seize the arsenal testified to its ordnance value and its strategic importance at the gateway to the Shenandoah Valley. Through the town ran the tracks of the Baltimore & Ohio Railroad, a vital supply line for the Union government. To strengthen its defenses and to bring order to the chaos among the volunteers at the site, Letcher and the state's military commander, Major General Robert E. Lee, assigned Colonel Thomas J. Jackson to the post during the final week of April 1861.[1]

Jackson, dressed in the blue uniform of a VMI faculty member, arrived in Harper's Ferry on the afternoon of April 29. A few of his former students at the institute recognized their former instructor and greeted him. The colonel took a room at a small hotel and established his headquarters at the home of the armory's superintendent. To his wife, Mary Anna, he confided that he had been given "the post which I prefer above all others . . . an independent command."[2]

The new commander was thirty-seven years old, a native Virginian who had been graduated from West Point in 1846 and had earned the brevets of captain and major in the Mexican War. In 1852, he had resigned from the army and had accepted a position on the faculty at the Lexington military school. As a professor, he was noted for dull lectures, strict adherence to a textbook, unbending discipline and integrity, and an intense religious devoutness. Self-discipline and piety formed the steel core of Jackson's being. He was a figure easily ridiculed by young men. The cadets dubbed him "Tom Fool," while swearing that he could see backward.[3]

Jackson was, according to an acquaintance, always in "dead earnest." Before he left Lexington, he warned a group of rowdy cadets, who were celebrating the attack on Fort Sumter by firing guns into the air, "The time for war has not yet come, but it will come and that soon, and when it does come, my advice is to draw the sword and throw away the scabbard." To him, the terribleness of civil war was God's will, and His faithful must accept it and do their duty. His faith, a biographer has averred, "permeated every action of his adult life." When he departed for the war, Jackson went as the Lord's servant and with unsheathed sword.[4]

A man of lesser faith might have questioned his Maker's will had he confronted the problems at Harper's Ferry that Jackson encountered. But in characteristic fashion, the colonel labored long hours to correct innumerable deficiencies. His orders from Letcher and Lee authorized him "to organize into regiments the volunteer forces which have been called into service," and to augment the command by issuing a call for additional companies from the Shenandoah Valley. At once, Jackson relieved all general and field officers of the militia, assigned campsites, instituted a daily regimen of formations and drills, assigned details to work on fortifications, began the organization of companies into regiments, and sent wagons laden with the men's unnecessary clothing and luxuries south to Charlestown. The latter directive moved one Valley recruit to grumble that Jackson "considered a gum cloth, a blanket, a tooth brush and forty rounds of cartridges as the full equipment of a gentleman soldier."[5]

Hundreds of other recruits evidently shared at first the Valley man's complaint. "Few had a good word to throw at the new man," contended Captain William Nelson, while Lieutenant Samuel Moore informed his wife that "the discipline is pretty strict." But Jackson would not bend, and as Nelson added, the volunteers' "notions of war were so completely revolutionized in a short time." The men might have understood him better had they read his words to Lee on May 7: "I am of the opinion that this place should be defended with the spirit which actuated the defenders of Thermopylae, and, if left to myself, such is my determination."[6]

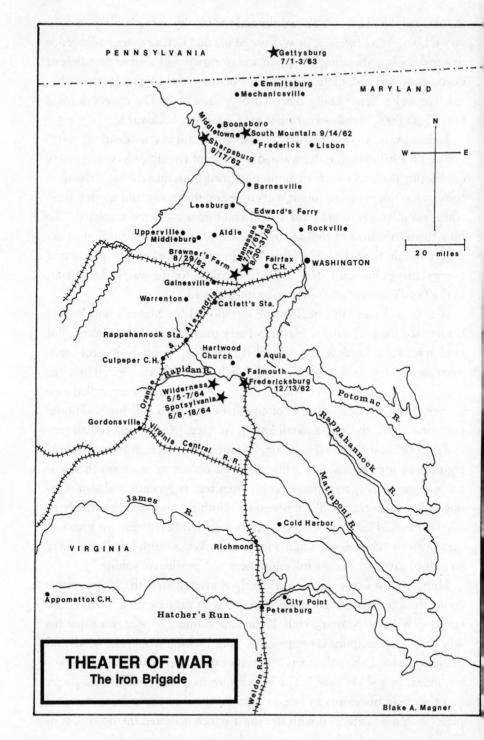

PENNSYLVANIA

★ Gettysburg
7/1-3/63

● Emmitsburg
● Mechanicsville

MARYLAND

Middletown

● Boonsboro
★ South Mountain 9/14/62
● Frederick   ● Lisbon

★ Sharpsburg
9/17/62

N
W ─── E
S

● Barnesville

Leesburg ●
● Edward's Ferry

Upperville ●
Middleburg ●
● Aldie
Manassas
7/21/61 &
8/30-31/62
● Rockville

20 miles

Brawner's Farm
8/29/62
Fairfax
C.H.
● WASHINGTON

● Gainesville
★

Warrenton ●
Catlett's Sta.

Rappahannock Sta.

Hartwood
Church
● Aquia

Culpeper C.H. ●
Rapidan R.
Falmouth
● Fredericksburg
12/13/62

Potomac
R.

Wilderness
5/5-7/64
★
Spotsylvania
5/8-18/64

Gordonsville ●
Virginia Central   R. R.

Rappahannock
R.

James   R.

Mattaponi R.

● Cold Harbor

VIRGINIA
Richmond ●

● Appomattox C.H.

● City Point
Petersburg

Hatcher's Run

Weldon R.R.

THEATER OF WAR
The Iron Brigade

Blake A. Magner

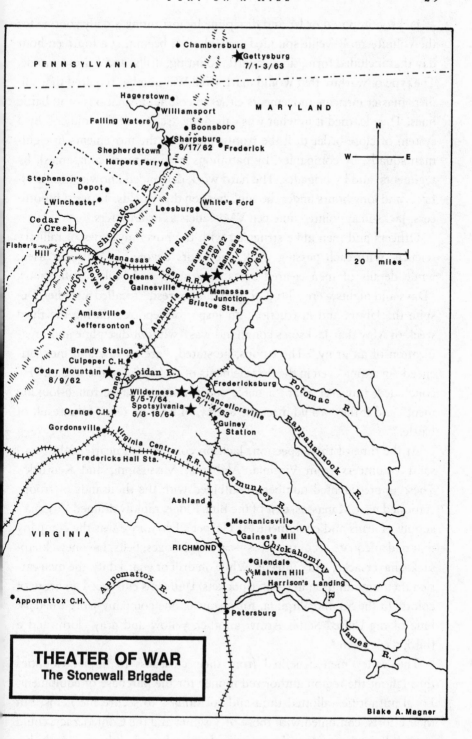

PENNSYLVANIA

• Chambersburg

★ Gettysburg
7/1-3/63

MARYLAND

Hagerstown •
• Williamsport
Falling Waters •
• Boonsboro
★ Sharpsburg
9/17/62   • Frederick
Shepherdstown •
Harpers Ferry •

Stephenson's
Depot •
• Winchester

Leesburg •   • White's Ford

Cedar
Creek

N
W   E
S

Fisher's
Hill

20   miles

Shenandoah R.

Front Royal
Manassas   White Plains
Gap R.R.   Brawner's
Orleans   Farm
Gainesville   8/29/62   Manassas
7/21/61   &
8/30-31
/62
Amissville   Manassas
Jeffersonton   Junction
Bristoe Sta.

Alexandria

Brandy Station
Culpeper C. H. •
Cedar Mountain ★
8/9/62   Rapidan R.

Wilderness ★
5/5-7/64   ★ Chancellorsville
Orange C.H.   Spotsylvania ★   5/1-4/63
5/8-18/64
Gordonsville •   Guiney
Station

Virginia Central R.R.
Fredericks Hall Sta.

Potomac R.

Fredericksburg

Rappahannock R.

Pamunkey R.

Ashland •

• Mechanicsville
• Gaines's Mill
VIRGINIA   RICHMOND •   Chickahominy
• Glendale
Malvern Hill
Appomattox R.   Harrison's Landing

• Appomattox C.H.

• Petersburg

James R.

THEATER OF WAR
The Stonewall Brigade

Blake A. Magner

Jackson imposed order and discipline by instituting a daily routine for the volunteers. Reveille sounded at 5:00 A.M., beginning a fourteen-hour day that included formations, guard mounting, drills, and a dress parade. The type of warfare that would mark Civil War combat required that soldiers master intricate movements either in column formations or in battle lines. They learned it in what was called the "school of the soldier." By a system of close-order drill the troops practiced the movements in eight-man squads, by companies, by battalions (two or more companies), by regiments, and by brigades. The hard work demanded knowledgeable officers and long hours under the sun's heat on dusty fields. To assist his officers, Jackson appointed nineteen VMI cadets as drillmasters.[7]

Officers and men alike struggled with the novel mysteries of military science. With each passing week, the hours devoted to drill increased, while details of men cleared acres of ground and built fortifications. "Days and nights were all full of work and unrest," recalled a soldier. Despite the labors and instruction, an inspector reported during the third week of May that Jackson's command was "without discipline and organization of an army." The troops, he stated, "are all raw and inexperienced—wanting even in the first elements of the school of the soldier." He concluded, however, that "a fierce spirit animates those rough-looking men," and if they would meet the enemy, "I have no fear of the result of battle."[8]

At the time of the inspection, Jackson commanded nearly eight thousand volunteers from Virginia, Alabama, Mississippi, and Kentucky. These unprecedented numbers, combined with the thousands of troops stationed near Manassas, east of the Blue Ridge, rapidly drained Virginia's supply of arms and equipment. At Harper's Ferry, rare was the company that had adequate accoutrements—cartridge boxes, belts, bayonets, knapsacks, haversacks, and canteens. While on drill or guard duty, the men carried their ammunition in trouser pockets. Uniforms embraced an array of colors. In the Second Virginia, for instance, one company wore the dark blue of the United States Army; another, yellow and gray cloth; and a third, dark green.[9]

The Valley men benefited from their closeness to home. Counties throughout the region authorized money for the purchase of equipment. Local authorities allotted thousands of dollars to secure the items; but their efforts, combined with those of Virginia and the Confederacy, could not fulfill the demands at this point in the war. In early July, two weeks before the Battle of Manassas, Jackson's ordnance officer, Lieutenant Alexander S. "Sandie" Pendleton, son of Captain William N. Pendleton of the Rockbridge Artillery, reported that the brigade of five Virginia regiments required 168 belts, 627 cartridge boxes, 733 percussion cap boxes, and 783 bayonet scabbards.[10]

The most critical deficiency, however, related to the variety and the quality of shoulder arms. For months before the war, agents from Southern states had been purchasing weapons in the North and in Europe, stockpiling them against the approaching storm. When the war began, the supplies of arms remained inadequate, and authorities acquired any type of available gun, including outmoded flintlock muskets. Consequently, within regiments, even companies, the troops received different arms in both caliber and firing range. The hodgepodge of weaponry compounded the ammunition supply problems and the training of the men.[11]

Records from the five Virginia regiments that would form the Stonewall Brigade illustrate the shoulder-arm problem in that command. In the Second Virginia, three companies carried .69-caliber muskets altered from flintlock to percussion; one company had .58-caliber smoothbore muskets; and another, .58-caliber rifled muskets, the preferred weapon. In the remaining five companies, men in each unit possessed either a .69-caliber or .58-caliber arm, some smoothbore, some rifled. Eight companies of the Fifth Virginia bore similar shoulder arms, but five of them had the .58-caliber rifled musket that would become the standard Civil War infantry weapon. The disparity of ordnance within the brigade would not be solved for months.[12]

Despite the want of equipment and arms, the volunteers had settled well into the daily routine with its rigors of work and discipline. They had ample food—"good fat beef," bacon, and "the best bread I ever saw," in the words of one of them. "The men were discontented and unmanageable at first," an officer wrote in a letter on May 24, "but are now very well satisfied." Recruits continued to enlist from the Valley. Two members of the Rockbridge Rifles of the Fifth Virginia deserted, however, only to be captured and confined in the town jail. Many complained of sickness at times, but the morale and the "fierce spirit" noted by the inspector remained steadfast. As a private in the Fourth Virginia put it, "we sleep ruff, and live ruff, and we hardly get enough of Scotch snuff, but we must be satisfied and hope for the better."[13]

On the afternoon of May 23, Brigadier General Joseph E. Johnston arrived in Harper's Ferry. A Virginian and West Point classmate of Robert E. Lee, Johnston was one of the Confederacy's most highly regarded and senior officers. He had been ordered by the War Department to assume command of the post and garrison. Unfortunately for the general, he had forgotten a written copy of his appointment, and no one in Richmond had informed Jackson of the change. A rigid adherent to proper, written orders, Jackson refused to relinquish the command until Johnston found a letter from Lee that included an endorsement: "Referred to J. E. Johnston, commanding officer at Harper's Ferry." Jackson stepped aside, and on the 27th, Johnston appointed the colonel to command of the Virginia regiments.[14]

Jackson's brigade consisted of the Second, Fourth, Fifth, and Twenty-Seventh Virginia Infantry—the Thirty-third Virginia lacked enough companies at the time to be organized into a regiment—and the Rockbridge Artillery. Although his responsibility and authority had been reduced, Jackson was where he wanted to be, with troops in the field, readying them for battle. Now he could personally oversee the drills, instill a firmer discipline, and imbue them with their commander's aggressive spirit. He knew the men; he had lived among them for nearly a decade, had taught many of them at VMI or in Sunday School class, and understood their attachment to the Valley and to Virginia. When he learned from his surgeon shortly after assuming command of the regiments that Johnston had derided aloud the mettle of the Second Virginia, Jackson asked: "Did he say that? And of those splendid men?" Pausing, he then affirmed, "The patriotic volunteer, fighting for country and his rights, makes the most reliable soldier on earth."[15]

"Drills and marches and work was the order of the day under our new commander," wrote a brigade member. Roll call at five o'clock in the morning was followed by the first of four hours of drill during the day. At sundown, the regiments marched in a dress parade. Jackson wore seemingly at all times a "grave, solemn countenance." "He was a man who had very little to say," asserted a private. An officer who was assigned temporarily to his staff during this time described his superior as "one of the most conscientious men I know, pious, determined and brave, I like him very much, very fair, very polite." From the beginning, the Virginia soldiers called him "Old Jack."[16]

While Jackson focused his labors on the brigade, Johnston wrestled with the broader responsibility of the Harper's Ferry post. From his arrival, the general regarded the place as indefensible. Sitting in the bottom of a bowl carved by the Potomac and Shenandoah rivers, the town was dominated militarily by surrounding heights, and the position could be easily turned by a Federal advance south up the Valley. By his estimate, the enemy had seven thousand troops at Williamsport, Maryland, upstream on the Potomac, and another two thousand at Romney, sixty miles to the west in the mountains. If the Maryland force crossed the river and combined with the Romney contingent, Johnston and his garrison could be trapped within the bowl.[17]

Johnston tried unsuccessfully to persuade Lee and others in Richmond of the place's vulnerability. In the capital, Harper's Ferry was viewed as indispensable to the defense of Virginia's borders, a symbol of Confederate resistance. Finally, after weeks of exchanged messages, the government acquiesced to Johnston's repeated demands, and on June 15, the garrison abandoned the post, but only after destroying the nine-hundred-foot metal railroad bridge across the Potomac and burning the arsenal works and buildings. Silently, Jackson opposed Johnston's decision. The only satisfaction that he received from the withdrawal was witnessing the spirit with which his brigade marched to meet a reported advance of the Federals. "But when they were ordered to retire," he informed his wife, "their reluctance was manifested by their snail-like pace."[18]

The Confederates retired to the Bunker Hill area north of Winchester. In this section of the Lower Valley, Johnston maintained a bold front for the next month, contesting Union incursions from Maryland. On June 19, for instance, Johnston ordered Jackson, who had been promoted to brigadier general two days earlier, to march with his brigade to Martinsburg, Virginia, west of Harper's Ferry, and to destroy the railroad shops.[19]

The Virginians started in the evening, marching into the night. Jackson pushed the men for several hours. In the heat and the dust, hundreds straggled, falling out of the ranks to rest in fence corners. A soldier described it as "a most wearisome and exhausting journey." An officer thought it was the "severest they have had yet," but the men "take what comes and in the main keep cheerful." When they reached Martinsburg, crews began the work of destruction, burning the shops and engines and cars. Jackson established Camp Stephens four miles north of the town, and here the brigade remained for nearly a fortnight.[20]

While at Martinsburg, Jackson hoped that the Federals would cross the Potomac and offer battle, writing to his wife that "our troops are anxious for an engagement." Confederate cavalry, under Colonel James E. B. "Jeb" Stuart, roamed along the river in Jackson's front to warn of an enemy advance. To keep the 2,300 members of the brigade busy, Jackson drilled them for six hours each day. "The Commander," a VMI drillmaster still with the troops wrote of Jackson, "is strict in requiring attendance at the camp, and wherever to military discipline."[21]

On July 2, while the men ate breakfast, orders came from Jackson to prepare to march. He had received a note from Stuart, who reported that a Union force was less than five miles away and advancing south. Jackson hurried Colonel Kenton Harper's Fifth Virginia and the battery toward the enemy. Harper's skirmishers, posted in the front, like a long knotted string of men, encountered the Northerners near Falling Waters at a bend in the Potomac. Harper pushed his other companies forward to a farmhouse, barn, and outbuildings. The Federals, a brigade of about three thousand troops, opened, in Harper's words, a "very heavy" fire on the Virginians. "My men, however, stood well to their ranks," the colonel stated. "Balls flew in every direction," wrote a private. When the Northerners outflanked the Fifth Virginia's position, the regiment withdrew, ending the minor engagement with a loss of eleven wounded and nine killed or captured.[22]

Falling Waters was the first combat experience for a unit in the brigade. Private George Ruse of the Fifth Virginia became the first member killed. In a letter to Mary Anna, Jackson wrote that "my officers and men behaved beautifully, and were anxious for a battle, this being only a skirmish." A private in the Second Virginia, which was posted in support to the rear, put the day's action in perspective: "The experience was helpful to all; it gave us some idea of what we should have to do, and braced our nerves for that which would surely come to pass."[23]

Jackson retreated after the engagement, and the Federals occupied Camp Stephens, seizing the tents of the Second Virginia that had been left behind mistakenly by the regimental quartermaster. By July 4, the brigade had returned to Winchester, where its plans for a celebration ended in disgust when a captain, who was a member of the Sons of Temperance, so diluted the whiskey "that no toasts were drunk that day." The regiments occupied a campsite in woods north of town and soon returned to the "monotony of camp life." "I have never in the whole course of my life been so utterly discouraged and disheartened," Lieutenant Samuel Moore grumbled in a letter. "A man in the army soon learns or ought to learn,"

Moore added, "to be like an old wagon horse, to obey his master's voice, without asking any questions."[24]

Many members of the brigade shared Moore's discontent and weariness. They had enlisted to defend Virginia, had seen Yankees only from a distance, except at Falling Waters, where only some of their comrades had tasted combat. They had had enough of being "an old wagon horse." "Our troops are eager for a fight," a captain wrote from the Winchester camp. "They are tired out with these two months marching and counter-marching." Fortunately for them, Jackson dispensed with daily drills at the new campsite, but the itch to do their duty, to test their manhood remained. They had not long to wait, however, because of events beyond the Blue Ridge.[25]

For weeks, Northerners and Southerners had watched the escalating prospects of a confrontation in northern Virginia, outside Washington. Confederate forces, under Brigadier General P. G. T. Beauregard, occupied Manassas Junction, where the Manassas Gap Railroad from the Valley connected with the Orange & Alexandria Railroad, which continued south into central Virginia. If the Union army, gathering in numbers outside the capital, planned an overland campaign against Richmond, the railroad junction was vital to the defense of northern Virginia. Here, Beauregard had the rail connections to combine his 22,000 troops with Johnston's 11,000 west of the Blue Ridge.[26]

On July 16, the 35,000-man Union army lumbered out of its camps, marching toward Manassas Junction. Its commander, Brigadier General Irvin McDowell, a West Point classmate of Beauregard, had resisted making a movement with such an untrained army. But Northern newspapers, politicians, and the public clamored for an advance, an "On to Richmond" movement. Abraham Lincoln prodded the general. McDowell relented finally, and his eager volunteers filled the road toward Beauregard's army. The march of slightly more than twenty miles consumed three days. On the 18th, units of each army clashed at Blackburn's Ford on Bull Run, a meandering stream behind which Beauregard planned to give battle. Early that morning, the War Department telegraphed Johnston to join Beauregard "if practicable."[27]

Johnston reacted swiftly. For weeks his opponent in the Valley, Union Major General Robert Patterson, a sixty-nine-year-old relic from the War of 1812, had shown no aggressiveness. Using Stuart's horsemen as a screen, Johnston marched east. Jackson's brigade, which had included the

Thirty-third Virginia since July 15, started at 3:00 P.M., pacing the march. At nine o'clock they forded the Shenandoah River, with the taller men carrying their shorter comrades on their backs across the current. The column passed through Ashby's Gap after midnight and halted outside Paris, where the men slept along the road.[28]

Jackson had them on the road again by four o'clock on the 19th. Two hours later, the men began loading onto freight and cattle cars of the Manassas Gap Railroad at Piedmont Station. One locomotive was available, and the thirty-five-mile ride with the heavy cargo took eight hours. While on board, Private Willie Page of the Liberty Hall Volunteers read a passage from the Twenty-seventh Psalm: "Though an host of men were laid against me, yet shall not my heart be afraid; and though there rose up war against me, yet will I put my trust in him."[29]

The Virginians joined their comrades behind Bull Run on the morning of the 20th, and were placed in line of battle near Blackburn's Ford. Many of them visited the scene of the fighting on the 18th. "A line of fresh graves was rather depressing," admitted one of them. That night in the bivouac area of the Thirty-third Virginia one soldier, attempting to shoot off a toe, ripped apart half his foot. The Virginians slept in a grove of pines. Sergeant Major Randolph Barton never forgot the night, writing years later, "to me there is something inexpressibly melancholy even to this date about the smell of pine woods."[30]

Beyond Bull Run, members of the Second Wisconsin Infantry examined their equipment and arms, filled canteens, and wrote letters home from their camp west of Centreville along the Warrenton Turnpike. At dress parade that evening, officers announced that the army would advance against the Confederates south of the stream at two o'clock next morning. For the Wisconsin men, it appeared that after nearly three difficult weeks in Virginia, they would meet the enemy.[31]

Troubles beset the regiment soon after its arrival at Fort Corcoran on the outskirts of Washington. During the weeks at Camp Randall, Colonel S. Park Coon drank whiskey freely, and evidently once the regiment reached Virginia, his indulgences increased, affecting his ability to lead the unit. His behavior so disgruntled the regimental officers that on July 10, all of them, except a captain, signed a petition, requesting Coon's resignation. The colonel was, according to Captain Andrew Langworthy, "completely unmanned" by the document, arguing that some of the signers were "greater sinners than he." At Langworthy's suggestion, Coon gave the petition to the brigade commander, Colonel William T. Sherman, who told the beleaguered colonel that when the army advanced on the Confederates he could serve on the brigade staff. Lieutenant Colonel Henry Peck could command the regiment if they engaged the enemy.[32]

The brigade to which the regiment had been assigned consisted of the Thirteenth, Sixty-ninth, and Seventy-ninth New York infantry regiments, and Battery E, Third U.S. Artillery. The Sixty-ninth was a regiment of Irishmen with an emerald green flag. The Seventy-ninth, known as "Highlanders," wore magnificent knitted Scotch dress uniforms. The Thirteenth was, in the words of a Wisconsin soldier, "only a common, everyday Yankee regiment like my own." As for the brigade commander, Colonel Sherman, the Western men left behind few comments about one of the army's future architects of victory. Sherman was forty-one years old, an Ohioan, West Pointer, and Mexican War veteran. He had been superintendent of a military academy in Louisiana until January 1861, when he returned North, and with the attack on Fort Sumter, secured a commission.[33]

While at Fort Corcoran, Sherman attempted to train the regiments but had to cancel drills on a number of days because of rainy weather. The troops managed some time at target practice with their shoulder arms. The Wisconsin men had the .69-caliber Harper's Ferry muskets, altered from flintlock to percussion, that had been issued to them in Harrisburg. The men were allowed to fire only two rounds a day, but those who shot more cartridges discovered that the musket overheated rapidly. The men dubbed the faulty weapons "gaspipes." On July 13, however, Company B received new .58-caliber Springfield rifles, apparently at the request of Brigadier General Daniel Tyler, division commander, who had inspected and drilled the regiment four days earlier.[34]

The campsite of the Second Wisconsin was, to a sergeant, "rather a poor one." It had good water, but dozens of men became ill. Here, they were introduced to hardtack or "hard bread," thick three-inch squares made from flour and water. "You might soak a biscuit in a cup of coffee six weeks," wrote a sergeant on July 10, "then you would have to have a good set of teeth to eat it. This kind of bread I suppose was made to *keep*." At night men sneaked away from camp into the countryside to forage for additional food. Some evenings, the regimental brass band played songs, most of which were "of excruciating melody." When the musicians accompanied the troops at a review, "no man," contended an officer, "excepting a broken-legged cripple, could possibly keep step."[35]

With the other units of the Federal army, Sherman's brigade marched west toward Manassas and the Confederates on July 16. In the Second Wisconsin, about one hundred reported unfit for duty and were left in camp under a lieutenant, "whose obesity was a guarantee of his inability to march." Most of the officers in the regiment hired private wagons to haul their dress uniforms and luxuries. They were certain of victory and wanted to be attired properly.[36]

The van of the Union army, Tyler's division, entered Centreville, roughly two miles east of Bull Run, on the morning of the 18th. Tyler had orders from Irvin McDowell to "observe well the roads to Bull Run and Warrenton," but not to "bring on an engagement." Local residents informed the brigadier that Confederate units had retreated west beyond the creek earlier that morning. Tyler decided to send a brigade toward Blackburn's and Mitchell's fords on a reconnaissance. About eleven o'clock Union artillery opened fire on a Southern force behind Blackburn's Ford, and within an hour, Tyler advanced his leading brigade.[37]

At Centreville, meanwhile, the Second Wisconsin and the New York regiments of Sherman's brigade listened to the roar of the heavy guns. It was the first time they had heard artillery fire in an engagement, and a Wisconsin soldier noted in his journal afterward that "it had a peculiarly pleasant sound, there being something so glorious in the thought of a battle for ones country and that battle at hand." Shortly, orders came for an advance, and Sherman's brigade went forward at the double quick after "some ignoramous," in an officer's words, had ordered that pace of march. In the afternoon heat, the men, carrying knapsacks on their backs, wilted under the three-mile march at the double quick. When the exhausted men reached the ridge above the crossing, they formed a battle line in nearby woods.[38]

Confederate artillerists across the creek rattled the woodlot with shells. Suddenly, the sound of cannon was not "so 'peculiarly pleasant'" to the Wisconsin journal writer. One shell burst killed Private Myron Gardner and wounded two other members of the Second. The Irishmen of the Sixty-ninth New York, however, had enough and raced to the rear. When Colonel Coon rode up with orders for the men to lie down, the Second stood erect. The Southern fire came in so rapidly that one Wisconsin soldier compared it to "the heaviest snowstorm in winter." With the Union thrust repulsed, Tyler ordered a withdrawal, and Sherman's brigade bivouacked one mile west of Centreville. A captain in the Second remarked later that the real danger in a battle was not a shrieking artillery shell but a bullet, "which reached one without note or warning."[39]

The Federals waited in their camps while McDowell and his generals plotted a battle plan. When the orders for a march filtered down to the ranks at dress parade on the 20th, the soldiers prepared. In the Second Wisconsin's camp, before lying down to sleep, Private George Davis wrote a letter to his parents. "It will be a great battle the greatest yet," the young private predicted. "God only knows how it will end who amongst us will stand the contest God can only disside should I live I will write as soon as it is over should I fall you will here in time the fate of war shall deside."[40]

Davis and his comrades stirred at two o'clock on Sunday morning, July 21. They carried muskets, canteens, haversacks, blankets, and forty rounds of ammunition. They were "equipped like pack horses instead of men," groused a captain. Thirty minutes later, they filed into a column of four abreast and marched west toward Bull Run. In the darkness, other units angled north and west in McDowell's planned turning movement of the Confederate position behind the creek. At daylight, Sherman's troops crossed Cub Run and soon afterward halted in woods that overlooked the Stone Bridge, where Warrenton Turnpike crossed Bull Run. They lay down, waiting to hear their comrades' attack from the north.[41]

Reveille sounded in the camp of Jackson's brigade before daylight on July 21. The Virginians answered to roll call, and officers inspected arms. Before five o'clock the Second and Twenty-seventh Virginia left their breakfast fires and hurried toward Blackburn's Ford in response to a request from Brigadier General James Longstreet for support. In the Second, several men from each company remained in camp to finish cooking the meals and to carry them to their comrades. Soon, Jackson received orders from army headquarters to move his brigade upstream to support a brigade at Mitchell's and Ball's fords, roughly four miles to the north. The brigadier formed the Virginians into column and sent a staff officer to recall the Second and Twenty-seventh regiments.[42]

The Virginians stumbled across the countryside, "feeling our way along," according to a lieutenant. They reached the position above the fords as cannon fire echoed down Bull Run from the north. From where

the Virginians stood, they could see the puffs from Union guns east of
Stone Bridge. Then after ten o'clock the air seemed to explode with volleys
of musketry to the northwest. Some men in the ranks grumbled that the
battle had begun and that they would miss it. Another hour passed, as the
fury beyond their view intensified. Finally, officers shouted orders to file
into a column. The men shouldered their weapons and stepped off—Jackson was leading them to the assistance of another brigade under attack.[43]

The brigade followed a narrow woods road toward the cannon fire and
musketry. Wounded from the morning's fighting soon appeared, hobbling
to the rear and claiming that the battle had been lost. "Such talk was very
[dispiriting] to raw troops," recalled a member of the Fourth Virginia. "It
was calculated to make a boy wish himself a thousand miles away and in
the trundle bed at his mother's home." When the Virginians emerged from
the trees, they halted at the base of a broad hill. Before them, unscathed infantrymen and artillerists with their guns were spilling over the crest. At
the head of three artillery crews came Captain John D. Imboden from
Staunton. When the artillerist learned the reinforcements were Jackson's
men, he vowed to return to the field, promising that "we'll have warm
work of it, I can tell you."[44]

The Confederate fugitives belonged to the remnants of three infantry
brigades that had been overwhelmed by the main assault of McDowell's
army. Among the fleeing troops were those of Brigadier General Barnard
E. Bee, who encountered Jackson. "General, they are driving us," exclaimed Bee. "Sir," Jackson replied calmly, "we will give them the bayonet." The South Carolinian spurred away to rally his men, while Jackson
turned to deploy the Virginians.[45]

Jackson posted the five regiments in a pine thicket along the southeast
or reverse slope of Henry House Hill, a broad rise that extended several
hundred yards in a roughly east-to-west direction and loomed above the
intersection of Warrenton Turnpike and Sudley Road. The home of
eighty-five-year-old Judith Henry, for whose family the hill was named,
sat on the northwest spur, while a smaller house, belonging to the Robinson family, lay six hundred yards to the northeast. Jackson's line fronted
the fallow fields between the two residences. If the enemy attacked, they
had three hundred yards of open ground to cross.[46]

The Thirty-third Virginia held the brigade's left, with the Second,
Fourth, and Fifth regiments extending the line to a hollow. To their front,
Bee and other officers were re-forming the broken units from the morn-

ing's action. The Twenty-seventh Virginia formed to the rear of the
Fourth. In the infantrymen's front, Jackson placed five cannon, including
three from Imboden's battery. The men lay down amid the pines, sheltered
and concealed by the trees. Jackson rode along the ranks, telling the regimental commanders to be prepared to use the bayonet. Private Thomas
McGraw of the Thirty-third had been telling his comrades throughout the
morning how he wanted a chance at the Yankees, but when he heard the
order about bayonets, he conceded that it meant closer quarters than he
had anticipated.[47]

The alignment of the brigade took an hour, during which time a lull in
the combat blanketed the field. The morning's victory had disorganized
the Federal units, and their officers needed time to reestablish the ranks
before resuming the attack. The initial Union thrust against Henry House
Hill rolled up the northwest slope near the Robinson house finally at 1:30
P.M. Two regiments of New Englanders drove past the building and were
met by a volley from the Fifth Virginia and the Hampton Legion. The
Confederates had advanced into open ground to meet the assault and
were soon pushed back into the woods. The Federals blasted the Southerners with musketry, but the Fifth stood and triggered a volley. Private
Billy Woodward of the Fifth shouted: "I will never retreat! Give me liberty
or give me death!" and died instantly with a bullet in the heart.[48]

The New Englanders recoiled and disappeared over the crest. The combat temporarily subsided, but within thirty minutes two batteries of Union
cannon unlimbered on each side of the Henry house, three hundred yards
from the Virginians. Behind them Federal infantrymen appeared. The
gunners rammed in charges and pulled the lanyards on the pieces. A gale
of iron seared the open ground and shook the pine thicket. Jackson, meanwhile, had gathered additional cannon, and the Rebel artillerists, including the Rockbridge Artillery, opened fire.[49]

For perhaps an hour the battery crews dueled across Henry House Hill.
In the pine thickets, the Virginians hugged the red clay ground. It seemed
like an "incessant shower of shot and shell" to a member of the Second
Virginia. Lieutenant John Lyle of the Fourth Virginia admitted later that
he was scared and uttered prayers, adding "the shorter catechism and
scripture for good measure." One shell killed Sergeant Charles Bell, Corporal William Paxton, and Private Benjamin Bradley, all in Lyle's company. Bell and Bradley had been childhood friends and roommates at
Washington College, and together they died. Men pleaded for the fury to

end. One soldier shouted: "Oh Lord! Have mercy upon me! Have mercy upon me!" Hearing his words, a comrade exclaimed, "Me too, Lord! Me too, Lord!" Speaking for many, one Virginian confessed that "doubtless I wished I was home, but I had to stick."[50]

Dressed in his blue VMI uniform, Jackson rode along the line, assuring the men: "All right my brave Boys this day we will drive the enemy beyond the Potomac." Earlier, a bullet or piece of shell had fractured the middle finger of the general's left hand. To his right, in the hollow beyond the Fifth Virginia, General Bee watched the punishment inflicted upon the Virginians. Turning to the mass of troops, he shouted: "Look, men, there is Jackson standing like a stone wall! Let us determine to die here, and we will conquer! Follow me."[51]

About three o'clock, Union Lieutenant Charles Griffin shifted two of his battery's cannon from south of the Henry house to a position opposite and within two hundred yards of the Thirty-third Virginia's left flank at the end of Jackson's line. The Union gunners raked the Southern batteries and the men of the Thirty-third. The Virginians had earlier been pressed by two enemy infantry regiments until Jeb Stuart's horsemen scattered the Northerners in a charge. If the Thirty-third broke under this new threat, Jackson's entire line would be endangered.[52]

Like all of Jackson's regimental commanders, Colonel Arthur C. Cummings had orders to withhold the men's fire until the enemy was within thirty yards. A VMI graduate and Mexican War veteran, Cummings could see that his eight companies—two had remained in the Valley on guard duty—could not withstand the artillery fire much longer. Many of them clamored for an attack, and finally, Cummings gave the order to charge. The Confederates emerged from the pine trees, crossing the open ground in a disorganized swarm. Seventy yards from the two cannon, whose gunners had withheld their fire, uncertain about the troops' identity amid the acrid smoke, the Virginians halted and unleashed a volley. In minutes, they were among the pair of guns, scattering or capturing the artillerists. The Virginians cheered; it was the first victory for Confederate arms on the field that day.[53]

Cummings and company commanders tried to restore order in the ranks. They failed, and it cost the Virginians dearly. Coming up the northwestern slope of Henry House Hill was the Fourteenth Brooklyn, a Chasseur regiment modeled after French troops, dressed in red trousers, blue jackets, and red kepis. At a murderous distance, the New Yorkers lashed

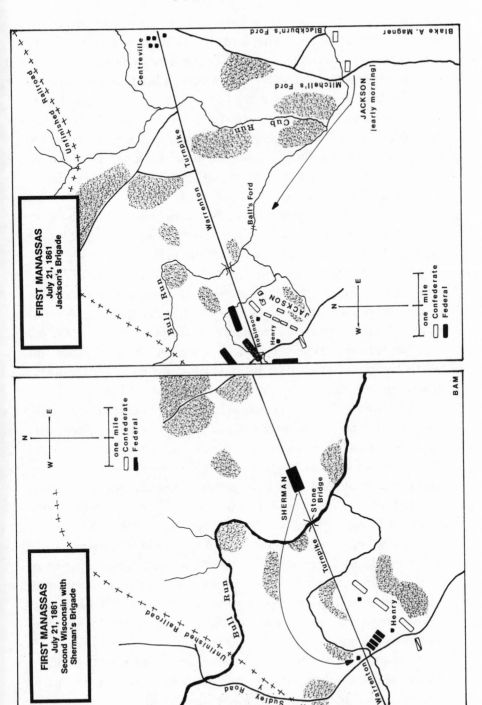

FIRST MANASSAS
July 21, 1861
Jackson's Brigade

FIRST MANASSAS
July 21, 1861
Second Wisconsin with
Sherman's Brigade

the crowd of Virginians with a fearful volley, "cutting us to pieces," claimed a member of the Thirty-third. The Valley men streamed for the shelter of the woods, and the Federals reclaimed the cannon.[54]

In the pines, the Second began to disintegrate when Cummings's fleeing men plunged through the Second's left-flank companies. According to Lieutenant Samuel Moore, in letters written within two weeks of the battle, Colonel James W. Allen, despite the pleas of the men, had refused to advance with the Thirty-third. Now, with the left flank uncovered and under increasing fire from the Chasseurs and Union cannon, a "bewildered" Allen shouted for the troops to "fall back, fall back." A tall man, the thirty-one-year-old colonel had lost sight in his right eye in a childhood accident, and during the action was temporarily blinded when a tree branch struck his left eye. Undoubtedly, it contributed to his bewilderment.[55]

In his report, Allen claimed that he had ordered only the three companies on the left to bend their line but the instructions had been misunderstood by others, resulting in the retreat of most of the companies. Moore's version of events seems more credible, even alleging that some of the soldiers "actually shed tears when the order was given." Evidently, about one hundred officers and men never heard the command nor saw in the thicket their comrades retire.[56]

The Fourteenth Brooklyn, meanwhile, redirected its attack toward the Confederate cannon. The Southern gunners reloaded their pieces with canister—one-inch iron balls, packed in cylinders of sawdust—and blasted the Chasseurs. Jackson ordered the Fourth and Twenty-seventh to open fire with musketry. The New Yorkers retreated, came on a second time and then a third, driving to within feet of the cannon before the Rebels finally blasted them rearward. Jackson directed the artillery crews to withdraw and then rode to the front of the pair of infantry regiments. To Colonel James F. Preston of the Fourth, he said, "Order the men to stand up." Officers relayed the instructions, and the Virginians rose from the ground. "We'll charge them now and drive them to Washington," Jackson stated. He then admonished them not to fire until within fifty yards of the enemy and to "yell like furies."[57]

The two regiments—the Fourth in front, the Twenty-seventh behind— cleared the pines, obliqued left to avoid the artillery crews, and prepared to charge. Many of the men's faces were stained with the red clay of Virginia. The Rebels surged forward, the ranks of each regiment mixed with those of the other. Across the plain, Griffin's and Lieutenant James B.

Ricketts's gunners switched to canister. The cannon mouths looked as "big as flour barrels" to the oncoming Virginians, who were, as ordered, yelling "like furies."[58]

Explosions belched from the cannon as a storm of canister slammed into the Virginians. Undaunted, the attackers closed, triggered a volley into the Federals' faces, and raced among the guns and crews. Some of the artillerists resisted. Men clubbed at each other. Private Joseph Neff of the Twenty-seventh, according to a witness, "knocked a Yankees brains out with the butt of his gun." Nearby, Private William Jennings lifted the Twenty-seventh's flag on a cannon and fell with two disabling wounds. A VMI drillmaster, John Daniels, picked it up, only to be shot in the right breast and left hip.[59]

The "dreadful charge" had secured the cannon, but the Federals were determined to retake them. During the next hour the Virginians clung to the captured pieces. Approximately one hundred men from the Second Virginia came in on their left, and the Fifth Virginia and Hampton Legion on the right. Five Union regiments in three successive counterattacks advanced against the Confederates. The carnage was "fearful," claimed an officer in the Twenty-seventh. "I never expected to see you again," a private in the same regiment told his wife. "The balls was falling around me like hail and I don't see how I ever did escape for the men was falling around me like cornstalks and still I was not touched." First Sergeant Henry Shanklin fired many rounds but reported to his parents that "I dont know whether I killed anyone or not."[60]

On the plateau of Henry House Hill, the Virginians bled and discovered a reality of combat. Amid the blinding, bitter-tasting smoke, the deafening crash of musketry and cannon fire, and the pitiful screams of the wounded, a man appeared frighteningly isolated, as if trapped in a cocoon. A soldier's reality covered only a small area around him, and like Sergeant Shanklin, rarely knew if he harmed an opponent. Shortly after the battle, Lieutenant Samuel Moore wrote of this experience. "The uproar of the fight," Moore related, "the excitement attending it, and the close attention required to the work immediately before him, so occupy him, that he has no time for observation beyond the immediate neighborhood in which he is himself placed."[61]

About four o'clock a final Union assault force emerged from the low ground along Sudley Road. The Federals belonged to the brigade of Colonel William T. Sherman—three New York regiments and the Second

Wisconsin. During the morning Sherman's troops had waited—some im-
patiently—east of Stone Bridge until McDowell's main force cleared the
ground west of the span. When the order came to advance, the men removed their haversacks and blankets and waded Bull Run above the
bridge. They marched across the countryside, arriving near the Warren-
ton-Sudley intersection as the struggle for Henry House Hill escalated.
The brigade formed a battle line in a column of regiments, with the Second
Wisconsin behind the Thirteenth New York and in front of the Seventy-
ninth and Sixty-ninth New York.[62]

Confederate batteries soon targeted the area, and Sherman's troops
flattened on the ground. Sheltered by a hollow in which they lay, the Wisconsin men were spared, although Corporal Horace Emerson told his
brother later that it was "awful to hear" the shells shriek over their heads.
Before long, the Thirteenth New York rose and began to ascend the hill.
Officers of the Second Wisconsin brought the men to their feet, waving
them forward. Dressed in the state-issued gray uniforms, the Wisconsinites crossed Sudley Road, halted, and dressed ranks. Ahead of them,
smoke obscured the crest.[63]

Either Sherman or division commander Daniel Tyler or both ordered
the Second Wisconsin to charge. Shouting an "Indian war whoop," the
men went up the slope at the double quick. A ravine bisected their path of
advance, and the regiment divided into two wings—four companies on
the right, six on the left. From the crest, the Confederates unleashed "the
most hellish shower of bullets you can imagine, if you try a month,"
claimed a Westerner. The Southern line overlapped the flank of the right
wing, enfilading the ranks of the four companies. Wisconsin men fell in
clumps, caught in nearly a circle of fire as the Seventy-ninth and Sixty-
ninth New York mistakenly fired into their rear. "Oh! It was dreadful,"
Captain George Stevens averred, "and I cannot see how not only myself,
but any of us, escaped with life." Many of the men fell to the ground and
returned the fire.[64]

Their comrades in the left wing endured a similar withering fire from
the Southerners. "Our men fell in every direction," recounted a private,
"some killed, some wounded, begging for us to kill them, and put them
out of their misery." "I saw men cut in all shapes and manners," lamented
Corporal Emerson. The Wisconsin men pushed up the slope through the
smoke, only to be hammered down the hillside. Few of them even saw the
enemy. The combat defied description, even understanding. "There is no

way I can tell you about the battle," a soldier told his friends at home, "so that you can get the fainest idea of it." He knew, however, "it was a sight to remember after it was over, but at the time I did not care anything about it."[65]

Sherman advanced his final two regiments, again incrementally, into what he described as "the severe fire" from the hill. These New Yorkers fared no better than their comrades, and the survivors abandoned the slope. The Wisconsin and New York soldiers tried to re-form along Sudley Road. Suddenly, from the south hundreds of fleeing, panic-stricken Federals appeared, driven north by fresh Confederate troops that had arrived on the field from the Valley and from the opposite end of the Southern line. Much of the Union army dissolved, racing toward Bull Run.[66]

The Second Wisconsin scattered with the rest of the army. Beyond Bull Run, a handful rallied by their fallen flag, repulsing an attack by Rebel cavalry. One of the Wisconsin men grabbed the colors and waved it at the enemy. He "is the bravest man I ever saw," contended one of his comrades.[67]

Many defeated soldiers stumbled through the night toward the capital. Members of the Second Wisconsin reached Fort Corcoran by noon on Monday, July 22. They heard later that Lieutenant Colonel Peck and Major McDonald were the first two officers to cross the Potomac with news of the disaster.[68]

In an old barn near the fort, with rain falling outside, the Second Wisconsin gathered and began counting the losses. Although the casualty figures vary, the most recent tabulation places the numbers at eighteen killed, seventy-six wounded, and seventy-six captured, out of an effective strength of about eight hundred. Like many units on both sides, it had been spared greater casualties because of the inexperience of each army. That night in the barn, Wisconsin most likely seemed far away.[69]

On the battlefield of First Manassas or First Bull Run—Confederates designated battlefields, generally by a nearby town, Federals by a geographic feature—on July 22, members of Jackson's brigade buried their comrades. "Horrible" and "awful" were the common descriptions of what they encountered. The details laid the dead, wrapped in blankets, in common graves near where they died, anticipating that family members would retrieve the remains. During the work, a soldier in the Fifth Virginia passed a field hospital, with its mounds of amputated limbs. At a distance, he thought, they "resembled piles of corn at a corn-shucking."[70]

The defense of Henry House Hill had incurred a fearful toll. The official count placed the cost at 119 killed or mortally wounded and 442 wounded, while a modern study listed 111 killed or mortally wounded and 373 wounded or missing, out of an estimated 2,600 in the brigade. Only three other regiments in the army suffered more losses than the Thirty-third, Twenty-seventh, and Fourth Virginia. Within the brigade, the Thirty-third had the highest figure of 146 killed, wounded, or missing. Of its dead, 33 came from Shenandoah County. No other Virginia county sustained a higher percentage of killed and mortally wounded in a single engagement during the war than did this Valley county at First Manassas.[71]

Combat generated its own form of democracy, inflicting punishment regardless of rank or stature at home. So it was with the Valley men, and so it would be. In the Fourth Virginia, Colonel James Preston and Lieutenant Colonel Lewis Moore fell wounded. Moore's injury was so crippling that he never returned to duty with the regiment. Captain William Lee, acting major of the Thirty-third, was killed, as were three of the VMI drillmasters, all members of the same class. In the Second Virginia, the Conrad brothers, Holmes and Henry Tucker, died beside each other. Their cousin, Lieutenant Peyton Harrison, was slain nearby. The Conrad brothers had enlisted without their Union sympathizing father's knowledge, and he did not hear of them until the news of their deaths reached the family's Martinsburg home. An unknown fatality in the Twenty-seventh Virginia was as "homely-looking dog as ever seen perhaps," who had joined the Rockbridge Rifles during its march to Harper's Ferry and had been adopted as a pet.[72]

The sacrifice had, however, "almost immortalized" the brigade, as an officer exclaimed in a letter of July 22. Its stand on Henry House Hill had been the turning point of the battle, and the brigade's and other units' capture and defense of the Union cannon insured the stability of the Confederate center. Even the modest Jackson confided to a friend: "You will find, when my report shall be published, that the First Brigade was to our army what the Imperial Guard was to the First Napoleon—that, through the blessing of God, it met the thus far victorious enemy and turned the fortunes of the day."[73]

In fact, the words of Barnard Bee, who fell mortally wounded later on

Henry House Hill, insured immortality for Jackson, and in turn, for his Virginians. Within a week of the battle, Bee's cry to his men had been published, and the general and his soldiers became known as "Stonewall." But that lay down the road; for the present, duty required attention. In the rain of July 22, officers "gathered up fragments" of their commands, in the words of a lieutenant's diary, "and started for the junction."[74]

3

✠

VIRGINIA AUTUMN

THE stench of death choked the air around Manassas Junction, Virginia, during the final days of July 1861. Three months earlier, blinded by illusions of glory and swift victory, Americans had released the terrible furies of civil war. But a Sabbath day along Bull Run revealed the shadows of darkness that would envelop the nation. The carnage sobered everyone as summer winds carried death's smell beyond the battlefield and into homes, North and South.

In the battle's aftermath, while Confederates celebrated the valor of Southern arms, Abraham Lincoln acted swiftly to retrieve the disaster. On July 27, the president relieved Irvin McDowell as commander of the defeated army and appointed Major General George B. McClellan. The thirty-four-year-old native Pennsylvanian had undertaken a successful campaign in the mountains of western Virginia, resulting in control of the Baltimore & Ohio Railroad in the region. With few choices, Lincoln turned to the young, dashing McClellan, who had been a classmate of Thomas Jackson at West Point.[1]

McClellan brought to the command organizational ability and inspirational leadership that would in time reforge the soon-to-be designated Army of the Potomac. For the present, however, the capital needed to be defended and the failures of Bull Run addressed. Few, if any, regiments in the army confronted the battle's legacy more swiftly than did the Second Wisconsin.

Company officers and the rank and file had shamed neither themselves nor their families in Wisconsin. They had endured the fury on Henry House Hill until they and the other regiments in the brigade could do no more. Caught within the terror of a rout, they had fled with the army. But Lieutenant Colonel Henry Peck and Major Duncan McDonald had issued no orders during the fighting and had outdistanced the regiment during the retreat. The two officers had been, in a sergeant's blunt words, "badly scared or frightened at Bulls Run."[2]

Within days of the battle, the regimental officers met with Peck, Mc-Donald, and Colonel S. Park Coon, who allegedly had been seen staggering drunkenly on the capital's streets after Bull Run, and asked all three to resign. Coon and Peck left the regiment by month's end, and McDonald by the second week of August. When the news of the resignations reached Madison, Governor Alexander Randall acted at once and traveled to Washington.[3]

Governor Randall visited the camp of the Second Wisconsin on August 2, presenting the troops with a blue silk state flag and introducing them to Coon's replacement, Colonel Edgar O'Connor. A short, darkly complexioned man with black eyes and hair, O'Connor was twenty-eight years old and an 1854 graduate of West Point. After service on the frontier, O'Connor had resigned from the army in 1859, returned to Wisconsin and opened a law practice in Beloit. He suffered, however, from health problems and seemed to be lethargic to fellow officers. Sergeant Davis thought him to be "a fair looking man and has the appearance of beaing a good Officer."[4]

To replace Peck as lieutenant colonel, Randall selected Captain Lucius Fairchild of the First Wisconsin. A native Ohioan, twenty-nine years old, Fairchild was a member of a prominent Democratic family in Madison. He had spent six years in California, searching for gold, farming, and speculating in land. When the war began, the governor offered Fairchild a lieutenant colonelcy, but he declined because of lack of experience. On August 17, the First Wisconsin's three-month term of enlistment expired, and three days later, Fairchild received his commission with the Second Wisconsin. A friendly, enthusiastic man, Fairchild became a popular officer in the regiment after his arrival in early September.[5]

The new major of the Second Wisconsin came from within the regiment. The officers recommended Captain Thomas Allen of Company I, and Randall appointed him to the rank on August 23. "Long Tom," as Allen was known, was a thirty-six-year-old former mine surveyor, teacher, state legislator, and clerk in the government land office. He had commanded the Miners Guard since its organization, and according to the regimental historian, "a more zealous patriot never commanded a company."[6]

During these command changes, the regiment was camped near Fort Corcoran, recovering from the battle, drilling, and serving on picket duty. On August 27, the Second Wisconsin marched across Aqueduct Bridge into Washington and joined the brigade of Brigadier General Rufus King. In the weeks ahead, McClellan created additional brigades, reassigned regiments, and added new units to commands. By mid-October, King's brigade consisted of the four regiments that would constitute the original Iron Brigade— Second, Sixth, and Seventh Wisconsin, and Nineteenth Indiana.[7]

The first of these three new regiments to arrive in Virginia was the Sixth Wisconsin. Like the Second, the Sixth had been recruited from across the state—its ten companies coming from eight counties. Seven of the companies contained a majority of native-born Americans in the ranks while the members of two companies were predominantly German, and a third, Irish. They had enlisted in their hometowns and went forth with names such as the Sauk County Riflemen, Prairie du Chien Volunteers, Citizens' Corps, Beloit Star Rifles, Anderson Guards, and Lemonweir Minute Men.[8]

Upon organization, the individual companies reported to Camp Randall in Madison. Facilities at the installation had improved since the Second's arrival in early May, but the Sixth's recruits still grumbled about the "poor fare" and the beds. On July 4, for instance, two companies threatened to leave when served "dry bread, cold soup, and spoilt meat" for dinner. The same cannon that awoke the men of the Second sounded the reveille for the Sixth. A day's routine had changed little, consisting of drills and formations. Regimental officers maintained "very strict" discipline in the camp, sparing the citizens of Madison from the rowdyism that had marked the Second's weeks at the facility.[9]

As each company arrived at Camp Randall, the three regimental field officers welcomed the recruits. Each officer had received his commission from Governor Randall on May 28. For the colonelcy of the Sixth, the governor appointed fifty-four-year-old Lysander Cutler, a Massachusetts native. A big, gray-bearded man with a gruff voice and manner, Cutler had made and lost two small fortunes in New England before emigrating in 1857 to Milwaukee, where he ran a grain brokerage business. Two decades earlier, he had led militia troops in the so-called Aroostook Wars in Maine. The volunteers soon learned that the colonel was, as an officer stated, "rigid in his discipline, and stern and unflinching in exacting the performance of all duties." When angered, Cutler "emitted a grunt, like an enraged porker."[10]

Governor Randall chose Julius P. Atwood, a Madison judge, for the lieutenant colonelcy. But Atwood resigned because of ill health in less than three months and was succeeded by Major Benjamin F. Sweet. A lawyer and state senator from Calumet County, Sweet proved to be a capable officer and eventually obtained the colonelcy of another regiment.[11]

Captain Edward S. Bragg of Company E replaced Sweet as major. A fellow captain believed Bragg to be "the brightest man in the regiment." A lawyer in Fond du Lac, the native New Yorker was a staunch Democrat and had been a delegate to the party's two conventions in 1860. He appeared to some to be inordinately ambitious and allegedly had actively sought the promotion.[12]

The company officers included a few Mexican War veterans, the son of a Regular Army officer who had learned drills from his father, and in the two German companies, four captains and lieutenants who either had attended a military school in Europe or had served in a Continental army. Captain Rufus R. Dawes of Company K, the Lemonweir Minute Men, was the twenty-two-year-old great-grandson of William Dawes, the Revolutionary War patriot who had sounded the alarm with Paul Revere on April 18, 1775. An Ohioan, Dawes had been visiting with his family in Juneau County when elected company commander.[13]

The final company to join the regiment arrived at Camp Randall in early July, and on the 16th, 1,070 officers and men of the Sixth Wisconsin were mustered into Federal service. Two days later, the regiment received a state flag, made of dark blue silk with the seal of the United States on both sides. Finally, on Sunday, July 28, the Sixth boarded a train for Washington. Its scheduled departure had been accelerated because of the defeat at Bull Run.[14]

While many of the men believed that the war would be ended in six

months, Private Julius A. Murray doubted that prediction. Three days earlier, he had stated in a letter that "in my opinion this war will not be
brought to a close as a great many immagine I think we will have some
hard and bloody fighting, and a great many Companies will lose some of
their number from the muster Roll before they return." Then, in a perceptive judgment, he added that "sickness will thin off our Ranks faster than
the enemy can."[15]

Among those who boarded the train was Lieutenant Edwin A. Brown
of Company E. Since leaving his wife, Ruth, and children in Fond du Lac,
Brown had written a number of letters to them. He assured Ruth that
when he left for Madison he had wanted to embrace her, but with the
crowd at the station, "it was pride that kept me up. I did not want people
to think that soldiers were baby's." Although he expected hardships and
danger: "I think my chances is as good to come back as any ones else, and
if I should see you again after doing my duty you would then be proud of
your husband." At the end, he asked her to kiss the children for him and
not to let them forget their father.[16]

The train clanged east through Milwaukee and on to Chicago, with
hundreds of civilians beside the tracks, cheering the soldiers. A sergeant
claimed that this leg of the trip "was as near a paradice as I ever expect in
this world." The regiment stopped at Fort Wayne, Indiana, before crossing Ohio into Pennsylvania. At Pittsburgh, the Wisconsin volunteers de-
trained again. "You can smell smoke, feel smoke & I will go so far as to
say you can taste it," one of them asserted about the city of foundries and
mills. The newsboys looked "as if they had [been] suspended over the fun-
nel of some blacksmith's shop."[17]

The Sixth Wisconsin arrived in Baltimore on the night of August 3. One
hundred armed policemen escorted the unarmed command through the
city to a park, where the troops repulsed an attack by a group of "Plug
Uglies" armed with clubs after midnight. The regiment stayed in camp until the 8th, when it boarded "filthy cattle cars" for the capital. The next
day the Western men marched to a camp near Georgetown, and army officers began issuing them accoutrements.[18]

The Nineteenth Indiana arrived in Washington via train from Baltimore on the evening of August 8, a few hours behind the Sixth Wisconsin.
Mustered into Federal service on July 29, the regiment consisted of 1,084
officers and men, representing eight counties in the state. Since the firing
on Fort Sumter, Indiana had raised one heavy artillery battery and sixteen

regiments of infantry by August 1. Like residents in other Northern states, Indianans answered President Lincoln's proclamation after Fort Sumter with thousands of volunteers.[19]

After Governor Oliver P. Morton issued the order organizing the Nineteenth Indiana on June 24, it took six weeks to recruit soldiers. Four counties, located north and east of Indianapolis, supplied half of the regiment's ten companies, while three counties surrounding and south of the capital raised four companies. The final unit, the Elkhart County Guards, hailed from the northern section of the state. Like the Wisconsin troops, the Indiana volunteers adopted company names—four contingents of "Greys," four of "Guards," the Selma Legion, and the Invincibles.[20]

When organized, each company reported to Camp Morton in Indianapolis. A private described their weeks at the camp as "not exactly a picnic," grumbling about the hot weather and the hours of drill. A daily routine for the companies had been established, with Lieutenant Colonel Thomas J. Wood of the First U.S. Cavalry conducting the drills. Unlike the Wisconsin recruits, few of the Indianans complained about either the accommodations or the food.[21]

Towering six-foot, seven-inch Colonel Solomon Meredith commanded the Nineteenth Indiana. Fifty-one years old, a friend of Governor Morton, Meredith was one of the state's leading Republican politicians. In the three decades since his family had relocated to Indiana from North Carolina, he had been a county sheriff, federal marshal, state legislator, a member of Congress, a railroad vice president, and a noted farmer and stock breeder. His ambition matched his imposing physique.[22]

Meredith's prominence and political influence fostered a host of enemies, none more important than Republican Congressman George P. Julian. Julian's supporters and other opponents of Meredith railed against the appointment, terming Morton's action as "brassy impudence and sublime effrontery" and a "damnable swindle." One wit suggested that the tall colonel "be cut in half so his lower, better half could be appointed lieutenant colonel." Meredith thought his political labors had been justly rewarded, and he saw the future political possibilities for a man with a distinguished military record. His efforts at advancement would be tireless.[23]

Governor Morton appointed Robert A. Cameron as lieutenant colonel and Alois Octavius Bachman as major of the regiment. Both men had been serving as captains in three-month regiments, whose term of service expired on August 2. Among the company commanders, only one had prior military service in the Mexican War. The captains included a doctor, lawyer, salesman, and cabinetmaker. Samuel J. Williams, John M. Lindley, and William W. Dudley were destined for higher rank.[24]

On the night of August 5, the officers and men of the Nineteenth Indiana boarded trains for Washington. The journey east took seventy hours, and along the route, the Hoosiers—the nickname was derived probably from the corruption of a French word that meant "outside the pale" of civilization—were feted in various cities. Armed at Camp Morton, the regiment passed through Baltimore without any problems, and on August 9 joined King's brigade at Camp Kalorama on the heights above Georgetown.[25]

Nearly two months passed before the fourth regiment that would comprise the renowned brigade, the Seventh Wisconsin, joined the other units in Washington. Recruited primarily from the communities of southern and central Wisconsin during the weeks of July and August, the Seventh was mustered into service at Camp Randall on September 2. Its original complement of officers and enlisted men numbered 1,022.[26]

According to a private, his comrades disliked Camp Randall and adapted to military life no better than the members of the Second and Sixth Wisconsin. The daily routine of cleaning barracks, drills, and dress parade was enlivened by considerable profanity. "There are a great many dissatisfied, dissatisfied in eating, drinking sleeping & in everything they do," he contended. "They are continuously grumbling." Except in his company, the Platteville Guards of Company C, "there is a great deal of trouble" with the officers. Camp Randall possessed seemingly few pleasant memories for the Wisconsin volunteers that passed through during the early months of its existence.[27]

A Hungarian aristocrat and émigré, Joseph Van Dor, commanded the Seventh Wisconsin. Following service in the Hungarian army, Van Dor came to the United States, eventually settling in Wisconsin. Governor Randall appointed him to the colonelcy evidently because of his background, but Van Dor proved to be a poor fit with the officers and men. Once the regiment reached Washington, he ceased active command of it, finally resigning in January 1862, to serve as American representative in Tahiti.[28]

Van Dor's successor as colonel was William W. Robinson, the regiment's first lieutenant colonel. A native of Vermont, graduate of Norwich

Academy, the forty-two-year-old Robinson had served as a lieutenant and then captain in the Third Ohio during the Mexican War. He had sought gold in California before eventually settling in Wisconsin.[29]

Governor Randall selected a Milwaukee attorney of famous lineage, Charles A. Hamilton, as the regiment's major. A grandson of Alexander Hamilton, the thirty-five-year-old officer was a native New Yorker who had practiced law in that state before relocating to Wisconsin in 1851. Upon Robinson's promotion, Hamilton succeeded to the lieutenant colonelcy.[30]

On September 21, the Seventh Wisconsin marched out of Camp Randall to the accompaniment of cannon fire and the cheers of civilians. At the train station, they loaded into cattle cars that had benches along the sides and at each end, and six inches of manure on the floor. A considerable number of the men were ill with measles but were evidently placed on board. The regiment received warm welcomes and good food en route, arriving in Washington on the 26th. They bivouacked for the night near the Capitol amid, as a corporal described it, "one sea of tents as far as you can see each way." The next morning the regiment joined King's brigade.[31]

Brigadier General Rufus King was one of Wisconsin's most renowned citizens. A member of a distinguished New York family, King was an 1833 graduate of West Point, but had devoted most of his life to the newspaper business and civic affairs. He moved to Wisconsin during the 1840s and founded the Milwaukee *Sentinel*. He helped to frame the state constitution and served as superintendent of the city's schools. When the war began, the forty-seven-year-old King withdrew as the minister to the Papal States and accepted a commission as a brigadier, to rank from May 17. He had been away from the army for nearly a quarter of a century.[32]

On the morning of October 5, King led his four regiments across Aqueduct Bridge over the Potomac River and into Virginia. Assigned to the division of Irvin McDowell, the defeated commander at Bull Run, they camped on Arlington Heights, with King using the antebellum home of Robert E. Lee as headquarters. Four days later, the division commander reviewed his new brigade and held a "grand inspection" of uniforms, arms, and accoutrements.[33]

The four regiments that passed in review for McDowell comprised the only distinctive Western brigade in the Army of the Potomac. The soldiers came from a section of the country that Easterners described as "way down beyond the sunset." Each regiment, except the Seventh Wisconsin, now wore the standard Federal uniform of a dark blue frock coat and light blue trousers. While the men in three regiments wore common forage caps on their heads, the members of the Second Wisconsin had been issued high-crowned, black-felt Regular Army or so-called Hardee hats. Each soldier cocked the left brim with a brass eagle and attached a black feather to the right brim. "They look as bold as a sheep," thought one of them on the day of the review.[34]

The Westerners also differed from their comrades in other regiments in their ethnic backgrounds. While nearly a quarter of all Union troops in the war were foreign-born, one half of the Wisconsin and Indiana men were immigrants. Germans and Irishmen comprised the largest segments, with handfuls of Scandinavians, British, Canadian, and Welsh in the ranks. Like a typical Civil War regiment, the majority of Westerners had been either farmers, craftsmen, or common laborers in civilian life. Their mean age, twenty-five, was probably that found throughout the army. Except for the immigrants in the ranks, the Badger and Hoosier state men were typical Union soldiers.[35]

Beyond demographic traits, Union soldiers shared bonds that had impelled them to enlist and would sustain them after more than the Bull Run veterans passed through the horrors of combat and witnessed a battlefield's terrible aftermath. Patriotism, duty, and honor motivated men to endure and to give meaning to their sacrifices. Like most Americans of their generation, soldiers believed that duty incurred an obligation to the country, a moral bond between the citizenry and its government. Union soldiers invoked the legacy of the Founding Fathers—an attachment to the Constitution and to the nation that required their defense.[36]

The Western men of King's brigade were infused with these motivating factors. As noted previously with the Second Wisconsin, the brigade members saw beyond the borders of a state with a nationalism that encompassed the entire country. For them, "the cause" meant the Union of states, or as one of them wrote in August, "we will ever stand by the Union stand by the Flag the homes of our Forefathers we will protect with the last of our blood." Their contemporary letters and diaries are replete with such sentiments. Although one private asserted that he had enlisted "not for my Country being nothing but a boy did not know what that meant. did not know what my duty to country was but for the sake of seeing the sunny south," he was among the minority in the command.[37]

They marched forth, as Lieutenant Edwin Brown averred, to suppress "this monstrous and unholy rebellion." "I can come to no other conclusion," wrote Private Julius Murray, "that should the Gen Government be overpowered there will be one continued scene of anarchy and confusion for the future and that it is the duty for every one that can possibly do so to Enlist willingly." To his family, sixteen-year-old Indiana farmboy Private Adam Juday wrote: "I have enlisted, and am going to stand as one that is for his country, I am determined to fight for my country. It seems hard to leave you, but I am very anxious to go, and feel it to do my duty."[38]

Before them lay the long road of war—the days of drill, the monotony of camp life, the homesickness, the exhaustion of forced marches, the terror of combat, and the deaths of comrades and kin. In the darkest of days ahead, something beyond themselves would have to sustain them. Their devotion to country, duty, and honor would make of them, in time, a remarkable body of soldiers. It was a simple matter in the end, perhaps, as a private saw it: "I had ambition to do something for the world *in which I found* myself living."[39]

These men from "way down beyond the sunset" came together while the warmth of summer still clung to Virginia. But despite their shared values, common backgrounds, and geographic bond, the Westerners were not "on the best of terms" in the beginning. Much of the difficulty arose evidently with the Second Wisconsin. The veterans of Bull Run sneered at their untested comrades in the other three regiments. They "put on an air of superiority over the rest of the brigade," contended members of the Sixth Wisconsin. They refused to drill, according to Lieutenant Brown of the Sixth, and told "big stories about their exploits" at Bull Run that were always "embellished with some tall swearing." Corporal Horace Emerson of the Second admitted that "this Regt is composed of the tough cusses of Wis," who "dont fear nothing" and "steal every thing they can bring away." The other regiments, said Emerson, called them "Devels."[40]

Before long, each regiment received a nickname from the other units. The Second Wisconsin became the "Ragged Assed Second," because of the condition of their trouser seats; the Sixth Wisconsin, the "Calico Sixth," because of alleged favoritism by King toward its members; the Seventh Wisconsin, the "Huckleberries," for their incessant talk about food; and, the Nineteenth Indiana became the "Swamp Hogs No. 19," because of their disdain for appearances and willingness to fight. Each had taken an early measurement of the others and had rendered an appropriate judgment in their view.[41]

Together, on ground that their government would eventually consecrate as a national cemetery, the Wisconsin and Indiana volunteers began the process of becoming a brigade. Throughout the army, training marked the day's routine, with King holding brigade drill two or three times a week. "They are trying to make *regulars* of us," groused a captain, "and the *ordeal* that we have to pass is *pretty severe."* Hundreds in the brigade could not participate as smallpox, measles, and dysentery raced through the units, confining the victims to city hospitals. When the first member of the Sixth Wisconsin, Private Edgar Ames, died, his comrades paid to ship his body home. His would be the only remains returned to Wisconsin.[42]

On Tuesday, October 22, Edwin Brown, now captain of Company E, Sixth Wisconsin, wrote a letter to his wife, Ruth. Earlier, he had complained often of the hardships but remained firm in his commitment. Now, as cold nights preceded cooler days, he stated: "I grieve much at the unfortunate condition of our Country. It seems as though the day of her deliverance from the machinations of traitors was far distant."[43]

"A great deal of sickness in camp," Lieutenant John Grabill of the Thirty-third Virginia recorded in his diary during August 1861. The "almost incessant rain" had confined men to tents, canceled drills, and overflowed the hospitals with soldiers. In four letters to his wife during the month, Captain James J. White of the Fourth Virginia mentioned the cases of illness, describing them in one letter as "very extensive and serious." An enlisted man with measles reported to a hospital and discovered that "the doctors cared but little for the sick, unless they cared something for the man before he became sick." In Lieutenant Grabill's regiment no surgeon had been appointed to minister to the men.[44]

For the heroes of Henry House Hill, it seemed as if the fates had mocked them in the weeks after their valiant stand. For ten days they were bivouacked on a wretched site near Manassas Junction that the men dubbed Camp Maggot. On August 2, the Virginians of Thomas Jackson's brigade moved to "a pretty camp" located one mile east of Centreville. Named for Jackson's quartermaster who chose the site, Camp Harman provided the troops with good, ample water. Jackson pitched headquarters tents on the grounds of the Philip Utterback farm, a half mile from the camp. Details of men built a guardhouse of upended logs and privies of bushes with board seats.[45]

Although Jackson believed that the official and public praise accorded his men's conduct at Manassas was deserved, he wrote to his wife during August that "still much remains undone that I desire to see effected." He granted few furloughs and ordered daily drills, but the inclement weather thwarted his plans. "General Jackson is rigid in his requirements," a captain wrote about the general, "although not more so than security requires."[46]

Despite Jackson's firmness and adherence to the rules of military conduct, discipline and command problems plagued the brigade. Colonel Arthur Cummings of the Thirty-third Virginia reported discipline in the regiment as "indifferent." In the Second Virginia, when Colonel James Allen assigned Lieutenant Samuel Moore to command of Company F, which "was in a state of disorganization" because of the absence of its officer, all but seven members of the unit "decamped" or deserted. Moore heard their complaints about Allen's refusal to approve the election of new officers, reported them to the colonel, and then asked to be relieved of the duty.[47]

The most serious problem in the brigade was the number of deserters. Men left either temporarily on a so-called French leave because they could not secure an authorized leave, or permanently because of demands at home, or of their dislike of soldiering. The ranks of the Twenty-seventh Virginia had been so depleted by sickness and absences during August, for instance, that the commander requested that it be transferred to the Valley. Regimental courts-martial sentenced those apprehended or those who returned willingly to a loss of pay and/or imprisonment. "Others will share the same fate," contended an officer, "until this practice is broken up." In fact, "this practice" never ceased; it only worsened, draining men away from the ranks and crippling the brigade's combat effectiveness.[48]

Command changes and dissension among officers compounded the difficulties within the brigade. Among the officers of the Second and Fifth Virginia the dissatisfaction appeared to be the worst. In the latter regiment, Colonel Kenton Harper resigned on September 5, citing "the peculiar condition of my family, which requires my immediate presence." Governor John Letcher promoted Lieutenant Colonel William H. Harman to the colonelcy, but the selection was opposed by the officers and most of the rank and file. They preferred Major William Baylor, former captain of Company L, over Harman, and the officers presented Harman with a petition, asking him to request reassignment to another regiment.

The colonel "treated it with contempt," according to Baylor, who was appointed lieutenant colonel, and Captain Absalom Koiner, major.[49]

Baylor was determined, as he stated, "to leave the responsibility of ruining one of the best regiments in the service upon him [Harman] for I feel that I cannot sustain it by any effort of mine whilst he is over it, and it would be suicidal in me to take any of the blame which rightly attach to him." Baylor threatened to resign but relented. Weeks later, however, he traveled to Richmond, seeking a commission in the Confederate regular army.[50]

Matters were even worse in the Second Virginia. Since the July 21 battle, disagreement over Colonel Allen's conduct on that day festered. When Allen's published report appeared in a Winchester newspaper, the regimental officers met and designated Lieutenant Samuel Moore to prepare a letter that corrected the colonel's alleged errors in the document. A day later, Allen agreed to amend the report. In turn, the officers prepared their version of the events, believing that the beleaguered commander would sign any statement to avoid a trial. A copy of Allen's report is among Moore's papers, but in it Allen maintained his assertion that he had ordered a charge and not a retirement, as Moore claimed in a letter after the battle.[51]

The modifications Allen agreed to remain unknown. The questions about his leadership persisted, however. According to Lieutenant Moore, whose writings seem credible, Major Lawson Botts told Moore confidentially that he had "no confidence" in Allen since the battle. Any field officer can make mistakes, particularly in an initial battle, but Allen's officers and men believed the colonel lacked personal courage. To Civil War soldiers, a leader had to demonstrate personal bravery by example in combat. To Southerners especially, leadership by example was linked to honor or one's public reputation. Allen failed, in his regiment's judgment, to act with courage at Manassas.[52]

The death of Lieutenant Colonel Francis Lackland of heart disease and pneumonia on September 4 exacerbated the discord within the Second Virginia. A group of officers endorsed Captain John Q. A. Nadenbousch over Major Botts for the vacancy, but Botts received the appointment, with Frank B. Jones promoted to major. An 1848 graduate of VMI, Jones had been serving temporarily on Jackson's staff.[53]

The other units in the brigade underwent command changes with apparently less rancor than in the Second and Fifth Virginia. In the Twenty-seventh Virginia, Colonel William W. Gordon, who had not led the regiment at Manassas, finally resigned, and was succeeded by the capable Lieutenant Colonel John Echols. Major Andrew J. Grigsby replaced Echols, and First Lieutenant Elisha Franklin Paxton received the commission as major. A Lexington attorney and farmer, Paxton was serving on Jackson's staff when appointed to the post. His company, the Rockbridge Rifles, had been organized originally as Company B, Fifth Virginia, then switched to the Fourth about July 1, but following the battle, authorities transferred it a second time to the understrength Twenty-seventh as Company H.[54]

In the Thirty-third Virginia, Captain John R. Jones of Company I, and First Lieutenant Edwin G. "Ned" Lee, former adjutant of the Second Virginia, were appointed lieutenant colonel and major, respectively. Jones was thirty-four years old and a VMI graduate who had organized his company in Harrisonburg. Unlike Jones's appointment, Ned Lee's raised questions. Twenty-five years old, an antebellum lawyer, Lee was the son-in-law of Colonel William N. Pendleton, now the army's chief of artillery, and had served briefly on Jackson's staff with his brother-in-law, Sandie Pendleton. His family connections appeared inappropriately fortuitous to other officers.[55]

A number of captains and lieutenants resigned during the weeks after Manassas, including Captain James White of the Liberty Hall Volunteers, Fourth Virginia. "Old Zeus," as his college student-soldiers called him, left the service because of ill health. In the Rockbridge Artillery, battery members elected First Lieutenant William McLaughlin to the captaincy as replacement for Colonel Pendleton. On August 14, the unit underwent further change with a reorganization into a six-gun battery.[56]

The men in the ranks, meanwhile, answered roll calls, policed the camp, walked guard duty, and served on picket details. The weather cleared during the final week of August, and Jackson resumed drills, with four per day. At month's end, the Virginians mustered for pay call by company. A paymaster examined muster rolls, marked men who were present, charged those who owed the government money for uniforms and equipment, and then settled accounts with each soldier. When the officer completed the settlements, he paid the men.[57]

Two weeks later, the Virginians vacated Camp Harman and marched east to Fairfax Court House, establishing a new campsite less than a mile from the village. By now, the Southern press and public had been referring to Jackson as Stonewall, and the men adopted readily the name of the Stonewall Brigade. Throughout the army it came into common usage, and the Valley men had a permanent distinction.[58]

The Stonewall Brigade had been sent to Fairfax to assume picket duty along the Confederate front. For two months the opposing armies had watched each other across the fields and woodlots between Fairfax's and Washington's defenses. The Confederates had neither the numbers nor the artillery to assail the Federals. Combat was reduced to occasional skirmishes and the constant dance between picket lines.

Headquarters assigned the Virginians to picket duty on Munson's Hill, an elevation about ten miles from their camp. From its crest, the Southerners could see the enemy forts, the Potomac River and the Navy Yard, and even the unfinished Capitol dome. Mornings and evenings, the Federals sent up an observation balloon that "looked as large as a tent and just as white" to the Virginians. It was "beautiful country" for such duty.[59]

Picket duty on Munson's Hill rotated, with two regiments assigned together for five days. The work involved more than sightseeing and could be deadly. Lieutenant Samuel Moore described it well in a letter home:

> Picket duty is the most disagreeable of all duties. I mean picketing in the very presence of the enemy—to lie in the fence corner, or behind a bush, for 24 consecutive hours, exposed to the weather, and to the enemy, with whom shots are exhanged every now and then, with nothing to eat save what you can carry in your haversack, and without being able to lift up your head for any purpose without the risk of having a ball sent at you, is by no means a comfortable situation. I would rather fight the battle of Manassas once again, then be on picket in front of the enemy for 24 hours.
>
> I am satisfied that in most cases where men lose their lives at their posts, it is either from want of vigilance in watching or from an imprudent exposure of the person.[60]

Moore then related the recent death of a private in the Second Virginia at Munson's Hill. Darkness seemed, at times, to be worse than the danger of exposure during daylight. According to a diarist, one night, while the Thirty-third Virginia manned the posts, "a good many men," were "frightened" by "the hooting of an owl."[61]

When not picketing at Munson's Hill, the Virginians drilled, stood for inspections, and marched in review for generals. At least one Valley man grumbled that "this eternal routine of drilling a little going on guard occasionally & cooking day after day & week after week must kill me." The war, he asserted, "will never be ended except by fighting & the sooner we do it the better." Details of officers and men checked military personnel for valid passes at the railroad station. Other squads went to the Valley to recruit and to gather up deserters. "Many of the men have come home" without leave, noted Lieutenant Moore in mid-October.[62]

On October 11, the Stonewall Brigade participated in a grand review for the army commander, General Joseph Johnston, other ranking officers, and foreign visitors. "The brigade behaved remarkably well," claimed a Virginian. Five days later, it abandoned its camp near Fairfax, marching to Centreville as Johnston retrenched the army's lines beyond Washington. Two weeks later, Governor Letcher, whom the men called "Old Whiskey Barrel," came from Richmond, and presented to each Virginia regiment a state banner that one officer described as "a beautiful blue flag with a white center (round) containing coat of arms."[63]

Jackson, meanwhile, had been promoted to major general, to rank from October 7, and assigned to command of the Valley District in the newly reorganized Department of Northern Virginia. Johnston, who now commanded the department, delayed ordering Jackson to the Shenandoah region until November 4. During that morning, the field and regimental officers of the Stonewall Brigade visited Jackson at his headquarters tent. Each officer shook the general's hand. He spoke a few words to the assembled group, reminding them of Manassas and expressing a hope that they could join him in the Valley. "The scene was very affecting indeed," stated a captain.[64]

At one o'clock, on a Virginia hillside, the Stonewall Brigade formed a hollow square to await Old Jack. Together, they had gathered to defend Virginia, had struggled with the demands of soldiering, had bled on another hill, and had earned a nickname that bound them as one. The men had not bent willingly at times to his stern dictates of discipline and of duty, but at Manassas, he had brought them victory and acclaim as heroes. So they stood, in close ranks, behind new flags, with a pride that they shared with him.[65]

Jackson soon appeared, accompanied by his staff, and rode to the front of the brigade. He was ill-suited for such occasions, and as he looked upon the faces before him, he tried to master the emotions within himself. Removing his hat, he began: "Officers and men of the First Brigade! You do not expect a speech from me. I come to bid you a heartfelt goodbye." He reminded them briefly of Harper's Ferry, of the "hard marches," and of the "imperishable honor" they had gained at Manassas. He then paused, struggling with his feelings as some men in the ranks wept. Finally, with arms raised, in a louder voice, he said:

> You were the First Brigade in the Army of the Shenandoah, the First Brigade in the Army of the Potomac, and the First Brigade in the Second Corps, and are the First Brigade in the hearts of your general. I hope that you will be the First Brigade in this, our second struggle for independence, and in the future, on the fields on which the Stonewall Brigade are engaged, I expect to hear of crowning deeds of valor and of victories gloriously achieved! May God bless you all! Farewell![66]

Jackson turned his horse around and spurred away. Behind him, the Valley men, many with tears, burst into a loud, rolling cheer. Most of them, if not all, wished as one wrote that "I could go with him, though my hardships should be more than doubled." As Jackson boarded a train toward the Blue Ridge, they returned to their tents. Around campfires, they probably spoke of him and of the Valley.[67]

4

✠

"DAMD HARD BUSINESS"

LIEUTENANT Samuel Moore rejoined the Stonewall Brigade at its camp near Centreville, a day or two after Stonewall Jackson said his farewell to the unit. Moore had been away from the command for several weeks on provost duty in the Shenandoah Valley, searching for deserters. He was disgusted by what he found in the brigade, complaining to his wife on November 7: "we have sort of a holiday time in our Brigade since my return there has been little done by the men but to eat, drink and be merry, which our soldiers seem to know how to do most thoroughly."[1]

The young officer wanted drills to resume and discipline tightened, but on the day he wrote his letter, a rumor swept the camp that the brigade had been ordered to the Valley with Jackson. Confirmation came the next day, and on the evening of the 8th, the five regiments marched to Manassas Junction to board trains. The holiday mood that Moore described increased with the prospects of a return home. "There is no place on this side of the Blue Ridge that I do like," contended a brigade member, undoubtedly speaking for many comrades. Even Moore admitted to his wife that the Valley was "the spot above all others that I want to defend."[2]

A steady, soaking rain fell as the Second, Fifth, and Twenty-seventh Virginia boarded cars at the station. The members of the Fourth and Thirty-third Virginia had to wait until the engine and cars returned from the Valley. For them, it would be a long, miserable night in the rain. The Irishmen in Company E, Thirty-third Virginia comforted themselves with whiskey, but after a few hours of revelry, a dispute ignited a brawl. The inebriated Irishmen slashed and stabbed each other with knives and bayonets before armed guards arrested the unscathed combatants and sent the wounded to doctors. Nearly a month later, Jackson was still complaining about the "unmanageable Irishmen."[3]

The first contingent of the brigade, meanwhile, arrived in Strasburg, south of Winchester, at 2:30 A.M. on the 9th. The men were soaked, cold, and hungry. They slogged through the mud in the darkness, seeking food among the town's residents. About six o'clock, the three regiments re-formed for the march to Winchester, but many, if not most, of the Virginians had decided that they had had enough of the war for a while and had gone home. In the Second Virginia, a number of officers refused to plod through the mud with the men, renting wagons and buggies to carry them into Winchester, where they spent the day at the Taylor Hotel.[4]

Many of those still in the ranks were drunk and were prodded along with rifle butts and bayonets by the rear guard. "Such a march in the rain I never had in all my life," grumbled Lieutenant Moore, who added that the men "behaved abominally." When the regiments approached Winchester, contingents of militiamen blocked the road. Jackson had issued orders for the brigade to camp south of town and for the men to be kept out of Winchester. When the orders were announced, however, entire companies mutinied, refusing to countermarch and to bivouac. "Jackson and all hell could not keep us out of Winchester," one Virginian avowed, and some of them, with fixed bayonets, scattered the militia guards and entered the town. "The difference between us and the militia was," recalled a brigade member, "that we had been in the first battle of Manassas."[5]

The final companies of the Fourth and Thirty-third Virginia filtered into the camp throughout November 10. The Rockbridge Artillery, meanwhile, marched overland to the Valley. Like their infantry comrades, the artillerists secured whiskey and celebrated. "The men seemed to have set out with the intention of making this march a sort of a spree" and "they succeeded pretty well in carrying out their intentions," claimed a battery member. So many were drunk after a night's "spree" that sober men who had never driven the teams handled the reins. They "knew no more about

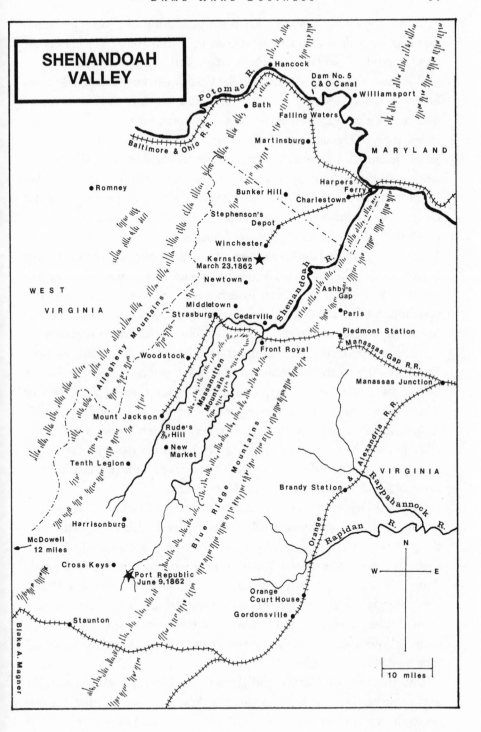

it," wrote a gunner, "than they knew about steering a balloon. The situation was disgusting; so much that it grew to be ludicrous." The battery arrived by the 11th, and with the foot soldiers settled into camp routine.[6]

Winchester's residents welcomed the Valley men, opening their doors to family members, friends, and strangers. "Our town is all astir in consequence of the arrival of Jackson's Brigade," noted Julia Chase, a Unionist, in her diary. "The citizens of Winchester feel perfectly safe now, I suppose." Eventually, Jackson and brigade officers herded the soldiers out of town, and before long, the general sent the command to Camp Stephenson, four miles north of Winchester. There, the brigade pitched tents and resumed drills. In nearby farmhouses, officers' wives and children, as plentiful "as black-berries in August," boarded.[7]

Jackson attributed the breakdown of discipline and organization in the brigade during the trip to the Valley to the lack of a commander. On November 11, he wrote to General Joseph Johnston's chief of staff that "it is very important that I should have a good Brigadier General in command of my old Brigade at this moment," describing some of the regiments as "greatly disorganized." "It is important," he continued, "that the Brig. Genl. should be with his command so as to know it and be in turn known before the battle." Jackson recommended either Colonel A. P. Hill or Brigadier General Robert E. Rodes, both of whom were Virginians, and in Jackson's view, capable officers. In fact, before he left the army at Centreville, Jackson had expressed to Johnston the notion that Hill "might be my successor." The Valley commander's choice of Hill would be ironic because of future difficulties between the two men.[8]

The War Department, however, chose neither of Jackson's recommendations and instead appointed Brigadier General Richard B. Garnett to the post on November 14. A Virginian from an aristocratic family, Garnett was a West Pointer and had spent nearly two decades in the Regular Army. He was forty-four years old, of medium height, blond and blue-eyed. Handsome and proud, he looked like an aristocratic man in uniform, but he possessed a personal warmth that in time would endear him to his officers and men. They came to regard him as "the soldier's friend," who tended to their welfare.[9]

Unfortunately for Garnett and Jackson, the latter did not welcome the appointment. The Valley commander believed apparently that Garnett owed the assignment to political influence. In time, Jackson came to regard the brigadier as a lax disciplinarian and disliked him personally. By

Jackson's rigorous standards, Garnett lacked the iron hand necessary in a brigade commander.[10]

The brigadier assumed command of the Stonewall Brigade on December 7. He went to work at once, holding an inspection of arms and battalion drill. In the evenings, Garnett rode through the regimental camps, speaking with the officers and men. "With our Genl," wrote an officer soon afterward, "there is not so much formality and pretention about him." On the 10th, Garnett reviewed the brigade before a large crowd of civilians from Winchester. "We were all dressed in our best uniforms," wrote a member, "& made quite an imposing display."[11]

Within a week of the review, Jackson started north down the Valley with the Stonewall Brigade, militia companies, and the Rockbridge Artillery. Jackson's target was Dam No. 5 of the Chesapeake & Ohio Canal along the Potomac River. Since the Confederates had halted traffic on the Baltimore & Ohio Railroad, the canal served as the transportation link for the Federals along the river. Constructed of stone-filled wooden cribs, the dam supplied water for twenty-two miles of the canal. While the waterway lay north of the river and guarded by Union troops, the dam was along the southern bank and vulnerable to Confederate raids. An earlier attempt by a detachment from the brigade had failed, so Jackson decided to advance in force against the site.[12]

The Confederates marched on December 16, camping at Big Spring, three miles south of Martinsburg. Companies of the Second Virginia had been posted in the town for two weeks, and when Lieutenant Moore saw Jackson on the streets, he wrote that "I knew Genl Jackson had not come for nothing." "I really was glad to see him," continued Moore, "and when there is serious work to do, I want him to be at hand." A private shared Moore's view, jotting in his diary that "all are delighted because Gen. Jackson is with us for all of us will follow wherever he may go."[13]

Despite Jackson's presence, the dam's structure and Federal troops across the river in Maryland defied Confederate efforts. For three days, the Southerners tried to break apart the wooden cribs with crowbars and axes while being subjected to artillery and musketry fire. On the 20th, Jackson feinted upstream with the militia, and the enemy followed, permitting work crews to make a minor breach in the dam. Jackson settled for this, and two days later, the command returned to the Winchester area.[14]

The members of the Stonewall Brigade celebrated the holidays at Camp

Stephenson. On Christmas Eve, three wagons, filled with "the good things of life" from Rockbridge County families, rolled into camp for the Twenty-seventh Virginia. The next day, the men feasted on "roast turkey, sausage, cakes, pies, fruits" and "had a royal time." In the Second Virginia, a majority of men sneaked out of camp to spend the celebrations in their Lower Valley homes.[15]

At year's end, some of the men reflected on the momentous preceding months. "A year ago," Lieutenant John Grabill of the Thirty-third Virginia confided to his diary, "we had not national existence now we look forward to be ranked as one of the nations of the world. May God grant that we be blessed with posterity equal to that which has been lavished upon us in the past." Adjutant James Langhorne of the Fourth Virginia thought of home, of parties, and of "how different will be the approaching New Years Day." He believed that instead of enjoying the warmth of family and friends: "I will be on a hostile march against those whom at this time last year I called 'brothers, countrymen & friends.'"[16]

Under a slate of bleak, gray clouds, Major General George McClellan watched with pride the passage of his creation. Since his appointment to command nearly four months earlier, "Little Mac," as the men called him, worked to forge an army from the defeated units of Bull Run and the dozens of newly formed regiments that had been hurried to Washington. He ordered countless hours of training, evening dress parades, and periodic reviews. With justification, he refused to advance against the Confederates near Centreville, but now, on November 20, he wanted to display his army for capital "big bugs" that included President Abraham Lincoln, cabinet members, and thousands of civilians.[17]

"It was by far the grandest thing I ever saw," exclaimed a private about the review of 70,000 troops and 120 cannon. When McClellan, Lincoln, and generals rode along the front of the arrayed columns, "cheer after cheer filled the air." An officer asserted that "such shouting you never heard." As the reviewing party passed the brigade of Brigadier General Rufus King, however, the Wisconsin and Indiana men stood in silence. "We have been taught and teach our men," explained Major Edward Bragg of the Sixth Wisconsin, "that perfect silence in the ranks is evidence of the true and well disciplined soldier."[18]

While McClellan enjoyed evident popularity with the rank and file, his regimen of strict discipline and drills had worn thin. Soldiering was, a private in the Second Wisconsin grumbled at this time, "damd hard business." The grand performance on the 20th marked the third review in less than two weeks for King's men. They were weary of and frustrated by the school of the soldier and the sham battles. They had volunteered to fight Southerners, and except for the Second Wisconsin's experience at Bull Run and the Nineteenth Indiana's skirmish or "sort of a scratch" at Lewinsville in September, the Westerners had only exchanged long-range picket shots with the enemy. An enlisted man described well the situation to his father, "no fighting, except a fist fight now and then."[19]

Other factors contributed to the sour moods. In the Sixth Wisconsin, Colonel Lysander Cutler had ordered examinations for selected officers that resulted in the resignations of four captains and six lieutenants. When the Nineteenth Indiana drilled, Colonel Solomon Meredith exposed "himself to the contempt of the officers," argued a member of the regiment, "and became a laughing stock to his men." Officers plotted either to have him promoted to brigadier or to resign but failed on both attempts. "Men can not will not fight," a lieutenant claimed, "when they think their officers dont know what they are doing."[20]

Four days after McClellan's grand review, Captain Edwin Brown, Sixth Wisconsin, painted a somber description of the army's morale. "I don't believe if the Army was disbanded, to be called *voluntarily* together again in a month," Brown alleged to his parents, "that one Enlisted man in twenty would re-enlist in this vast army of ours. I don't believe that one third of commissioned officers would stay if their pride did not keep them. The discipline is very strict. The hardships are many now, and most every one thinks of the cheerful faces & blazing fires of *home* with a very strong desire to be there."[21]

Whether Captain Brown's dismal portrait was accurate is difficult to assess—his letters reveal a man given to pessimism, complaint, and homesickness. He assured his parents that "you need not fear anything dishonorable from me," nor would have most parents from their sons in the army. The weeks of drills, guard and picket duty, work details, and inspections undoubtedly eroded spirits with the prospects of months of more labor and of cold weather ahead. Without the experience of combat, few officers and men accepted the value of training and of discipline.[22]

During the initial weeks of December, McClellan's Army of the Potomac prepared for the advent of winter. On Arlington Heights, King's troops built log huts with brick fireplaces. Some of the bolder men sneaked into the countryside, confiscating furniture and mirrors from civilian residences for the huts. When not restricted to camp by duties, groups of men visited the Capitol to "see what Congress does." After a visit to the Senate, Captain Brown described its members as looking like "bald headed Methodist Class leaders with just about brains *enough to howl & blat* without much substance to their speech."[23]

The wearisome routine of camp life still filled the days. "We are perfectly tired of doing nothing but drill, drill and no fighting," a Wisconsin corporal muttered on the 19th. "If we could only hear the long roll beat, I tell you every man would jump out of his boots to go." Companies from each regiment rotated picket duty at the front. One night members of the Seventh Wisconsin fired at "shadows," which elicited sneers from the other regiments. But on another night, pickets of the Sixth Wisconsin saw "a barn advancing on them," as a corporal in the Seventh recorded it, and "they all fired on it and retreated back into the woods." "I don't know," he scoffed, "whether the barn followed them or not." Despite the humor of the incidents, picketing was, the corporal said, "rather risky business."[24]

Fifty-one members of King's brigade, meanwhile, had volunteered for service with Battery B, Fourth U.S. Artillery. Unlike the volunteer units, Battery B had a military lineage that dated from 1821. Its members had fought in the Seminole Wars in Florida, in the conflict against Mexico, and on the Western frontier. When the Civil War began, the battery was stationed at Camp Floyd, Utah Territory. Orders summoning it east did not arrive until July, when the camp's contingent of artillery, infantry, and cavalry began the 1,200-mile trek to Fort Leavenworth, Kansas. From there, they marched across Missouri to St. Joseph, boarded trains, and arrived in Washington in October. The War Department assigned Battery B to Brigadier General Irvin McDowell's division.[25]

Captain John Gibbon commanded the battery, and McDowell appointed him chief of artillery for the division. To fill Battery B's depleted ranks, Gibbon visited each regiment in the division, including King's four Western units, and obtained 150 volunteers, who he stated were "of the finest material for soldiers I ever saw." Gibbon had a Regular Army officer's prejudice against volunteers but admitted that his recruits possessed "quick intelligence." McDowell attached the battery with its new members to King's brigade, beginning an association that would last over a year. In the Second Wisconsin, Company K was reorganized into a heavy artillery battery and assigned to the capital's defenses. By the end of December, however, a new company, the Swiss-German Rifles, from Wisconsin replaced the departed unit in the regiment.[26]

Christmas passed quietly on Arlington Heights for the Wisconsin and Indiana men. "The camp is uncommonly still," a soldier noted in his diary, with the troops enjoying "a splendid Christmas dinner" of boiled beef, beans, and bread. Fifer Ludolph Longhenry, a German immigrant in the Seventh Wisconsin, confided to his diary that "here Christmas pleasures are very rare." He believed he knew why, adding that "it is because Americans do not have any *gemutlichkeit* [generosity], Americans are a materialistic people, and are interested only in making money and raising hell."[27]

During the year's final week, the Westerners participated in a sham battle with the division, buried a comrade in the Seventh Wisconsin and the wife of an Indiana soldier, and went on picket duty. On New Year's Eve, the army celebrated with cannon and rifle fire at midnight. Before he slept that night, Captain Brown wrote to his wife, remarking that "we have not killed any of the enemy yet but I feel like a veteran of 100 battles."[28]

Campfires flickered in the winter wind as soldiers huddled together and stomped the ground in a vain effort to resist the frigid temperatures that cut deep into a man. Some of them even double-quicked back and forth to allay the numbness in their bodies. They had marched eight miles that day from their camps near Winchester toward a destination none of them knew. With Old Jack they expected secrecy, but they had not expected a campaign in weather that could punish man and beast.[29]

Since his arrival in the Shenandoah Valley in November, Stonewall Jackson had been planning and working on this operation. "I deem it of very great importance," he wrote to the Confederate secretary of war on the 20th, "that Northwestern Virginia be occupied by Confederate troops this winter." Specifically, he wanted to occupy Romney, forty-three miles west of Winchester, and if possible, retake the portions of the state lost to the Federals during the early fall. At the time, four thousand Union troops, under Brigadier General Benjamin F. Kelley, held Romney, with several thousand more, under Major General Nathaniel P. Banks, stationed in Maryland along the Potomac River, opposite the Valley.[30]

Jackson counted barely five thousand officers and men with the Stonewall Brigade, inadequately armed and trained militia companies, and several companies of cavalry under the dashing and fearless Lieutenant Colonel Turner Ashby. To undertake a movement against Romney, Jackson required more troops. He requested the three brigades of Brigadier General William W. Loring stationed to resist a Union force in southwestern Virginia. The War Department acquiesced, ordering Loring to Winchester. It took nearly a month for all of Loring's roughly five thousand troops to join Jackson, who issued instructions for the march on the year's final day. The district commander planned to advance on Bath (now Berkeley Springs, West Virginia), and Hancock, Maryland, across the river, dispersing the enemy and securing his flank and rear before he turned toward Romney.[31]

The Confederates marched from Winchester on New Year's Day in weather that reminded the men of early spring, but after nightfall the temperature plummeted, and the troops sought warmth around fires. They had no tents, and those who tried to sleep did so under blankets on the ground. Snow fell on January 2, with the winds driving it into the men's faces. Wagon and artillery teams struggled on the frozen, icy roads. Night brought little respite and less sleep, but by the 3rd, the column approached Bath and its garrison of 1,400 Federal troops.[32]

Jackson planned to trap the enemy, but his army did not, probably could not, respond. Loring's units floundered, and when Jackson came upon the Stonewall Brigade halted in the road and drawing rations from wagons, he sought out Richard Garnett, demanding an explanation.

"I have halted to let the men cook their rations," the brigadier said.

"There is no time for that," responded Jackson, undoubtedly with his blue eyes ablaze.

"But it is impossible for the men to march farther without them," Garnett countered.

"I never found anything impossible with this brigade," asserted Jackson.

Garnett ordered the men back into column, and the march resumed. Another snowstorm blew in during the night. Shielded by it, the Federals abandoned Bath on the 4th.[33]

"It has been the worst march in every respect we have ever taken," Sergeant Hugh A. White informed his father in a letter on the 4th. Nevertheless, Jackson pushed toward Hancock on the 5th, halting the column three miles south of the Potomac. Details of men destroyed a bridge over the Big Cacapon River, wrecked a section of B & O Railroad track, and burned a warehouse. At eight o'clock that night another heavy snowfall began. The next morning, before most of the men awoke, the scene, according to a diarist, "was that of a country graveyard, the hillocks resembling graves covered with snow, each representing a live Confederate." Another soldier described it simply as "a horrible night."[34]

On January 6, Jackson abandoned his attempt to capture Hancock and withdrew the troops back to Bath. The Confederates began a countermarch south toward Unger's Store on the afternoon of the 7th, continuing into the morning of the 8th. Conditions were probably worse than before as temperatures plunged and a northwest wind "cut like a knife" into the men. They slipped and fell often on the frozen road, and drivers struggled to keep wagons and artillery pieces on the surface. At Unger's, Jackson halted his army, and there it remained for the next four days.[35]

From Unger's, Captain Samuel Moore wrote to his wife, Ellen, "I seem to be farther away from home than I ever have been since the beginning of the war." A private told his sister that the men were "weak and poor and can not stand much hardship." In fact, hundreds were sick from the exposure, and wagons hauled them to Winchester. The suffering did not escape Jackson, and he issued furloughs to an officer, a noncommissioned officer, and two privates in each company. He also granted leaves to three regimental commanders in the Stonewall Brigade and sent a fourth, Colonel James Allen, to Winchester on court-martial duty.[36]

The Confederates began their three-day march to Romney on January 13. Their accounts of the march describe a harrowing ordeal. Many marched barefoot because their shoes had burned as they attempted to warm their feet. An artillerist recalled how sad it was "to hear the *chorus* of *coughing* that rose from the lines of the poor fellows" as the regiments passed the cannon. The icy road jammed often with the wagons, forcing the infantrymen to stand for hours "freezing & imprecating the cause of our delay." They had little to nourish themselves, except crackers. One enlisted man estimated that between a fourth and a third of the command were either disabled or sick. A major argued that "two battles would not have done us as much injury as hard weather and exposure have effected."[37]

Jackson and the Stonewall Brigade entered Romney on the evening of January 15, during a sleet storm with "the men encased in ice & icicles hanging from the visors of their caps." The Federals had withdrawn hastily, abandoning supplies and tents. During the next two days, Loring's men dragged themselves into the village that a soldier in the Fourth Virginia described as "this hog pen." Jackson quartered his old brigade in houses and Loring's troops in the tents.[38]

The aggressive Jackson contemplated an advance farther into the mountains but thought better of it because, as he reported, Loring's command had "become very much demoralized." In fact, the discontent and low morale extended into the Stonewall Brigade. An officer in the Rockbridge Artillery wrote later that nothing during the war compared to the "physical and mental suffering" that they endured on this campaign and that "the expedition seemed to everybody to be a dismal failure. Our confidence in our leader was sorely tried." When the Valley men heard the order for their return march to Winchester, they shouted.[39]

The Stonewall Brigade marched out of Romney on January 23, with "no one shedding a tear," noted a private in his diary. Jackson left behind Loring's brigades to occupy the region. As the Virginians filed past, Loring's men watched in angry silence. They derisively called Garnett's soldiers "Jackson's Pet Lambs," while members of the Stonewall Brigade likened Loring and his men to "a scared turkey." The animosity between the two commands had resulted in a number of fistfights while in Romney. "The Stonewall Brigade," argued a lieutenant, "reserved to itself the exclusive right to cuss 'Old Jack.'"[40]

The Valley men reached Winchester on the 25th, bivouacking on its outskirts. Adjutant James Langhorne of the Fourth Virginia summarized aptly their feelings after nearly four weeks of soldiering in freezing temperatures and snow, without adequate shelter and food: "I have witnessed and experienced all of a winters campaign that I desire. . . . I have endured & seen others endure that which if a man had told me 12 months ago that men could stand such hardships, I would have called him a fool." By one estimate, three hundred of their comrades lay in Winchester hospitals, with many dying from the pneumonia that drowned their lungs. Others, who had been spared, deserted. Three weeks after the brigade's return, Colonel William Harman reported that at least in the Fifth Virginia there were "a general & thorough demoralization" and "the rapid thinning out of our numbers."[41]

Despite the hardships and apparent failure, Jackson had succeeded in the overall objective of occupying Romney, damaging the railroad, and preventing an advance by the Federals into the Valley. The weather and its toll on men and animals thwarted his more ambitious plans. Unfortunately, all that had been achieved seemed to unravel, when on January 31, Jackson received a telegram from Secretary of War Judah P. Benjamin, instructing the district commander to order Loring's brigades "back to Winchester immediately." Stunned and angered at Benjamin's interference with his command and authority, Jackson submitted his resignation within an hour.[42]

Loring and his brigade commanders had convinced the secretary that Jackson had abandoned them in the forsaken village and that they were in danger of being assailed by a Union counterthrust. Benjamin then issued the order, igniting a dispute that embroiled Jackson, Benjamin, President Jefferson Davis, General Joseph Johnston, and Governor John Letcher. In the end, Letcher and Congressman Alexander Boteler, a friend of Jackson, convinced him that Virginia and the Confederacy required his services, and Jackson withdrew his letter. The War Department promoted Loring, dispatching him to southwestern Virginia, and parceled out his brigades, with Jackson retaining the Virginia units.[43]

The members of the Stonewall Brigade were "excited and enraged" by the controversy. "They all cling to their gallant commander & protest against the very thought of his leaving the Valley," stated a Virginian. "No man in the Confederacy can ever gain the confidence of the people so entirely as Jackson does. Hence no one can fill his place." Major Frank Jones informed his mother while the events unfolded that "Romney is evacuated, so is Bath, Genl Jackson has resigned I declare I believe the world is turned up side down."[44]

While the government officials and generals feuded, the Stonewall Brigade settled into winter quarters on Pughtown Road about five miles north of Winchester. The Valley men built log huts, enjoyed ample food, and recovered from the Romney Campaign. During February, the soldiers discussed the Confederacy's offer of a fifty-dollar bounty and a thirty-day furlough to reenlist for the duration of the war. Opinions varied, but most of the men signed up and departed for home. Jackson limited the number of leaves to one third of the rank and file at a time. A private summarized most of his comrades' attitudes when he wrote, "No, never do I intend to desert the flag of my country, so long as the abominable flag of despotism hovers over a fort on Southern soil." They knew that with warmer weather Old Jack would file them into column and lead them on another road.[45]

✝

Beyond the Blue Ridge, in the forts and camps that ringed Washington, Union troops plodded through "mud mud and upon mud." The snow that blanketed the northwestern Valley and the mountains either turned to rain or melted quickly in the East. The weather, however, still limited training and confined men to their log huts.[46]

On Arlington Heights, like their comrades in other units, the Wisconsin and Indiana men of Rufus King's brigade endured the tedium of winter quarters. Their incessant complaint of the autumn echoed through their letters during the weeks of January and February. "There is considerable discontentment in the army here," Sergeant James Converse of the Sixth Wisconsin wrote typically, "the boys say they enlisted to fight not to lay around here in the mud." When Corporal Orson Parker of the Second Wisconsin learned that recruits were enlisting in his hometown, he cautioned that "they will learn a good lesson but I should advise [any] man that knows his gate to stay at home."[47]

A daily routine formed their lives, with three or four days of picket duty interspersed every three weeks. Experience had taught them to prepare flavorful concoctions from the army issue of hardtack, salt pork, and beef. Some men liked a sandwich of raw pickled pork between two pieces of hardtack, while a brigade favorite consisted of pieces of hardtack cooked in a little water in a skillet, or a "spider" as men called it, and seasoned with pork fat. They dubbed the dish a "son-of-a-bitch." Their "perpetual beverage" was coffee "for breakfast, dinner, & supper."[48]

King and regimental commanders restricted passes into Washington, and the guardhouses had a constant flow of occupants who had violated the orders or had committed other crimes. City bawdy houses—Washington "abounds in women of easy virtue," grumbled Captain Edwin Brown—enticed some of the men. Others visited frequently a nearby camp of German soldiers, who distilled their own whiskey. The imbibers attached names to the various drinks, such as "Slow Torture," "Death Bed Confession," and "Kill at the Counter," the latter designating a brand that killed the drinker before change could be made. The whiskey ignited numerous fights and piled more soldiers in the guardhouses.[49]

Officers enjoyed a wider latitude of freedom and movement. Lieutenant Colonel Lucius Fairchild of the Second Wisconsin spent many afternoons and evenings in the company of a number of women, including an eighteen-year-old, a widow, and the wife of a hotel owner. In the Seventh Wisconsin, Lieutenant Hollon Richardson courted Leonora Robinson, who was visiting her father, Colonel William Robinson. Colonel Robinson objected vigorously to the relationship, forbidding his daughter from seeing the young officer. Leonora defied her father, and in the spring the couple eloped. In time, Richardson proved to be a fine officer and rose to the rank of lieutenant colonel.[50]

When the skies cleared and the mud dried, the officers conducted two hours of drill each day, followed by dress parade at sunset. Bayonet exercises augmented the regular company and battalion drills. Such training moved one private to write that "it is strange predeliction we have for injuring our brother man, but we learn the art of killing far easier than we do a hard problem in arithmetic."[51]

During the third week of February, the three Wisconsin regiments received new .58-caliber Springfield rifles, the Union army's standard shoulder arm. The new weapons "look as if they were made for service," asserted a private. But almost any gun would have been better than the Austrian, Belgian, and converted Harper's Ferry muskets they had been carrying. A sergeant claimed that his old weapon reminded him "of Sam Edward's 'Dog Gun,' which he says will 'kick' a man down, and 'kick' *at* him six times after he is down." "Our boys think they can whip any amount of Secesh," boasted another soldier after they obtained the Springfields.[52]

Sickness stalked the camps, a relentless companion. A report by the army's medical director for January noted 263 men as sick out of an aggregate of 3,669 in the brigade. Fatalities from disease took almost sixty men in the Nineteenth Indiana and seventeen in the Seventh Wisconsin. Surgeons discharged from service eighty-five men in the Sixth Wisconsin alone. When measles felled some in early February, officers and men received vaccinations. The prediction from a volunteer months earlier that disease would take more lives than bullets seemed ominously real.[53]

On February 22, the army and the city celebrated George Washington's birthday with cannon, church bells, dress parades by the troops, and the reading of the first president's Farewell Address. Earlier, Lincoln had ordered an advance of the Union armies on or before that date, but in Virginia, McClellan countered Lincoln's instructions with a strategic proposal that left his army in place when the deadline came.[54]

The inactivity rubbed harder into the Western men. "I would not go home now if I could," vowed Corporal Horace Emerson, a veteran of Bull Run. "I want satisfaction out of Secesh they made me run (and dident I) and I will endeavor to make them do the same." He thought that "it would be a disgrace" if the war ended before they could redeem themselves. A private in the same regiment complained that "I am tired" of camp life, and "I shall be glad when the word comes for us to go on to Battle."[55]

About this time a comrade of Corporal Emerson penned a group portrait of the four Western regiments. His own regiment, the Second, he described as "probably the hardest set of boys, but good natured and easy to get along with. They wear an air of fearless carelessness wherever found." The Sixth Wisconsin, he thought, "is more stately, and distant, and march to slower music than we do," while the Seventh Wisconsin "puts on the least style and crow the least." The Seventh "is the truest friend the 2d ever found." As for the Hoosiers of the Nineteenth Indiana, "they pride themselves on their fighting pluck—which is undoubtedly good—more than their drill." The Nineteenth "is an indifferent, don't care regiment." He concluded that "as a brigade we get along finely together."[56]

5

✣

"If This Valley Is Lost"

THE familiar landmarks along the road enlivened the spirits of the Confederate soldiers. Although officers prodded them to keep the ranks closed up, the men knew that Stonewall Jackson was leading them north, down the Shenandoah Valley, and toward the Yankees. It was Saturday, March 22, 1862, a cold, blustery day with patches of snow pockmarking the ground. At nightfall, they halted north of Strasburg, along Cedar Creek. The exhausted troops had covered twenty-six miles during the day, with hundreds unable to keep pace. The stragglers stumbled in as their comrades warmed themselves around fires and shared the rumor that the Federals had evacuated Winchester, an easy day's march to the north.[1]

Less than a fortnight before, the Confederates had passed this way en route south. During the first week of March, nearly 24,000 Union troops under Major General Nathaniel Banks had advanced on Jackson's forces in their winter quarters around Winchester. A prominent Massachusetts politician without military experience, Banks probed the Southern position cautiously. Jackson reacted boldly—"I never saw a finer feeling or more enthusiasm since I have been in the army," claimed a Confederate staff officer about Jackson's men—but he barely mustered 3,600 troops to oppose Banks. On March 7, Colonel Turner Ashby's cavalrymen had clashed with Federal units five miles north of Winchester, but the blue-clad soldiers withdrew.[2]

On the day of Ashby's encounter, to the east, Brig. General Joseph Johnston began the evacuation of the Centreville-Manassas area with the Confederacy's main army in Virginia. Anticipating an advance by McClellan, Johnston decided to pull his army closer to Richmond. The department commander had been in communication with Jackson about operations west of the Blue Ridge, opposing a stand in the Lower Valley by his aggressive subordinate. Johnston expected Jackson to conform with his movements and to prevent Banks from detaching units to McClellan.[3]

While Johnston's army marched away from Centreville, Jackson sought to assail a weak segment of Banks's lines. Jackson's boldness stalled the Federals, but at last the Confederate commander ordered reluctantly the abandonment of Winchester. "I have only to say that if this Valley is lost Virginia is lost," he told a friend. Shielded by darkness, the Confederates marched through Winchester on the night of March 11–12, with the Stonewall Brigade as rear guard. From behind windows and in doorways, women of the town wept.[4]

The Confederates filed up the Valley Pike for the next five days, eventually camping along the Shenandoah River, four miles north of Mt. Jackson. The Northerners trailed to Cedar Creek and then halted when the Rebels contested the crossing. A Stonewall Brigade private summarized graphically to his sister the recent movements. "Old Banks thought to distinguish himself by bagging 'Old Jack,'" he wrote, "but he finds an affinity between Gen Jackson & the Irishman's flea—'when he goes to put his finger on him he ain't thar.' & I'll bet my head agin' a rotten rail that if old Banks comes up the Valley very far he will get into a bag himself."[5]

Banks had no intention of doing that; in fact, he had received orders from McClellan to leave the region and march to Manassas. On March 21, Ashby reported to Jackson that the troops of Brigadier General James Shields's division were retreating north toward Winchester while wagons were rolling east toward the Blue Ridge. Jackson reacted at once, as he explained later: "Apprehensive that the Federals would leave this military district, I determined to follow them with all my available forces."[6]

The Confederates marched north on the afternoon of the 21st, as rain, mixed with snow, fell. They did not look like an army. As a militiaman with them remembered, they "were dressed in every conceivable style," with slouched, beaver, and homemade hats, and were "uniformly dirty."

March 22 brought the twenty-six-mile forced march in which "a great many give out & dident get up until late at night," according to a lieutenant. Reveille sounded at five o'clock on the 23rd, and within two hours, the troops started toward Winchester. "I & every one else thought," claimed a Valley man, "just to walk in and take possession" of the town.[7]

The march continued for seven hours until Jackson halted the column just south of the small village of Kernstown. Stragglers trailed the main body once again, and orders came to bivouac. Ahead, Ashby's horsemen confronted Union artillery and infantry posted on both sides of the Valley Pike near the town. When the cavalry officer reported that he opposed only a brigade, Jackson decided to attack. Federal cannon held Pritchard's Hill just west of the turnpike. The elevated ground dominated the terrain around it, but a mile or so farther to the west, wooded Sandy Ridge extended north to Winchester. If the Southerners could secure Sandy Ridge, they could outflank the enemy position and seize the Valley Pike in its rear. Conversely, if they waited, the Federals could be reinforced and assault them the following day. Jackson issued the orders.[8]

March 23 was a Sabbath, a day Jackson believed was for the Lord's work, not a warrior's. Later, when Mary Anna Jackson questioned him about it, he responded, "I was greatly concerned, too; but I felt it my duty to do it, in consideration of the ruinous effects that might result from postponing the battle until the morning." Assuring her that he hoped and prayed "that I may never again be circumstanced as on the day," he believed that "as far as our troops were concerned, necessity and mercy both called for the battle."[9]

It was about three o'clock when the Confederate infantry and artillery advanced toward battle. Jackson did not clarify, however, his plans to subordinates. Confusion hampered Southern movements and dispositions from the outset. Consequently, the Rebels stumbled into a fierce engagement with a Federal division, not a brigade.[10]

Colonel Samuel V. Fulkerson's brigade of two regiments led the attack column. Behind Fulkerson came Brigadier General Richard Garnett's four regiments of the Stonewall Brigade—Jackson had detached the Fifth Virginia as a reserve. Garnett counted fewer than eleven hundred rank and file in the four regiments and had orders to support Fulkerson. More than that, Garnett did not know.[11]

Artillery batteries dueled as the Confederate infantry entered wooded

Sandy Ridge. The Twenty-seventh Virginia had been ordered forward personally by Jackson and opened the engagement. On its left, Fulkerson's men closed. Before the Southerners, Colonel Erasmus B. Tyler's Union brigade, backed by cannon, opened fire. An Ohio regiment raced ahead toward a stone wall, but the Thirty-seventh Virginia of Fulkerson's command reached the wall first and blasted back the Federals. "Soon volleys of musketry seemed to shake the hills with their incessant roar," recounted an officer of the Fourth Virginia. "I could but wonder how any one could escape."[12]

Garnett brought the Second, Fourth, and Thirty-third Virginia into line between Fulkerson's men and the Twenty-seventh Virginia. The combat escalated into a seemingly unbroken sheet of musketry and artillery fire. Descriptions of the fury are uniformly similar—"incessant fire"; "the most terrific fight of musketry that can be well conceived"; and "the most desperate time I was ever in." For an hour and a half, the opponents hammered each other on Sandy Ridge.[13]

The Stonewall Brigade endured the worst punishment from Tyler's brigade and Colonel Nathan Kimball's. Lieutenant Colonel John Echols of the Twenty-seventh fell from a bullet that shattered an arm bone, while Lieutenant Colonel Charles Ronald of the Fourth was badly injured when his horse spooked, and he was thrown to the ground. In the Second, seven color-bearers were either killed or wounded. Finally, Colonel James W. Allen seized the flag, encouraging the men and erasing questions about his bravery at First Manassas. "Col. Allen fought like a man," Captain Samuel Moore stated three days later. "He has gained wonderfully with his regiment." A colonel avowed that "men never behaved better." Across the ground, a Union regiment counted twenty-nine bullet holes in its flag.[14]

Federal numbers began to prevail. Earlier, when Jackson had learned of the size of the enemy force, he told a staff officer that "we are in for it." During the combat, Jackson oversaw the artillery, moved Colonel Jesse Burks's brigade into line beside the Stonewall Brigade, and encouraged the men to stand firm. If his outnumbered army could, as he testified later, "hold the position on the hill till after dark," he could extricate the units under the cover of night.[15]

For Richard Garnett, night could not descend too soon. His four regiments in the center of the Confederate line had been subjected to concentrated enemy fire. The Valley troops had withstood the punishment

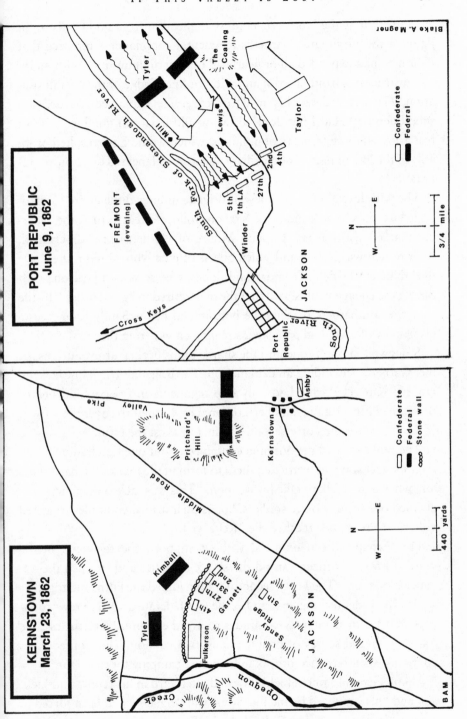

Blake A. Magner

PORT REPUBLIC
June 9, 1862

Confederate
Federal

3/4 mile

Cross Keys

FRÉMONT
(evening)

South Fork of Shenandoah River

Mill

Tyler

The Coaling

Lewis

Taylor

5th
7th LA
27th
2nd
4th

Winder

JACKSON

Port
Republic

South River

KERNSTOWN
March 23, 1862

Confederate
Federal
Stone wall

440 yards

Valley Pike

Pritchard's Hill

Middle Road

Kernstown

Ashby

Kimball

Tyler

Garnett
4th
27th
33rd
2nd

Fulkerson

Sandy Ridge

5th

JACKSON

Opequon Creek

BAM

valiantly, but as the Northerners pressed ahead in front and on the right flank of the Virginians, Garnett's regimental commanders reported that their men had expended all or nearly all of their ammunition. Without direct instructions from Jackson and without knowledge of the overall situation, Garnett ordered his men to retire. He explained his decision subsequently: "Had I not done so, we would have run imminent risk of being routed by superiority of numbers, which would have resulted probably in the loss of part of our artillery and also endangered our transportation."[16]

The withdrawal of the Stonewall Brigade unhinged the entire Confederate line. Fulkerson's and Burks's troops followed rearward as the Federals charged with cheers. Captain Moore of Garnett's brigade claimed, "our retreat was a slow and sullen one as of men who would rather have died than left the field." Major Frank Jones, who served on Jackson's staff during the engagement, stated that the men retired in "good order." By the time the Southerners reached the bottomland below Sandy Ridge, however, many of them had panicked, streaming away from the pursuers.[17]

Stonewall Jackson rode into the shards of his broken army. Furious, he met Garnett, demanding an explanation. The brigadier tried, but Jackson ignored him. The army had only two regiments in reserve, and one of them, the Fifth Virginia, had been ordered by Garnett to cover the retreat. Jackson sent for the Forty-second Virginia to assist the Fifth.[18]

The ranks of the Fifth Virginia contained about one hundred unarmed recruits. Jackson had instructed them to form in the rear of the battle line, and when a man fell, to take his weapon. "This was Jackson's tactics," exclaimed one of the novice soldiers. So, as their armed comrades triggered volleys, the recruits screeched the "Rebel yell."[19]

For perhaps fifteen minutes, without support, the regiment, in the words of a staff officer, "stood the shock of battle and stopped the advance of the foe." The Forty-second Virginia joined the Fifth, and together stalled the Federals long enough for the Confederate artillery crews to escape and for their infantry comrades to avoid capture. Nevertheless, the Yankees bagged scores of prisoners and two cannon. The Confederates continued their retreat south six miles before camping for the night.[20]

Union General James Shields boasted afterward in his report that Jackson and "his supposed invincible 'Stonewall Brigade'" had been forced to retreat "in disorder." The Federals had inflicted a decisive tactical defeat upon their opponent, inflicting more casualties than incurred. Jackson sustained losses of 451 killed and wounded and 286 captured or missing. Casualties for the Stonewall Brigade amounted to 65 killed or mortally wounded, 137 wounded, and 155 captured or missing, more than Fulkerson's and Burks's commands combined. The five regiments of Garnett's brigade averaged a casualty rate of nearly twenty-five percent. Conversely, the Southerners killed or wounded 574 Federals.[21]

Once again, on March 24, the Confederates followed the Valley Pike south, eventually reaching the former campsite near Mt. Jackson, on the 27th. Their reactions to Kernstown ranged from a private's "overpowered by numbers," to a captain's "I dont know what Genl Jackson was thinking of when he made the attack." An artillerist concluded that "Jackson must have been fooled by the Yankees." Although many of the officers and men questioned Jackson's decision to engage the enemy, their confidence in Old Jack, according to another officer, "is undiminished, and we will follow him with as much enthusiasm as ever."[22]

To the Valley commander, however, the primary responsibility for Kernstown rested with one man—Richard Garnett. In the days after the battle, Jackson convinced himself that Garnett was guilty of "neglect of duty." Twice during the battle, Jackson had sent aides with orders for the brigadier, and each time, the staff officers could not find him. The subordinate also had countermanded an order by halting the Fifth Virginia and posting it to cover the retreat. Finally, and most importantly, Garnett had withdrawn the brigade without authority, resulting in the collapse of the Confederate line. On April 1, Jackson ordered Garnett's arrest and relief from command.[23]

Jackson's acting chief of staff, Lieutenant Sandie Pendleton, delivered the order to Garnett. "I am exceedingly sorry for it," the twenty-one-year-old officer informed his mother two days later, "and was utterly amazed by it." Garnett had not "behaved in any but the most gallant manner," Pendleton explained, "but he was guilty of a breach of orders and partly to his mismanagement it is owing that we did not gain victory." The Stonewall Brigade, he added, "is in a very bad humour at [Garnett's arrest], for he was a pleasant man and exceedingly popular."[24]

"A very bad humour" did not begin to describe the brigade's reaction. Like Garnett, they were stunned and furious. "It fell like a thunderbolt on our Brigade," stated Major Frank Jones, who had been "closely" queried about orders at Kernstown by Jackson. Lieutenant Henry Kyd Douglas claimed that the officers and men "almost unanimously differed with"

Jackson's action. Their anger was, Douglas contended, so intense and universal that it "amounted almost to insubordination." An artillerist wrote that Garnett's "conduct enjoys the universal commendation of our Infantry." They believed, as Garnett had, that their withdrawal at Kernstown spared them from greater casualties. Lieutenant Colonel Andrew Grigsby was asked several weeks later if the brigade could have held their position for five minutes longer; he growled, "No sir, they could not have stood a damned second longer."[25]

When the officers heard the news, they gathered at Garnett's tent "to express our astonishment and sorrow to lose so valuable and so gallant an officer." Evidently, a number of them professed a willingness to testify on his behalf at a court of inquiry. They might have protested openly, but as Major Jones expressed to his wife: "our cause was too sacred to jeopardize [or] there would have been considerable commotion made amongst us." Instead, for the next three weeks, whenever Jackson passed the brigade, silence greeted him.[26]

Garnett left the army immediately, as Sandie Pendleton thought, "virtually ruined for the war." He traveled to Richmond, where he tried for months to secure a court of inquiry. The War Department suspended his arrest in June, and on August 6 the court convened. Only Jackson and Pendleton testified before Jackson ordered a movement of his command that resulted in the suspension of the inquiry. The court never reconvened, and on July 3, 1863, at Gettysburg, Garnett died at the head of a brigade in George Pickett's division.[27]

In the Valley, meanwhile, the Stonewall Brigade took the measure of a new commander. To the more perceptive among them, Jackson's dismissal of Garnett demonstrated Old Jack's stern and uncompromising adherence to his interpretation of proper conduct and performance. "Genl. G.'s fault was a blunder," wrote Pendleton, and in Jackson's army, a blunder would not be tolerated, particularly from the commander of the army's best brigade. But Jackson's aggressive tactics altered Union plans in Virginia, causing the administration in Washington to suspend Banks's departure from the region. The war in the Shenandoah Valley would continue.[28]

Like an awakened giant, the Union Army of the Potomac lumbered out of its winter camps on March 9, 1862, marching on the road to Centreville, Virginia. The column stretched for fifteen miles when all the units filed into formation. It was a massive, powerful weapon, the pride of its commander, Major General George McClellan. For months the officers and men in the ranks had waited for this day, but with McClellan, the road led toward specters.[29]

At Centreville, empty fortifications, guarded by fake cannon, made of wood and painted black, abandoned cabins, and deserted farms welcomed the Federals. Confederate General Joseph Johnston had begun the evacuation two days earlier, and by the time of McClellan's advance, the Southerners left behind discarded supplies and scarred earth. A Yankee soldier grumbled that the Rebels "lived better than we did last winter."[30]

The Federals occupied the Centreville-Manassas area for a week. Parties of soldiers roamed the countryside, foraging for chickens, pigs, and other foodstuffs, despite having "plenty to eat" and whiskey rations in the camp. While officers attempted to stop the foraging, most volunteer soldiers refused to accept the Regular Army's strictures against the practice. They came to resent Southern civilians and viewed the confiscation of civilian property as just punishment for the populace's support of treason and rebellion. Before long, foraging became common and widespread.[31]

The Wisconsin and Indiana troops of Rufus King's brigade raided the farmsteads. One corporal corraled six pigs himself during one night's excursion. The Westerners wanted, however, "to go on to Dixie." "We are ready to do anything," one of them told his parents, "for the sake of getting at the enemy." The men wagered that "the war will be closed up" by June, and they would miss their chance.[32]

While at Centreville, McClellan reorganized the army into corps, and received President Abraham Lincoln's final approval for an offensive against Richmond, via the Peninsula between the York and James rivers, east of the Confederate capital. The general and the president had discussed the plan for weeks, with Lincoln consenting at last only if Washington and its defenses were guarded with sufficient forces. The chief executive limited McClellan's authority by relieving him as general-in-chief of the Federal Armies while retaining him as commander of the Department of the Potomac.[33]

McClellan's plan required hundreds of transport vessels and ships to carry the army down the Potomac River and into the Chesapeake Bay to Fort Monroe at the tip of the Peninsula. The embarkation of troops, horses, mules, cannon, and mountains of supplies began on March 17, at Alexandria. In McClellan's reorganization, Major General Irvin McDowell assumed command of the First Corps, with Rufus King promoted to divisional command. King's senior colonel, Lysander Cutler of the Sixth Wisconsin, served temporarily as the brigadier's successor. With the rest of the army, Cutler's brigade marched to Alexandria for the journey by water.[34]

While the Westerners waited their turn to board the vessels, the news of Stonewall Jackson's attack at Kernstown reached Washington. Lincoln reacted by redirecting Nathaniel Banks back into the Valley and detaching McDowell's divisions from McClellan's movement. In turn, government officials created the Department of the Rappahannock and appointed McDowell as commander. On April 4, the First Corps, including Cutler's four regiments, started south, following the route of Johnston's Confederate army.[35]

The march took nearly three weeks as the corps followed the tracks of the Orange & Alexandria Railroad for part of it. The men foraged while en route. "We sampled this captured grub and liked it," recalled a Wisconsin soldier. "Yes we did!" At night, they used their recently issued shelter or "pup" tents. The tents consisted of two halves, each five feet, six inches square. Two men buttoned the halves together and crawled inside for the night. One Westerner concluded that the shelter halves had been invented by "some preacher who was desirous of getting the boys on their knees occasionally and thought this was a sure way."[36]

McDowell's troops arrived at Falmouth, opposite Fredericksburg, on the Rappahannock River, on April 23. A beautiful old colonial town, Fredericksburg lay on the river's southern bank, midway between Washington and Richmond. Here, McDowell could guard the overland approaches to the Union capital, and if needed, advance from the north in support of McClellan on the Peninsula. If Banks requested reinforcements in the Valley, McDowell could utilize the numerous gaps in the Blue Ridge.[37]

The Yankees had entered a section of the Old Dominion that most, if not all, had never seen before. Amid the natural beauty, splashed with the colors of spring blossoms and flowers, they began occupation duty. Few of Cutler's Westerners probably clung to the idea that the war would be over in several weeks. Captain Edwin Brown had become convinced that "the Seceded States can [not] be brought back into the Union without *Conquering the people of those states.*" So the Wisconsin and Indiana men performed their duties and waited for a new brigade commander. Unknowingly, their fates would be linked in the forthcoming weeks to events beyond the Blue Ridge, with those of Stonewall Jackson's troops.[38]

Brigadier General Charles Sidney Winder deserved better. A member of a prominent Maryland family, the thirty-two-year-old Winder was a West Pointer and former Regular Army officer who had resigned his commission on April 1, 1861. He had watched the bombardment of Fort Sumter and then received the colonelcy of the Sixth South Carolina. Confederate authorities promoted him to brigadier general on March 7, 1862, and when Stonewall Jackson dismissed Richard Garnett, Winder journeyed to the Valley to assume command of the Stonewall Brigade, arriving on April 2.[39]

A physically striking man, Winder carried himself with the air of a Regular Army officer. He believed in strict discipline, and as a Virginian noted later, had "a will as inflexible as that of Jackson himself." Unlike Garnett, Winder would earn Jackson's respect as a brigade commander, although the brigadier would adapt slowly to the secretive ways of Stonewall. Theirs would be an uneasy relationship for months.[40]

Winder's appointment, however, infuriated the Stonewall Brigade. Not only had Jackson treated Garnett wrongly, he chose an outsider, a Marylander, to command the Virginians. To demonstrate their disapproval, the regimental commanders refused initially to visit Winder's headquarters. Eventually, Colonel William Harman of the Fifth Virginia came to talk with Winder. The others soon followed, with Andrew Grigsby of the Twenty-seventh—"a bluff soldier given to swearing," according to one of Winder's staff officers—sitting often at night around the campfire and chatting with the brigadier.[41]

The rank and file greeted the Marylander with "sulky and resentful silence." A private claimed that "he was a kind of fancy General" and that "the boys all took a dislike to him from the start, and never did like him afterwards." They hissed him when he rode past until Winder told the colonels that he would hold them responsible for the "bad state of discipline." When Jackson ordered a reduction in the wagon train, which required the men either to discard items or carry them, the men blamed Winder. For days afterward, as he rode along the column or through the camps, the soldiers chanted: "More baggage, more baggage." He tried to have the culprits arrested, but none could be identified. His response only alienated the men further.[42]

Winder's arrival coincided with an influx of recruits into the brigade. The Furlough and Bounty Act passed by the Confederate Congress in December 1861 had resulted in reenlistment of an estimated thousand men in Jackson's command during January and February 1862. The recruits were either volunteers or militiamen whose units had been ordered into service until the Confederate Congress passed for the first time in American history a national conscription law on April 16. With some exceptions, all white Southern males, aged eighteen to thirty-five, were now subject to a draft. If a man volunteered, however, he could join a regiment of his selection.[43]

Jackson enforced the legislation with characteristic vigor. When he heard about bands of militiamen and deserters hiding in the mountains, he detached companies to flush them out and return them to the army. His efforts and those of recruiters increased the army with hundreds of new men. In the Stonewall Brigade, the Second Virginia added 274 soldiers, and the Thirty-third, 370. By the end of April, the brigade counted nearly 3,600 present for duty. A month earlier, only 1,400 had stood in the ranks at Kernstown.[44]

In the legislation, the Confederate Congress granted enlisted men the right to elect their company and regimental commanders. Before the Valley units could reorganize, however, Nathaniel Banks's Federals advanced south to Mt. Jackson, where Jackson had been camped since Kernstown. Confronted by this force, Jackson withdrew up the Valley, eventually halting at the foot of Swift Run Gap in the Blue Ridge, on April 19. During the next week, the members of the regiments exercised their right to elect new officers.[45]

Civil War officers earned their men's support primarily by tending to the welfare of those in the ranks and by leading through example in combat. The rank and file were impressed by an officer's willingness to share the hardships of a march and in camp. They resented an officer who flaunted his rank and exercised petty authority over them. In nearly all regiments, officers and men knew each other before the war, attended school and church together, worked in the same fields, and courted the same young women. Independent-minded, these Americans accepted being led, not compelled, by friends. Among the roughly two hundred infantry regiments in the Confederate forces in Virginia that spring, enlisted men voted out 155 field officers.[46]

Ranking officers voiced opposition to the law, arguing that merit, not the preferences of enlisted men, should govern promotions. Within the Stonewall Brigade, the members elected officers who seem to have earned the men's respect. In the Second Virginia, all three field officers retained their posts. Colonel James Allen had redeemed himself with the rank and file by his performance at Kernstown. Both Lieutenant Colonel Lawson Botts and Major Frank Jones had demonstrated their capabilities.[47]

The death of Colonel James Preston on January 20 opened the colonelcy of the Fourth Virginia. Lieutenant Colonel Charles Ronald had succeeded to the command in February, and was elected to the colonelcy by the men in April. Captains Robert D. Gardner and William Terry received the promotions to lieutenant colonel and major, respectively.[48]

The elections in the Fifth Virginia settled an old dispute. When Kenton Harper resigned the colonelcy in September 1861, Major William Baylor believed then that he deserved the post, but it went to Lieutenant Colonel William Harman, an unpopular choice with the officers and men. Jackson regarded Baylor highly and appointed him inspector general on his staff in November 1861. He was, wrote a fellow officer, "a first rate good fellow, good natured and accommodating." On April 21, the men voted unanimously for Baylor as their colonel, and a day later, he wrote to his wife, "I will have a fine regiment—one that loves me & will do every thing I can to make it a proud & noble defender of the country."[49]

Two company commanders received promotions to lieutenant colonel and major in the Fifth. Twenty-four-year-old Captain John Funk, an antebellum physician, was voted to the former rank, while Captain Hazael Williams replaced Absalom Koiner as major. Williams turned thirty-one years old a week after his election and had been a farmer and contractor before the war.[50]

One of the brigade's colorful figures, Lieutenant Colonel Andrew Grigsby, commanded the Twenty-seventh Virginia. Impulsive, brave, headstrong, and gruff, Grigsby was "a stern disciplinarian," but as a soldier asserted, "his regiment was devoted to him, and would follow him anywhere." Except for Major John Harman, Jackson's wagonmaster, Grigsby was the army's finest swearer. Although he was one of the first officers to visit Winder, Grigsby had been a firm supporter of Garnett and expressed a willingness to testify on the general's behalf.[51]

Since the Twenty-seventh lacked a full complement of companies, the regiment did not undergo reorganization. During the autumn of 1861, Jackson had detached Company A, the Alleghany Roughs, from the

Twenty-seventh and converted it into an artillery battery. The Roughs' first commander, Captain Thompson McAllister, had resigned after the Battle of Manassas because of ill health. When Jackson reorganized them into artillerymen, he selected a former VMI cadet, Joseph Carpenter, as captain. Jackson remembered Carpenter as an excellent artillery student and recommended the twenty-seven-year-old's appointment. The conversion of the company, however, further reduced the smallest regiment in the brigade.[52]

The Thirty-third Virginia's popular and capable Colonel Arthur Cummings refused to stand for election. Among the regimental commanders, Cummings bristled the most under Jackson's disciplinary methods and his treatment of Garnett. Evidently, the colonel wanted out from under Jackson's authority and chose not to be a candidate in the reorganization. The officer who had unleashed his men against the Union cannon on Henry House Hill left the brigade and was dropped officially from the rolls on June 14. Returning to Washington County, Cummings won election to the state legislature.[53]

The rank and file of the regiment elected Adjutant John F. Neff as Cummings's successor as colonel. Neff was, wrote an artillerist, "a young man of no remarkable fitness." The son of a Dunkard preacher, he had forsaken the family's pacifist beliefs and was graduated from VMI, class of 1858. He studied law and had practiced the profession in New Orleans and Memphis until the war began. He was twenty-seven years old and had become a popular officer with the men.[54]

Neff's surprising election, however, angered Major Ned Lee, who was voted lieutenant colonel. Lee's brother-in-law, Sandie Pendleton, described his reaction as "troubled about having to take a place under [Neff] who was so lately his junior." Pendleton and Cummings convinced Lee to accept the post. His health problems—Lee "was bad all the time," wrote a soldier—may have contributed to the election's outcome. His predecessor, Lieutenant Colonel John Jones, stood for all three positions and lost in each vote.[55]

The members of the Thirty-third selected Captain Frederick Holliday of Company D as major. Holliday was thirty-three years old, a distinguished graduate of Yale University and law school graduate of the University of Virginia. He had been serving as commonwealth's attorney for Frederick County when Virginia seceded. Although captain of Company D, Holliday had spent most of the war's first year on provost marshal duty in the Valley. His election returned him to active field command.[56]

The Rockbridge Artillery underwent two reorganizations during these weeks. Recruits to the battery swelled its ranks to 250 men. Consequently, Jackson submitted a plan to divide it into three battalions, but the War Department rejected it. Against the protests of the artillerymen, Jackson then ordered that its numbers be reduced to 150, with the members who joined initially to be given the first choice to remain or join an infantry regiment. The members elected William T. Poague as captain to succeed the recently promoted Major William McLaughlin. The battery's complement of guns was reduced from eight to six.[57]

The reorganization of Jackson's army occurred during miserable, rainy weather. April had been unusually wet, and the rains continued while the troops were camped at Swift Run Gap. Whenever the skies cleared, the men drilled and held a dress parade in the evening. Morale remained high as recruits trained beside veterans. The men indicated in their letters that they had come to accept the burdens of a soldier's life. One Virginian explained their attitude well when he wrote: "I am not fond of the army. Indeed many things in it are hateful to me; but nothing is so much so as the invader of my native soil."[58]

Although Jackson defied understanding, his imprint had been pressed even deeper into the fabric of the army. The men, particularly in the Stonewall Brigade, saw his unflinching will after Kernstown. The "Stonewall General" was, a private stated, "not to be trifled with." To Jackson, the influx of recruits offered possibilities. As he confided to his wife, Anna, earlier in the month, "Our gallant little army is increasing in numbers, and my prayer is that it may be an army of the living God as well as of its country."[59]

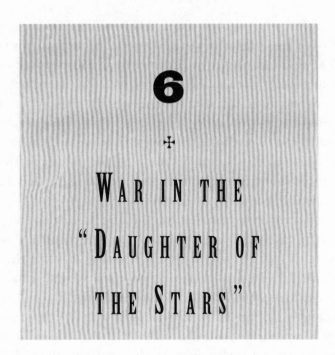

6

+

WAR IN THE "DAUGHTER OF THE STARS"

JOHN GIBBON was a man, wrote a private, whom "you'll just feel that you hadn't better call him Johnnie." Regular Army to the soul, Gibbon had adapted to military life, it seemed, as easily as a man slipped into an old boot. The army had been his home for nearly two decades, since his cadet days at West Point in the class behind Thomas Jackson. A stern, nononsense officer, Gibbon believed that the quality of a unit could be measured by its adherence to discipline, its proficiency in drill, and its soldierly appearance. On May 7, 1862, at Falmouth, Virginia, John Gibbon assumed command of the four Wisconsin and Indiana regiments formerly belonging to Rufus King.[1]

Gibbon and the Westerners were not strangers to each other. During the previous autumn, he had visited their camps, recruiting volunteers for Battery B, Fourth U.S. Artillery. Since then they had seen him occasionally in his role as chief of artillery for Major General Irvin McDowell. They might have heard that the thirty-five-year-old officer, although born in Pennsylvania, had grown up in North Carolina, and had family in the Confederate army.[2]

McDowell had urged Gibbon's promotion to the War Department for weeks, and Secretary of War Edwin Stanton appointed the artillery officer to brigadier general on May 2. Although Gibbon preferred assignment to an artillery command, he welcomed the appointment to King's former brigade. As he wrote later, he "had been strongly impressed with the high character of the material composing them by observation of the men I had obtained from them the previous fall." "All they needed," he was convinced, "was some discipline and drill to make them first class soldiers."[3]

Like Jackson, Gibbon began to impose his imprint upon the brigade at once. During his first week in command, he reviewed each regiment individually and then held a brigade review—"the first time we passed the reviewing officer at double quick," wrote a sergeant. To his wife, whom he called Mama, Gibbon stated soon afterward that although he had "an excellent brigade," he was "hard at work trying to knock the *kinks* out of it and indoctrinate the officers and men into the ways of the regulars."[4]

Gibbon addressed all aspects of the brigade's routine, discipline, and training. He discovered that reveille was "a mere farce," as he put it, so he required all officers and men to form on the regimental colors each morning in his and his staff's presence. The rank and file delighted in seeing the officers tumble out of bed with them. He also learned that sentinels on guard duty saw little sense in pacing back and forth, as required from sentries on duty. One day, when a sentinel did not present arms in a salute to Gibbon, the general had him relieved of duty and placed on a barrel head in camp for several hours. "I never had more trouble after that," he wrote.[5]

The new commander leavened punishments with rewards. He issued an order that the three best dressed and accoutered men who reported for guard mounting would be relieved and granted a twenty-four-hour pass. Soon, the attire of guards improved noticeably, with most of the soldiers using the pass to hunt blackberries.[6]

As a veteran artillery officer, Gibbon had limited experience with infantry drill, but he believed that it was fundamental in molding volunteers into good soldiers. Initially, he allowed regimental officers to conduct the training until he overheard two soldiers saying that as an artillerist the general knew nothing about the school of the soldier. Gibbon then studied a manual at night, and before long, he led brigade drills. The Westerners spent hours on the field under the watch of the former gunner. "There were early morning drills, before breakfast, forenoon drills, afternoon drills, evening and night drills, besides guard mounting and dress parades," complained a brigade member.[7]

In his memoirs, Gibbon stated that "the habit of obedience and subjection to the will of another, so difficult to instill into the minds of free and independent men became marked characteristics in the command." In time, that was true, but in May 1862, the "free and independent men" of Wisconsin and Indiana scowled under the discipline and training. "As an officer," wrote a Westerner of Gibbon, "he is arbitrary, severe, and exacting, requiring a complete subservience to his caprices as the condition of his favor. As a man he is distant, formal and reserved, standing very much on dignity of position." Another soldier said it more bluntly, "Probably no brigade commander was more cordially hated by his men."[8]

They resisted, as they viewed it, the commander's determination to make them into Regular Army troops. "While we could and did take on the soldierly bearing largely," an Indianan explained later, "we viewed ourselves in a different light from that of the regular army. We were in the army for business—that of putting down the rebellion, and not particularly for military display, and we expected to as soon as that was accomplished to return to our several homes, to our knitting, our plows, our shops, our counters, etc., and live in peace."[9]

To Gibbon, however, soldierly appearance could boost morale, instill pride, and give a unit a distinctiveness that would matter someday on a battlefield. Shortly after he assumed command, Gibbon authorized the issue of new uniform items to each soldier in the brigade. He wanted the standard Regular Army or so-called Hardee hat and long dark blue frock coats worn by Regulars. It would prove in time to be a brilliant idea that singularly marked the brigade and gave its members an identification that would become a badge of honor.[10]

Records and photographs indicate that the brigade members never wore identical uniforms. Although Gibbon preferred the longer frock coats, the men had both them and the shorter and more common sack coats. The members received reissues of both styles, but at no time did they all wear the frock coat. Conversely, each soldier was issued white leggings, which elicited considerable protests. Gibbon required their use, however, until one morning he discovered his horse with four of them on its legs.[11]

The brigade members accepted readily the new hats that would become the unit's symbol. When Gibbon adopted them for the brigade, men in the Second and Seventh Wisconsin were already wearing them. The brigadier then issued the hats to the Sixth Wisconsin and Nineteenth Indiana. The

Hardee hat had been the standard headgear in the Regular Army for nearly seven years and was named for now-Confederate General William Hardee, who had served as secretary of the board that had recommended it.[12]

The black Hardee hat had a crown that measured six and a quarter inches high and a brim of three and a quarter inches wide. The Westerners fastened either the left or right brim to the crown with a stamped brass eagle and adorned the opposite side with a black ostrich plume. Some of the men preferred to keep the brim flat. A twisted wool cord of light blue in color encircled the crown's base. Most of the men attached the infantry's traditional brass horn, a company letter and regimental number of brass, and later, a cloth corps badge to the crown. Adornments varied within regiments, even companies, according to individual preferences.[13]

Although the Westerners grumbled that the cost of the new items would count against their annual forty-two-dollar clothing allowance, they boasted in their letters about the new uniforms. "We have new hats," wrote a member of the Sixth Wisconsin, "they are black with a feather in them, and they look gay. It makes our Regt. look better than it did." After a dress parade, an officer in the same regiment stated that the men were "in 'fine feather.'" An Indiana soldier bragged that "they look splendid, with new legings on, the best in the Brigade." When fellow soldiers in other regiments derisively called Gibbon's men the "bandbox brigade," they responded that it was better to wear leggings than to be dirty and lousy. An Indiana officer claimed to his father that Gibbon's troops were regarded "as the Best disciplined Best drilled and finest looking Brigade in the great army of the Potomac."[14]

Among the brigade's regiments, Gibbon regarded the Second and Sixth Wisconsin as the best in drill and discipline because of their colonels, Edgar O'Connor of the Second and Lysander Cutler of the Sixth. O'Connor shared the bond of a fellow academy man with Gibbon while Cutler and the brigadier had served together in the Regular Army. Gibbon described Cutler as "a natural soldier" but admitted that the latter could be "arbitrary and dictatorial" with subordinates. Soon after he took command, Gibbon became embroiled in a festering dispute between Cutler and Lieutenant Colonel Edward Bragg, an officer as ambitious as Cutler was abrasive. Bragg wanted redress for an alleged falsehood that Cutler had written in an order, and the colonel wanted charges preferred against the subordinate. Gibbon resolved the matter to neither man's satisfaction by refusing to forward the papers for an inquiry or court-martial.[15]

While Gibbon respected O'Connor and Cutler as officers, he despised Colonel Solomon Meredith of the Nineteenth Indiana. "Long Sol" embodied, to Gibbon, the worst kind of officer, a political appointee who saw the war as a personal opportunity for office and prestige. Although the Nineteenth "had the finest material in it in the whole brigade," the brigadier testified later before a congressional committee, "and yet it was the worst regiment I had." The Indiana colonel "had not the first principle of a soldier in him," Gibbon asserted. "He was altogether disqualified for his position." In his memoirs, Gibbon described the officer as "not being anything of a soldier and too old to be made one." For his part, Meredith protested openly about a Regular Army officer's appointment to the command and tried to have the Nineteenth transferred out of the brigade. Neither man mollified his opinion of the other.[16]

The war, meanwhile, continued. For McDowell's corps at Falmouth, it meant long days of arduous labor, rebuilding railroad tracks to Aquia on the Potomac River, constructing a bridge for trains across the Rappahannock, and manning iron foundries, machine shops, and grist mills. On May 18, two trainloads of supplies arrived from Aquia, and within a few days the bridge across the Rappahannock carried locomotives and cars. President Lincoln and Secretary of War Stanton visited with McDowell, reviewing the corps and discussing strategy. Gibbon told his wife privately that he thought the president was "the *ugliest* white man I ever saw," but believed "him to be a most excellent and *honest* man."[17]

Lincoln, Stanton, and McDowell undoubtedly discussed in their meetings events on the Peninsula. As they spoke, McClellan's Army of the Potomac approached Richmond's outer defenses. For two months, the Federals had crawled up the land between the York and James rivers, pursuing Confederate General Joseph Johnston's troops. Believing his army was outnumbered, McClellan moved cautiously, reaching the Chickahominy River, where he shifted part of his forces north of the stream. The army commander had deluged Washington with requests for McDowell's corps to advance overland on Richmond from the north. Before he left the capital for Fredericksburg, Lincoln had ordered McDowell south and granted McClellan operational control of the corps. The president and the secretary returned to Washington on May 23.[18]

Within twenty-four hours, however, Lincoln suspended McDowell's movement when he learned of Nathaniel Banks's retreat north down the Shenandoah Valley before the Confederates of Stonewall Jackson and

Major General Richard S. Ewell. The president directed McDowell and Major General John C. Frémont in western Virginia to dispatch troops to the region, stating that "your object will be to capture the forces of Jackson & Ewell." McDowell responded by sending Brigadier General James Shields's division west.[19]

Rufus King's division, including John Gibbon's brigade, marched south from Fredericksburg on May 25. A small contingent of Southerners— "damed rascals" to a Wisconsin soldier—opposed the Federals with skirmishing and by burning bridges. The Northerners covered eight miles and then camped, staying there for three days. From his tent, Gibbon wrote to his wife on the 27th that the administration was "awfully stampeded" by events in the Valley. "I get more and more disgusted every day with the way they manage things," he stated, adding that "we ought to be 'thundering'" in the Confederate rear at Richmond.[20]

While camped south of Fredericksburg, Gibbon's men encountered for the first time significant numbers of runaway slaves or contrabands. The fugitives came into the camps "in droves," telling the soldiers that the war was being fought to free them. One Wisconsin soldier fumed to his sister that "the more I see of them the more I hate them. I wish that the Niggers' lovers in Boston were down here and had to take charge of them." He thought that the contrabands "are no better than cattle." He was not alone in his sentiments.[21]

On May 29, McDowell ordered King's division toward the Valley, or as Gibbon noted, "to help bag Jackson." The countermarch began, according to a Wisconsin sergeant, "to our deep mortification as we thought we soon should join the army at Richmond." The Federals marched seventeen miles that day, and twenty-seven more on the 30th and 31st, reaching Catlett's Station on the Orange & Alexandria Railroad.[22]

The final leg was a forced march in "melting hot" weather. Hundreds of men wilted in the heat, discarding clothing and dropping by the roadside. "Well it is enough to kill any man," a corporal avowed, "the loads we had to carry." Despite the conditions, some men kept up their spirits by singing a song with a favorite refrain:

> We'll freeze to Old Stonewall
> When the Johnnies go to sleep;
> Put 'simmons in his whiskey
> And mustard on his feet.

When they arrived at Catlett's, some Irishmen of the Sixth Wisconsin discovered whiskey in a railroad car and drilled through the floor into the barrels, celebrating their good fortune in a drunken revelry.[23]

During the next week, Gibbon's Westerners marched to Warrenton, enduring heat and heavy rainstorms. Gibbon thought the Warrenton area was "one of the most beautiful spots I ever saw." A sergeant even noted in his diary about the flower beds in the town. The residents were decidedly hostile, opening few, if any, doors to the blue-clad visitors. The Northerners departed on June 9, returning to Fredericksburg on the 11th. The next day Gibbon held a review of the brigade.[24]

The two-week excursion brought almost universal grumbling from the Wisconsin and Indiana troops. An officer called it "a wild goose chase," while a private complained, "we have now marched 150 miles for nothing at all." Another enlisted man griped that they "dont have any fighting to do the rebels run away every time we have advanced."[25]

Much of the discontent centered upon Gibbon. While he thought that "the experience and marching were valuable to our new troops," they simmered to a boil over his orders about stragglers and discarded clothing. Upon their return, he required an accounting in each company, charging those who requisitioned new clothing. In a letter of June 13, an Indiana sergeant contended: "We have one of the meanest Brigadier Generals that ever lived. There ain't a man in the regiment but what hates him. Gibens is his name. He is a regular and if we ever get in a fight, he will be the first to fall. Everybody hates his very name."[26]

The Westerners' moods worsened during June's final weeks. Diarrhea of "a serious character" afflicted many, requiring hospitalization in Washington. On June 20, Private Homer C. Sillie of the Sixth Wisconsin drowned in the Rappahannock while bathing. At his burial, many of his comrades were "almost in tears."[27]

Their letters reflected common themes during these weeks. They were the old grumbles about being left out of the fighting, the discipline, and the routines of camp duty. "I think all that this part of the army is good for is for a show," wrote a soldier. Captain Edwin Brown argued that "we are getting quite discontented" because of the severity of Gibbon's discipline and of the "hopelessness" of contributing to the conflict's end. In another letter, he told his wife, "Ruth, there is neither honor or profit in being in 'Kings Division and McDowells Corps.'"[28]

"We would rather be on the advance," asserted Private William G.

Davis, "and have a chance to establish our name amongst those who are now crowning their names with so much honor in their Countries cause." Davis referred to the men with McClellan. But for him and his comrades, "the advance" was approaching with a swiftness. The war would not elude them.[29]

Stonewall Jackson's "army of the living God" slogged through the knee-deep mud, shouldering mired wagons forward as rain and snow soaked man and beast. The men cursed the weather, their fates, and perhaps most of all, Old Jack. His intentions had left them "entirely bewildered." The wagonmaster, Major John Harman, growled that "Jackson is a strange man," adding that "as sure as you and I live Jackson is a cracked man and the sequel will show it."[30]

Conditions worsened throughout the day, April 30, 1862, and the following one. The column of 8,500 infantry and 1,000 cavalry struggled along the road from Conrad's Store, near Swift Run Gap, to Port Republic. An officer called it "the worst road I ever saw," with the Southerners only managing five miles a day. Despite the mud, the hardships, and the oaths, the soldiers plodded on, or as one of them had affirmed, "we have come to be veterans—have no tents, carry our knapsacks and blankets . . . obey orders implicitly without inquiring the why or wherefore, and, in case of necessity can live on half rations and not think it anything remarkable."[31]

May 3 dawned with clear skies and with the warmth of a spring day in Virginia. Jackson's troops marched east through Brown's Gap in the Blue Ridge and out of the Valley. Rumors darted from regiment to regiment as to their destination, with speculation centering upon Richmond. By late afternoon, the Confederates reached Mechum's River Station on the Virginia Central Railroad, which connected Staunton in the Valley to the Confederate capital. After dinner, members of the Stonewall Brigade bathed in a mountain stream, "washing off the mud of the three days of wading from Conrad's Store." Before they slept, most likely the men argued about Jackson's mysterious ways.[32]

Jackson had brought them to the depot east of the mountains to deceive his Valley opponent, Nathaniel Banks, whose main force of nineteen thousand Federals was posted at Harrisonburg, nearly thirty miles north of Staunton. For weeks the Confederate commander had been corresponding with General Robert E. Lee, military advisor to President Jefferson Davis in Richmond, about the mounting pressures against Southern forces in the Old Dominion. Lee had watched closely the Union corps of Irvin McDowell at Fredericksburg, fifty miles north of the capital. If McDowell combined his troops with those of McClellan on the Peninsula, Johnston's defenders could be crushed between an anvil and hammer of Union numerical power, and Richmond would be lost.[33]

Lee had available for an operation Jackson's forces in the Valley, Brigadier General Edward Johnson's 2,800-man command in the mountains west of Staunton, and Major General Richard Ewell's nine thousand infantry and cavalry near Gordonsville in central Virginia. Consequently, on April 21, Lee suggested to Jackson, "If you can use General Ewell's division in an attack on General Banks, and to drive him back, it will prove a great relief to the pressure on Fredericksburg." Another letter followed four days later from Lee in which he admonished, "The blow, wherever struck, must, to be successful, be sudden and heavy."[34]

With Lee, Jackson saw opportunity, and by April 29, had settled on a plan which he outlined to Lee. He would march to join Johnson in the Alleghenies beyond Staunton, assail the vanguard of Major General John Frémont's Union forces, and then with Johnson and Ewell would descend upon Banks. Jackson confided in no one, and when he conferred personally with Ewell on the 28th, he told him only to cross the Blue Ridge, camp at Conrad's Store, and threaten Banks's flank if the Federals advanced toward Staunton. Ewell's men entered the Valley on the 30th, occupying the abandoned bivouac sites of Jackson's troops.[35]

With his flank protected, Jackson piled the sick and disabled men on trains at Mechum's on May 4, and started the able-bodied on the road toward the Valley. The locomotives hissed and heaved under the loads, while the passengers cheered when they saw the direction. The general and his staff entered Staunton that evening. Alarm among the residents had changed to celebration at the sight of Jackson and the trainloads. While the main body of Confederates came in during the 5th, Jackson received a haircut and a new gray regulation coat of a Confederate general and trousers to replace his worn, blue VMI uniform. The suit was ill-fitting and homespun.[36]

The Confederates marched west out of Staunton on May 7. By nightfall, they were halted six miles east of Edward Johnson's troops, who lay at Shaw's Fork, about eight miles from McDowell. On the 8th, Jackson resumed the advance and occupied Sitlington's Hill above the town. Union Brigadier General Robert Schenck offered battle although outnumbered. For four hours the Southerners repulsed Federal sorties on the hill, and after nightfall, Schenck disengaged and abandoned McDowell, having inflicted more casualties than he had incurred. The Stonewall Brigade held a reserve position during the fighting and was not engaged. Major Frank Jones of the Second Virginia walked across the battlefield about 10:30 that night, and wrote in his diary afterward, "O, the dead! The dying! The screams of the wounded! I have never seen so much of it."[37]

The Confederates pursued deeper into the mountains during the next four days. Slowed by the miserable mountain roads, woods set on fire by the fugitives, and occasional ambushes, they never overtook the enemy. The pursuit exhausted officers and men and frayed tempers. Jackson and Charles Winder, commander of the Stonewall Brigade, clashed verbally over a misunderstanding.[38]

On the 13th, with the enemy safe within Frémont's lines at Franklin, Jackson began the sixty-seven-mile countermarch to Staunton. Heavy rains slowed the pace, but by the 17th, the Southerners were camped north of Staunton, within ten miles of Harrisonburg. During the return march, seventeen members of the Twenty-seventh Virginia demanded a discharge, claiming their one-year enlistment had expired. Jackson reacted by ordering the regiment into line with loaded rifles and offering the mutineers, as he saw them, the opportunity to return to duty or be shot. They rejoined the ranks.[39]

Richard Ewell rode to Jackson's headquarters, and the pair of generals conferred on Sunday, May 18. Ewell had been driven to distraction during the past two weeks, wrestling with conflicting orders from Jackson and Johnston. The bald-headed general, with bulging eyes, reminded some people of an eagle, others of a buzzard. He suffered from dyspepsia, and it worsened as his frustrations rose. At one point, Ewell stormed to an officer: "Did it ever occur to you that General Jackson is crazy? I tell you, sir, he is as mad as a March hare." When he received a directive from Johnston to march east, Ewell went to see Jackson.[40]

The two generals plotted the campaign's next phase. Banks had withdrawn his Union forces north, posting 6,500 troops at Strasburg, about twenty miles south of Winchester. Opposite Strasburg, Massanutten Mountain—"the glory of the Valley," to a Confederate general—rose like a slumbering giant, extending south forty-five miles to Harrisonburg and dividing the Valley proper from Luray Valley on the east. Only New Market Gap notched the giant's spine and was the geographic key to operations in this section of the region. By holding it, an army could advance down either the main valley or the narrower Luray Valley, threatening the front and/or flank of an opponent. In Massanutten's shadow, Jackson changed the course of the war in Virginia.[41]

The Confederates marched on the 19th, down the "Daughter of the Stars." When they passed through Harrisonburg, Jackson had all unnecessary equipment stacked in the court house. "We knew there was some game on hand then," a Stonewall Brigade member asserted, "for when General Jackson ordered knapsacks to be left behind he meant business." They covered fifteen miles that day, bivouacking at Tenth Legion, where Brigadier General Richard Taylor's brigade of Ewell's division joined them the next day. The son of former president Zachary Taylor, the thirty-six-year-old general commanded four regiments and a battalion of Louisianans. Taylor's men would fight anyone, friend or foe, with a fierceness that made them superb in combat and unruly in camp.[42]

A rain during the night dampened the road as the Louisianans led Jackson's troops toward New Market on May 21. The men marched fifty minutes in each hour, halted, stacked arms, and then rested for ten minutes. At New Market, the column turned east toward Massanutten's notch. Up through the gap the Confederates climbed. Randolph Barton of the Rockbridge Artillery looked behind him and recalled the scene later: "The army in the far off curves of the road looked like a great snake with shining back, twisting along its sinuous path." By nightfall, the troops were camped in Luray Valley, with Ewell's other two brigades a few miles to the north.[43]

The Confederates stirred again before sunrise. The day's march down the valley covered nearly twenty miles, with the column halting ten miles south of Front Royal, where a Union detachment of a thousand troops guarded the northern entrance to Luray Valley. Jackson planned to seize the small force the next day, positioning himself on Banks's flank. He issued instructions for the men to cook three days' rations and to be awakened at 2:30 A.M. on the 23rd.[44]

When the order filtered down to Lieutenant Colonel Lawson Botts, who was temporarily in command of the Second Virginia, he replied in writing that the commissary had only a day's rations. Duty required him to report that "the men are much fatigued by the constant marches they have recently made & need rest, that, were it possible to issue the rations, at once, it would be impossible for the men, with the limited supply of cooking utensils, to cook them & obtain any rest tonight. This loss of rest, followed by a forced march tomorrow, would so exhaust them as to hazard the hard-earned reputation of the Regiment." The physical condition of men in other units must have been similar to that in the Second Virginia.[45]

Botts's Second Virginia and the rest of the Stonewall Brigade were spared from the fighting at Front Royal on May 23, posted in a reserve position. Ewell's troops, with the First Maryland in the lead, drove the First Maryland, U.S.A., through the town to Cedarville, where Confederate cavalry swept in, bagging nine hundred of the "homemade Yankees," as the Rebels called them. As Jackson reported, "the enemy's flank was turned and the road opened to Winchester."[46]

At Strasburg, roughly fifteen miles to the west, Nathaniel Banks hesitated to react when he learned of the attack at Front Royal. He and his senior officers debated the options throughout the night. At three o'clock on the morning of the 24th, Banks started the sick and wounded toward Winchester, eighteen miles to the north. Seven hours later, the main body of troops marched down the Valley Pike with cannon and wagons. It had become a race for Winchester.[47]

The Confederates spent the morning of the 24th poised to advance along two roads to Winchester. When Jackson received a note about noon that his cavalry had attacked a Federal wagon train at Newtown, south of Winchester, he ordered Ewell's division forward on the Front Royal–Winchester road while he led his division west to Middletown on the Valley Pike.[48]

The Stonewall Brigade marched in the van of Jackson's division toward Middletown. As the Valley men approached the village, the ranks were "thrown into regular parade march, the flags were uncovered and unfurled, the bands played, and the loyal inhabitants went wild with delight." A brigade member thought that "everything in Middletown turned out to greet us, men, women, girls, children, dogs, cats and chickens." Confusion over the location of the enemy necessitated a countermarch as Winder's regiments turned initially south toward Strasburg. Everywhere the Confederates saw the wreckage of a fleeing army, and Jackson pressed the pursuit north. He wanted to seize the hills south of Winchester before Banks could fashion a defensive position on the heights. As darkness settled in, the Stonewall Brigade pushed ahead.[49]

It was a harrowing ordeal for the men. Colonel James Allen described it as "continual skirmishing with an invisible enemy." Exhaustion and hunger overcame many. The colonels of the Twenty-seventh and Thirty-third Virginia reported that they had fewer than three hundred men combined in the ranks. Three weeks earlier, while at Mechum's, Jackson had listed nearly twelve hundred in the two regiments. The campaign's exertion had reduced the numbers by a staggering seventy-five percent.[50]

"General Jackson seemed determined not to be stopped," an officer wrote of the night. Federal ambushes flashed in the darkness, stunning the Southerners and further impeding the pursuit. About three o'clock, Jackson relented and halted the troops, giving them two hours' rest. At daylight, "we rose," recounted a brigade member, "shook the dew from our limbs, and moved forward."[51]

May 25 "was a lovely Sabbath morning," remembered Brigadier General Richard Taylor. Shortly after daybreak, the Stonewall Brigade advanced, scattered enemy skirmishers from a ridge, and then met a wall of fire from the main Union line farther north on a second ridge. The Virginians clung to their position as Federal volleys and cannon fire seared the ground. A gunner in the Rockbridge Artillery asserted that "it was by far the hottest and most destructive fire this battery has ever been under." The artillerymen were so tired that they could barely work the cannon. Jackson extended Winder's left with a second brigade, but Banks's troops fought tenaciously.[52]

Finally, Jackson rode to Taylor, and pointing to the ridge, said, "You must carry it." The brigadier spurred ahead to examine the ground, while the Louisianans followed. Union gunners spotted the column, punishing it with shell fire. The Louisianans shifted into battle line, adjusted ranks, and stepped off. The enemy fire increased, but in view of both sides, the Rebels ascended the slope, sweeping the blue-coated soldiers off the crest. Along the Confederate lines, the units closed on the retreating enemy. Banks's army disintegrated into a mob. "I have never seen sutch a grand sight in my life," avowed a Virginian, "as that was to see the Yankees a runing and throughing away thir knapsacks and guns." The Southerners harvested more than three thousand prisoners, nearly ten thousand small arms, and an immense cache of quartermaster and commissary goods. It could have been worse for the Federals, but the Confederate cavalry were too dispersed to undertake the pursuit.[53]

In Winchester, the residents flooded into the streets to welcome and to cheer the victors. "I have never seen such an exhibition before," marveled Captain James K. Edmondson of the Twenty-seventh Virginia. A private in the same regiment reported that "the whole town seemed mad [with] delight, cheering us at every step—the ladies meeting us at every door with refreshments." An artillerist described "our passage through Winchester" as "perfectly glorious." Even Jackson admitted to his wife that "our entrance into Winchester was one of the most stirring scenes of my life. The town is much improved in loyalty to our cause."[54]

Human limitations ended the pursuit a few miles beyond the town. The Confederates were numbingly exhausted. A soldier in the Stonewall Brigade put it frankly in a letter the next day: "We done a grate deal of hard marching to git them but we got them at last. I am so tired I hardly can write." But when Jackson appeared along the road, the news that "Old Jack's coming" raced through the ranks, and the men had enough left to emit a "deafening" cheer and to wave their hats. "I never saw a more thrilling scene," remarked a Rockbridge Artillery member. A private in the Fourth Virginia summarized his comrades' feelings, "My estimate of Jackson's generalship has risen a hundred degrees."[55]

Jackson suspended movements on May 26, for the army to rest and "for the purpose of rendering thanks to God." The troops enjoyed the spoils, but when Ashby's men mistook infantrymen dressed in captured Federal uniforms for the enemy, Jackson forbade the use of any article of Union clothing. Guards prevented entry into Winchester unless an officer or enlisted man carried a pass. Surgeons worked on the wounded from both armies, including more than three hundred Southerners. Casualties in the Stonewall Brigade amounted to fewer than seventy.[56]

On Wednesday, May 28, four regiments of the Stonewall Brigade, artillery, and cavalry marched toward Harper's Ferry. Jackson wanted to mislead the enemy into believing that he planned to threaten the town and the enemy position along the Potomac. At Charlestown, a detachment of Federals fled after a brief shelling from Confederate cannon, and Winder pitched camp. On the 29th and 30th, the Southerners occupied Bolivar Heights west of Harper's Ferry, while the Second Virginia rejoined their comrades and pushed on to Loudoun Heights to the south of the town.[57]

At Winchester, meanwhile, Jackson learned on the afternoon of May 30 that a Union force had seized Front Royal and that the leading elements of John Frémont's command were approaching Strasburg from the west. If the enemy units combined, the Southerners would be trapped in the Lower Valley, confronting overwhelming numbers. Preparations for a retreat up the Valley began at once. Jackson's greatest concern was for the troops before Harper's Ferry, and at three o'clock on the morning of the 31st, he sent Jedediah Hotchkiss, his mapmaker, to recall the Stonewall Brigade. In Hotchkiss's account, the general told him, "I will stay in Winchester until you get here if I can, but if I cannot, and the enemy gets here first, you must bring it around through the mountains." Jackson's anxiety for his old brigade's safety was evident to the staff officer.[58]

Hotchkiss met Winder as the brigadier was riding to the front. When Hotchkiss described "the state of affairs," Winder hurried a courier to bring back the Second Virginia from Loudoun Heights and staff officers to alert the other regiments. The brigadier had probably fewer than sixteen hundred rank and file, including the First Maryland, which had been attached temporarily to the brigade. When the Second returned, the column started. Each man knew the circumstances.[59]

Few in the ranks spoke as one mile followed another. False reports of approaching Yankees intensified the men's apprehension. The pace was relentless, draining away a body's strength and testing a man's soul. One private estimated that about five hundred fell out, and in small groups headed for the mountains. They passed through Winchester well after dark and were greeted by women with slices of bread. Most of them had not eaten all day; the members of the Second Virginia, for two days. A cold rain began falling as Winder called a halt at Newtown. The men collapsed on the ground, ignoring the drenching storm. They had completed one of the war's greatest marches—roughly thirty-five miles in fourteen hours.[60]

Winder gathered up the remnants of his brigade and started south at 5:30 A.M., on June 1. "It was a silent and gloomy column that trudged along the turnpike that morning," recalled a member of Winder's staff. "Officers and men were silent as the grave—occupied all with the same gloomy apprehensions." About eight o'clock, cannon boomed ahead. Most of those left in the ranks believed that the Yankees had cut them off from Jackson. As they neared Strasburg, however, they learned that Old Jack had waited for them, and the guns were theirs, contesting Frémont's advance from the west. "From that hour we never doubted him," a staff officer wrote of Jackson.[61]

Throughout the day, the Confederates parried the Federals, giving the wagon train a head start south and allowing stragglers to stumble in.

Sandie Pendleton admitted to his father in a letter that day that "our force is too small and too much broken down by constant marching to do much good work for some little time against an overwhelming force." After dark, Jackson resumed the march up the Valley.[62]

Through Woodstock, Mt. Jackson, and on to Rude's Hill below New Market—hometowns to many in the Stonewall Brigade—the Confederates plodded during June 2 and 3. Rain soaked them. On the 2nd, the Valley men protected the rear but were relieved, as one of them stated, because "we were more worn out than any other." One soldier wrote home that "I never saw so many barefooted men with their feet all swollen and bleeding." From Rude's Hill, Captain Edmondson informed his wife that "I never saw the Brigade so completely broken down and unfitted for service as our Brigade is now." Major John Harman believed that they could "whip" the enemy "if our men were not so tired."[63]

Jackson rested the army on June 4, while he considered its next move. Frémont's troops harried his rear, while the division of Brigadier General James Shields from Fredericksburg was advancing up the Luray Valley. If Jackson could destroy a bridge over the South Fork of the Shenandoah River near Conrad's Store, he could isolate the two forces, and by posting his troops fifteen miles south of Conrad's Store at Port Republic, where the North and South rivers formed the South Fork, he could, if necessary, give battle against either opponent. Consequently, he dispatched a cavalry detail to destroy the bridge and continued the march south that afternoon.[64]

At three o'clock on the morning of the 5th, the Southerners filed once again into column and stepped off. Before noon, they reached Harrisonburg and turned southeast on the road to Port Republic. Rain resumed near nightfall as the Stonewall Brigade bivouacked a mile from the village. They had covered twenty-one miles, moving Winder to jot in his diary, "Jackson is insane on these rapid marches." Behind them, other units and teamsters camped along the road, reaching back to Harrisonburg. Throughout the miserable night, stragglers came in, "all exhausted," according to Winder.[65]

The famed "Pathfinder" and former Republican presidential candidate John Frémont probed the Confederate lines throughout June 6 and 7. In an afternoon skirmish on the 6th, Jackson's cavalry commander, Turner Ashby, suffered a mortal wound. Winder described the dashing officer's death as "a great loss to us & our cause." On the 8th, however, the com-

bat escalated at Cross Keys, northwest of Port Republic. Jackson left the
direction of the fighting to Richard Ewell, whose troops repulsed the
Union attacks and held the ground. Frémont hoped for news from James
Shields, whose troops were following the South Fork toward Port Republic.[66]

Jackson had spent the three days awaiting Federal movements. Like his
men, said Sandie Pendleton, "General Jackson is completely broken
down." Early on the morning of the 8th, 150 Union horsemen rode unde-
tected into Port Republic, surprising the entire Confederate army and
nearly capturing Jackson. The Yankees belonged to Shields's advance contingent and had orders to secure the covered bridge over the North River.
Southern infantry cleared the village of the bold Federals, who retreated
across the South River to their infantry supports. The Northerners retired
to Lewiston, the estate of John Francis Lewis, located two miles northeast
of Port Republic.[67]

Following the abortive raid, Confederates piled into and around Port
Republic throughout the day. Ewell's division remained posted at Cross
Keys, confronting Frémont's troops. Jackson had decided to advance
against Shields on the 9th, and during the night of the 8th–9th, conferred
with officers and directed his engineers to construct a makeshift bridge
across the South River. He directed Ewell to retire toward the village, delaying Frémont, while the rest of the army engaged Shields. He sent cavalry to insure that the road was open to Brown's Gap, and issued
instructions for an early movement across the South River. At four o'clock
on the 9th, the pioneers completed the bridge of stone-laden wagons and
of planks from a nearby sawmill. Within two hours, the Southerners, with
the Stonewall Brigade in the lead, filed over the span.[68]

Charles Winder's exasperation with the army commander had increased during the past two days. In his diary on the 7th, he jotted, "grow-
ing disgusted with Jackson." The brigadier was as bone-weary tired as his
men. "You have no idea how completely exhausted our troops are,"
wrote a brigade member on June 7. Now, the Stonewall Brigade was moving to battle without one regiment, since the Thirty-third Virginia was detached on picket downstream on the western bank of the South Fork.
Winder counted fewer than eleven hundred men in the ranks of the four
regiments.[69]

The Lewis family farmland was rich with nature's fertility, nourished by
the floodwaters of the South Fork. Its fields extended from a wooded spur

of the Blue Ridge to the river. It was a place to glean a harvest's bounty, not for the killing fields of warriors. But on this warm spring day, men gathered to reap a fearful crop.[70]

Before Winder's Virginians, three thousand Federals, under Brigadier General Erasmus Tyler, waited along a farm lane, Lewiston Lane, that ran from the Lewis home to a mill beside the South Fork. On a ninety-foot-high knoll, called the "Coaling," six cannon supported the infantrymen. The Lewises had used the elevation to make charcoal for the farm. From the Coaling Union artillerists dominated the terrain, their fire sweeping the fields like wheat harvesters with scythes.[71]

The Federal gunners opened the engagement as the Confederate infantry and two artillery batteries deployed behind a lane on the Andrew Baugher farm, three-fourths of a mile southwest of Lewiston. The artillerists of Captain Joseph Carpenter's battery (the former members of Company A, Twenty-seventh Virginia) and the Rockbridge Artillery answered. Jackson soon ordered Winder to outflank the enemy at the Coaling. The brigadier responded by sending the Second and Fourth Virginia and Carpenter's guns to the right. The two regiments crossed the open fields under shell fire and entered the woods, while Carpenter shifted two pieces forward in support.[72]

While the nearly five hundred Virginians in the two regiments groped through the thickets and woods, the Fifth and Twenty-seventh Virginia endured a punishing fire on the plain. "I was badly scared," admitted a recruit in the Fifth. It took the two regiments on the mountainside more than an hour to close on the Union cannon. When the Second Virginia reached a bluff across a ravine from the Coaling, the Northern gunners switched to canister and blasted the Virginians off the hill, throwing the ranks into confusion. "It was some time before they were reformed," stated Colonel James Allen. On the Second's right, Colonel Charles Ronald of the Fourth became disoriented in the "very dense wood and laurel thicket," and never found the enemy battery. Both regiments pulled back into the woods.[73]

On the fields of the Baugher and Lewis farms, Winder led the Fifth and Twenty-seventh Virginia in an attack against Tyler's regiments along Lewiston Lane. The Yankees unleashed a "withering fire." Although the Valley men "fought gallantly and desperately, as our holy cause urged them to do," reported Winder, they fell back to the Baugher lane. Jackson, meanwhile, had brought up Richard Taylor's Louisianans and added the

Seventh Louisiana to Winder's command. For a second time, the Southerners charged.[74]

The three regiments advanced en echelon—one after another on an off-
set front—across the bloody fields. "A terrific fire" exploded into their
faces, but they drove ahead, reaching a worm fence that ran parallel to
Lewiston Lane and about one-fourth of a mile from it. Here, the Southerners fought for thirty minutes, "exposed to a murderous cross-fire,"
claimed Lieutenant Colonel John Funk of the Fifth. The Twenty-seventh's
Colonel Andrew Grigsby had his mount killed under him. Finally, under a
"perfect shower of bullets," pieces of the line broke and fled rearward, unraveling the Confederate line. The Yankees counterattacked, driving the
Virginians. Grigsby had lost a third of his command, including Major
Daniel McK. Shriver, the wealthy Wheeling officer who had recruited the
Shriver Grays and had brought them to Harper's Ferry after a 298-mile
trek.[75]

Confederate reinforcements repulsed the Yankees, stabilizing Jackson's
line on the plain. To their right, on the wooded mountainside, Taylor's
Louisianans charged the Coaling. As they had at Winchester, the
Louisianans would not be denied, and swarmed among the surprised gunners. "Men ceased to be men," claimed a Southerner. "They cheered and
screamed like lunatics—they fought like demons—they died like fanat-
ics." Tyler hurried infantry supports to the knoll, but the Louisianans finally held the Coaling after taking it for the third time.[76]

Below the combatants, Jackson's other units, including a portion of the
Thirty-third Virginia of the Stonewall Brigade, surged toward Lewiston
Lane. Tyler's line dissolved under the onslaught, fleeing north on the road
to Conrad's Store. In Port Republic, the smoke and flame from the burning covered bridge over the North River signaled that all of Jackson's
troops had passed the stream. Behind them, Frémont rolled cannon onto a
ridge and ordered the crews to fire. It did not matter; he could get no
closer, and Tyler's men were in flight away from the battlefield. At last, the
Confederates were beyond the grasp of their enemy.[77]

The fighting at Cross Keys and Port Republic cost Jackson's army 239
killed or mortally wounded, 928 wounded, and 96 missing for a total of
1,263. In the five Virginia regiments of the Stonewall Brigade the casualties amounted to 17 killed or mortally wounded, 142 wounded, and 33
missing, totaling 192. Only George H. Steuart's brigade and Taylor's
Louisianans incurred higher figures. The Union losses exceeded 1,900,

with 272 killed or mortally wounded, 849 wounded, and 782 missing.[78]

The Confederates held the warriors' fields northeast of Port Republic until sunset. Then, in a pattern that had marked the entire campaign, they filed into column and marched toward another destination. They followed a set of "old coal roads" into the folds of Brown's Gap. As the night deepened, members of the Rockbridge Artillery covered the headless corpse of a Second Virginia man with a white handkerchief, placed it on the rear caisson, and used the cloth as "a sort of guide." Lieutenant Colonel Funk reported that many of his men "fell at the road-side, wornout and exhausted." He allowed them to sleep where they lay as did other officers. Once again, rain worsened the men's plight, but by midnight, most of the army was asleep.[79]

The irony may have escaped most of the men in Jackson's division, but they had come full circle to Brown's Gap. Thirty-eight days ago, they had snaked through the mountain defile, taking the first steps in a campaign that would alter Confederate fortunes in Virginia and make their commander a Southern hero. By one estimate of a member of the Rockbridge Artillery, they had been on the march on thirty-two of the days, covering about four hundred miles, much of it in the rain and mud. Often, the troops stayed up until ten o'clock at night to cook rations and to brew coffee. Reveille sounded usually at 3:00 A.M. the next morning. With pride and justification, they had begun to call themselves Jackson's "foot cavalry."[80]

Numbers reveal the staggering toll that the long days, short nights, and seemingly endless miles had exacted from body and flesh. On May 3, according to Jackson's figures, 3,681 officers and men comprised the Stonewall Brigade. At Port Republic, on June 9, Winder counted roughly 1,500 in the five regiments. Until that battle, the Virginians had suffered fewer than one hundred combat casualties. If the original numbers are accurate, approximately two thousand members either fell out of ranks temporarily, were subsequently captured, or deserted during the campaign. The figure amounted to fifty-four percent of the command, an astonishing proportion.[81]

Comparative figures for the other two brigades in the division are unknown, but a modern study of the campaign has estimated that Taylor's Louisianans incurred twenty-five to thirty percent nonbattle losses. The evidence indicates that no other command in Jackson's army was so plagued and affected by either straggling or desertion as the Stonewall Brigade.[82]

The campaign carried the brigade members through their hometowns and by their farmsteads. The enticements of home for exhausted and hungry men were more readily at hand for them than for any other troops in the army. But the amount of absenteeism denotes a crippling lack of discipline in the brigade. At no other time during the war would so many members stand in the ranks of the Stonewall Brigade as they did on May 3, 1862. Nearly six weeks later, the thinned ranks at Port Republic testified to the campaign's hardships and the unit's cohesion as a combat command. Old Jack had asked more of his old brigade than he knew.

7

✠

VIRGINIA SUMMER

HISTORY often comes to a place at a certain time as an unwanted intruder. It tarries, passes on, and in its wake, leaves a mark. At times, history's visit alters forever the meaning of a place, but at other times, its passage isn't perceived until later. It was the latter when shortly after noon, on June 1, 1862, General Robert E. Lee assumed command of the Army of Northern Virginia outside of Richmond.[1]

Lee was fifty-five years old, a member of one of the Old Dominion's most renowned families. The son of Revolutionary War hero Henry "Light Horse Harry" Lee, he was an 1829 graduate of West Point, an engineering officer in the antebellum army, who had distinguished himself on the staff of Winfield Scott during the Mexican War. When his native state seceded, the authorities offered him command of its forces, and Lee resigned from the army, leaving his home on Arlington Heights, opposite Washington, forever. He led troops in western Virginia during the fall of 1861, and most recently, had served as President Jefferson Davis's military advisor.[2]

When General Joseph Johnston fell wounded during the Battle of Seven Pines or Fair Oaks, on May 31, Davis turned to Lee. Even Davis or the most sanguine Confederate supporter could not have foreseen that Lee's appointment would recast, before long, the conflict's course in the East. Unknowingly to Southerners, history would be a welcome visitor on this day.[3]

"No one could meet Lee," wrote an artillery officer, "and fail to be impressed with his dignity of character, his intellectual power, and his calm self-reliance." Handsome, kind, devout, and gentle by nature, Lee possessed enormous talents as a man and as a soldier. Endowed with exceptional intelligence, he had an aptitude for war. Where others groped to visualize strategy and tactics, Lee saw, as if crystallized, opportunities across a theater of operations and possibilities upon a battlefield. Moreover, as an acquaintance of the general remarked to an officer, Lee was "audacity personified. His name is audacity, and you need not be afraid of not seeing all of it that you will want to see."[4]

When Lee succeeded Johnston, who most in the army thought would return to command after his wound healed, George McClellan's Union Army of the Potomac stood poised beyond Richmond's defenses. Earlier when Johnston had broached the possibility of the capital's abandonment during a meeting, Lee affirmed with uncharacteristic fervor, "Richmond must not be given up; it shall not be given up!" Although McClellan believed mistakenly that he confronted superior numbers, Lee understood correctly that the disparity favored his opponent. In order to save Richmond, Lee concluded, he must strike the enemy. Like Johnston at the end of May, he saw the chance while the Federal units remained divided by the Chickahominy River. Johnston had assailed McClellan's left wing south of the river; Lee would attack the opposite end, and for this he would need Stonewall Jackson's troops from the Shenandoah Valley.[5]

During the first three weeks of June, consequently, Lee fashioned a battle plan. On the 23rd, he conferred with his senior division commanders— Jackson, James Longstreet, A. P. Hill, and D. H. Hill. Jackson had arrived at mid-afternoon after a nearly sixty-mile horseback ride. The commander outlined his proposal for an offensive against McClellan's right flank near Mechanicsville, relying on information gathered by Jeb Stuart on a spectacular four-day ride around the entire Union army. When he finished, Lee left the room, allowing the four generals to discuss the details. Since Jackson would initiate the attack with his troops, he fixed the time as daylight on the 25th. Lee returned, further discussion ensued, and the attack was moved back twenty-four hours to the 26th. Jackson departed to hurry his command forward. He had given himself less than sixty hours to be in position.[6]

While Jackson rode west, his foot cavalry was en route to Richmond. Since their twin victories at Cross Keys and Port Republic, the officers and men had been given some time to heal and to recuperate from the campaign's exhausting rigors. Even so, few stragglers rejoined their commands, and more continued to sneak away. A Stonewall Brigade officer contended in a letter to his father on June 16 that "a few more marches and fights will ruin his Old Brigade unless he allows them to recruit now." The officer reported that Jackson's men "have had three days rest in the last two months."[7]

Jackson's relentless demands during the campaign moved the brigade's commander, Charles Winder, at last, to submit his resignation. Throughout the operations, the brigadier complained in his diary about the marches and shortage of sleep. In a typical entry, he wrote on June 11, "Oh how tired I am of this constant moving—really worn out—slept badly." He asked initially for a transfer, but when Jackson rejected it, Winder requested a temporary furlough for personal business. Jackson denied that, and Winder resigned. Richard Taylor, who described the Marylander as "an accomplished soldier and true brother-in-arms," interceded between the two generals and resolved the dispute, convincing Jackson to speak personally with his subordinate. Winder withdrew his letter but did not obtain his leave.[8]

During the week after the Valley Campaign's conclusion, Jackson proposed, in fact, a renewal of the offensive in the region. He corresponded with Lee, who accepted Jackson's arguments and dispatched eight thousand troops to him for a feint. But Jackson reconsidered his plans, telling Lee that "we should not attempt another march down the Valley to Winchester until we are in a condition under the blessing of Providence to hold the country." He asked for an additional forty thousand men, but Lee could not possibly detach such a force without losing Richmond. Instead, Lee decided to bring Jackson to the capital, and on June 18, the foot cavalry crossed the Blue Ridge.[9]

While the units that Lee had sent to Jackson traveled by railroad, the Valley veterans marched on foot, reaching Gordonsville on the Virginia Central Railroad. Jackson rested the men on Sunday, June 22. Early the next morning he departed for the capital and his conference with Lee to plan strategy, while his troops followed the railroad line east. The commander rejoined them on the morning of the 24th, at Beaver Dam Station. He had expected all of his brigades to be nearby; instead, they were strung out for miles to the west, crawling through mud and rain. It took much of the day and night for them to reach the station, and it was after sunrise on the 25th before the columns resumed the march. In blistering heat, the soldiers covered twenty miles, halting for the night near Ashland, six miles short of where Jackson had planned to camp. That night, Jackson sent a message to Lee, noting that he would start earlier, received a letter from the army commander about possible routes of advance, and conferred with his ranking subordinates.[10]

Nothing went well for Jackson and his troops on June 26. His ill temper indicated that exhaustion had begun to drain his strength and cloud his mind. Hours behind schedule, Jackson's men struggled along the roads, finally making contact with troops from Lee's army about 9:00 A.M. The brigadier, however, did not relay the information to army headquarters. Jackson's progress continued to slow as contingents of Federal troops harassed the Confederate van. Late in the afternoon, following a sixteen-mile march, Jackson halted the ranks at Hundley's Corner, where he expected to find elements from the main army. None were there, and to the south, ripples of gunfire sounded ominously, like the growl of an angry giant.[11]

At Mechanicsville, meanwhile, Confederate units assailed entrenched Federal troops on a plateau behind Beaver Dam Creek. Major General A. P. Hill had initiated the attack after failing to hear from Jackson, whose advance was intended to outflank the Union position. The Northerners repulsed the assaults, but Hill's action began the main operations of the so-called Seven Days' Campaign, which had begun on the 25th, with feints by Confederate forces against the Union front south of the Chickahominy. For the next five days, Lee's army drove the enemy across the Peninsula, with McClellan retreating and changing his base of supplies from the Pamunkey River to the James River. As had happened on the 26th, Confederate operations were hampered by poor staff work, bad maps, misunderstood orders, and flawed performances by officers. The campaign has generated historical controversy ever since, with much of it focused on Jackson and on McClellan. In the end, the Confederate army's reach exceeded its grasp.[12]

For the men in the ranks, the campaign brought them to three bloody battlefields after the engagement on the 26th—at Gaines's Mill on the 27th, at Glendale or Frayser's Farm on the 30th, and at Malvern Hill on July 1. In each of the battles, the Confederates attacked the Federals. The work was costly, with Lee's army incurring more casualties than its opponent. For Jackson's troops, the combat drew them in at Gaines's Mill and Malvern Hill.[13]

The Stonewall Brigade advanced to battle late on June 27, at Gaines's Mill. It had taken hours for Lee's units to deploy before nearly thirty thousand Federals stacked in three lines on a wooded plateau behind Boatswain's Swamp. Once again, A. P. Hill's division began the Confederate attacks, followed later in the afternoon by James Longstreet's brigades. Hill's and Longstreet's men assailed the enemy's center and left front while Jackson brought his units into position opposite the Union right front. Late in the day, the Southerners launched a final charge along much of the line.[14]

Charles Winder aligned his Virginia regiments from left to right—Second, Fifth, Fourth, Twenty-seventh, and Thirty-third. Colonel William Baylor believed that only eight hundred men stood in the brigade's ranks as scores of Virginians had fallen out during the day's march. At the outset, the regiments passed through underbrush and a swamp, disrupting the ranks. When they emerged into an open field, the Second and Fifth were well ahead of the other three regiments, coming under the concentrated fire of Union batteries. The pair of regiments advanced across the rising ground and suffered for it. Union infantry triggered volleys. "The bumshells was bursting over our heads," wrote a private in the Fifth, "and the miney balls was whisling on every side of us it was the awfullest time that I ever saw."[15]

The Virginians ascended the slope, leaning into the iron and leaden storm. They closed to within 150 yards of the enemy ranks and fired a volley. The Yankees unleashed more fury into the Rebels. Colonel James Allen of the Second crumpled to the ground with a bullet in his head. He never regained consciousness and died ninety minutes later on the field. At Kernstown, four months ago, he had erased all questions about his courage and had won his men's respect. Nearby, a canister round mangled the knee of Major Frank Jones. Later, surgeons amputated the leg, but the Frederick County man could not stay the darkness, dying on July 9. "If there ever lived a pure man," wrote Colonel Baylor, "he was Frank Jones."[16]

Behind the Virginians' opponents, the Union line was unraveling as other Confederates pierced a hole in the Northern ranks, swarming over the crest. The Valley men surged ahead, capturing two cannon and handfuls of prisoners. The entire Federal position collapsed under the attacks with the blue-coated soldiers retreating south across the Chickahominy River. Lee's victorious units gathered up twenty-eight hundred prisoners and twenty-two artillery pieces.[17]

The other three regiments of the Stonewall Brigade joined their comrades on the plateau. The units had suffered few casualties, with the Twenty-seventh not even firing a shot. The Second and Fifth bore the bulk of the losses, which were listed as thirteen killed or mortally wounded and sixty-two wounded. While the casualties amounted to less than ten percent of the command, the dead or fatally wounded included Allen, Jones, two captains, and a surgeon. In his report, Winder described the Second's colonel as "a true soldier and gentleman, whose loss to his regiment, country, and friends will be long mourned, though falling in so sacred a cause." As for Major Jones, the brigadier wrote, "His mild and gentlemanly manner had long since endeared him to all, and deeply is his loss felt and regretted." Winder concluded by citing the conduct of his troops, stating, "I cannot speak too highly of the officers and men of my brigade."[18]

The Confederates slept on the battlefield that night. The Fifth Virginia's Private James Gabbert remembered the hours of darkness for a long time. "The Battle field was a horrible sight," recalled Gabbert. "To hear the wounded and dieing moaning and calling for water and for some one to take them away. We layed rit in amongst the dead & wounded on the field. It was the dreadfulest night I ever spent."[19]

Lee rested his army and searched for evidence about McClellan's move during the 28th. Late that night, the Confederate commander received a report that the Federals had abandoned their supply base. He reasoned that the enemy must be in retreat toward the James River and issued orders for a pursuit. Both north and south of the Chickahominy River, Lee's units moved on the 29th. It was not until June 30 that elements of the Southern army intercepted McClellan's columns at Glendale. Jackson's divisions remained in place during the fighting, sparking the sharpest of several controversies about Jackson's performance in the campaign. The Federals repulsed the assaults, and by the afternoon of July 1 were deployed on Malvern Hill, a one-mile-wide and one-and-a-half-mile-long bluff that rose one hundred feet above the surrounding terrain. McClellan held a formidable position, with his flanks anchored by ravines and marshes.[20]

The Confederates stumbled into a terrible slaughter among the fields of ripened grain below Malvern Hill's crest late on July 1. A misunderstanding triggered the assaults. Into a gale of artillery fire and musketry the Southern brigades advanced only to be swept away. Major General D. H. Hill said later that "it was not war—it was murder." Another member of the army shuddered at the memory of "the rivers of good blood that flowed that evening all in vain." A Virginian asserted, "At no other time did I so realize the horrors of a battle field." The rebels never had a chance, although with valor they tried.[21]

Few Confederate units that advanced toward the enemy were spared on this day. The Stonewall Brigade went forward after six o'clock, barely mustering five hundred rank and file. Union batteries blanketed the air above them with shell bursts. The metal shards knocked down men individually and in small clusters. One shell mortally wounded Captain Louis J. Fletcher of the Fifth Virginia with "the most frightful wound I ever saw," reported Colonel Baylor. For nearly two hours, the Virginians endured the cannon fire and long range musketry. One bullet wounded Colonel Andrew Grigsby, and two spent balls bruised Colonel John Neff. Only darkness ended the punishment that had killed thirteen and wounded seventy-two.[22]

"This fight beggars description," Captain James Edmondson of the Twenty-seventh Virginia told his wife in a letter four days after Malvern Hill. "It has been most horrible. I have never before witnessed anything to compare to it and I pray God that I never witness anything like it again." The "mangled dead" lay in piles. "Oh, my dear wife," he continued, "I do wish this terrible war would cease. I have never felt so gloomy and so low spirited as I do now." As a precaution, he informed her, he had prepared a will.[23]

Like Edmondson, an enlisted man in the Thirty-third Virginia contended after Malvern Hill "I never want to witness such a scene again." As for the Peninsula region, "I never was more tired of any country as that," he wrote. Although the Valley men would have preferred to be back beyond the mountains, Lee's campaign had saved Richmond and pushed McClellan down the Peninsula to the security of Union gunboats on the James River. In its aftermath, the Lincoln administration reopened closed recruiting offices. It would be nearly two years before another Union army came so close to the Southern capital.[24]

The Fourth Virginia's Captain Hugh White believed that their recent successes could be explained, in part, because the Northern soldiers "are not actuated by the spirit that animates ours." To the Southerners, wrote White, "our earthly all is at stake."[25]

Fireworks arced through the night skies above Fredericksburg, Virginia, on July 4, 1862. The display marked the end of celebrations for the troops in the division of Rufus King. Drills had been suspended, allowing the men to enjoy cannon firing in the morning and activities in the afternoon. In the brigade of John Gibbon, the Wisconsin and Indiana volunteers held "a great mule race" with a purse of forty dollars to the winner. The entire brigade watched and howled as some of the mules "went one way and some the other some threw their riders and some tumbled head over heels." An animal from the Seventh Wisconsin won the prize amid cheers from the regiment.[26]

After the festivities ceased, Ordnance Sergeant James Converse of the Sixth Wisconsin wrote to his family. It had been a year ago, the sergeant remembered, since his company had passed through Madison to Camp Randall. A few weeks later they boarded trains for the nation's capital, and during the intervening months had been in Virginia "without ever seeing a battle or even an armed rebbel." "It is hard for us," Converse stated, knowing about the fighting on the Peninsula, "to lay here within sixty miles and not have a chance to assist" George McClellan's troops.[27]

To the sergeant and his comrades, they had been misled or "sold," in army slang, too often during the past two months. Each time it appeared that they might join McClellan, the order was countermanded. An officer in the Sixth Wisconsin described the brigade members as nothing "more than ornamental file-closers." He believed that in drill, discipline, and soldierly bearing "we do not yield the palm to the regulars in any service." But with McClellan's army driven away from Richmond, the Western men saw little chance that they would meet "armed rebels" in the near future. They had the suspicion that they would be sold again by countermanded orders before they met the enemy on a battlefield.[28]

The Westerners blamed unfairly their corps commander, Irvin McDowell, for the avoidance of battle. An Indianan argued that McDowell "seems to shun every thing that would promote the 'cause.'" When the major general visited Fredericksburg a week after the celebrations on the Fourth, the troops greeted him during a review with "disgust and contempt appearing on every coutenance." McDowell had been governed, however, by instructions from the War Department. Although not an energetic commander, he enjoyed no independent control of his command. Authorities in Washington had sold the brigade members.[29]

John Gibbon knew of his men's frustrations, having heard them no doubt from his regimental commanders. Like them, he chafed under the routine of garrison duty. As noted previously, he had been "more and more disgusted" with the administration's management of military affairs. But as July's heat and humidity smothered the Virginia countryside, Gibbon continued the brigade's preparations for a day of battle.[30]

Gibbon conducted brigade drill every day unless rain canceled it. Often in sweltering heat, the officers and men performed the evolutions for two to three hours. On July 17, "the General got mad," wrote a sergeant, "because we done so poorly." Two days later, however, he complimented them, remarking that the "drill would do honor to veteran troops." Following two long days of training on the 21st and 22nd, an enlisted man scribbled in his diary that "it appeared that Gibbon determined to prepare us for sanguinary conflict." On another occasion, he ordered the command to form a battle line at the double quick and rode along it, timing the men. Their progress pleased him, as he noted in a letter to his wife: "They have now pretty much concluded that if they are able to perform all the movement I can put them thru they will do pretty well!"[31]

The old Regular also required all officers and men to form in "light marching order" each morning after reveille. Every member had to appear with weapons, accoutrements, canteens, and haversacks on them. "This order don't trouble the boys so much," contended a private, "but it hurried some of our officers considerable to get out."[32]

Some of the initial dislike of and resentment toward Gibbon had subsided. While Captain Edwin Brown carped to his wife that "it would take me a *month*" to list his complaints about Gibbon, King, and McDowell, most officers and men probably shared Lieutenant Colonel Lucius Fairchild's assessment of their commander. "We have a splendid Brig. Genl.," asserted Fairchild about Gibbon. "He is regular old fire on strict discipline—no officer or man can leave the ranks on the march—or the camp—without his permission. He attends to his troops very closely, knows all that is going on, in fact he is a model Genl."[33]

Gibbon's relations with some officers, however, still caused difficulties for him. During June, he had become involved in a dispute over the selection of a new major in the Sixth Wisconsin. Lieutenant Colonel Benjamin Sweet had received the colonelcy of a new Wisconsin regiment and left the Sixth. Major Edward Bragg had succeeded Sweet, creating the vacancy. Gibbon and Colonel Lysander Cutler supported Lieutenant Frank Haskell, the brigade's able and ambitious adjutant, for the post, but the regiment's captains endorsed Captain Rufus Dawes of Company K. Believing that Haskell would win, Cutler ordered a caucus of regimental officers. But the subordinates voted, 14–13, for Dawes, who agreed afterward to submit the decision to Wisconsin governor Edward Solomon. Haskell's supporters in Madison besieged Solomon on the lieutenant's behalf, but the governor disliked the lobbying effort and appointed Dawes to the rank.[34]

No officer in the brigade, however, riled Gibbon more than Colonel Solomon Meredith of the Nineteenth Indiana. Their mutual dislike had not abated; if anything, it had deepened. Long Sol continued his efforts to arrange the transfer of the regiment, presenting his case to King, McDowell, and political friends in the capital. While King seemed to sympathize with the colonel, the division commander told Meredith that he was "most unwilling to part with the 19th Indiana." The regiment stayed in the brigade, and the relationship between Gibbon and Meredith festered like an open sore.[35]

On the evening of July 31, the approximately 2,800 officers and men of the brigade signed their payroll forms. "The camp was lively and jubilant" that night, according to a member. The next day, they received their pay, drilled under Gibbon's direction, and held a review for King. Drill and an inspection followed on August 2 and 3. During the night of the 4th, orders came to prepare for a march. Around the campfires, they most likely speculated about whether they would be sold again.[36]

A Virginian in the Stonewall Brigade described the fortnight after the Battle of Malvern Hill as "the halcyon days of Jackson's troops." Camped three miles north of Richmond along Mechanicsville Turnpike, the soldiers enjoyed "well earned rest, good rations, abundant supplies from their valley homes, proximity to the capital with its varied attractions, the praises and admiration of its people for Stonewall and his followers." All of these pleasures, he wrote, "combined to make it most pleasantly remembered ever afterwards."[37]

Lieutenant General Thomas J. "Stonewall" Jackson, first commander of the Stonewall Brigade. Jackson and the brigade earned their immortal nickname on Henry House Hill during the First Battle of Bull Run or Manassas, July 21, 1861. This is the last known photo of Jackson, taken two weeks before he received his mortal wounds at Chancellorsville, May 1863.

Elisha F. "Bull" Paxton, a commander of the Stonewall Brigade. Paxton was killed leading the brigade at Chancellorsville, May 3, 1863. Picture is of Paxton as a lieutenant in 1861 or 1862.

Prewar view of William S. H. Baylor, colonel of Fifth Virginia, who was killed at the head of the Stonewall Brigade on August 30, 1862, in the Second Battle of Bull Run or Manassas.

Prewar view of V.M.I. cadet John F. Neff, who was elected colonel of the Thirty-third Virginia in April 1862, and was killed at Brawner's Farm in engagement with the Iron Brigade, on August 28, 1862.

Private Samuel S. Sours, Second Virginia, dressed in attire typical of Confederate soldiers early in the conflict.

Postwar view of Henry House Hill, at First Bull Run or Manassas, looking west from the position of the Stonewall Brigade. Henry house on left, Robinson house on right. Across this ground the Virginians charged and captured Union cannon.

Winter camp in 1862 of Second Wisconsin outside of Washington, D.C. View shows typical winter quarters of Civil War soldiers.

Postwar view of Brawner's Farm, looking west toward Confederate position on Stony Ridge.

Postwar view of Antietam battlefield, 1885, looking east toward Antietam Creek and South Mountain.

Postwar view of Hagerstown Pike–Smoketown Road intersection, Antietam battlefield, looking east from Dunker Church. John B. Hood's Texas Brigade formed in field marked by telegraph pole and attacked toward left of photo, meeting the Iron Brigade and other Federal units.

Culp's Hill, Gettysburg. Confederate troops, including the Virginians of the Stonewall Brigade, confronted this terrain in their attacks on July 2–3, 1863.

Painting by Thure de Thulstrup of the attack by Union troops on Dunker Church, morning of September 17, 1862, Battle of Antietam.

Brigadier General John Gibbon, second commander of the Iron Brigade. Gibbon was a West Pointer and Regular Army officer, who issued to the Westerners the black Hardee hats that became their distinctive badge. He led them from Brawner's Farm through Antietam.

Brigadier General Solomon Meredith, Gibbon's successor as commander of the Iron Brigade. As colonel of the Nineteenth Indiana, Meredith clashed frequently with Gibbon, who despised the politician-turned-soldier. Meredith led the brigade at Gettysburg, where he was wounded.

Brigadier General Lysander Cutler, first colonel of Sixth Wisconsin who commanded the Iron Brigade and then a division.

Lieutenant Colonel Rufus R. Dawes, Sixth Wisconsin. Dawes led the regiment in the attack on the railroad cut at Gettysburg, July 1, 1863.

Colonel William W. Robinson, Seventh Wisconsin. As senior colonel, Robinson commanded the Iron Brigade from July 1863 to March 1864. Pictured with the Hardee hat with a plume.

Private George H. Cole, Seventh Wisconsin. Cole is dressed in the state-issued gray uniform and is carrying musket, pistol, knife, cap, pouch, and canteen.

Private Edward Ranney, Seventh Wisconsin. Ranney is holding the Hardee hat, with infantryman's horn, Company K letter, regimental number, hat cord, and plume. It is an excellent view of one of "those damn black hats."

A previously unpublished sketch, drawn by Private Sullivan Green of the Twenty-fourth Michigan, of two officers by a campfire and a tent.

The welcome interlude resulted from the Confederates' strategic victory in the Seven Days' Campaign. Although the Southerners had suffered a tactical defeat at Malvern Hill on July 1, the Union Army of the Potomac had abandoned the field, and since then, had huddled under the protection of gunboats at Harrison's Landing on the James River. Confederate units conducted constant reconnaissances along the enemy lines, looking for any indication of a Federal withdrawal down the Peninsula. Occasionally, the Yankees probed forward, igniting brief skirmishes between the opponents. But George McClellan had no intention of becoming entangled with the Rebels.[38]

In Washington, meanwhile, the administration had created the Army of Virginia by merging the Mountain, Shenandoah, and Rappahannock departments. President Abraham Lincoln appointed Major General John Pope to command of the roughly fifty-thousand-man force, including the division of Rufus King at Fredericksburg. Confident, boastful, and aggressive, Pope promised to advance against the Confederates. The forty-year-old general had achieved some modest success along the Mississippi River, and when he assumed command in the East, he announced to the troops: "Let us look before and not behind. Success and glory are in the advance."[39]

While King's division remained posted at Fredericksburg, Pope marched with the bulk of the army south, following the Orange & Alexandria Railroad. On July 12, the vanguard entered Culpeper Court House, located between the Rapidan and Rappahannock rivers in central Virginia. Thirty miles to the south lay Gordonsville, where the Orange & Alexandria and Virginia Central railroads intersected. Foodstuffs from the Shenandoah Valley flowed along the latter's tracks. If Pope occupied Gordonsville, the vital railway would be severed.[40]

When General Robert E. Lee learned of the Federal entry into Culpeper Court House, he reacted at once. On July 13, he ordered Stonewall Jackson, with two infantry divisions and artillery, northwest to confront the new threat. Jackson had approximately eleven thousand troops, but Lee would within two weeks augment the force with Major General A. P. Hill's division. "I want Pope to be suppressed," Lee told Jackson.[41]

Reveille sounded in the camps at 2:30 A.M. on July 14. At sunrise, the men filed into columns and marched. "Nothing known as usual as to where we were going," noted a captain in the Stonewall Brigade. The day's movement brought them to the tracks of the Virginia Central Railroad, whose officials were unprepared for the floodtide of manpower. For the next two days seventeen freight trains of roughly fifteen cars each hissed and clanged around the clock, transporting the men, animals, and cannon west to Frederick's Hall. From there, the Confederates traveled on foot to Gordonsville, with the leading elements reaching the town on the 18th. By the 20th, Jackson's force occupied the railroad junction and guarded the tracks both east and west of the village.[42]

During the march, Charles Winder tried to reduce straggling in the Stonewall Brigade by having rolls called when the men bivouacked for the night. Those absent would be either bucked or gagged the next day, if they were not marching, from sunrise to sunset. Bucking consisted of tying a man's wrists together, slipping them over his knees, and inserting a stick under the knees above the arms. A man was gagged by placing a bayonet in his mouth and tying it in place. One of the guilty members alleged subsequently that one half of the soldiers punished in this fashion deserted. The officers complained to Jackson, according to a member, and he ordered Winder to stop the measures. Some of the Virginians swore that they would kill the brigadier in the next battle.[43]

Straggling and desertion, however, remained a serious problem with the brigade. Colonel John Neff of the Thirty-third Virginia estimated that about 350 members of the regiment were absent without leave. "I wish men at home would send these deserters back," he complained to his parents. "We never can keep up an army as long as men run off as they have been doing. I think some of them will very likely be shot for desertion." Captain Samuel Moore heard a report that some of the Second Virginia's men had refused to return to duty, with one of them openly running a store in Newtown. The command lost additional troops when a number of conscripts received discharges.[44]

Jackson kept his troops posted around Gordonsville until A. P. Hill's large division arrived during the first week of August. With the reinforcements, Jackson's force amounted to about 22,500 infantry, artillery, and cavalry. Pope had with him at least twice that number, but the Union general had shown little aggressiveness since his occupation of Culpeper County. Skirmishes between cavalry units characterized the action between the opponents. On August 6, Jackson learned that Pope had divided his force, advancing with a portion of the command south of Culpeper Court House. The next day, the Confederates marched north toward the enemy.[45]

Sweltering heat drained away the stamina of the marchers on August 7 and 8. Confusing orders, fatigue, and snarls of wagons slowed the pace. Jackson and Hill clashed on the 8th over the order of march, each blaming the other for the confusion that delayed the latter's division. August 8 was a terrible day for the men and animals as temperatures peaked at ninety-six. By nightfall, however, Richard Ewell's and Winder's divisions bivouacked north of the Rapidan River, while Hill's brigades camped south of the stream. Less than ten miles to the north, the Confederates' old Valley foe, Major General Nathaniel Banks, had his troops bedded down near Cedar Mountain.[46]

Ewell's three brigades paced the march on August 9, followed by the four brigades of Jackson's former division. The army commander assigned his senior brigadier, Alexander R. Lawton, to the wagon train guard, giving command of his brigades to Charles Winder. The Marylander had been ill for several days, and on this morning, he could barely ride his horse. He had refused a surgeon's recommendation that he relinquish command. Colonel Charles Ronald of the Fourth Virginia succeeded Winder at the head of the Stonewall Brigade.[47]

The stifling heat and jammed wagons slowed the movement along Culpeper Road. Captain Samuel Moore described the march as "slowly feeling our way for 7 or 8 miles." About 1:00 P.M., Jackson ordered Ewell's leading brigade to advance against the enemy, who were posted south of a branch of Cedar Run at the foot of Cedar Mountain. About a mile from the Union line, Culpeper Road bent east, with farmland extending south of the road to Cedar Mountain and with fields and woods covering the ground north of the roadbed. When the Southerners appeared, Banks had about nine thousand troops on the field.[48]

Confederate artillery batteries rolled into position south and east of Culpeper Road and opened the battle against their opposing gunners. Behind the Southern cannon, Brigadier General Jubal A. Early's brigade deployed in the fields while Ewell's other two brigades covered the flank along the mountain. Winder aligned his four brigades in woods along the road. For the next two hours, the battlefield belonged to the begrimed gun crews as shell bursts rained down upon the waiting infantry ranks on both sides.[49]

During the artillery contest, Winder, who looked "very pale and badly," watched the action near a battery posted beside the road. Suddenly, a piece of shell ripped through the general's left arm, plowing through his body and exiting near the spine. The brigadier, according to an eyewitness, "fell straight back at full length, and lay quivering on the ground." He remained conscious for about ten minutes, muttering, "My poor, poor wife." "My little pets." Stretcher-bearers carried him to the rear, where he died within an hour.[50]

The bearers passed the Stonewall Brigade with the dying general. When the Virginians recognized their commander, they "said nothing," wrote Moore, "but seemed sternly to resolve that for every drop of his blood, they would pour out a gallon of Yankee blood." While many of the men never liked Winder, Captain Hugh White probably reflected the majority's view of the general when he stated a few days after the battle, "He was a most gallant soldier, and by his admirable discipline, was not only keeping the Brigade efficient, but was making it better, I think, than it ever was before."[51]

Winder's fall coincided with an escalation of the combat. The brigades of Brigadier General William B. Taliaferro and Colonel Thomas S. Garnett extended Early's line north of Culpeper Road into the woods. Colonel Ronald brought the Stonewall Brigade forward by columns of regiments, but his confusion in the woods had delayed the Virginians' arrival. They formed in the woods on Garnett's left along a stake-and-rider fence that marked the edge of a brushy field. Ronald had about twelve hundred men in the ranks and began aligning the five regiments, from left to right—Fourth, Second, Fifth, Thirty-third, and Twenty-seventh.[52]

The Virginians leveled the fence while under artillery fire from enemy cannon. Before the line was completed, a Union brigade, under Brigadier General Samuel W. Crawford, advanced through a wheatfield toward Garnett's men. The Federals slammed into Garnett's front and left flank, driving the Southerners toward Culpeper Road. William Taliaferro, who had succeeded Winder, ordered Ronald to attack. The colonel rode to the front of the Virginians, shouting, "First Brigade, prepare for a charge bayonets." The Valley men stepped forward, clearing the trees and dense underbrush into the brushy field.[53]

On the brigade's right, the Thirty-third and Twenty-seventh Virginia advanced to a fence at the northwest corner of the wheatfield. Two of Crawford's regiments lashed the Virginians' line. The combatants blasted each other with volleys. The Twenty-seventh Virginia counted barely 130 men and was commanded by Captain Charles L. Haynes. When the Northerners overlapped its right flank, raking the Virginians, the Twenty-

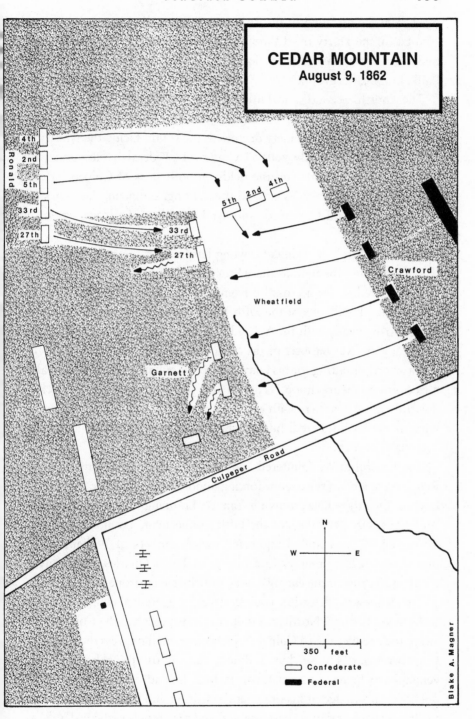

CEDAR MOUNTAIN
August 9, 1862

Ronald

4th
2nd
5th
33rd
27th

5th   2nd   4th

33rd

27th

Crawford

Wheatfield

Garnett

Culpeper   Road

N

W ——— E

350   feet

◻ Confederate
■ Federal

Blake A. Magner

seventh broke and fled in disorder into the woods. Lieutenant Colonel Ned Lee of the Thirty-third Virginia—Colonel John Neff had been placed under arrest over a trifling policy dispute by Winder—refused his right flank, holding the ground.[54]

The Fourth, Second, and Fifth Virginia, meanwhile, advanced "with great deliberation, loading and firing," into the brushy field. The three regiments then wheeled ninety degrees to the south, facing the wheatfield and triggering "a deadly volley." Crawford's Federals reeled under the musketry. In the woods and the fields on both sides of Culpeper Road, two of A. P. Hill's brigades entered the fighting, stabilizing Jackson's faltering lines. Behind Crawford, another Union brigade drove across the wheatfield.[55]

The three Virginia regiments swung left to meet the oncoming Union troops, stopping them amid the wheat shocks. To the south, Crawford's men staggered under a crossfire from the Virginians and Hill's soldiers. Major Hazael Williams of the Fifth Virginia ordered a charge. The regiment drove ahead, with the Second and Fourth Virginia trailing. Color Sergeant John M. Gabbert of the Fifth rushed to the front with the flag and a sword, shouting for his comrades to follow him. Some of the Valley men emitted a "war whoop." The Yankees fired at the attackers, knocking down Sergeant Gabbert with wounds in the leg and shoulder. The left wing of the Fifth faltered, but Adjutant Charles S. Arnall rallied it. The Virginians kept coming.[56]

The Federal ranks splintered and then dissolved. Within minutes, the Rebels were among the enemy, forcing hundreds to surrender. "One small boy" in the Fifth chased down a Yankee, grabbing him by the belt. The Virginians seized the flags of the Fifth Connecticut, Twenty-eighth New York, and an unidentified regiment. Some members of Williams's regiment claimed later that Private Narcissus Finch Quarles, Company E, grabbed all three of the enemy colors and nineteen prisoners.[57]

The Stonewall Brigade's counterattack triggered a counterthrust of Jackson's entire line. North and south of Culpeper Road the Confederates swept the enemy toward Culpeper. Jackson wanted to press the pursuit to Culpeper Court House, but darkness and his troops' exhaustion prevented it. As he had at Kernstown, Jackson had advanced to battle without solid knowledge of his opponent's position and numbers. But on this sweltering August day, he had reserves, and they repulsed the Federals' assaults, counterattacked, and secured the victory. The Southern commander's aggressiveness—"Jackson marched us hard [and] fought men hard," in the words of a Valley man—had inflicted another defeat upon a Union foe. "It was in battle," asserted one of his soldiers, "that the men showed their great love for, and confidence in, General Jackson."[58]

Instrumental to the battle's outcome was the performance of the Stonewall Brigade. "Men never behaved better in battle," Colonel Ronald boasted in his report. To his wife, Captain Moore avowed that "the 'Stonewall' lost none of its reputation." Except for the Twenty-seventh Virginia, the regiments had fought tenaciously and spearheaded the counterattack that won the day. In defense of the Twenty-seventh, it should be noted that it was the smallest regiment with only seven companies and was commanded by a captain. Although the unit rallied and reentered the fighting, it broke and fled initially. Its disorderly flight sparked an eventual controversy in which A. P. Hill's troops claimed inaccurately that the entire brigade had abandoned the field.[59]

The Valley men suffered relatively minor losses of ten killed, fifty-one wounded, and one missing. For Jackson's entire army, the casualties amounted to 1,418, while Banks's losses totaled 2,403, one fourth of whom were prisoners. Among the wounded in the Stonewall Brigade was Major Frederick Holliday of the Thirty-third Virginia. A bullet shattered his right arm, which surgeons amputated. Holliday's service had ended, and upon his return to Frederick County, he was elected subsequently to the Confederate Congress. Since the April reorganization, the "gallant" Holliday was the fourth field officer in the brigade either killed, mortally wounded, or permanently disabled.[60]

The brigade's most grievous loss was that of Charles Winder. "There was no better Brigadier General in our Army," believed Captain Moore. In his report Jackson described the fallen general with whom he had had stormy confrontations as "richly endowed with those qualities of mind and person which fit an officer for command and which attract the admiration and excite the enthusiasm of troops, he was rapidly rising to the front rank of his profession. His loss has been severely felt." General Robert E. Lee called Winder "that noble and accomplished officer and patriot."[61]

The Confederates held the torn fields and woodlots near Cedar Mountain throughout August 10, expecting a Union advance. It never came, and on the 11th, the Federals asked for a truce to gather their dead and wounded. While the blue-coated details searched for comrades, the Southerners prepared to withdraw. They marched during the afternoon and night, halting finally at Orange Court House. A seventeen-year-old private in the Stonewall Brigade, who had enlisted during the previous winter, remembered the spring and summer months with the command and summarized the time by stating, "Battles became a habit."[62]

Heat rose from the ground as if the fires of hell were just beneath the surface. Overhead, a relentless sun burned men's flesh while the humid air pressed upon them. For the Wisconsin and Indiana soldiers of John Gibbon's brigade, each mile on the road brought further agony. They had been on the march since three o'clock on the morning of August 5, in what the general called the "hotest day I have seen." Gibbon tried to quicken the pace but abandoned the attempt as scores of his men collapsed to the ground. Their comrades revived the unconscious ones by pouring water on their chests. "It became so hot," wrote a sergeant, "that it seemed nearly to melt everything."[63]

Before noon, Gibbon halted the command in a section of woods for a respite. When the order came to resume the march, however, members of the Sixth Wisconsin refused to move until threatened with bayonets. More men fell out of the ranks until the Sixth "looked like the *skeleton* of a Regiment." Similar numbers in the other three regiments lay along the roadside, many suffering from sunstroke. A soldier in the Seventh Wisconsin estimated that 460 of his comrades had been stricken by the heat. About noon, after fourteen miles, Gibbon stopped the march. The rest of the day, he said, "was spent in doctoring our poor broken down men."[64]

Men dragged themselves into camp throughout the afternoon and into the night. It might have gone better with the soldiers if they knew that a battle lay at road's end. Instead, they had been ordered south from Fredericksburg to wreck the tracks and facilities of the Virginia Central Railroad, which the Confederates had been using to shuttle troops west to confront soldiers of John Pope's Army of Virginia.[65]

At 2:00 A.M., on August 6, the officers and men of the Sixth Wisconsin filed into column. Gibbon had selected them to push south to the railroad while their comrades in the other three regiments moved on another road and pressed back Southern horsemen, who had harassed the Federals on the 5th. Before the regiment started, Lieutenant Colonel Edward Bragg told them that the day's march would be worse than yesterday's, and all who could not stand it should stay in camp.[66]

"We now commenced a march," a sergeant in the Sixth jotted afterward in his diary, "that will be remembered by every man that went through it." As Bragg predicted, the suffering in the heat increased. More of them straggled and fell out of the column. While their fellow Westerners with Gibbon and troops from Brigadier General John P. Hatch's brigade clashed with enemy cavalrymen, the men of the Sixth covered seventeen miles, reaching Frederick's Hall Station late in the afternoon. Assisted by runaway slaves, details soon began their work of destruction, lifting up rails and burning supplies, a bridge, a turntable, and a warehouse. After dark, they withdrew nine miles and bivouacked.[67]

Bragg had his troops on the road north by four o'clock on the morning of the 7th. They plodded along at a "steady pace" in the "terrible" heat. By nightfall, the Sixth were camped along the Mattaponi River, eighteen miles from their previous bivouac site. Ahead of them, Gibbon and Hatch had withdrawn to near Spotsylvania Court House, where Bragg's regiment rejoined them the next day. During the march's final miles, officers lost control of the men, who broke ranks and either halted or proceeded at their own pace. Few of the exhausted officers even tried to restore order and discipline.[68]

The raid cost Gibbon's brigade one killed and fifty-nine captured by Confederate cavalry. The damage inflicted upon the railroad was minimal and easily repaired. The men needed time to recover—"we had a damed hard time of it," recounted a soldier—but news of the Battle of Cedar Mountain reached Fredericksburg on the night of the 9th. Pope wanted reinforcements, and at four o'clock on the morning of the 10th, King's division headed west.[69]

"The atmosphere was like a great hot sponge," recalled a lieutenant, "which sucked the moisture out of every pore of the soldier's body." By noon, stragglers trailed the column for miles. Carrying their pants, shoes, accoutrements, and rifles above their heads, the troops crossed the Rappahannock at Kelly's Ford after dark and camped. They started again at 3:00 A.M., on the 11th, covering twenty-eight miles under "a boiling sun" during the day. When they halted near the Cedar Mountain battlefield that night, "men collapsed" on the ground, according to Gibbon. A private in the Sixth Wisconsin scribbled in his diary that he was "just about as tired and sleepy as I ever wish to be."[70]

On August 14, Pope and McDowell reviewed King's division. When it was finished, the army commander "declared my Brigade *the best one in the division,*" Gibbon informed his wife that same day. "As I have always said," added the brigadier, "I knew that before, but was glad to have it acknowledged by high authority." About the same time, a soldier in the Second Wisconsin told his mother that "Gen Gibon is a bully man."[71]

While camped near Cedar Mountain, the Westerners roamed across the torn farmlands and woods, hearing stories about the fighting and seeing the freshly dug graves. For over two months, these soldiers in the tall black hats had been caroming across the Virginia countryside in response to alarms caused by Stonewall Jackson and the foot cavalry. The Confederate general and his legions never seemed far away, but always beyond the reach of the men from Wisconsin and Indiana. But one thing seemed certain to them, or as Private Lyman Holford of the Sixth Wisconsin put it in his diary after the review, "I do knot know where Jackson is now but I expect he will be giving us another race before long."[72]

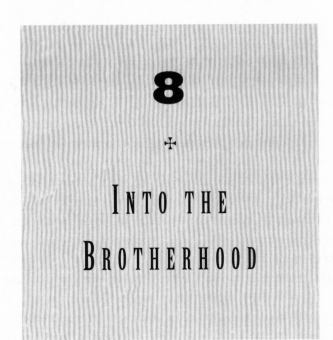

8

✠

INTO THE
BROTHERHOOD

A N evening's sun edged beneath a mountain crest. On a large boulder beside a country road, a solitary figure stood. With the dying sun's rays bathing his face, he looked larger than life, a giant in Confederate gray. Below him on the road, ranks of weary soldiers passed by. Enjoined to be silent, they doffed their hats, bowed their heads, or saluted. Turning to an aide near the boulder, Stonewall Jackson said, "Who could not conquer with such troops as these?" It was late in the day of August 25, 1862, outside Salem (present-day Marshall), Virginia, and as a Wisconsin soldier predicted, the elusive Stonewall was giving the Federals "another race."[1]

Barely two weeks had passed since the Battle of Cedar Mountain, and in that interim, the war in the Old Dominion had shifted to central Virginia between the Rapidan and Rappahannock rivers. Within two days of Jackson's victory, General Robert E. Lee, convinced that Union Major General George McClellan's army at Harrison's Landing on the Peninsula posed no threat to Richmond, began shuttling units to Gordonsville. Lee followed on August 15, and with the bulk of his army at hand, discussed with Jackson and Major General James Longstreet how to assail Major General John Pope's Army of Virginia, posted between the two rivers. The generals agreed on a plan, scheduling it for the 18th. But the offensive miscarried, and that night, Pope learned from captured documents of Lee's operations and began withdrawing his army across the Rappahannock.[2]

The Confederates pursued, halting south of the river, whose opposite banks brimmed with Union cannon and infantry. Skirmishes flared along the river for three days. On the night of August 22, Jeb Stuart's Confederate horsemen raided into Catlett's Station in the Federal rear, seizing prisoners, horses, and Pope's personal baggage, including a dispatch book. Stuart forwarded the documents to Lee, whose suspicions were confirmed that elements of McClellan's army were en route to Fredericksburg to reinforce Pope. To President Jefferson Davis, Lee wrote on the 23rd, "If we are able to change the theater of the war from James River to the north of the Rappahannock we shall be able to consume provisions and forage now used in supporting the enemy."[3]

Lee chose the audacious road, explaining after the war that "the disparity . . . between the contending forces rendered the risks unavoidable." On the 24th, he conferred with Jackson, directing the subordinate to take his three divisions and artillery, roughly 24,000 men, march up the Rappahannock, swing beyond the enemy flank, and sever the Orange & Alexandria Railroad, Pope's main supply and communication line. Longstreet's troops would feint along the river and then follow Jackson's. Lee hoped to maneuver Pope out of the region, avoiding a battle, and if an opportunity beckoned, threatening Washington.[4]

Jackson's soldiers rolled from beneath their blankets at three o'clock on the morning of August 25. They were "confident and in fine spirits," but knew that Old Jack meant business. Orders had come down the night before to discard knapsacks, cook three days' rations, and carry sixty rounds of ammunition. They were also informed that straggling was forbidden, and when crossing a stream, shoes and clothing would not be removed. They speculated about their destination, but as Private James Hendricks of the Second Virginia admitted, "I do not believe that there was a man in the corps that knew our destination except Jackson. It looked like madness to march away from our supplies and support, but we had learned to obey and to blindly follow."[5]

The pace was relentless with no ten-minute breaks each hour. Through Jeffersonton and Amissville, across the Rappahannock at Hinson's Mill Ford, and to Orleans and Salem, the marchers plodded. Officers prodded the men, "Close up." "Close up." When Jackson watched them pass south of Salem, the van of the column had covered nearly twenty-five miles. As an officer wrote of Jackson, "the glory of belonging to his army is great & so is the *labor.*" Darkness found the troops strung out on the road from Salem back to Orleans.[6]

August 26 dawned with the portent of a hot summer's day. The Confederates were on the move before sunrise, turning east at Salem toward White Plains, and beyond it, Thoroughfare Gap in the Bull Run Mountains. Despite the orders, stragglers accumulated, victims of the billowing heat, dust, and miles. Cavalrymen reported that the gap was clear of the enemy. Before four o'clock in the afternoon, the Southerners descended the defile, reaching Gainesville, where Jackson directed the column toward Bristoe Station on the Orange & Alexandria Railroad. At the depot, the Rebels derailed one train and narrowly missed capturing two others. Stuart and two brigades of cavalry overtook the column, and Jackson dispatched some horsemen and two infantry regiments to seize Manassas Junction, Pope's supply base, five miles up the tracks.[7]

The veteran soldiers had completed one of the war's most renowned marches—fifty-four miles in thirty-six hours. They were astride Pope's lines of communications and held the Federals' major cache of supplies. One of Longstreet's staff officers stated afterward that the Rebels' efforts "in swiftness, daring, and originality of execution, were almost extraordinary." Jackson knew, however, that the train crews had sounded the alarm up and down the railroad. In fact, Union scouts had notified army headquarters of the movement at 9:00 A.M. on the 25th, but Pope misinterpreted this as a withdrawal into the Shenandoah Valley. It would be another day before the army commander grasped the magnitude of the disaster in his rear.[8]

Leaving Major General Richard Ewell's division at Bristoe Station to guard his rear, Jackson marched with his former division, under Brigadier General William Taliaferro, and Major General A. P. Hill's division to Manassas Junction on the morning of August 27. Soon after their arrival, a Union brigade approached, advancing under the false information that they opposed only Southern cavalry. It proved to be a bloody mistake as Jackson's artillery and infantry blasted apart the enemy ranks, inflicting more than 130 casualties and capturing 300. "The enemy seemed to run, every man for himself," claimed a Rebel, "and we ran right after them, shooting as we ran." The fugitives carried their mortally wounded commander with them to the north.[9]

At Manassas Junction, meanwhile, the hungry Southerners feasted on a cornucopia of foodstuffs. "What a time was that . . ." asserted a member of the Stonewall Brigade, "half-starved and worn out, we suddenly found ourselves turned loose among car loads of everything good to eat and drink and smoke." The men grabbed shoes, clothing, candles, and before details destroyed it, whiskey. What food the troops could not consume, they stuffed into pockets and haversacks, or carried on their backs. Late in the afternoon, Ewell's division arrived, having retreated before oncoming Union forces at Bristoe Station. His soldiers took their shares, and at midnight, with the remaining stores ablaze, the Confederates marched away.[10]

Jackson's habitual secrecy, errant guides, and the darkness scattered the divisions across the countryside. But by mid-morning on the 28th, most of the units had gathered on a wooded ridge north of Warrenton Turnpike near Groveton. Here Jackson held good defensible ground that concealed his units and was located in such a way that Lee and Longstreet, who were en route with the rest of the army, could link up with him. As the hours passed, Jackson received a string of reports about Pope's army, which was converging on Manassas Junction. For the men in the ranks, including the Virginians in the Stonewall Brigade, the inactivity allowed them to rest and to enjoy the previous day's bounty. For once, with Old Jack, the war might have seemed remote.[11]

The roads north from the Rappahannock River in central Virginia appeared from a distance to be moving cordons of blue on August 27. Down to the men in the ranks, the word had filtered that once again Stonewall Jackson and his foot cavalry had emerged from shadows and wreaked havoc with Union plans. The reports stated, a private noted in his diary, "that the enemy had outflanked us and were trying to get in our rear." Their commander, John Pope, had been outwitted again, and it must have seemed if his army were chasing ghosts in butternut and gray uniforms.[12]

Although "straggling almost became a mania," remembered a participant, the Union army of fifty thousand responded well to the day's exertions. A portion of it had engaged the Rebels at Bristoe Station, grabbing some prisoners, who located Jackson's forces near Manassas Junction. At headquarters, Pope spoke confidently of bagging the raiders and prepared orders for a convergence of his units on Manassas the next day. While he knew that a large Confederate force—Longstreet's wing of Lee's army—had reached Salem, Pope issued no instructions to delay it or to prevent it from joining with Jackson. With single-minded myopia Pope focused on Manassas, where he assumed Jackson would be waiting to give battle. So, as campfires marked the bivouac sites of his army, John Pope must have anxiously awaited the dawn.[13]

Among the troops camped in fields by the roads were the Wisconsin and Indiana volunteers of John Gibbon's brigade. They had marched fourteen miles that day, from beyond Warrenton to where Warrenton Turnpike crossed Broad Run at Buckland Mills, five miles west of Gainesville. Although they had recovered slowly from the terrible marches during the month's initial two weeks, their "wonderful discipline and high morale," claimed a member, had limited straggling on this day. Whether they would admit it or not, the Westerners bore Gibbon's stamp. They retained also their devotion to the cause, or as an Indianan told his sister at home, "If I was there now it would only be a source of annoyance to me; to know that all most all of the young men of my age were rallying under the flag of their country and I safe at home."[14]

Gibbon's four regiments—numbering slightly more than 1,900 officers and men—filed on to Warrenton Turnpike with the other three brigades in Brigadier General Rufus King's division before daylight on August 28. The morning's march was slow and tedious as the various units of the army approached Manassas Junction, only to discover the charred rubble left by the enemy. Conflicting strands of information inundated army headquarters, and Pope vacillated. Jackson was allegedly at Centreville, and Union cavalry reported that Longstreet was approaching Thoroughfare Gap in the Bull Run Mountains. Pope spent much of the afternoon wrestling with the choices of concentrating against either Jackson or Longstreet, while the army halted.[15]

For the troops of King's division, Pope's indecision offered them a few hours of rest and a meal of freshly butchered cattle. At noon, they camped south of Warrenton Turnpike and west of Pageland Lane and roasted the beef over fires. They had time to lie in the grass and sleep or talk with comrades. About five o'clock, their corps commander, Major General Irvin McDowell, who was nearby, received Pope's new instructions to march to Centreville. Aides relayed the orders; officers shouted to re-form ranks, and the afternoon pleasures ended.[16]

Brigadier General John Hatch's brigade led the march of King's division, followed by Gibbon's, and those of Generals Abner Doubleday and Marsena Patrick. The men advanced at "route step" on Warrenton Turnpike, carrying their weapons "at will." McDowell accompanied Hatch in the column's van, and when they neared the homestead of John Brawner, the corps commander ordered the brigadier to send a regiment through the fields north of the pike to flush out any Confederates who might be there. Earlier in the day, some Rebels had fired upon a passing column from the fields and ridgeline. Hatch called upon the Fourteenth Brooklyn, a Chasseur unit that over a year before had fought against Jackson's Virginians on Henry House Hill. The New Yorkers spread out across the ground, found nothing, and rejoined the column, which had continued on toward Groveton.[17]

Minutes later, a Confederate battery emerged from the woods beyond the Brawner farm, deployed, and fired at Hatch's column. The Union general hurried a battery forward to oppose the Southerners. Up the pike came Gibbon's Westerners—the Sixth Wisconsin, Second Wisconsin, Seventh Wisconsin, and Nineteenth Indiana, from front to rear—and Battery B, Fourth U.S. Artillery. At the sound of the artillery fire, Gibbon spurred ahead to a knoll north of the roadbed and east of Brawner's woods. The brigadier scanned the trees on the ridge with field glasses, but as he wrote later, "not a moving thing was in sight." He searched the woods with the glasses again when he saw a team of horses appear. "I had scarcely time to think," he stated, "whether they belonged to friend or enemy . . . when I was struck by the fact that the horses presented their flanks to view. My experience as an artillery officer told me at once what this meant; guns coming into 'battery'!"[18]

Within minutes, the enemy gun crews had deployed north of the farm buildings and pulled the lanyards on their cannon, sending shells over the pike. In the roadbed, the Westerners heard the discharges, and as one of them wrote home later, "a minute after, 'whiz,' an old shell would come right over our heads. Every head was down in an instant, till the missle struck the ground, when the heads were all up again and laughing at each other for dodgeing." Gibbon summoned forward Battery B. As the artillerists lashed their horses, the infantrymen scrambled off the road. The Union gunners unlimbered on the knoll and answered in kind.[19]

Gibbon watched the effect of Battery B's fire, believing that they opposed a battery of horse artillery. In front of him, the ground rose to the ridge, which stood about seventy feet above the pike. To Gibbon's left, woods extended approximately four hundred yards from the pike. Beyond the trees, a log farmhouse, a small barn, a few outbuildings, and an orchard of apple and peach trees marked the Brawner homestead. A farm lane ran from the house to the pike, while an old, narrow road passed through the woods. Several old fences gave the ground a symmetry. If the Rebels were in force on Stony Ridge and gave battle, the terrain favored the enemy.[20]

Abner Doubleday joined Gibbon. After viewing the ground and the Confederate battery, he suggested an attack. "By heaven, I'll do it," exclaimed Gibbon. The pair of generals separated, with neither one knowing that division commander Rufus King had been stricken with an epileptic seizure for the second time in six days. The fight belonged to the brigade commanders.[21]

Gibbon rode back to the pike, reining up before Colonel Edgar O'Connor and the Second Wisconsin. The brigadier selected the Second to make the attack because he respected the former West Pointer as an officer and the regiment had been tested at First Bull Run. Officers brought the men to their feet, formed the ranks into a column, and with Gibbon and O'-Connor at the head followed the woods road up the slope. Beyond the treeline, in the fields below the Brawner house, the Second shifted into a battle line, with skirmishers in front. The experience of that Sunday in July seemingly so long ago and the endless hours of training expedited the maneuver. The color guard stepped forward, and Colonel O'Connor, mounted before the flag, waved the regiment forward.[22]

Ascending the slope, the Wisconsinites neared the southern edge of the crest, halting in a broom-sedge field. Ahead of them, a line of Confederate infantry emerged from the trees, with five battle flags denoting the number of regiments. The blue-coated skirmishers fell to the ground, and in the description of one of their comrades to the rear, "the remaining companies in line firmly awaited the charge of the rebels, the men grasping their pieces with a tighter grasp." Some of them muttered, "Come on, God damn you." Down the slope, their fellow Westerners watched and waited. Would the Second fight alone and brag about it for months, or had their time come at last? In the dying of an August day, volleys of musketry exploded. Time quickened for the men from "way down beyond the sunset."[23]

When the red-trousered Fourteenth Brooklyn cleared the Brawner fields, Stonewall Jackson rode out of the woods on Stony Ridge. Alone and sil-

houetted against the foliage, he sat his horse and watched the ranks of
Federals pass by on Warrenton Turnpike. All day he had wanted to strike
the enemy, and now the time had come. Turning his mount around, Jackson reentered the trees, halted before a group of subordinates, and said,
"Bring up your men, gentleman!"[24]

The wooded ridge leaped seemingly to sudden life as officers shouted
for infantrymen to form ranks and battery crews prepared to roll forward
into the fields. On the Confederate right, William Taliaferro ordered the
Stonewall Brigade to advance against a Union regiment that was moving
toward the Brawner buildings. The Virginians "had nearly given out the
idea of a fight," wrote a captain in the Thirty-third Virginia, "as the sun
was fast sinking in the west." The brigade counted upward of nine hundred officers and men, only one fourth of the number who had been in the
five regiments on May 3, 1862.[25]

Colonel William Baylor stepped to the front of the brigade. As senior
colonel, the thirty-one-year-old Augusta County man had succeeded to
temporary command after the death of Charles Winder at Cedar Mountain. A popular officer, he had been elected unanimously as commander of
the Fifth Virginia in April, and his performance since then had enhanced
his stature within the brigade. Consequently, on August 15, the command's field officers prepared and signed a letter to the War Department,
recommending Baylor, "who is in every respect qualified to lead and command the Brigade." In the past, they argued, the brigade "has had several
different commanders all of whom were brought from other commands,"
and as "an act of justice" the Virginians deserved one of their own for promotion.[26]

Baylor confided to his wife, however, that he felt "my inability for such
a responsible position & rely only on heaven for wisdom & strength in the
discharge of my Duties." Evidently, Jackson had approached the colonel
about promotion before the officers had written the letter, and Baylor said
he did not want it. In turn, Jackson endorsed another officer but told the
brigade officers to forward the petition to Richmond. The matter remained unsettled as Baylor led his Valley men from the woods on Stony
Ridge.[27]

The Virginians cleared the trees, adjusted ranks, and stepped on. They
advanced steadily as opposing artillery crews created a thunder of shell
bursts. Ahead of them, blue-coated skirmishers and even some men in the
distant ranks of a regiment fired wild shots at the Valley men. They re-

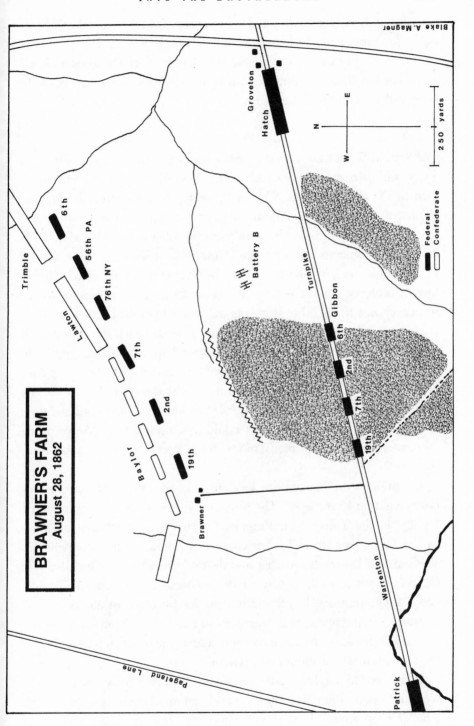

Blake A. Magner

BRAWNER'S FARM
August 28, 1862

Trimble
Lawton
Baylor

6th
56th PA
76th NY
7th
2nd
19th
Brawner

Groveton
Hatch

Battery B
Turnpike

Gibbon
6th
2nd
7th
19th

Warrenton
Patrick

Pageland Lane

N
W — E

250 yards

Federal
Confederate

sponded with a ragged volley and kept coming. Few, if any, of the Confederates probably remarked about who these Yankees were, except to note perhaps that they wore high-crowned black hats. As the Virginians closed to within less than two hundred yards, the enemy leveled their rifles. In both ranks, men braced themselves.[28]

The Second Wisconsin waited until the oncoming Rebels were 150 yards away, and then unleashed a volley. Enemy soldiers staggered and crumpled to the ground as the Westerners reloaded, with ramrods clanging against the barrels. The Virginians surged toward a fence eighty yards from the Federals and were hit with a second volley. "We halt—all seem to be falling," remembered a private of the Second Virginia. "The rain of bullets is like hail." From the fence, the Southerners emitted a yell, followed, as one of them stated, by "a sheet of flame [that] seemed to go out from each side to the other along the whole length of the line."[29]

For twenty minutes the opposing lines pounded each other in what a Union officer described as "a fair square stand up face-to-face fight." On both sides, men described the severity of the musketry as "intensely concentrated," "terrific," and a "great fury." Behind the fence, many of the Virginians, according to one of them, "would lie down, load and fire, and it seemed that every one who would raise up was shot." Some of the Westerners knelt, while many more stood erect amid the fearful combat.[30]

A captain in the Thirty-third Virginia believed it to be "the severest infantry fighting I ever saw." The price of valor in such ferocity mounted rapidly. In the Thirty-third Virginia, Colonel John Neff died instantly from a bullet that struck his left cheek and exited through his right ear. The son of a Dunkard preacher and devoutly religious—"The bible was the man of his council," wrote a fellow officer—Neff had refused a surgeon's suggestion that he relinquish command because of illness and exhaustion. One company in the regiment lost eleven of seventeen members. Captain Philip T. Grace assumed command as the other two field officers were absent due to sickness and a wound.[31]

In the Second Virginia, Colonel Lawson Botts fell with a mortal head wound. Captain John Nadenbousch took command and went down with a bullet in the groin. The Berryville lawyer and frequent letter writer Captain Samuel Moore hobbled away with a thigh wound. In the ranks, Private Albert Saville, who had enlisted only sixteen days ago, died beside his new comrades.[32]

Down the slope, the carnage among the Wisconsin men was equally grievous. Colonel Edgar O'Connor reeled in the saddle and toppled to the ground with a fatal wound. As some troops carried him off the field, he implored his soldiers to do their duty. Lieutenant Colonel Lucius Fairchild took command. Walking behind the line with rolled-up shirtsleeves and a sword in hand, Fairchild urged the men to sustain their "good name." Major Thomas Allen suffered a wound, and seven of the eight members of the color guard were either killed or wounded. Although hit in a leg, Color Corporal Joseph L. Minor held the flag. Eighteen-year-old Private Frank Cole was killed, surrounded by seven or eight rifles he had been using. One soldier asserted that "in moving we had to be careful where we placed our feet to prevent stepping on" fallen comrades.[33]

Colonel Baylor, meanwhile, sent the Fourth Virginia to the Brawner outbuildings, where the Southerners raked the Federal left flank. A Wisconsin man claimed the lines were so close that "it was almost a hand to hand fight." Private Gustavus Horn rushed forward and captured a Virginian at bayonet point. Behind the Northerners, however, the Nineteenth Indiana was ascending the slope, dispatched by Gibbon to secure the Second's flank. As the Indianans advanced, Colonel Solomon Meredith shouted to them, "Boys, don't forget that you are Hoosiers, and above all, remember the glorious flag of our country!"[34]

Meredith had 423 officers and men, and they went in with a yell on the Second Wisconsin's flank. The Virginians initiated these new Yankees into the brotherhood with a volley. An Indianan thought afterward that the explosion of musketry was "like a cat that has unexpectedly met a big dog, bowing up its back and spitting fire at him." The Hoosiers responded, and the killing and maiming escalated. Individual rifle shots blended into a continuous discharge, sounding as if an enraged titan was ripping apart a huge cloth. Bravery was a shared commodity at such close range.[35]

The Confederates advanced a battery of horse artillery, supported by infantry, against the Nineteenth Indiana's left flank. While refusing companies to meet the threat, Colonel Meredith had his mount shot from under him. The animal fell on the colonel. Semiconscious, with fractured ribs, Meredith relinquished command to Lieutenant Colonel Alois Bachman, who detached two companies against the Rebel artillerists. The units forced the gunners to retire, but the Confederate infantry on the Nineteenth's left advanced. Gibbon ordered Bachman to withdraw to a fence in the regiment's rear, and here the Hoosiers repulsed the sortie.[36]

Like their comrades in the Second Wisconsin, the Indianans incurred casualties that approached half their numbers as men fell in clots. Major Isaac May collapsed with a head wound while Private Morris Gilmore watched his twin brother, John, drop to the ground with a disabling wound. Private Stephen Padgett was killed, leaving behind a widowed mother and his brother, Gideon, who was a member of the Sixty-ninth Indiana and who would die within months. The life of Sergeant Thomas Benton oozed away with wounds in the bowels and lungs. Weeks earlier, he had told his sister that if he were home, it would be an "annoyance" to him to be safe while others defended the flag.[37]

The pressure against the two Union regiments mounted as Jackson brought forward Brigadier General Alexander Lawton's Georgia Brigade of Richard Ewell's division on the left of the Virginians. The Federals stood their ground, however, as the Georgians directed their fire toward the Second Wisconsin. Gibbon reacted to the Georgians' arrival by ordering up the Sixth and Seventh Wisconsin. No member of the brigade would be spared any longer from the brotherhood of warriors.[38]

The two regiments moved forward in concert, with the Seventh marching through Brawner's woods in column while the Sixth passed in front of Battery B. In the fields, the Sixth, wrote Major Rufus Dawes, "advanced without firing a shot, making a half wheel to the left in line of battle as accurately as if on the drill ground." As the Seventh emerged from the woods, Colonel William Robinson ordered them into line. Three hundred yards to the east, Colonel Lysander Cutler had halted the Sixth. Together, the pair of units numbered nearly eleven hundred.[39]

At a distance of less than one hundred yards, the Seventh Wisconsin triggered a volley into Lawton's Georgians. The blast scythed through the Confederate ranks. A Georgian believed that he and his comrades would be "overwhelmed and cut to pieces." The two lines were, claimed a Westerner, "within a hailing distance of each other." "My God, what a slaughter!" he added. "No one appeared to know the object of the fight, and there we stood one hour, the men falling all around."[40]

"Jacksons men fight like Devils," a Wisconsin soldier claimed in a letter. "They think Jackson can do anything he undertakes." Colonel Robinson and Lieutenant Colonel Charles Hamilton of the Seventh suffered wounds, although Hamilton stayed on the field. About one man in three in the regiment went down. "During my 46 battles of the war," recalled a private, "I never heard a more incessant rifle fire for 40 minutes. And it was deadly too!"[41]

On the Seventh's right, three hundred yards across the fields, the Sixth Wisconsin also raked the Georgians. As the regiment advanced up the slope, one private recalled that he had "a queer choking sensation about the throat." Ahead of him and his comrades they saw the Rebels in the fading light. The enemy appeared "like a black mass or ridge of ground thrown up and not more than fifty yards away." The Wisconsinites halted in a swale. The Confederates seemed either not to have seen the Federals or mistook them for fellow Southerners. "Get ready, boys, for the fun is coming," shouted Colonel Lysander Cutler, who then gave the order to fire. The rifles flashed, and more Georgians were caught in a furious gale. The Westerners cheered.[42]

From the woods on Stony Ridge now came four regiments and a battalion of Alabamians, Georgians, and North Carolinians, under Brigadier General Isaac R. Trimble, a redoubtable sixty-year-old fighter. Trimble's men advanced to a fence barely eighty yards from the Sixth Wisconsin. "The work of death commenced at short range," stated a Georgian. Volleys exploded along each line. With the roar of artillery, a Wisconsin sergeant thought that it seemed "as if the heavens was a furnace." Major Rufus Dawes declared that the Westerners "loaded and fired with the energy of madmen." Before long, the Seventy-sixth New York and Fifty-sixth Pennsylvania from Doubleday's brigade filled the gap between the Seventh and Sixth Wisconsin, having been sent in when Gibbon requested assistance.[43]

On John Brawner's fields, around the outbuildings, and among the apple and peach trees, the combat blazed from one end of the two lines to another. It was "a roaring hell of fire," claimed a participant. Trimble contended later that "I have never known so terrible a fire." A Georgian captain compared it to "a regular slaughter house." Union officers shouted repeatedly, "Give them hell! boys, give them hell!" Despite the deafening upheaval, a member of the Seventh Wisconsin swore afterward that he heard a Rebel colonel call the Yankees "sons of Bitches," and yell at his men to fire until "every God damned man of them are killed and make them take their breakfasts in Hell."[44]

Lawton pushed forward the Twenty-sixth Georgia in an attack on the Seventh Wisconsin. Some of the Confederates closed to within thirty yards when the Wisconsinites fired. The Georgians "fell from ranks by the dozens." The color guard disappeared, and eight of ten company commanders fell. A member of the Seventy-sixth New York witnessed the bloody work and wrote home subsequently: "Gibbon's men did not run. Those western men are not easily scared." The Georgians stumbled back across the ridge with only sixty members left in the ranks.[45]

"It would be hard to say," Lieutenant Colonel Edward Bragg of the Sixth Wisconsin informed his wife later, "how much a man, with a good strong purpose can endure if obliged to." They had been obliged to endure more than expected for troops in their first battle, but it was not finished. They could barely see through the smoke and darkness, but over the fence in their front came the Twenty-first Georgia and Twenty-first North Carolina in an attack.[46]

The Confederates screeched the Rebel yell. The men in the Sixth had never heard it so close before, and they would not forget the sound. "There is nothing like it this side of the infernal region," as a member of the Sixth described it years later, "and the peculiar corkscrew sensation that it sends down your backbone under these circumstances can never be told. You have to feel it, and if you say you did not feel it and hear the yell you have *never* been there."[47]

Trimble had wanted his entire brigade to charge, but the order never reached the troops on the left. Instead, the Georgians and North Carolinians advanced against the Sixth Wisconsin and Fifty-sixth Pennsylvania. The Southerners' bravery carried them forward, but it could not overcome the withering musketry of the Federals. "The blazes from their guns seemed to pass through our ranks," professed a Georgian. The gunfire nearly annihilated the Twenty-first Georgia, inflicting upon it losses of over seventy percent. In one company, only five of forty-five members escaped unscathed. When Colonel Sanders Fulton tried to urge on his North Carolinians by seizing the flag, he died. Finally, they retreated, and with the repulse of Lawton's troops in the center of the Confederate line, the terrible, violent convulsions ended.[48]

Mercifully, darkness shielded the horrors upon the Brawner farm. But night could not hide the "pitiful cries" of the wounded. "O, God," "O, mother, mother" resounded in the blackness. Friends on each side gathered up their own, guided by the wails. The "groans were the most pitiful sounds I ever heard," a Wisconsin soldier confided in his diary. "A fresh battlefield is a painfully interesting sight, though a terrible one," confessed a Confederate staff officer, who rode over this one after the Federals withdrew, "and darkness by stimulating the imagination increases inexpressibly its gloomy grandeur." The dead, he recollected, defined the battle lines in "dark rows of bodies." A corporal in the Second Wisconsin asserted that "we found all our dead and wounded along a line a rod or two in width."[49]

Gibbon's men removed their wounded comrades from the field before they retreated, carrying them to field hospitals south of Warrenton Turnpike. For the Westerners who had never seen them or had never been wounded, a new terror awaited in the hospitals. They were wretched places, where surgeons and their assistants were overwhelmed after a fight such as this. The heavy, soft-leaded Civil War minié ball created ghastly wounds, particularly when it struck a bone. Surgeons could do little with abdominal wounds and usually dismissed them as fatal, giving their attention to patients who required amputations. The doctors probed, cut, sawed and stitched on improvised operating tables amid pools of blood, gore, and filth.[50]

The casualties in Gibbon's brigade were staggering: 725 killed, wounded, and missing, or nearly forty percent of those engaged. Every regimental commander fell in the fighting, including Colonel Lysander Cutler of the Sixth Wisconsin, who was wounded in the thigh near the battle's conclusion. Of the other eight field officers, four were either killed or wounded. Among the regiments, the losses varied in intensity. The Sixth Wisconsin incurred the fewest casualties because the low ground in which it fought shielded it, while the numbers in the Second Wisconsin approached a rate of nearly two out of three engaged. When Lieutenant Colonel Fairchild viewed the thinned ranks after the engagement, he choked back tears. Some companies were mere shadows. In the Nineteenth Indiana, the casualties exceeded fifty percent. A member of the Second Wisconsin summarized the battle's cost bluntly: "The regiment is all cut to pieces. The whole brigade is badly cut up."[51]

That night as Gibbon received the initial casualty figures from his officers, he bowed his head and wept. His relationship with the brigade had been difficult during the early weeks as he implemented a rigorous program of drill and training, imposed discipline, and tried to make them worthy of Regular Army troops. They balked, complained, and grumbled about their general's safety in battle. But on this day, they conducted themselves with a battlefield discipline and personal valor that belied their combat inexperience. They stood "up to their work like old soldiers," Gibbon wrote subsequently, adding that "I was exceedingly proud of my command." In turn, the rank and file recognized how Gibbon's leadership had prepared them for the demands of a warrior's trade. At Brawner's Farm, the general and the brigade forged a bond amid the terribleness that was tested but not broken.[52]

Gibbon believed, however, that "my single brigade was left almost alone to sustain itself against a division of the enemy." To his wife, he complained that "my men were literally slaughtered" in the "desperate fight." Gibbon blamed, in particular, Marsena Patrick, who had refused to send reinforcements, or as Gibbon put it in his report, "Patrick's brigade remained immovable and did not fire a shot." With Rufus King's incapacity, the brigade commanders operated without overall direction. Ironically, it was Abner Doubleday, an officer whom Gibbon disliked personally, who responded to the requests for support. The situation was, Doubleday wrote, "a very dangerous one, for the Rebel lines overlapped ours," and he reacted by filling a critical gap in Gibbon's line with two regiments, probably saving the Westerners from defeat.[53]

Brigade members shared Gibbon's pride and his criticism of others in the division. Lieutenant Colonel Bragg affirmed in his report that "it were hardly possible to be placed under a hotter fire, but there was no confusion, no faltering. The regiment fought as brave men only can fight." An Indianan boasted to his father that "every man was at his place in the 19th. The Rebels said they fought the best of any troops they ever fought against and theirs is the best troops in the Rebel service." But Major Dawes wondered about the worth of the sacrifice, writing later, "The best blood of Wisconsin and Indiana was poured out like water, and it was spilled for naught."[54]

On Stony Ridge, meanwhile, the Federals' opponents counted the day's toll. In the Stonewall Brigade, the losses amounted to 340 killed, wounded, and missing. Two regimental colonels—Neff of the Thirty-third and Botts of the Second—were either dead or dying, while Colonel Andrew Grigsby of the Twenty-seventh had been wounded. Neither the Second nor the Thirty-third had a field officer with the regiment. Only one captain and one lieutenant remained in the Second Virginia. Writing two days after the engagement, a member spoke for many in the command about the losses: "The old Stonewall suffered on Thursday. . . . Oh, how we suffered in the loss of noble, valuable men and officers."[55]

The casualties resulted, some of the men believed, from their commanders' willingness to use them when a battle offered. "Our brigade," a Virginian grumbled shortly afterward, "it seems is almost always put in front, and has suffered very much in nearly every fight." But their sacrifice elicited praise. In his report, division commander William Taliaferro, referring to First Manassas, stated, "The First Brigade was more exposed than any other, and more than sustained the reputation which, under the leadership of the major-general commanding on the same field over twelve months ago, it achieved, and which has distinguished its veteran troops in many of the hardest-fought battles of the war."[56]

In some of the other units of Jackson's command, the losses exceeded those of the Stonewall Brigade. The Twenty-first Georgia of Trimble's brigade and the Twenty-sixth Georgia of Lawton's suffered casualties of more than seventy percent of their effectiveness in the battle. Only two other regiments in Lee's army would incur a higher percentage of loss in a single engagement during the war. Gibbon's and Doubleday's men had ravaged the pair of Confederate units. The combat also cost Jackson the services of Taliaferro, Richard Ewell, and Isaac Trimble, all three of whom suffered wounds that would disable them for months. Ewell's injury necessitated the amputation of a leg. "Never before, or after that, during the war," claimed a Georgia officer, "did Stonewall Jackson's old Corps suffer so severely in the same length of time."[57]

The Confederates had little, however, to show for the grievous casualties. Neither Jackson, Ewell, Taliaferro, nor Trimble handled the action well. Although the Southerners enjoyed a superiority in numbers and the advantage of higher ground, the brigades, even regiments, attacked piecemeal, negating their edge. In the end, the Yankees and the Rebels settled for a tactical draw. As both sides withdrew, the Brawner farm belonged to neither, only to the dead and the maimed.[58]

Stonewall Jackson had disclosed his location to John Pope with the attack at Brawner's farm. While Federal units, including elements from George McClellan's Army of the Potomac, converged throughout the morning of August 29, Jackson adjusted his lines that extended for one and three fourths miles along the embankment of an unfinished railroad. A. P. Hill's brigades held the left of Jackson's front, with the flank anchored on a rocky knoll where Sudley Road crossed Bull Run. On Hill's right, Ewell's division, under A. R. Lawton, covered the center. Taliaferro's units, commanded by Brigadier General William E. Starke, protected the right.[59]

Along a section of Starke's line, the railroad bed had been carved through high ground, creating a "Deep Cut," as it would come to be known. It provided the defenders a natural protection, while elevated wooded ground behind the railway gave Confederate gunners a platform for cannon. Jackson's position was formidable, but not impregnable.[60]

The Southern position was solidified before noon when the van of James Longstreet's wing arrived on the field, coming in on Jackson's right flank. Longstreet's units spilled off the road from Thoroughfare Gap into woods that concealed them. When completed, Lee's reunited army covered a front of more than three miles. Although Longstreet's position lacked the natural features of Jackson's, it offered the Southerners good terrain for launching an attack or counterattack.[61]

While Longstreet's men completed their deployment, Pope's long-anticipated assault "to crush Jackson" rolled forward against the railroad embankment. The Northerners charged with spirit, driving toward Hill's position on Jackson's left. The attackers stormed up the rocky hill, only to be pounded back by Confederate reserves. The fierce combat ended late in the afternoon. Later, at sunset, Longstreet undertook a reconnaissance-in-force against the Union left south of Warrenton Turnpike that resulted in a snarling, confusing brawl until darkness.[62]

August 30 dawned clear, with a silence across the old killing ground at Bull Run. "The morning was so still and quiet," remembered a Southerner, "that everybody seemed to be on his good behavior." Perplexed by the Union inactivity, Lee conferred with Jackson and Longstreet, deciding to await a Federal movement. If Pope did not renew the offensive, Jackson would withdraw after nightfall and march beyond the enemy right flank, interposing his units between Pope and the capital in Washington. Longstreet would demonstrate against the Union left front, and if the Northerners retreated, would pursue. But if Pope offered battle again on the 30th, Lee's army would fight.[63]

The morning's quiet resulted from confusion at Union army headquarters. Throughout the campaign, Pope had either misinterpreted intelligence reports or misjudged his opponent's intentions. The same failings plagued him throughout the morning of the 30th, as conflicting information that had the enemy either retreating or still in force behind the embankment flooded headquarters. He knew of Longstreet's presence since

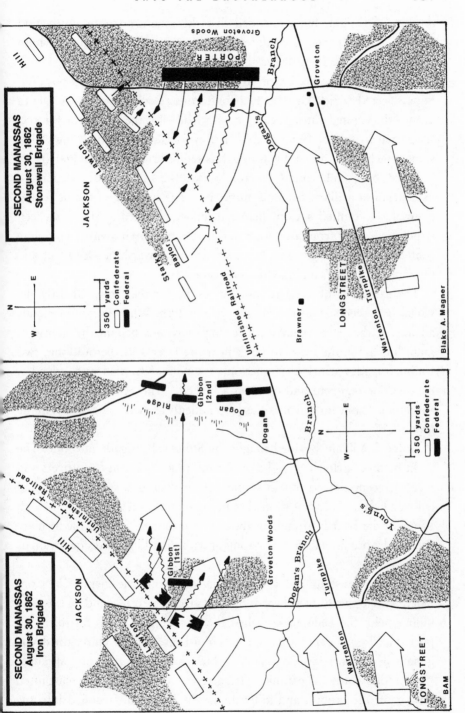

SECOND MANASSAS
August 30, 1862
Stonewall Brigade

Blake A. Magner

SECOND MANASSAS
August 30, 1862
Iron Brigade

BAM

the previous night, but concluded that the general's troops lay behind Jackson's. Finally, after a conference with senior officers, some of whom offered objections, Pope deduced that the enemy was in retreat.[64]

About 3:00 P.M., the Union assault rolled toward Jackson's position. Pope selected Major General Fitz-John Porter's corps from McClellan's army—the Confederates' foe at Gaines's Mill—for the main attack force, supported by Major General John F. Reynolds's and Rufus King's divisions. The latter command was under its senior brigadier, John Hatch.[65]

Emerging from beyond Groveton Woods, the Yankees advanced into a maelstrom of artillery fire and musketry. "The first line of the attacking column," recounted a Confederate defender, "looked as if it had been struck by a blast from a tempest and had been blown away." The blue-coated soldiers kept coming, however, driving toward the Deep Cut and the ranks of Starke's and Lawton's divisions.[66]

The explosion of combat ended a respite for the Stonewall Brigade, which had been spared the fighting of the 29th. When Porter's Federals advanced, the Valley men were resting in woods behind the division's main line along the railroad bank near the Deep Cut. Before long, two Union brigades struck the junction of a pair of Confederate brigades, routing one regiment and creating a breach. "The Federals," recalled a Virginian, "came up in front of us [as] suddenly as men rising up out of the ground."[67]

Colonel William Baylor brought the Stonewall Brigade into line. The night before, Baylor had held a prayer meeting at his tent for officers and men. A recent convert to Christianity, Baylor had quit swearing and had enjoyed hours of conversation about religion. He had told Captain Hugh White of the Fourth Virginia at the prayer meeting, "I know the men are tired and worn but I cannot rest tonight without asking God's mercy on us for tomorrow."[68]

The Virginians plunged down the hillside toward the enemy. The Confederates had two hundred yards of open ground to cross, and on this easy killing field, the Federals scorched the attackers. It "was terrible," reported a Virginia captain. When the color-bearer of the Thirty-third Virginia fell, Colonel Baylor rushed to him, seized the flag, and shouted, "Boys, follow me." The Yankees triggered another volley. The blast lifted Baylor off the ground and killed him. The Virginians recoiled into the woods.[69]

When Captain White saw Baylor's body on the field, he ran to his friend. A devout young man, White had graduated from Washington College and then trained for the ministry. He had led the services at the previous night's prayer meeting. Now, with Baylor dead, White grabbed the flag, yelling, "Come on! Come on!" to the troops. A handful followed the captain, but White had gone only a few steps before rifle fire killed him instantly. Later a staff officer retrieved White's bible and letters for his family.[70]

In the woods, Colonel Andrew Grigsby—"the gallant Grigsby, who knew no fear," in an officer's words—assumed command of the brigade and rallied the men. Once more, the Virginians charged toward the railroad bank. This time, they were not denied, driving out the Federals and filling the gap. Here, they "stood like demons" against more Union attacks. When Grigsby sent a captain to Jackson for reinforcements, the brigade's old commander admonished the officer, "Go back, give my compliments to them and tell the Stonewall Brigade to maintain her reputation."[71]

Pressure abated against Jackson's lines after four o'clock when the Federals found themselves outflanked and under assault by Longstreet's troops. Pope's miscalculations had endangered his entire army as Longstreet sprung his wing in a massive counterattack. "My whole line was rushed forward at a charge," reported Lee's senior major general. "The troops sprang to their work, and moved forward with all the steadiness and firmness that characterizes war-worn veterans." When Jackson's soldiers saw the battle flags of their comrades, they cheered. Lee sent orders for Jackson to advance.[72]

Among the Union troops caught in the billowing storm were John Gibbon's Westerners. Like the Stonewall Brigade, Gibbon's command had been spared from the combat on the 29th, supporting a battery until darkness. Exhaustion had overtaken many—"I never saw men more in need of sleep," claimed a sergeant. Whenever the brigade halted, the troops lay down. Due to the casualties on the 28th, Gibbon had consolidated the Second and Seventh Wisconsin into one unit, under Lieutenant Colonel Lucius Fairchild. Brawner's Farm "had eradicated our yearning for a fight," asserted Major Dawes later. They would be ready if called upon, "but never again anxious."[73]

The Wisconsin and Indiana men had spent the morning of the 30th relaxing and cooking meals. After noon, they advanced into Groveton Woods as support for Porter's assault columns. The density of the trees protected them and restricted their range of vision. They learned of the collapse of Porter's attack and Longstreet's offensive when fugitives bolted through the woods toward the rear. The Westerners tried to staunch the flood of men, but unsuccessful, they retreated to Dogan Ridge, where two batteries braced for the oncoming fury.[74]

From the elevated ground, the Westerners watched the Confederate ranks approach the patchwork Union line. "The shot & shell tore thro' the air," as Gibbon described the situation to his wife, "and bullets whistled around our ears in a most astonishing way." The brigadier had stacked the Sixth Wisconsin and Nineteenth Indiana behind the Second/Seventh Wisconsin. The Rebels—Alabamians, Mississippians, and North Carolinians under Colonel Evander M. Law—"were pretty close" when the Wisconsinites rose and squeezed triggers. The Southerners reeled, fired a volley, and then were lashed with canister from the Federal batteries. The blasts, wrote a Northerner, "piled the dead and mangled in rows like hay raked in windrows in a hayfield."[75]

The black-hatted Federals spilled down the ridge. One of their officers shouted, "Come on boys, God damn them we can keep them back!" Standing in an orchard, the Confederates fired another volley, but the bullets flew over the heads of the Yankees "like [a] shower of hailstones." The counterattack pushed Law's men down the hillside to the base of the ridge. Gibbon ordered a recall, and the Westerners retired to the crest. To his wife, the general boasted, "My men behaved splendidly & by their coolness & courage set a good example to some less inclined to be steady."[76]

The Union position on Dogan Ridge became untenable, however, as Longstreet's en echelon attack outflanked the elevated ground with other units. Gibbon's brigade covered the withdrawal of the artillery crews, and then retreated toward Henry House Hill, where corps commander Irvin McDowell assigned them to rear-guard duty near the Robinson house. Other Union commands stopped Longstreet's troops short of the critical Warrenton Turnpike–Sudley Road intersection. For reasons never fully explained, Jackson did not join in the counteroffensive until six o'clock, allowing Federal commanders to shift enough units to oppose Longstreet and save Pope's army from disaster.[77]

Gibbon's four regiments crossed Bull Run at eleven o'clock and then slept. Rain fell during the night. On the morning of August 31, Pope consolidated his units around Centreville, where two corps of McClellan's army joined them. The Federals waited all day for a Confederate assault. On September 1, Pope began a withdrawal toward Washington. Late in the afternoon, Jackson's troops assailed the Union rear guard near Chantilly but were repulsed during a violent thunderstorm. Thunder and lightning, as if a sign, ended the Second Manassas or Bull Run Campaign.[78]

John Gibbon's veterans slogged through the mud toward the capital with their comrades in the defeated army. They were dispirited, and like nearly everyone else in the columns, blamed Pope and other senior generals. Lieutenant Henry F. Young of the Seventh Wisconsin summarized the campaign tersely, writing that Pope had the army "scattered from Hell to breakfast," and the Confederates had taken advantage of that fact.[79]

For the Westerners in the Sixth and Seventh Wisconsin and Nineteenth Indiana, however, the campaign had marked their entry into the brotherhood of men who had been in combat. They had wished for it for a year, but when it came, it was terrible. Their losses in the three days amounted to nearly nine hundred killed, wounded, or missing, approximately forty-five percent of their numbers. The Second and Seventh Wisconsin and the Nineteenth Indiana were among the dozen Union regiments that sustained the highest casualties in the army. The price had been indeed high, but as a Hoosier told his father in words that could embrace the entire brigade: "We have not yet disgraced our flag. It is torn & riddled with Balls. The staff is shattered. But it is not dishonored."[80]

To the west, the Virginians of the Stonewall Brigade, like all of Lee's soldiers, could comfort themselves with the knowledge that their sacrifices had brought another victory. But the price was undeniable; it could be seen whenever they formed ranks. On August 31, according to a surgeon, the Valley men "paraded under but one flag instead of 5," adding that "the 27th Rgt may be regarded as broken up," and the Fourth Virginia "has not more than a good Company present."[81]

The brigade mustered probably fewer than 450 officers and men. Casualties among field- and company-grade officers had been so severe as to cripple the command's effectiveness. William Baylor possessed the qualities to be an outstanding brigade commander, while John Neff and Lawson Botts were fine colonels, and all three were gone. Since the reorganization in April, only one regimental commander, Andrew Grigsby of the Twenty-seventh, remained with his unit. Three had been killed in combat, and the Fourth's Charles Ronald was absent on leave.[82]

On August 31, when the Virginians marched under one flag, Private B.

B. Weirman of the Thirty-third wrote home to his brother. "It is heart rending to think of the misery etc. that has been produced by this sad civil war," Weirman despaired. "Would that it soon cease." He hoped that they would follow up "our present victories" and win a peaceful settlement to the conflict. "I am getting real tired of a soldier's life," he concluded, "and want to get home once again. It seems as though I would not then care if I ever saw a gun or any other war material hereafter."[83]

9

✝

"Corn Acres of Hell"

THE banners of a revolution waved in the bright sunlight, marking a passage. Behind them, in ranks of four, Stonewall Jackson's soldiers waded into the river's shallows. "I never expect as long as I live," wrote staff officer Thomas G. Pollock, "to witness so imposing a spectacle." "Nobody spoke," explained Pollock, because "it was a time of great feeling." He spurred his mount into the current beside the moving column. Halting in the stream, Pollock turned in his saddle. As far as he could see stretched an unbroken string of infantrymen. "I felt," he told his father in a letter two days later, "I was beholding what must be the turning point of the war."[1]

Before Pollock passed the vanguard of Confederate nationalism as it crossed into Maryland, at White's Ford on the Potomac River, north of Leesburg, Virginia. It was September 5, 1862, less than a week after the victory at Second Manassas or Bull Run. In two months, General Robert E. Lee and the Army of Northern Virginia had carried the war from Richmond's doorstep to Northern soil upriver from Washington. Perhaps, as the young staff officer believed, the conflict was following a new road.

Lee understood that an offensive beyond the Potomac was "attended with much risk." But, as he argued to President Davis on September 2,

"The present seems to be the most propitious time since the commence-ment of the war for the Confederate Army to enter Maryland." Such a movement would give the Old Dominion a respite from the war's ravages, contended Lee, allow the Confederates to garner supplies and recruits from Maryland residents, and perhaps force the enemy into a crucial bat-tle. If the operation proceeded well, the commanding general planned to extend the raid into Pennsylvania.[2]

Despite the victory at Manassas, however, Lee's legions suffered from critical shortages on the eve of what could be a lengthy movement. They lacked shoes and clothing—the Southerners "were the dirtiest men I ever saw, a most ragged, lean and hungry set of wolves," claimed a young boy who saw them enter Maryland. The operations during August also had outpaced the commissary. Lee anticipated that the army could seize sup-plies in the North, but if the Confederates met the enemy in battle, the low levels of ammunition and ordnance stocks could be critical to the combat's outcome.[3]

The opportunity accorded the Confederates by their recent victory gave Lee the strategic initiative. With Jackson's command in the lead, the army of about fifty thousand men marched into Maryland. By September 6, Lee's entire force was camped at Frederick, where the Southerners paused until the 10th, while Lee, Jackson, and Longstreet formulated the opera-tion's next phase.[4]

The discussions among the army's three senior generals focused upon the Union garrison at Harper's Ferry. Lee wanted it eliminated as a threat to the army's communications and rear if he advanced into Pennsylvania. The enemy command of approximately fourteen thousand troops was vulnerable if the Confederates could seize the heights above the town. Lee proposed a division of the army to accomplish the task, but Longstreet, and perhaps Jackson, objected to the plan, arguing that the entire army should be used in the operation. Lee rejected the idea, and on September 9, issued Special Orders No. 191, which designated assignments for each of the army's nine infantry divisions and Jeb Stuart's cavalry.[5]

Lee committed six divisions to the capture of Harper's Ferry. Jackson and three divisions would recross the Potomac into Virginia upstream from the village and seal the western approaches; two divisions would march through Pleasant Valley and secure Maryland Heights to the north of Harper's Ferry; and the final contingent would reenter Virginia to the east, occupying Loudoun Heights. Longstreet and two divisions, meanwhile, would cross South Mountain with the army's main wagon train, as the division of D. H. Hill acted as rear guard. With the surrender of Harper's Ferry, which Lee projected for September 12, the army's scattered units would reunite at Boonsboro or Hagerstown, Maryland, before advancing into Pennsylvania.[6]

The Confederate army marched away from Frederick on the 10th. Lee had undertaken a bold gamble that counted upon a swift execution of his plans and the slow advance of the Union army from Washington. But the fates, it seemed, conspired against the Confederates. It was not until the 14th that the three elements of the army had closed on Harper's Ferry, having encountered delays attendant upon the movement of units, and some stiff enemy resistance on Maryland Heights. More critically to the army, the Federals had assailed D. H. Hill's troops on South Mountain during the 14th. Only a valiant stand by Hill's brigades and reinforcements from Longstreet prevented a possible disaster. That night, Lee prepared for a withdrawal from Maryland, informing a subordinate, "The day has gone against us and this army will go by Sharpsburg and cross the river."[7]

Cheers resounded along the blue-coated column in a thundering of voices, with the news rolling back along the ranks like a well-timed volley—"Little Mac is back!" Men shouted, leaped into the air, and tossed their caps in celebration. When John Gibbon announced it to his Westerners, "they were perfectly wild with delight," emulating their comrades by hurling their black hats into the air. It seemed inexplicable, perhaps, but George McClellan's hold on the hearts of his men was undeniable. As one of them said tersely, "A Deliverer had come."[8]

In the wake of the bitter defeat at Second Bull Run, the Federals needed a "Deliverer." Even John Pope had recognized the signs of a dispirited army, informing the War Department on September 2 that "unless something can be done to restore the tone to this army it will melt away before you know it." Within the army, the officers and men blamed Pope—"a complete failure," in Gibbon's words—and Irvin McDowell.[9]

In Washington, Abraham Lincoln reacted to the crisis by turning to McClellan. The president did so with reluctance and against the protests of the cabinet. The department heads believed that McClellan had imperiled Pope's army deliberately by his slow withdrawal from the Peninsula.

Some cabinet members tried to persuade Lincoln to dismiss the general from the service, but the president refused. As Lincoln saw it, he had no other choice and gave McClellan command of the Army of the Potomac and Pope's Army of Virginia. Like the army, Lincoln hoped that the Union had its savior.[10]

While the army camped around Washington, McClellan responded to the situation with a renewed spirit and energy. He rode through the bivouac sites for the men to see him, acknowledging their cheers by doffing his cap. He restructured the army into three wings, assigning two corps each to two wings and a corps and a division to the third. As for Robert E. Lee's Confederates, McClellan accepted slowly the intelligence reports and civilian accounts that placed the Rebels at Frederick. Characteristically, however, he believed the reports that estimated his opponent's numbers at 120,000, nearly three times Lee's actual strength. On September 7, the Union commander began shifting more of his units into Maryland, northwest of the capital, and relocated his headquarters to Rockville. Two days later, the 85,000-man army began the pursuit of the enemy.[11]

Federal units filled Maryland roads along a broad front, marching deliberately in the heat and dust for three days. On September 12, two days after the Confederates had departed, the advance elements of McClellan's right wing entered Frederick to the jubilation of its residents. More troops filtered in throughout the day and on the 13th. The soldiers bivouacked in the fields outside town, where on the latter day, two members of the Twenty-seventh Indiana discovered a copy of Lee's Special Orders No. 191, wrapped around three cigars. They gave it to their company commander, who carried it to regimental headquarters. From there, it passed through the chain of command to McClellan.[12]

When McClellan read the contents, he grasped its importance at once. In fact, he held in his hands one of the greatest intelligence finds in American military history. He wired Lincoln at noon, "I think Lee has made a gross mistake, and that he will be severely punished for it. . . . I have all plans of the rebels, and will catch them in their own trap if my men are equal to the emergency." Later in the day, Brigadier General John Gibbon visited his old friend at army headquarters, and according to Gibbon in his recollections, when McClellan saw the subordinate, he waved the copy of the order and said, "Here is a paper with which if I cannot whip Bobbie Lee, I will be willing to go home." McClellan then added, "Tomorrow we will pitch into his centre and if you people will only do two good, hard days' marching I will put Lee in a position he will find hard to get out of."[13]

While McClellan and Gibbon conversed, the latter's brigade was camping along the Monocacy River, southeast of Frederick. As noted previously, the Wisconsin and Indiana troops had welcomed enthusiastically McClellan's return. At Brawner's Farm and Second Bull Run the war had overtaken them at last, and they had learned, as a sergeant put it, the Rebels "fight like so many devils." Since their initial days at camps Randall and Morton, they had waited for their time, and although the Second Wisconsin had experienced it early, the other three regiments had spent a year in the army, grumbling constantly that the conflict would elude them. But the fury had embraced them, extracting a price of over nine hundred comrades or nearly one half of the brigade's membership.[14]

Despite the casualties and the campaign's rigors, Gibbon told his wife on September 3 that the brigade was in "excellent condition." With the rest of the army, the Westerners marched four days later. The 7th was a Sunday, and a Hoosier soldier complained that there was "nothing to remind us . . . of the holy Sabbath, nothing but long lines of soldiers, weary and faint traveling along through heat and dust." During the next five days, they passed through Mechanicsville, Lisbon, and New Market. "This is beautiful country," a Wisconsinite noted, "with great farms and beautiful girls." An unusually high number of men fell out of the ranks. A surgeon believed that the proportion who straggled exceeded that of any previous march, but once they reached Frederick, he claimed, "the spirits of the men began to assume more buoyancy."[15]

One of those whose spirits were not renewed by the arrival at Frederick was Captain Edwin Brown of the Sixth Wisconsin. He commanded Company E, which had been reduced to thirty-four members. "The Rebels are in force in Maryland, we are 'massing' to meet them," Brown informed his wife, Ruth, in a letter of September 13. "I am weary & sick if the enemy was off from our soil I should go to Hospital. Honor requires that every one *who has any patriotism left* should meet the insolent foe. Should I live to drive them out of this State & away from Washington, *I will have rest at some rate.*" Continuing, he admitted, "*I feel as though I was alone.*" Brown ended with an unusual, "Good Bye."[16]

Captain Brown and his comrades in Gibbon's brigade marched at 6:00 A.M. on September 14, crossing the Monocacy River, before entering Frederick. Like other units before them, the Westerners received the populace's cheers. They followed the old National Road through Middletown, halted to eat a midday meal, and about three o'clock in the afternoon approached South Mountain, from whose eastern slope smoke could be seen and the sounds of combat heard. Gibbon soon received an order to report with the brigade to wing commander Major General Ambrose E. Burnside.[17]

Since mid-morning the Federals had been ensnared in a fight for the 1,300-foot-high hill, held by D. H. Hill's five Confederate brigades. Hill's men guarded Turner's Gap, through which passed the National Road, and Fox's Gap, a mile to the south, where the Old Sharpsburg Road crossed the mountain. Three smaller roads branched off from the main routes over South Mountain. The terrain favored the defenders, however, with ravines, hollows, and knolls covered with trees, underbrush, and thick, entangled patches of mountain laurel. Hill was one of Lee's finest combat officers, and the Confederate army needed such a man on South Mountain on this day.[18]

By the time Gibbon's brigade reported to Burnside, the combat on South Mountain extended from south of Fox's Gap to north of Turner's Gap. McClellan had committed eighteen brigades in seven divisions to the fighting, while Hill had received reinforcements from Longstreet, bringing the total of Confederate brigades engaged to fourteen. At four o'clock, the entire Union First Corps, except for Gibbon's brigade of John Hatch's division, launched an assault against the Confederate left flank north of Turner's Gap, using Old Hagerstown Road and a farm road. Wanting to assist the corps, now commanded by Major General Joseph Hooker, Burnside directed Gibbon to advance directly up the National Road toward the front of Turner's Gap, or as he stated in his report, "for the purpose of making a demonstration upon the enemy's center."[19]

Gibbon aligned his four regiments on both sides of the old highway upon which countless numbers of Americans had traveled west. The Nineteenth Indiana deployed south of the road in a battle line, with the Seventh Wisconsin parallel to the Hoosiers north of the roadbed. In double columns the Second Wisconsin formed behind the Nineteenth and the Sixth Wisconsin behind the Seventh. Each of the latter units detached two companies to the front as skirmishers, while an Indiana company covered the attackers' left flank as skirmishers. Before the Westerners advanced, ten officers and forty-one enlisted men of the Second Wisconsin "were compelled" to fall out because of exhaustion and sickness. If other men in the remaining regiments did likewise, it went unreported.[20]

The eastern face of South Mountain appeared dark green, even black, as the sun sank beneath the crest when the Westerners moved forward. Steadily, in ranks worthy of troops in a review, the roughly twelve hundred Federals pressed ahead through open fields. Behind them, Gibbon watched their progress with pride, writing later that "the occasion was one to exhibit admirably, the drill and efficiency acquired by the brigade whilst lying at Fredericksburg." To the demanding brigadier, they looked like Regulars.[21]

On the mountain, Confederate artillery crews saw them coming and opened fire. One shell exploded in the Second Wisconsin, killing four and wounding three. Ahead of the Nineteenth Indiana, Rebel skirmishers fired from the windows of a farmhouse. Colonel Solomon Meredith requested artillery support, and a section—two guns—of Battery B, Fourth U.S. Artillery deployed in the road, sending a round into the upper story of the house. The Rebels scattered, Meredith reported, in a "general stampede." When the Hoosiers passed through the farmyard, they grabbed turkeys and chickens, according to the reminiscences of one of them. The owner protested the thievery, but the soldiers rebutted that the fowl were "obstructing our forward movement."[22]

From among the trees, Confederate infantry triggered a volley into the Nineteenth. The Southerners were Alabamians and Georgians under Brigadier General Alfred H. Colquitt. They had held the position across the road all day, spared from the combat until now. They knew who the Federals were, calling them "damned black hats." Most likely, they knew that it would be a fight.[23]

"The fire became general on both sides," Meredith stated. His Indianans unleashed a volley, cheered, advanced, and repeated the sequence. The colonel thought "it was a most magnificent sight" to witness his men moving forward with shouts. Colonel Lucius Fairchild brought up the Second Wisconsin, joining the Hoosiers in the combat. A member of the Second described the Confederate artillery and infantry fire as "murderous." Shielded by trees and stone walls, Colquitt's Rebels held their position.[24]

North of the National Road, the Seventh Wisconsin crested a knoll and were blasted at a range of forty yards by the Twenty-third and Twenty-eighth Georgia. A Federal described it as "a most terrific fire," adding that "it seemed no one could survive." The Georgians enfiladed the Seventh on

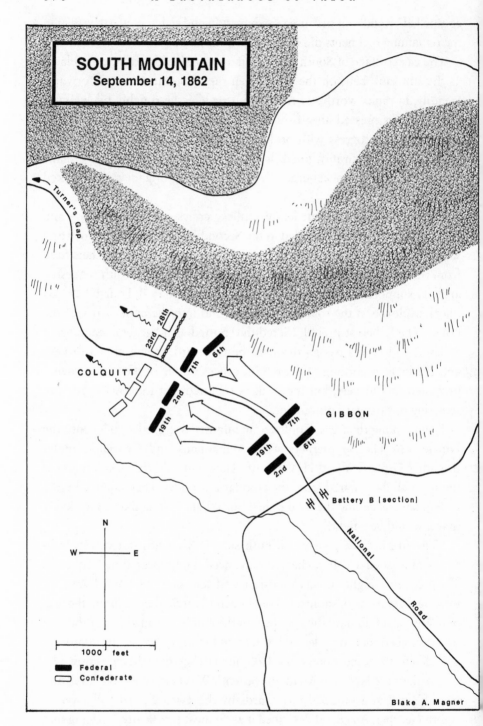

SOUTH MOUNTAIN
September 14, 1862

Turner's Gap

28th
23rd

7th
6th

COLQUITT

2nd

GIBBON

7th

19th

19th

6th

2nd

Battery B [section]

N

W   E

National

Road

1000 feet

Federal
Confederate

Blake A. Magner

both flanks. The Yankees clung to the knoll, firing as rapidly as they could reload.[25]

With the explosion of musketry in front of the Seventh, Lieutenant Colonel Edward Bragg rushed the Sixth Wisconsin forward at the double quick. The Sixth's right wing came into line on the Seventh's right flank, with the left wing stacked behind it. Bragg's men relieved the pressure against the Seventh, engaging the Twenty-eighth Georgia. Before long, however, Gibbon ordered Bragg to turn the Confederate flank.[26]

Bragg was, in the estimate of Major Rufus Dawes, an officer of "a remarkable quick conception and instant action." When he received Gibbon's directive, Bragg went to Dawes, who commanded the right wing, and instructed the major to have his men fire a volley and then lie down. "I am going over you," Bragg said, referring to the left wing. Dawes complied, and Bragg led the other half of the regiment up the slope, ordering his troops to fire a volley and fall to the ground. Dawes followed with his wing and repeated the tactic. The Sixth ascended the mountain, with one wing leapfrogging the other. "In a long experience in musketry fighting," Dawes contended later, "this was the single instance I saw of other than a fire by file in battle."[27]

The Sixth "poured volley after volley into the enemy." The gunfire on both sides was "incessant and forcible." Sergeant George Fairfield believed that "the artillery roared to beat anything I had yet heard." South of the worn roadway, the Second Wisconsin wheeled to the right, raking the flank of the Georgians across the road. It was so dark that neither opponent could see each other. The men aimed at the rifle flashes. The "sides of the mountain seemed in a blaze of flame," avowed a Federal.[28]

The combat raged in the darkness until nine o'clock. The Second Wisconsin expended all its ammunition, and Colonel Meredith brought forward the Nineteenth Indiana to relieve the Second. In the Sixth and Seventh Wisconsin, the men searched the dead and wounded for cartridges. When Gibbon learned of the situation, he ordered a cease-fire, but admonished the officers to "hold the ground at the point of the bayonet." In a final spasm, the Georgians crept toward the Sixth and Seventh only to be lashed by a final volley. Bragg's men emitted three cheers, and as the lieutenant colonel said, "the enemy was no more seen."[29]

Before midnight, troops from Massachusetts, Minnesota, and New York replaced Gibbon's men, except for the Sixth Wisconsin, at the front. It was not until eight o'clock on the morning of the 15th before Bragg's regiment filed off the mountainside. The engagement had cost the "damned black hats" 37 killed, 251 wounded, and 30 captured or missing, for a total of 318, a quarter of the brigade's strength. Among the dead was Captain Wilson Colwell of the Second Wisconsin. Described as "a general favorite of the regiment," Colwell fell while commanding the skirmishers. "His place can hardly be filled," reported Colonel Fairchild.[30]

When the brigade had passed through Frederick earlier in the day, Private George Miles of Company A, Sixth Wisconsin remarked to comrades that he had had a premonition of his death. His fellow soldiers reassured him otherwise, but when the regiment formed for battle, some of them asked Captain David Noyes to assign Miles to other duty. Noyes approached the private, who refused, saying that he would do his duty. As the wings of the regiment climbed the mountain, fighting the Georgians, the Reedsburg, Wisconsin, volunteer was killed.[31]

In a letter to his wife, written the next day, Gibbon confided, "Every one, from Genl. McClellan down, speaks in the highest terms of my gallant Brigade and I of course am proud." First Corps commander Joseph Hooker had not witnessed the struggle between Gibbon's and Colquitt's troops, but stated subsequently that the Westerners' list of casualties "speaks for itself." Wing commander Ambrose Burnside, who watched the fighting with McClellan, described it as "a most brilliant engagement." In his report, Gibbon boasted, "The conduct of the officers and men was during the engagement everything that could be desired, and they maintained their well-earned reputation for gallantry and discipline acquired in the engagements of the 28th and 30th of August."[32]

In the fields of Brawner's Farm, on the crest of Dogan Ridge, and at the base of South Mountain, the Black Hat Brigade, as the Wisconsin and Indiana troops had come to be known in each army, demonstrated how inexperienced combat soldiers could answer the fearful summons. Imbued with patriotism and tempered by discipline and training, the Westerners had stood amid the terribleness with a valor that had marked them among both comrades and enemies. They were warriors now, these men in tall, black hats.

During the battle at South Mountain, as Gibbon directed the brigade's movements, the general stopped one of his men. The soldier had been wounded earlier in the action, and with an arm in a sling and a rifle in the other, was returning to his regiment. "My man where are you going?" asked Gibbon.

"Back to my regiment, sir," replied the brigade member.

"But you can't handle your musket in that fix," Gibbon rebutted.

"Yes I can, sir," the Westerner affirmed.

Gibbon let him pass to the front, and as he informed his wife, "I had nothing more to say."[33]

The Confederates dragged themselves off South Mountain during the night of September 14–15. In Boonsboro, at the western base of the mountain, Robert E. Lee conferred with several of his ranking subordinates. "After a long debate," the officers decided to retreat to Sharpsburg, Maryland, on the 15th. Lee anticipated that the army would have to abandon the operation north of the Potomac River, and the route through Sharpsburg led to a good ford. But later that night, Lee received a message from Stonewall Jackson, who indicated that Harper's Ferry would fall to his troops within a day. Perhaps the army could hold at Sharpsburg until its scattered divisions could be reunited.[34]

While the troops with Lee marched to Sharpsburg on the morning of the 15th, Jackson sealed the fate of the Union garrison at Harper's Ferry. Southern artillerists on the heights above the town opened fire once the morning's fog lifted. Union gunners responded, but after an hour, the Federals requested a truce. Before nine o'clock the garrison's commander surrendered the post, 12,500 troops, 73 cannon, thousands of weapons, and hundreds of wagons and animals. All that had eluded the grasp of the Rebels was a 1,300-man cavalry contingent that had escaped during the preceding night, finding an unguarded road below Maryland Heights.[35]

Jackson hurried a letter to Lee, informing the army commander of the victory. Much had to be done at Harper's Ferry, however, before Jackson could rejoin Lee at Sharpsburg. The Confederates feasted on the enemy's foodstuffs as they had at Manassas Junction on August 27, while officers began the process of paroling prisoners and starting the ordnance supplies and arms south. Leaving A. P. Hill's division behind to finish the details, Jackson started with his other two divisions before midnight for Sharpsburg. The Southerners marched all night without cessation, crossing the Potomac at Boteler's Ford near Shepherdstown, and arriving late on the morning of the 16th at Sharpsburg, seventeen miles from Harper's Ferry. Lee greeted Jackson and escorted his subordinate to headquarters, where they discussed the situation.[36]

Lee's decision to seek an engagement before the army returned to Virginia was arguably the worst of his career. The terrain provided few natural advantages to the defenders. If his army suffered a defeat, it would have to retreat across the Potomac about four miles to the west. The town lay less than a mile west of Antietam Creek amid rich limestone soil. The encircling farmland undulated from the crests of ridges to the bottoms of hollows. Hills of various heights jutted above the creek's western bank while rock outcroppings and woodlots splotched the fertile fields. For decades the land had nourished farm families and townsfolk, but now if Lee were to make a stand before he abandoned Maryland, it had to be here on ground more suited for the labors of a farmer than those of a warrior.[37]

The strategic and tactical weaknesses of the position were compounded by the reduced numbers in Lee's army. Straggling was, according to a historian, "unprecedented" during the campaign. Men abandoned the ranks in droves, impelled by the hardships and by the invasion of Northern soil. The troops suffered from heat, dust, lack of shoes, and the collapse of Lee's commissary. A Shepherdstown woman who saw the Rebels pass through her town testified later to the condition of the army. "When I say that they were hungry," she asserted, "I convey no impression of the gaunt starvation that looked down from their cavernous eyes." She watched soldiers from both sides march by for four years, but during the Maryland campaign, "never were want and exhaustion more visibly put before my eyes, and that they could march or fight at all seemed incredible."[38]

A considerable number had either refused to cross the Potomac, or once in Maryland, returned to Virginia, believing that they had enlisted to defend their homeland and not to carry the conflict beyond its borders. A critical shortage of officers hampered efforts to enforce march discipline and to keep the stragglers or the disenchanted in the ranks. While precise figures cannot be determined, the Confederate army at Sharpsburg, when all units were on the field, probably numbered fewer than forty thousand, perhaps as low as thirty to thirty-five thousand.[39]

A recent estimate has calculated the average Confederate regimental strength at 166 and comparative Union numbers at 346. In the Stonewall Brigade, the figures were starkly worse. Jackson had detached the Second Virginia and assigned it to provost duty in Martinsburg, Virginia, reducing the brigade's regiments to four. Colonel Andrew Grigsby commanded the Virginians, with a lieutenant colonel, a major, and two captains serving as regimental commanders. The brigade's reported strength at Sharpsburg was 250 officers and men, an average of slightly more than sixty per regiment.[40]

Private John Garibaldi of the Twenty-seventh Virginia claimed in a letter written after the battle, however, that only a dozen members were with the regiment on the field at Sharpsburg. When Jackson's troops returned to Maryland after the fall of Harper's Ferry, most of the Twenty-seventh's men "never went across the river," according to the private. Although Garibaldi was absent during the campaign, he learned this from comrades upon his return to the regiment. If the number is accurate it indicates the breakdown of discipline in the unit, the campaign's hardships, and/or the Valley men's refusal to risk their lives in an invasion of Union territory. In less than five months, the Stonewall Brigade had seen its strength reduced by more than ninety percent. Casualties exacted a share, but the majority of losses had resulted from desertion.[41]

On ground that favored an aggressive opponent, with an army outnumbered two to one, and with his back to a river, Lee stood at Sharpsburg. If he held the field, he could achieve little more than a drawn battle, but if the Federals broke the Southern lines, Lee risked the destruction of his army. He explained his decision after the war, stating that "it was better to have fought in Maryland than to have left it without a struggle." He was convinced also that he could defeat his opponent, George McClellan.[42]

Boonsboro, Maryland, sat hard by the western foot of South Mountain. A small village of stone, log, and clapboard houses, Boonsboro framed the National Road as it debouched from the mountain through Turner's Gap. Its residents had heard the sounds of battle tumble down the mountainside and had watched Confederate troops race up the road toward the gap on September 14. During the ensuing night, they had witnessed the retreat of the Southerners. Now as September 15 lengthened, ranks of bluecoated soldiers descended South Mountain, pursuing the Rebels toward Sharpsburg, seven miles to the west.[43]

The townsfolk with Union sympathies welcomed the passing troops. Major Rufus Dawes remembered that a "respectable old gentleman" approached him and exclaimed, "We have watched for you, Sir, and we have prayed for you and now thank God you have come!" When George Mc-

Clellan clattered into the village, amid a cloud of staff officers, the civilians joined the troops in cheering the general. Earlier, he had telegraphed the War Department, stating, "I am hurrying everything forward to endeavor to press their retreat to the utmost." McClellan added that "the *morale* of our men is now restored."[44]

Throughout the 15th, the Army of the Potomac closed upon Sharpsburg. A member of the Black Hat Brigade reported that as the Westerners marched past troops from the Second Corps their fellow soldiers opened ranks and presented arms in a salute to the brigade. By mid-afternoon, John Gibbon's regiments and many units of the army were halted in fields along the Boonsboro–Sharpsburg road. On the hills west of Antietam Creek, Confederate artillery and infantry barked at any Union troops who appeared across the stream. McClellan's aggressiveness at South Mountain had surprised Lee, who learned only later of the so-called Lost Order. The Confederate commander resorted to a bold stand on the 15th, testing his opponent's determination while he waited for his army's scattered units to reconcentrate at Sharpsburg.[45]

Lee's bluff succeeded, and resuming his cautious generalship, McClellan and the army bivouacked for the night beyond the creek. Fog shrouded the ground on the morning of September 16, delaying McClellan's examination of the enemy position. Once the mists cleared, he studied the terrain west of the creek from his headquarters at the Philip Pry residence, situated on a knoll north of the Boonsboro road. Although the general could acquire only a limited knowledge of the ground and Lee's troop dispositions from this vantage point, he fashioned an offensive plan for the 17th. He decided to strike with his main assault force Lee's left or northern flank, where the terrain appeared favorable to such a maneuver. On the Confederate right, where the hills abutted the creek, McClellan intended to force a crossing at Rohrbach Bridge, either as a diversion or as a full-scale attack. If the flank movements succeeded, he would crush Lee's center astride the Boonsboro road. Once more, however, McClellan miscalculated his opponent's strength, inflating the numbers.[46]

McClellan committed three corps—First, Second, and Twelfth—to the attack north of Sharpsburg. Late in the afternoon of the 16th, the corps began the march toward their assigned areas, crossing the creek at Upper Bridge. Major General Joseph Hooker's First Corps, including the Black Hat Brigade, led the movement. Hooker's van brushed aside Rebel skirmishers, angling northwest and halting in the fields between the Joseph and Samuel Poffenberger farms, east of Hagerstown Turnpike and roughly a thousand yards from the Confederate lines in this section of the field. The Twelfth bivouacked to the north and east of Hooker's troops, while the Second Corps remained east of Antietam Creek.[47]

John Gibbon's Westerners bedded down north of Joseph Poffenberger's house and barn. During the march, they had passed a Confederate beef butcher site, and the men cut strips of fat from the discarded intestines to grease their rifles and to prevent rust. While applying the fat to his weapon, a corporal in the Nineteenth Indiana accidentally discharged it, with the bullet striking the brim of his hat.[48]

A drizzling rain began to fall after dark. The Westerners slept on the ground beside their greased rifles. "The night was dismal," recalled Major Dawes. "Nothing can be more solemn then a period of silent waiting for one's summons to battle, known to be impending. Such was this night." Earlier in the evening, they learned that the brigade "will have the honor to open the battle." When one man heard the news, he growled, "To Hell with your honors!"[49]

Hooker had approximately 8,600 troops in three divisions. His assault would follow the axis of Hagerstown Turnpike toward Sharpsburg. The corps's target was a plateau east of the roadbed opposite a whitewashed brick German Baptist Brethren or Dunker Church. Midway between the church and the Federals' bivouac sites was the farm of David R. Miller, whose buildings lay on both sides of the turnpike. South of the farmhouse Miller's cornfield—the "Cornfield" as it would be known—covered thirty acres east of the roadbed, and beyond it, a forty-acre pasture, shaped like a pie wedge, extended to the intersection of the turnpike and Smoketown Road, opposite the church. The soon-to-be-christened West Woods ran for nearly fifteen hundred yards from south of Dunker Church to the northern edge of the Cornfield. East of Miller's fields, East Woods sprawled for eight hundred yards along a section of Smoketown Road. It was a benign landscape whose features were about to be seared into America's collective memory.[50]

Hooker's troops awakened on Wednesday, September 17, before daybreak, with fog filling the hollows, woods, and fields. North of the Poffenberger farm, Gibbon formed the four regiments of his brigade into a column of divisions or in eight lines of five companies each, stacked one behind another. A recent recruit in the command described the brigadier, writing that he "is of medium height, fair complected, light hair, wears a long mustache, has a keen eye and is bold as a lion, is respected by his men, who have great confidence in his abilities as a leader."[51]

Despite the concealing mists, Confederate artillerists were at their posts and began hurling shells toward the Poffenberger farm. The first round missed the Westerners, but a second one burst above the Sixth Wisconsin, severing the foot of Captain David Noyes and killing or wounding a dozen men. The unscathed soldiers left "the mangled bodies of their comrades on the ground," and continued forward. Once they passed through North Woods, the Sixth Wisconsin in front deployed into line of battle, pushing two companies ahead as skirmishers. Southern gunners continued to fire upon the Federals while Rebel infantry pickets sniped at the oncoming brigade from the Miller outbuildings. When the Westerners neared the farmstead, the enemy fled south toward the stalks of standing corn.[52]

When the Sixth reached Miller's, the right wing of the regiment swung wide of the farmhouse as the left wing clogged up at a board paling fence that surrounded the family garden. Unable to level the barrier, Major Rufus Dawes hurried the men through a gate. Bullets from enemy skirmishers pockmarked the boards. As each company cleared the garden, officers re-formed the men into line. Captain Edwin Brown lifted his sword and shouted for his Company E to file into ranks. Suddenly, Brown shrieked and collapsed to the ground, hit by either a bullet or a piece of shell. He lived for only a short time. Brown had always been a reluctant soldier, concerned about his wife, Ruth, and their children in Fond du Lac. He "could scarcely walk" that morning, but duty kept him in the ranks. In his final letter, he assured Ruth that he would secure a furlough when the campaign ended. All he wanted was some rest, and now it would be a permanent one.[53]

With ranks realigned, the Sixth advanced toward the Cornfield. The right wing overlapped the turnpike in fields next to West Woods while the other wing plunged into the corn. Behind them, their comrades in the Second Wisconsin rushed ahead to come in on the Sixth's left. For the fourth time in less than a month, the Westerners faced combat's fearful truth. Why men went forward into battle "cannot be easily explained," admitted a captain in the Second. "All this is business like," he contended. "All understand the situation. The touch of elbows, the step, the alignment are more accurate, more perfect than usual, showing that every man is alive to the duty of the occasion. Right here description ends."[54]

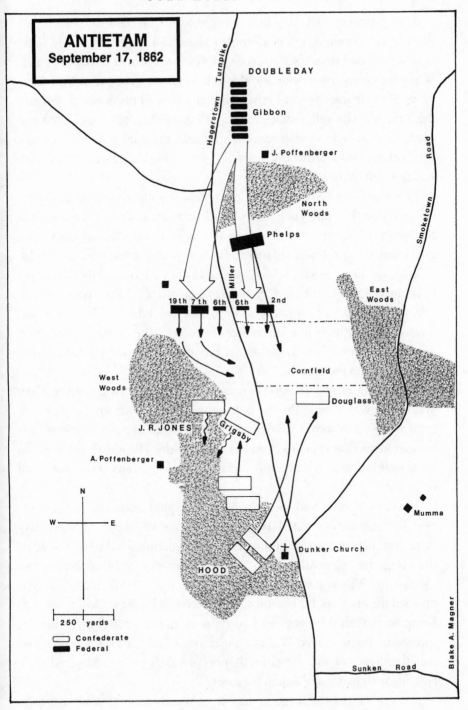

ANTIETAM
September 17, 1862

DOUBLEDAY

Gibbon

Hagerstown Turnpike

J. Poffenberger

North Woods

Phelps

Miller

East Woods

19th 7th 6th 6th 2nd

West Woods

Cornfield

Douglass

J. R. JONES

Grigsby

A. Poffenberger

Mumma

N
W   E

HOOD

Dunker Church

250 yards

☐ Confederate
■ Federal

Smoketown Road

Sunken Road

Blake A. Magner

A rail fence rimmed the southern edge of the Cornfield, and behind it a brigade of Georgians, under Colonel Marcellus Douglass, waited. These Southerners had stood face-to-face with Gibbon's men at Brawner's Farm. When the Georgians saw their old foes in black hats close to within thirty yards of the fence, the Southerners rose and opened the doors of hell into the Yankees. The volley staggered the Wisconsinites, but they halted and fired. As if staked to the ground, immovable, the opposing lines ravaged each other. "Men, I can not say fell," wrote Major Dawes, "they were knocked out of the ranks by dozens."[55]

The noise was deafening; the killing and maiming, unending. Dawes believed that the bullets seemed as "thick, almost, as hail." One soldier in the Second Wisconsin was struck by five balls. Private Gustav Eltermann died instantly as a bullet splattered his brains and blood over the stalks. "He did not know what hit him," wrote Corporal Horace Emerson of the German volunteer. But after three engagements, a soldier "becomes callous to those falling around you dead and wounded," a Westerner informed his daughters in a letter after the battle. "Under the Excitement," he claimed, men ignored "the shells bursting over your heads the solid balls tearing up the ground."[56]

Along Hagerstown Turnpike, meanwhile, the right wing of the Sixth Wisconsin was caught in "a murderous enfilade" from Confederate troops in West Woods. Like their comrades in the Cornfield, they had encountered familiar enemies from Brawner's Farm. The Rebels belonged to Stonewall Jackson's old division, including the Virginians of the Stonewall Brigade.[57]

The Confederates had spent the previous night bivouacked in the fields near the Smoketown Road–Hagerstown Turnpike intersection. At daylight, staff officers moved among the men, ordering them to cap their rifles. Brigadier General John R. Jones, a former field officer in the Thirty-third Virginia who had lost his post in the April elections, commanded the division. He had missed the Second Manassas Campaign, suffering from typhoid fever, but had rejoined the command at Frederick, succeeding the wounded William Taliaferro. On this day, Jones reported that the division's four brigades numbered barely sixteen hundred rank and file, with many of the men barefoot.[58]

Jones advanced the division into West Woods soon after daylight. At the southwest corner of the Cornfield, West Woods bent west. Between the treeline and the corn lay a clover field and farther north, opposite

Miller's field, a rock ledge jutted up, less than one hundred yards from the turnpike. Near this elbow of West Woods, Jones formed his former brigade and the Stonewall Brigade in the front line and his other two brigades as support deeper in the woods. The entire division was sheltered and concealed among the trees.[59]

As the fog dissipated, the Confederates saw the Yankees coming. A Valley man recalled the scene, "In apparent double battle lines, the Federals were moving toward us at charge bayonets, common time, and the sunbeams falling on their well polished guns and bayonets gave a glamor and a show at once fearful and entrancing." When the enemy neared the southern border of the Cornfield, Jones's brigade and the Stonewall Brigade stood up and fired a volley into the Sixth Wisconsin. The Southerners emerged from the woods, sweeping into the clover field. The 250 members of the Stonewall Brigade, commanded by Colonel Andrew Grigsby, occupied the division's right front near the turnpike.[60]

The blast of musketry lashed the flank and front of the Wisconsinites. The Sixth's commander, Lieutenant Colonel Edward Bragg, shouted to the two right companies to refuse the flank and sent an aide to Gibbon for help. While standing in the roadbed, Bragg took a bullet in the left arm, above the elbow, that damaged the ulnar nerve. He refused to relinquish command until the loss of blood so weakened him that he nearly fainted. He sent for Major Dawes to assume command and was then carried to the rear. In a letter to his wife, written four days after the battle, Bragg averred that the Rebels "fought like demons," adding that "officers and men, are all alike—in filth & rags."[61]

John Gibbon and division commander Abner Doubleday reacted to Bragg's request by ordering forward reinforcements. Doubleday led the division because John Hatch had been wounded at South Mountain. To assist the Westerners, Doubleday selected Hatch's former brigade, now under Colonel Walter Phelps, Jr. The Second U.S. Sharpshooters arrived first, bolstering the right front of the Sixth Wisconsin. Behind them, Gibbon shifted the Seventh Wisconsin and Nineteenth Indiana into the fields west of the turnpike and ordered them to charge toward West Woods. The brigadier also brought forward a two-gun section of Battery B, Fourth U.S. Artillery to the knoll thirty yards from the turnpike, opposite the northwest corner of the Cornfield. The Union gunners unlimbered among straw stacks.[62]

The combat grew as these Federals entered the action. The pair of Confederate brigades pushed farther into the clover field into a wall of musketry and artillery fire. "The fighting was terrible," stated a captain in the Thirty-third Virginia. Jones fell with a wound from an artillery shell and was succeeded by Brigadier General William Starke. In the turnpike, the Wisconsin men and Sharpshooters sheltered themselves behind the rail fence along the roadbed. Dawes grabbed six rifles, firing them in succession. Men on both sides fell in clusters. Starke added the division's final two brigades to the fury, leading them toward the Cornfield and the pasture south of it. Within minutes, Starke was killed, hit by three balls, and Colonel Grigsby assumed command of the division.[63]

The advance of the Confederates deeper into the clover field exposed their left flank, and toward it came the Seventh Wisconsin and Nineteenth Indiana. Over the Federals' heads, their comrades in Battery B hurled canister into the Southern ranks. The Westerners closed to within thirty paces, raking the Rebel line. The Virginians reeled and then fled toward the woods. Lieutenant Henry Young of the Seventh Wisconsin described the action in a letter, bragging, "Our brigade whipped Jackson's famous Stonewall Brigade, at the battle of Antietam in a fair and square fight. It was them we met in the morning, they fought well, but we hurled them back, broken and in perfect confusion." In West Woods, the "fearless" Grigsby rallied the "shattered columns." The Confederate division appeared to be "no larger than a good regiment!"[64]

Jackson's entire line between the turnpike and Smoketown Road in the pasture began now to unravel. From the Cornfield the Federals clawed themselves over the fence only to be blasted back. "Every body tears cartridges, loads, passes guns, or shoots," as Dawes described the fighting. "Men are falling in their places or running back into the corn. The soldier who is shooting is furious in his energy." Union reserves, including the red-legged Chasseurs of the Fourteenth Brooklyn, bolstered the lines, and then with a surge, the Yankees, "crawling, climbing, and scrambling," scaled the fence, cheering as they charged across the pasture. Ahead of them, they saw the whitewashed Dunker Church, the target of the morning's assault.[65]

The Sixth and Second Wisconsin, Second U.S. Sharpshooters, and Fourteenth Brooklyn spearheaded the attack. The Yankees' guns had become so fouled that they had to pound each new round down the barrel. Suddenly, through the smoke, in a field north of Smoketown Road a Confederate division appeared. The Rebels were Brigadier General John B.

Hood's two brigades of Southerners from six states, and when Federals come into range, they screeched their yell and fired a volley. The musketry was, Dawes wrote, "like a scythe running through our line." The Yankees lurched to a halt and recoiled. "It is a race for life that each man runs for the corn-field," as the major recounted it.[66]

One of the Federals killed by Hood's troops was Captain Werner Von Bachelle of Company F, Sixth Wisconsin. A former officer in the French army, Von Bachelle had emigrated to America, settling in Milwaukee. "He was a true soldier, a gallant officer, and a faithful man," in the words of Bragg. The captain had a pet Newfoundland dog that had been in the regiment since his master enlisted. The dog could salute and was never far away from Von Bachelle. When the officer fell, the Newfoundland sat beside his master, and there he was found dead two days later. The captain's men buried them together.[67]

Hood's Confederates pursued the remnants of the Federal line, driving toward the Cornfield. On the division's left, the Texas Brigade, comprised of Texans, Georgians, and South Carolinians, followed the turnpike. From west of the roadbed, the Seventh Wisconsin and Nineteenth Indiana saw the enemy counterattack. Lieutenant Colonel Alois Bachman stepped to the front of the Hoosiers, drew his sword, and shouted, "Boys, the command is no longer forward, but now it is follow me." The two regiments of black-hatted men ascended a slope west of the pike. When the Southerners discovered them, three of the regiments wheeled toward the roadbed to confront them head-on.[68]

The opponents exchanged gunfire at a murderous distance that one officer estimated at less than two hundred feet. Lieutenant Colonel Bachman fell mortally wounded in the initial discharge. "We got into a hornet's nest," stated a Hoosier, and were "nearly cut to pieces." Three color-bearers in the Nineteenth Indiana were slain, and only the bravery of Lieutenant D. S. Holloway saved the flag. Private Morris Gilmore died. At Brawner's Farm he had watched his twin brother, John, fall with a wound. Unable to endure more, the Westerners retreated to the protection of the rock ledge and fought.[69]

Among the men in the Seventh Wisconsin was Private George Partridge, Jr. After the battle, his sisters wrote to him, inquiring if he had fired at the Rebels. "I took aim at one several times," Partridge answered, "but they always fell before I could fire." Several times he drew a bead on one Southern soldier only to have another come into view. "But to tell the truth," he admitted, "I could not tell wether I killed any or not as they fell so fast . . . but I know I tryed as hard as I could to kill some of them." If he did not succeed, many of his comrades did.[70]

The slaughter in the pasture, along the turnpike, and amid "those corn acres of hell," as a Southerner termed Miller's field, stunned the soldiers. "I thought I had seen men piled up and cut up in all kindes of shape," asserted Corporal Horace Emerson of the Second Wisconsin, "but never anything in comparison to that field." Another corporal in the Sixth stated that "the dead was piled in winrows on both sides." It was "dreadful" to see so many dismembered bodies. Adjutant Frank Haskell of Gibbon's staff argued that the command's three previous engagements "were but skirmishes in comparison to this at Sharpsburg." He compared the combat's sound to "a roaring hell of fire" and "a great tumbling together of all heaven and earth." A quarter of a century afterward, Dawes put it simply, "Whoever stood in front of the corn field at Antietam needs no praise."[71]

The struggle rushed now toward a climax in the Cornfield and along Hagerstown Turnpike. The First Texas swept into the battered acreage, clearing the ground of the shattered ranks of the Sixth and Second Wisconsin and Phelps's brigade. The Texans advanced to the northern edge of the field in a remarkable display of bravery. Federal reserves and some of the Wisconsinites waited beyond the rows and savaged the Lone Star troops. A cauldron of flame and thunder decimated the Texans. Their casualty rate exceeded eighty percent. No other regiment in Lee's army incurred a higher percentage of loss in a single battle during the war.[72]

To the Texans' left, along the turnpike, the Eighteenth Georgia charged toward Battery B, Fourth U.S. Artillery. Earlier, Gibbon had ordered forward all of the unit's guns to the knoll, where the one section had been posted. The six cannon were a prize, and the Georgians raked the gun crews from behind the post and rail fence that divided the road from the Cornfield. The Rebels killed or wounded dozens of the gunners, including the battery commander, Captain Joseph Campbell. "It seems almost incredible that any man could have escaped," wrote a battery member. The surviving artillerists blasted the enemy with canister, splintering the rails and leveling cornstalks.[73]

Three times the Georgians charged toward the guns, and three times they were repulsed. Union infantry west of the battery ripped apart the attackers' flank, and the artillerists unleashed more canister. Gibbon, the old gunner, directed the battery's fire, sighting a cannon and urging, "Give them hell, boys." Finally, the Georgians could withstand the punishment no longer, and as more Union infantry piled into the Cornfield, Hood's wrecked division retreated toward West Woods and Dunker Church. When asked later where his command was, Hood replied, "Dead on the field."[74]

Like a dying beast, the combat had ceased in one final convulsion. It was 7:30 A.M., and in ninety minutes of almost unparalleled butchery, Jackson's and Hooker's men had decimated each other. Neither opponent had much left to give. Hooker's corps abandoned the bloody ground as additional units moved toward a renewal of the carnage. Fresh Confederate reserves replaced Jackson's troops and prepared for the approaching onslaught.[75]

The savagery of the Cornfield proved to be only a harbinger as the two armies killed and maimed each other in numbers unprecedented in American history. Before the battle ended, in West Woods, around Dunker Church, before Bloody Lane, and above Rohrback or Burnside's Bridge, more than 23,000 Americans had fallen or were captured. When A. P. Hill's division, arriving from Harper's Ferry, repulsed the final Union assault, September 17, 1862, became—and remains—the bloodiest single day in the country's annals.[76]

At nightfall, Lee's veterans clung to the scarred landscape around Sharpsburg. McClellan had withheld thousands of troops during the fighting, men that might have destroyed the Confederate army. Defiantly, Lee stayed on the field on September 18, but after darkness retreated across the Potomac into Virginia. A clash occurred on the 20th between Lee's rear guard and McClellan's pursuit force at Shepherdstown, adding more casualties to the lengthy bill. But two days later, Abraham Lincoln, seizing upon the Confederate withdrawal from Maryland as a victory, redefined the conflict by issuing the preliminary Emancipation Proclamation. A different trumpet sounded the advance of Union armies.[77]

In the Shenandoah Valley of Virginia, the members of the Stonewall Brigade counted Sharpsburg's toll. There had been so few of them in the ranks, but as John Jones boasted, they and their comrades in the division "fought with gallantry that has never been surpassed and rarely equalled." They had withstood the furnace of artillery fire and musketry until enemy numbers drove them from the clover field. Later, they reentered the struggle, assisting in the repulse of two Union divisions in West Woods. By then, the Virginians had expended nearly all of their ammunition. The Battle of Sharpsburg or Antietam exacted a cost of eighty-eight killed or wounded, or over a third of their numbers.[78]

Among the Valley men who did not recross the river was a soldier identified only as Robbie. He had been wounded in the right leg, above the knee. In the weeks ahead, Union surgeons would amputate the limb, and he would be confined to a Baltimore prison. He was young, "a boy" when he enlisted, and had been married for a brief time. Lying on a prison cot, he must have looked at the stump of his leg, thought of his wife, and wondered how she would accept a one-legged man.

It was weeks before he wrote to her, perhaps needing time to find the courage. "I trust and pray that my injury does not disgust you nor relinquish your love for me," he implored. "I'm still all the man you married. When I get home if I get home, I will never stop loving you. I hope to attach an artificial leg so I can plow the land and fix the house." What he had seen and had experienced had made him "older, tired, resigned." "You must never know what my eyes have seen gentile [sic] woman," he ended it. "War is too gruesome a sight to describe in words." But if he returned, she must have seen each day in his eyes and as he worked, Sharpsburg's price.[79]

On Friday, September 19, like thousands of others in the army, the men of the Black Hat Brigade walked across the battlefield at Sharpsburg. They searched for their wounded comrades left on the field and buried their dead. The carnage appalled them; it seemed unending, inexplicable. Corporal Horace Currier claimed that a man could walk "in one straight line" for a mile and not step on the ground. The slain were piled three and four deep at points. Along Hagerstown Turnpike—"this road of fearful carnage," in a Hoosier's words—there were "frightful" heaps of dead men. Sergeant James Converse wrote home that he could never give "a full description" of what he saw, but it was "a horrorable view that in my opinion never ought to be witnessed by any human being."[80]

Even John Gibbon was stunned by it. "I am as tired of this horrible war as you are," he confessed to his wife, "and would be perfectly willing never to see another battle field." In another letter, he told her that "forty eight hours after a battle the most intimate friend cannot recognise the features of the dead."[81]

Gibbon knew that "the men stood like iron," as Major Dawes avowed, and such valor carried a grievous cost. The brigade suffered casualties of 68 killed, 275 wounded, and 5 missing, for a total of 348. They had had roughly nine hundred in the ranks at the battle's outset. In Battery B, the losses amounted to two killed and thirty-eight wounded, a figure that would rank them third in casualties among light artillery batteries in a battle. One of those wounded in the battery was a sergeant, who killed himself with a bullet to the head while lying in a hospital.[82]

When Gibbon learned a few weeks later that his wife had been visiting some of the brigade members in Washington hospitals, he asked her to bring delicacies for them to eat. "They are as brave a set of fellows as ever lived or died," he explained. Although some of the wounded had told him that they wanted to heal and "try it again," most of the Westerners shared Gibbon's view that they had seen enough of war after Antietam. A Wisconsin corporal spoke for many: "I tell you it makes a person think of home & their dear Parents & wish to be there."[83]

10

✛

"THIS WAR IT SEEMS CANNOT END"

WHEN nightfall came at last to the bloody and scarred landscape around Sharpsburg, Maryland, on September 17, 1862, John Gibbon commanded the remnant of one of the army's finest brigades. In three weeks, from Brawner's Farm to Antietam, the Westerners had suffered approximately sixteen hundred casualties, while standing "like iron." Their conduct on four battlefields had earned them respect and admiration from both comrades and opponents, and within days of the slaughter at the Cornfield, a new appellation, Iron Brigade.[1]

According to tradition, Major General Joseph Hooker applied the sobriquet to the Wisconsin and Indiana volunteers after their performance at South Mountain. The corps commander in conversations with George McClellan during the day and night of September 14 allegedly used the phrase "they are iron," and called Gibbon's command "my Iron Brigade." This seems improbable. Hooker had not witnessed personally the Westerners' fight with the Georgians at the base of Turner's Gap, and no credible evidence exists that the conversation between the generals ever occurred.[2]

In fact, the most reliable evidence indicates that McClellan, not Hooker, conferred the name upon the four Western regiments. On September 21, Captain Alexander Gordon, Jr., of the Seventh Wisconsin wrote home, "General McClellan has given us the name of the Iron Brigade." Five days later, Private Hugh Perkins of the same regiment noted in a letter, "Gen. McClellan calls us the Iron Brigade." Neither man, however, offered further explanation or described how or from whom the members learned of it.[3]

Consequently, when and under what circumstances McClellan used the term as praise for Gibbon's brigade cannot be resolved. Unlike Hooker, the army commander had watched with Ambrose Burnside the unit's advance and engagement at South Mountain. During the Battle of Antietam or Sharpsburg, McClellan had remained east of Antietam Creek and could only have learned of the fearful struggle along Hagerstown Road from reports of officers. If, indeed, McClellan called the Wisconsin and Indiana volunteers the Iron Brigade, most likely he used it in reference to South Mountain, not Antietam.[4]

Gibbon's postwar recollections, however, cloud the name's origins. It would seem reasonable that the brigadier would have remembered if his old friend McClellan had bestowed such an honor upon the brigade, but Gibbon admitted in his memoirs that "how or where the name of the 'Iron Brigade' was first given I do not know." But he added that "soon after the battle of Antietam the name was started and ever after was applied to the brigade."[5]

Gibbon wrote his account over two decades after the war, while Captain Gordon and Private Perkins penned their letters within ten days of Antietam. All three agree, however, that by the end of September the Westerners had received a distinctive honor from a superior officer, a name worthy of their sacrifices and valor, the Iron Brigade.

In time, the Westerners' comrades in the New York brigade of Colonel Walter Phelps, Jr., disputed the claim that the Wisconsin and Indiana men were the original Iron Brigade. A recent study of the controversy concludes that "ample contemporary and postwar evidence" supports the New Yorkers' assertion that the honor belonged to them. According to the historian, the sources indicate that the name was given to the brigade because of its marching ability, and during and after the war the members used the sobriquet. Nevertheless, as a symbolic name for courage and steadfastness in combat, Iron Brigade became associated with the black-hatted volunteers of John Gibbon.[6]

For the present, however, Gibbon's Iron Brigade and its comrades in the

Army of the Potomac required time to heal and to replenish the ranks in Antietam's aftermath. McClellan deluged the capital with requests for more units, supplies, and equipment. On October 1, Abraham Lincoln arrived at Sharpsburg, in an unexpected visit. The president stayed for four days, conferring with McClellan and his generals, talking with the wounded in hospitals, touring the battlefield, and reviewing the troops. One of Gibbon's men wrote that "the President was dressed like any farmer but looked careworn. His dress and looks bore a marked contrast to that of the gay and dashing officers who accompanied him." A Hoosier recorded in his diary that although the president had "a rough camp look" about him, "altogether he is the man to suit the soldiers."[7]

Before Lincoln's visit to the army, authorities in Washington had responded to McClellan's petitions by dispatching wagonloads of supplies and designating twenty new infantry regiments for assignment to the army. Earlier, before South Mountain, when the Federals were in Frederick, Gibbon approached McClellan about his need for another unit in the brigade. The army commander promised the brigadier that "the first western regiment he received" would be placed in the latter's command. Consequently, perhaps, when the Twenty-fourth Michigan arrived at Sharpsburg during the first week of October, it was assigned to the Iron Brigade.[8]

The formation of the Twenty-fourth Michigan resulted from a riot in Detroit in mid-July. When the federal government reopened recruiting offices after the Seven Days Campaign, Governor Austin Blair of Michigan issued a proclamation on July 12, calling for six new volunteer regiments. Three days later, in Detroit, Major William C. Duncan and local dignitaries convened a recruitment rally at Camp Martius in the city's downtown.[9]

From a flag-draped grandstand, speakers intoned with patriotic oratory until some in the crowd began to jeer and shout, convinced that the meeting had been organized to propose conscription. Henry A. Morrow, judge of Wayne County's Recorder's Court, tried to quell the disturbance with a speech, but many in the crowd suddenly rushed the platform, scattering the dignitaries and wrecking the grandstand. The mob spilled into the street in pursuit of two prominent businessmen. Finally, Sheriff Mark Flanigan and deputies cornered the rioters at gunpoint. A city newspaper described the affair as "one of the most melancholy spectacles it was ever our lot to witness."[10]

Humiliated and shocked by the appearance of disloyalty, city and county officials decided to organize a seventh regiment. A week later, civil leaders gathered for a second meeting, attended by artisans and laborers, many of whom were armed with clubs. Judge Morrow and Sheriff Flanigan announced that they would lead the recruitment efforts, and businessman Duncan Stewart pledged his own money to assist volunteers who had families of three or more children. Other wealthy citizens offered contributions, and with the federal bounty of $100, a volunteer received $120 for enlistment.[11]

From the city and surrounding Wayne County, men flooded into the regiment. In the village of Redford, the holder of a lien on the Methodist Church promised to cancel the notes of each individual mortgagor if the man enlisted. All of them did, and each note was canceled. On August 11, at Wyandotte, a meeting garnered enough volunteers to complete the regimental quota of 1,030 officers and men. Four days later, the Twenty-fourth Michigan was mustered into the service.[12]

Authorities assigned the regiment to the State Fairground, also known as Detroit Riding Park. The overwhelming majority of the recruits had come from the city and Wayne County, while four nearby counties supplied 123 volunteers. Slightly over seven hundred of them were native-born Americans, with German and Irish immigrants comprising the largest number of foreign-born members. Nearly a quarter of the enlistees had been born in New York.[13]

Farmers and laborers comprised nearly one half of the regiment's numbers, while another 159 members listed their occupations as either carpenter, clerk, sailor, or blacksmith. The average age of the recruits was between twenty-five and twenty-six years old. James Nowlin at seventy was the oldest, and drummer boy Willie Young at thirteen, the youngest. One hundred thirty-five pairs of brothers stood beside each other in the ranks. Although the bounty probably induced many of them to enlist, most joined, as one of them asserted, to "fight for the Union and maintain the best government on earth."[14]

Governor Blair appointed Judge Morrow as regimental colonel and Sheriff Flanigan as lieutenant colonel. A native Virginian, born in Warrenton, in 1829, Morrow had fought in the Mexican War, and had served as a page to Michigan's Lewis Cass in the Senate. He settled in Detroit in 1853, opened a law practice, and four years later was elected as the first judge of the Recorder's Court. Flanigan, a native of Ireland, was thirty-seven years old, a butcher before being elected Wayne County sheriff in 1860. At six feet, four inches tall, the Irishman was a powerful man with a reputation for fearlessness.[15]

When the regiment arrived in Washington, Colonel Morrow selected Henry W. Nall for the major's vacancy. Born in England, the thirty-one-year-old Nall had served as a captain in the Seventh Michigan until his promotion. As in most volunteer units, men of local prominence were chosen as captains or company commanders. A majority of these officers had been either attorneys, businessmen, or building contractors. Captain Albert M. Edwards of Company F had been a college student when he enlisted in the First Michigan in 1861. Captured at First Bull Run and later exchanged, Edwards was the only company commander with military experience. Captain William J. Speed of Company D had served as a cadet in the Detroit Light Guard, a militia company. The other eight captains would have to learn the rudiments of the trade along with their men.[16]

Morrow and his officers had little time for training before the regiment departed for Washington. On August 26, in a ceremony at Camp Martius, the volunteers received from city and county officials a national flag, made by a local firm and inscribed with "24th Michigan Infantry." Three days later, they boarded a steamer, *Mary Queen*, for Cleveland, where they boarded trains for the East. Citizens in Pittsburgh and Baltimore fed the soldiers during the trip, which was marked by "a great deal of trouble and disturbance" because of liquor. The regiment arrived in the capital on the evening of September 1, and was ordered across the Potomac into Virginia.[17]

As they marched, the novice soldiers passed "streams" of ambulances from Second Bull Run and the disgruntled ranks of John Pope's army. "It was indeed enough to make ones heart blood run cold," Private John E. Ryder wrote, "to see the wounded soldiers mangled in every direction, with arms and legs off, and heads swollen, and eyes blowed out." The regiment bivouacked near Fort Lyon, four miles outside Alexandria. "This is hard looking country," thought Ryder. "There is no fences, no crops."[18]

The Twenty-fourth Michigan spent a week at Fort Lyon. On September 8, as the Army of the Potomac marched in pursuit of the Confederates into Maryland, the regiment relocated to Camp Shearer near Fort Baker, having been assigned temporarily to a brigade in the corps of engineers. Here, Private George B. Parsons of Company D died of delirium, the regiment's initial fatality. Officers detailed three companies each day to fell timber for the fortifications, while the remaining companies trained in the school of the soldier, conducted by Regular Army sergeants, whom Morrow had secured from another unit. "I find that soldiering is the great importance of the day," as Private Ryder put it on September 11.[19]

The work and the drills went hard with the Michigan volunteers. "The men know most of the time just as much as the officers & they dont put on many airs," remarked a private. During one training session, an enlisted man flattened a captain with a rifle butt "for some real or fancied wrong," and the soldier was not punished. One night, Morrow and the officers ordered the men out of their tents and into a line of battle as a test. Many of the troops believed it was an actual engagement, and "when the call was given some of the boys was so scared that they shook and laid down." With the drilling, the work details, and almost daily "sham" battles, the men soon learned the reality of army life, or as one of them grumbled, "The fact is a soldier has no right to have business of his own, as he is not his own master at all."[20]

Many of them admitted in their letters to kinfolk and friends, however, that "we are perfectly contented." Hospital steward Elmer Wallace told his mother, "We live here first rate; good fresh bread, coffee, tea, sugar, fresh beef, pork, rice, and milk we can buy at 10c a quart." The men liked Morrow, who "will talk as common as a private." They were impressed with the fortifications and defenses—"Look where you will," contended Wallace, "forts may be seen in any direction." When they received passes into the capital, they returned quite unimpressed, or as a private described Washington, "a very shiftlest city it nothin that is apparent."[21]

By month's end, the volunteers "have got so now that we understand it purty well," Private Ryder believed about drills. On September 28, Morrow assembled the companies and read an order that directed the regiment to Frederick. The colonel added "that we were going to fight," and the men cheered. "If we went into a battle," Morrow responded, "we would have something to cheer for." The troops reacted with "a thundering cheer," spooking the colonel's horse.[22]

The Twenty-fourth Michigan marched on September 30, arriving in Frederick two days later. Since the regiment's organization, its ranks had been reduced by desertions before it had left Detroit and by illness in Virginia, bringing its strength down to 898 officers and men. Leaving Frederick on October 6, the command followed the army's route to Sharpsburg. At South Mountain, the men discovered an unburied Confederate, and as one noted, "Some old rags saturated with blood still lay on the ground." They joined the army on the 8th, and were assigned to the Iron Brigade.[23]

The Michigan volunteers formed ranks in their new uniforms and with polished Springfield rifles the next day. Contrary to traditional accounts, John Gibbon did not inspect his new regiment because he was in Baltimore, enjoying a leave with his family. Lucius Fairchild, now colonel of the Second Wisconsin, welcomed the regiment as senior officer present with the brigade. Before the Michiganders stood the veterans of the Iron Brigade in worn uniforms and with their distinctive black hats. They had heard the rumor that their new comrades were "bounty men" and Democrats.[24]

Colonel Morrow, whom a Wisconsin private described as "an elegant man," addressed the four regiments, extolling his men's qualities as soldiers. When he finished, the black-hatted veterans reacted with silence. "A pretty cool reception, we thought," wrote a Michigander. "We had come out to reinforce them, and supposed they would be glad to see us. Neither was satisfied with the other."[25]

Gibbon's veterans resented the bounties given these new volunteers, but there was more to it. Once, not long ago, they also wore new uniforms and carried brightly polished rifles and thought of themselves as soldiers. Since then, however, they had stood in the fields at Brawner's Farm, had clawed their way up South Mountain, and had leaned into the withering hellfire of the Cornfield. Like the Michiganders, they had full ranks, but then the war found them, and like a scourge, took many of them. Before these proud veterans would accept the newcomers these fellow Westerners would have to prove that they possessed the mettle of iron.

An Indianan confessed later that he and his comrades had shown an "unbrotherly spirit" toward Morrow's troops, taunting and cursing them in camp. But to Major Rufus Dawes the new volunteers were "a splendid looking body of men," adding that "their ranks are full now, and they are, as we were, crazy to fight." Another officer was willing to wait and see, noting, "if they fight as well as they look, our Brigade will give the Rebs a warm reception when we meet them."[26]

Gibbon returned from leave about a week later. On the afternoon of the 16th, he inspected the Twenty-fourth and later that day wrote to his wife that he "was very much pleased indeed with its appearance, and from its bearing have no doubt it will not be very long before it will be a worthy member of the Black Hats."[27]

When Gibbon returned from his leave, it had been almost exactly a month since the Battle of Antietam. Despite Lincoln's visit to the army and the president's suggestions for a forward movement against the Confederates, McClellan refused to order an advance, providing Washington with a list of needs before he could undertake an operation. When the general sent a report that the cavalry's horses were "absolutely broken down from fatigue and want of flesh," an exasperated Lincoln replied with a barbed inquiry, "Will you pardon me for asking what the horses of your army have done since the battle of Antietam that fatigues anything?"[28]

Finally, on October 26, a day after Lincoln sent his telegram about the army's mounts, the Army of the Potomac marched away from Sharpsburg, moving down the Potomac River in a rainstorm. The Iron Brigade abandoned its campsite during the afternoon and covered ten miles before bivouacking for the night. Evidently, the brigade had not been performing its duties to Gibbon's satisfaction, because on the 25th, the brigadier had "to *pitch in* in a way which makes people open their eyes somewhat." What caused Gibbon's outburst he did not specify, only noting to his wife that the officers and men had been "ding-donging" for some time.[29]

When the Westerners camped on the 26th, they were "colors of clay from top to bottom." Few slept that night as the rain poured down. In the Twenty-fourth Michigan, "the boys were sick enough, some was a going to desert, and others wanted to go into a battle to get shot." Sickness had reduced their ranks further to six hundred fit for duty.[30]

The Union army slogged through mud on the 27th. With the Confederate army positioned in the Shenandoah Valley, McClellan directed his units east of the Blue Ridge into the Virginia Piedmont. But his troops seldom marched with alacrity, and it was not until the end of the month before the Federals had crossed the Potomac and reentered the Old Dominion. Skirmishes ignited in the mountain gaps as Robert E. Lee shifted his army to confront and to interdict his opponent's advance. On November 2, the Iron Brigade hurried to the support of other units engaged at Snicker's Gap. Many of Gibbon's men discarded clothing from knapsacks and "were pretty tired" when they halted for the night.[31]

On November 4, while the Iron Brigade was camped at Bloomfield, Major General John Reynolds, commander of the First Corps, approached Gibbon and offered the brigadier command of the corps's Second Division. Gibbon accepted, but as he stated in his memoirs, with misgivings. The promotion meant separation from the brigade and Battery B. "In the two united," he wrote afterward, "I had the most implicit confidence, always knowing I could depend upon them." Now, because of the casualties to regimental commanders, the untested Colonel Henry Morrow was senior colonel. It was, as Gibbon put it, "as if trusting a cherished child in the hands of a strange and inexperienced nurse." Gibbon asked Morrow to waive his seniority, but the Michigan officer declined. The brigadier then discussed the matter with division commander Abner Doubleday, who approved of Morrow as brigade commander.[32]

That night Gibbon prepared a farewell address "to the Black Hatted Brigade *almost* with tears in my eyes," as he informed his wife. When the members learned of his promotion, they expressed regret and said that "they desire to go with me." "I would rather take them into action than any Division I know of," he confessed, "but cannot expect to keep them always, so may as well give them up now, tho' I think they might let me have them as a part of my new command."[33]

The next morning he had his address read to the Westerners, and then as they followed another road, John Gibbon sat his horse and watched them pass. From the beginning of their association, he had recognized their character as men and had taken that material and had forged them into soldiers. They had bent unwillingly, opposing his desire to recast them into Regulars. He dressed them up, gave them a black hat, and instilled in them a unit identification and pride. They gave back, of themselves, at Brawner's Farm, Second Bull Run, South Mountain, and Antietam. He had led them into the brotherhood, and when he spurred away to command other men, they lost the finest commander they would ever know.[34]

The Iron Brigade marched to Warrenton—"a general look of desolation pervades the whole country," thought a Hoosier. For Colonel Morrow, it was a homecoming. Here he had been born and lived as a child, and here his mother was buried. On November 7, Colonel Lysander Cutler of the Sixth Wisconsin rejoined the brigade although not fully recovered from his Brawner's Farm wound. He outranked Morrow in seniority and assumed command of the brigade. That same day, in a heavy snowstorm that lashed Virginia, a general came from Washington with orders that relieved McClellan of command and replaced him with Ambrose Burnside.[35]

Lincoln's patience with the popular general had unfrayed at last. Cabinet officers and Republican members of Congress had been clamoring for months for McClellan's removal. When the president learned that Lee had interposed units between McClellan's army and Richmond, Lincoln decided that he and the country could no longer afford the cautious general. Later, Lincoln explained the removal to one of his secretaries, stating that "I began to fear he [McClellan] was playing false—that he did not want to hurt the enemy." In the capital, officials worried that the army commander might not relinquish the position and lead the army to Washington and overthrow the civil authority.[36]

McClellan, however, accepted the decision, believing as he told his wife, "They have made a great mistake." When the officers and men learned of it on the 8th, they were, in Gibbon's word, *"thunderstruck."* Some voiced a desire to descend on Washington and unseat those responsible. "There is but one opinion upon this subject among the troops," argued Gibbon, "and that is that the Govt. has gone mad. It is the worst possible thing that could have been done." On November 10, the army passed in review for their beloved Little Mac for a final time. The "excitement was perfectly wild" when he rode along the ranks. He said his farewell in a published address, and on the 11th, he boarded a train for Trenton, New Jersey, where he had been directed to await orders. They would never come, and George B. McClellan, a general seemingly ill fitted for the bloody convulsions of civil war, was gone from it.[37]

In the Iron Brigade, "there is considerable dissatisfaction expressed by the rank and file," affirmed a Hoosier about McClellan's dismissal. Officers in the Second Wisconsin tendered their resignations, but Colonel Cutler asked them to reconsider their decisions. "Finally," wrote Captain Loyd G. Harris, "we came to the conclusion that we were fighting for the country, and not for any individual, and withdrew our resignations."[38]

The Stonewall Brigade came home to the Shenandoah Valley in Sharpsburg's aftermath. Nearly six months earlier, the Virginians had counted more than 3,600 men in the ranks. Now there were barely one tenth of them with the brigade, if that. Colonels James Allen, John Neff, Lawson Botts, and William Baylor were gone forever, along with scores of the captains, lieutenants, sergeants, and privates who had answered the summons in the spring of 1861. Few probably cared that once they had been Rockbridge Rifles, Southern Guards, Tenth Legion Minute Men, Liberty Hall Volunteers, and Montgomery Highlanders. The names must have seemed too distant, too naive perhaps, to matter as they returned to the Valley to heal and to be restored.

Like the Virginians, the entire Confederate army required time to recover from the previous month's campaigns. When the Southerners had recrossed the Potomac on September 18–19, they were little more than a specter of an army. Sharpsburg's fury had taken many, but the "evil" of straggling, as Robert E. Lee termed it, had eliminated thousands from the ranks. Those who had stood on those fields of slaughter had saved the army from possible annihilation by courage and fighting prowess. They were exhausted, in need of shoes, clothing, and food. With the enemy beyond the river, Lee paused in the Valley to refashion an army.[39]

The army recovered its strength rapidly. Stragglers resurfaced by the thousands, swelling the ranks to more than 62,000 by the end of September. Within another ten days, officers counted 78,204 present, and by October's end, more than 80,000 stood in the ranks, almost doubling the army's size within six weeks. Lee, meanwhile, acted to prevent a recurrence of the serious problem, ordering daily roll calls at reveille and the posting of guards in the rear of each brigade during a march.[40]

While the army increased in manpower, Lee attended to its supply needs and restructured commands. Depots forwarded clothing, footwear, equipment, and foodstuffs but could not meet the army's requirements. The artillery had incurred crippling losses, so Lee disbanded some batteries, parceled out serviceable cannon and horses, and organized the batteries into battalions. On October 1, the Rockbridge Artillery was assigned to the battalion of Colonel J. Thompson Brown, dissolving its organizational association with the Stonewall Brigade. They had been together since June 1861, and had fought beside each other from Henry House Hill to West Woods. "We are all sorry to part with old friends," wrote a battery member.[41]

The most significant organizational change in Lee's army was the creation of two official corps. On September 18, President Davis had approved a law that provided for the appointment of lieutenant generals and the formation of corps. Lee recommended James Longstreet and Stonewall Jackson for the new rank and for command of the First Corps and Second Corps, respectively. The two generals were disparate individuals who approached war from vastly different perspectives. Jackson saw war as a moral imperative, a testing of a man's character, while Longstreet relied upon preparation and caution to conserve lives. Both men had earned the promotions; during the second week of October, they were appointed.[42]

The refitting, refurbishment, and reorganization consumed weeks, characterized by an unusual interlude of peace. "The army was never so quiet as now," a Virginian noted on October 5, "a general impression prevailing that we contemplate no advance upon the enemy and that he contemplates none upon us." Drills resumed, but the rank and file were spared from forced marches and combat. Their spirit or morale had endured despite the Maryland Campaign. "We are beginning to feel like farm cocks again," contended Longstreet early in October, "and some begin to wish for the chance to convince the Yanks that Sharpsburg is but a trifle to what they can do." Another officer described the army a week later as "in splendid condition."[43]

The Stonewall Brigade was camped near Bunker Hill in the Lower Valley during these weeks. Like other units, the brigade's ranks swelled with the return of stragglers and men who had journeyed home on a French leave or temporary unauthorized absence. Desertion or permanent absence, however, still plagued the command. For the present, the Virginians welcomed the respite in the Valley, but as one of them admitted, "we can't tell much about old Jacksons movements."[44]

On October 17, the brigade became ensnared in "a pretty sharp little fight" near Shepherdstown. Sent down the Valley to wreck a section of the Baltimore & Ohio Railroad, the Virginians collided with a superior Union force. The Fourth and Fifth Virginia incurred the worst punishment from enemy infantry and artillery. "I thought at one time," said a member of the Fifth, "that we would nearly all be cut down." Ordered to withdraw, the Confederates hurried south, leaving their killed and wounded on the field. Colonel Charles Ronald of the Fourth suffered a disabling thigh wound that ended his service. Casualties amounted to forty-eight killed and wounded. A week later, a private grumbled that "I am getting pretty tired of this mode of wasting our lives. this war it seems cannot end, oh how earnestly I hope we may have peace ere another Spring dawns."[45]

A day after the Virginian hoped for peace, on October 26, the Federals began their movement into Virginia east of the Blue Ridge. Lee had anticipated an enemy advance for some time. When he learned of it, he ordered Longstreet's First Corps east toward the mountain gaps. Until he knew the extent of the Union operation, Lee held Jackson's Second Corps in the Valley, drawing the units closer to Winchester. The Confederate commander waited a few days and then joined Longstreet and the latter's troops at Culpeper Court House, between the Rapidan and Rappahannock rivers in central Virginia, on November 5. Two days later, Ambrose Burnside succeeded George McClellan.[46]

Jackson's troops remained in the Valley around Winchester until November 22. During those weeks, the Stonewall Brigade bivouacked on a farm four miles north of the town along the Valley Pike, naming the site Camp Baylor. The Virginians numbered probably about fifteen hundred. An epidemic of smallpox, however, raced through the Fourth Virginia, causing surgeons to quarantine the members and to cancel leaves. Some of the Virginians still lacked blankets and none had tents as the nights became increasingly chilly. More men deserted. Those who stayed held revival meetings during the evenings. At one gathering, thirty-five converts accepted the faith.[47]

While at Camp Baylor, the brigade received its new commander. Since Charles Winder's death at Cedar Mountain on August 9, no officer had been appointed to permanent command of the unit. Colonel William Baylor had led the Virginians at Second Manassas until he was killed. His temporary successor, Colonel Andrew Grigsby, commanded the brigade and then the division at Sharpsburg. Grigsby retained the position in the weeks after the engagement.[48]

Although the new brigadier, Elisha Franklin Paxton, was a Valley man and a former officer in the brigade, his selection by Jackson caused another furor within the unit. The Virginians expected that the appointment would be given Grigsby, whom they thought deserved it. Fearless, combative, and highly capable, Grigsby had distinguished himself with the Twenty-seventh Virginia from the war's outset. John Nadenbousch of the Second Virginia claimed "that no bolder or more daring officer ever led troops into a fight, or managed them better when actually engaged" than Grigsby. Major General A. P. Hill, who had his own difficulties with Jackson, described the colonel as the "bravest among the brave." He was "all and all as good a fighting leader as the service can turn out." Even Paxton wrote subsequently that Grigsby "has been distinguished for the fearless exposure of his person and utter disregard of danger."[49]

When Grigsby learned of Paxton's appointment, he was "as mad as thunder." It was believed at the time that the old Presbyterian warrior Jackson bypassed Grigsby because the colonel was, in the words of an officer, "such an awful swearer." Undoubtedly, Jackson disapproved of the habit, but he had retained as wagonmaster the excellent Major John Harman, whose ability to emit a string of oaths appeared to be unmatched, even by Grigsby. Perhaps Jackson remembered the fiery Grigsby's outspoken support for Richard Garnett when the commander removed the brigadier after Kernstown. Jackson explained to Lee that he had not chosen Grigsby or another officer in the brigade "because I did not regard any of them as competent as another."[50]

Grigsby resigned on November 12, writing to the secretary of war that "I cannot longer hold the position consistently with honor." He told a fellow officer that he would not serve under Paxton. Grigsby left the brigade that day, but instead of returning home to Rockbridge County, he traveled to Richmond, where he pleaded his grievance with President Davis. The meeting deteriorated into an argument between two proud men, and at one point, Grigsby cursed. "Do you know who I am?" asserted an offended Davis. "I am President of the Confederacy."

"And do you know who I am?" stormed the officer. "I am Andrew Jackson Grigsby of Rockbridge County late colonel of the Bloody Twenty-seventh Virginia of the Stonewall Brigade, and as good a man as you or anyone else, by God!"[51]

Grigsby went home. In the winter of 1863, he visited the army, soliciting recommendations for a promotion to brigadier general. His efforts failed to secure the rank, and while he was with his former comrades, he was "drunk nearly all the time." An officer who had served with Grigsby wrote, "I would rather be shot at a good many times by the Yankees than have a quarrel with such a man." The Stonewall Brigade had lost one of its most indomitable warriors.[52]

Frank Paxton joined the brigade on November 14. Thirty-four years old, a native of Rockbridge County and a cousin of Grigsby, Paxton was a graduate of Washington College, Yale University, and the University of Virginia. He had practiced law in Lexington until failing eyesight ended his career. He bought a farm nearby, and when the secession crisis came, Paxton became an outspoken advocate of states' rights. Physically powerful, he had a body that looked like the cleaved trunk of an ancient oak tree. Because of his booming voice, Paxton was known as "Bull."[53]

When Virginia seceded, Paxton enlisted as a lieutenant in the Rockbridge Rifles. Later that year he was promoted to major of the Twenty-seventh Virginia, but he lost the April 1862 reelection for the post. Three months later, Jackson appointed him as a volunteer aide on his staff. Paxton held this position until his promotion to brigadier general. An artillery officer believed Paxton to be "the best specimen of a Scotch-Irish soldier given by Rockbridge to our cause."[54]

William Nelson Pendleton, Lee's artillery chief and the former commander of the Rockbridge Artillery, knew the general well, both in Lexington and in the army. Writing soon after the appointment, Pendleton described it as "a blunder." "Paxton is a fearless man," continued Pendleton, "but very obstinate and impracticable. Sure to be disliked & so far not to be fully efficient. It is in such matters that Jackson makes mistakes. His prejudices and partialities misled him as to the merits or demerits of individuals."[55]

The Virginians received their fellow Valley man with coolness, but not with the open hostility they had given to Winder. After one day in command, Paxton confessed in a letter that "I go where there is much thankless work to be done and much responsibility to be incurred. I am free to admit that I don't like the change. Yet there is no help for it." He had only a week to reacquaint himself with the officers and men before Jackson's corps left Winchester to rejoin Lee's army east of the Blue Ridge.[56]

It was the old road, the Valley Pike, that the Confederates followed south on November 22. Snow covered the ground, and cold air braced the column. A Winchester woman saw them pass and wrote: "They were very destitute, many without shoes, and all without overcoats or gloves, although the weather is freezing. Their poor hands looked so red and cold holding their muskets in the biting winds." In the Thirty-third Virginia, eight members from Hampshire County refused to leave the Valley and deserted, telling their comrades before they left that they would join the cavalry. "All good soldiers," recalled Private John Casler, "but they were tired of the infantry."[57]

The Hampshire County men guessed right. Their comrades struggled through rain, snow, sleet, and mud for ten days. Many were without shoes, "thinly clad," and lacked tents. One soldier called it "one of the longest and hardest marches on record." Paxton stated proudly that straggling in the Stonewall Brigade had been minimal. He promised himself that during the forthcoming winter he would try "to make my brigade the best in the army" by "teaching them all the duties of soldiers, and in instilling into them the habit of obeying orders." En route, Jackson was notified that his wife had given birth to their second child, a daughter, Julia. Four years earlier, the couple had lost another daughter soon after childbirth.[58]

Since Lee and Longstreet had left the Valley to counter the Union advance at the end of October, the war in Virginia had shifted to Fredericksburg on the Rappahannock River. There Jackson's corps went, with all units present by December 1. Lee used Jackson's divisions to extend his lines south down the river. Across the stream, Ambrose Burnside had massed the Army of the Potomac. If the Yankees crossed, the Confederates would give battle. Lee held a formidable position on hills beyond the town, where he had placed Longstreet's corps. Jackson's lines covered a wooded ridge and fields farther south. Until Burnside committed himself to an operation, the Southerners had to defend the various river crossings along a front of more than a dozen miles.[59]

Jackson posted his former division, under Brigadier General William Taliaferro, who had recovered from his Brawner's Farm wound, near Guiney Station, about a dozen miles south of Fredericksburg. Division members, including Paxton's Virginians, began building temporary huts because they had few blankets. "The men suffer a good deal," wrote a captain of the Twenty-seventh Virginia, "but seem to be quite merry." Along the river, the opposing pickets agreed not to fire on each other without an advance warning. The generals would decide when the killing would resume.[60]

The road from Warrenton to Fredericksburg was, in the opinion of a member of the Iron Brigade, "very pleasant—being lined with cedars, and packed down very smooth—with but few stones." And on it filed the Army of the Potomac in mid-November, ordered toward the old colonial town on the Rappahannock by its new commander, Major General Ambrose Burnside. George McClellan's successor knew that the administration expected an advance against the Confederate Army of Northern Virginia, and within a week of his promotion, Burnside received the president's approval to move toward Richmond via Fredericksburg.[61]

Burnside's movement appeared to a Michigan private to be "evidently a big thing." Rain hampered the march of the huge army as the "very pleasant" road became "as slippery as grease." By November 17, the vanguard arrived opposite Fredericksburg at Falmouth, where Burnside expected pontoon bridges to be waiting for the army. But the inclement weather delayed their arrival, and as more rain fell, Burnside only watched as the river's waters rose. Some generals argued for a crossing at one of the numerous fords, but the commander demurred. When Longstreet's men filed on to the heights west of Fredericksburg on the 21st, Lee barred the route to Richmond. From the town, women and children fled.[62]

The Union camps sprawled across the fields and hills around Falmouth. In the Iron Brigade, sickness continued to level the newest members from Michigan. Dozens filled the army hospitals while the worst cases were sent to the capital. During the march to Falmouth, one soldier in the Twenty-fourth fell out of the ranks, ill and exhausted. When officers prodded him to get up, he took his rifle and shot himself in the heart. Others died in agony or quietly in the hospitals. Private John Ryder, a nineteen-year-old farmer from Livonia, believed he could secure a discharge because of illness but refused, writing, "it is my duty to help preserve my country and then I can enjoy my home."[63]

While the Michiganders saw their ranks "dribble away," their comrades in the other regiments welcomed back field officers who had been absent with wounds. Colonel Lysander Cutler and Lieutenant Colonel Edward Bragg returned to the Sixth Wisconsin, and Colonel William Robinson and Lieutenant Colonel Charles Hamilton rejoined the Seventh. As senior colonel, Cutler held temporary command of the brigade.[64]

Cutler's service ended, however, on November 27, when Solomon Meredith rejoined the Westerners, wearing the star of a brigadier general. Long Sol had been away from the brigade for over two months. Health problems had kept him off the field at Antietam, and four days later he left the Nineteenth Indiana for Washington to seek medical treatment. While in the capital, Meredith met with Secretary of War Edwin Stanton and General-in-Chief Henry W. Halleck about his promotion to brigadier general. Undoubtedly, he contacted Indiana politicians to promote his aspirations. Finally, on October 21, he learned that his rank had been approved, to date from October 6.[65]

The promotion had not brought with it an assignment to a brigade, so Meredith journeyed to Indiana. On November 6, in Indianapolis, the new general "spent the day settling with Mr. Morton and others," as he recorded it in his diary. It would appear that he gave money to the governor and other Republicans for their political patronage. Meredith still retained the civilian position of clerk of the court, and this could be related to these accounts. By November 18, he was back in Washington, where he soon received the assignment to command of his old comrades. John Gibbon's reaction to the news was most likely unprintable.[66]

Although Gibbon despised Meredith and his political machinations, the rank and file of the Nineteenth Indiana had liked and respected him as regimental commander. Meredith had attended to their needs, and at Brawner's Farm and at South Mountain, he had led them with courage. "The men who carried the knapsacks," asserted a Westerner, "never failed to place an officer just where he belonged, as to his intelligence and bravery." Meredith had passed that test with his Hoosiers, and his promotion to brigadier general and to command of the brigade "pleases the boys," in the opinion of one of them.[67]

Two weeks after Meredith's return to the brigade, Burnside decided to cross the Rappahannock and assail the Confederate position. He had probed along the river for crossing sites, finally settling on three points directly opposite and below the town. He believed that Lee would be "surprised" by such a movement.[68]

With the pontoons at hand, Federal engineers began laying the spans on December 11. Fierce Confederate resistance from the town caused Burnside to order a bombardment of Fredericksburg. For over two hours, 150 cannon unleashed their fury upon enemy soldiers and civilians who had refused to abandon their homes. Buildings shook, walls collapsed, and victims clung to each other in terror. When the guns ceased, the Rebels reemerged and once again drove away the pontoon builders. Finally, Union infantrymen piled into boats, poled across the stream, and secured the streets after a house-to-house struggle.[69]

The next day, December 12, the Federals came in long cords of unbroken blue-clad ranks. It was a magnificent display of Union might. West and south of Fredericksburg, the enemy watched in admiration. Never before, however, had the Southerners held such a superb killing ground. Lee's left and center embraced three hills and were manned by Longstreet's corps. Marye's Heights in the center loomed above an open plain that extended to the town. On its slope and crest, Longstreet had stacked cannon, and at its base, he had piled infantry behind a stone wall that edged a sunken road. Earlier, referring to the position on Marye's Heights, an artillery officer told Longstreet, "General, we cover that ground now so well that we will comb it as with a fine-tooth comb. A chicken could not live on that field when we open fire."[70]

If the Confederate position had a vulnerable sector, it was on the right, where Jackson's divisions held a wooded ridge west of the Richmond, Fredericksburg and Potomac Railroad. Although trees concealed and protected the Rebels, the ground possessed no dominant feature. On the morning of the 12th, Jackson had only A. P. Hill's division at hand, but orders had been sent to William Taliaferro, Jubal Early, and D. H. Hill to hurry their divisions north from downriver. When A. P. Hill aligned his six brigades, a six-hundred-yard gap loomed across his center. Perhaps Hill and Jackson concluded that the marshy ground there could not be penetrated by the Federals. At the gap's rear, two brigades covered the terrain, but if a Union force drove into the breach, Hill's front line could be enfiladed. Jeb Stuart's horse artillery protected Jackson's right flank around Hamilton's Crossing.[71]

A dense morning fog clung to the woods, hollows, fields, and hills around Fredericksburg on December 13. Like a huge curtain pulled by frayed ropes, the thick mist lifted slowly. Beneath it, men waited, bracing themselves for the drama about to be staged. It was to be a tragedy scripted, it would seem, by Lucifer himself.[72]

When the fog dissipated, artillery crews in each army opened the battle. About noon, on the plain south of Fredericksburg, a division of Pennsylvania Reserves initiated the Union assault, advancing toward the woodland held by Jackson's troops. Smoke from thousands of muskets billowed up from the trees as the Confederates lashed the Pennsylvanians. The Yankees kept coming, striking the Confederate line at the gap and pouring into the woods. The opponents raked each other at close range. Jackson rushed forward reserves as a second Federal division entered the maelstrom.[73]

Among the troops hurrying forward to seal the breach was the Stonewall Brigade. Frank "Bull" Paxton had slightly more than twelve hundred officers and men in the ranks. The Second Virginia spearheaded the brigade's counterattack, coming under enemy rifle fire. Union batteries in the rear shook the trees with shell fire. One piece of metal tore into the face of Lieutenant Colonel Robert Gardner of the Fourth Virginia, and a shard penetrated his lung. The Virginians held firm, "doing their duty as only veterans know how." Their losses amounted to fewer than fifty killed and wounded.[74]

Jackson's reserves hammered back the Northerners and secured the Confederate line. To the north, meanwhile, Burnside hurled seven divisions against Longstreet's ranks of iron, bronze, and steel. The Yankees never had a chance. One Union division commander stated that his line "melted like snow coming down on warm ground" before the Rebel position. Another general described the field as "a great slaughter pen," adding that his men "might as well have tried to take Hell." At one point in the fearful butchery, Longstreet told Lee that if he had enough ammunition, "I will kill them all before they reach my line." At last, with "piles and cross piles" of his dead and wounded covering the ground, Burnside stopped the carnage.[75]

Late in the afternoon, at the southern end of the battlefield, the Iron Brigade became ensnarled in a nasty fight with Confederate skirmishers and artillery crews. The Westerners had spent the day in support of batteries and troops engaged with Jackson's troops. About three o'clock, Solomon Meredith received orders from division commander Abner Doubleday to flush out enemy skirmishers between the river and Bowling Green Road. Meredith posted the Twenty-fourth Michigan in front, one hundred paces ahead of the other four regiments. Battery B, Fourth U.S. Artillery added its firepower to the infantry's.[76]

Southern gunners saw the Westerners coming and targeted them with a barrage of shell fire and solid shot. "The old soldiers of our brigade," reported a Michigan soldier, "says the worst & hardest shelling they ever saw." Some of the brigade veterans bolted and ran, including nine Hoosiers who were accused later of cowardice and desertion. In the Twenty-fourth Michigan, Private John Bryant had an arm ripped off by a cannon ball. He was the regiment's first battle death. Nearby, another solid shot decapitated eighteen-year-old Private Louis Hattie. The untested soldiers began to waver, so Colonel Henry Morrow put them through the manual of arms to steady them under the storm. Another Confederate round killed a lieutenant and three soldiers.[77]

Morrow's men pushed forward through a ravine to the edge of woods. Suddenly from behind the trees, Rebels "came out like red squirrels to aggravate us." The enemy skirmishers stung the Yankees with rifle fire. They caught the Federals in a crossfire "at any point they chose." The other regiments advanced in support of the Michiganders, who "made a good appearance," in the view of Major Rufus Dawes. Meredith stated in his report that Morrow's officers and men "showed themselves to be worthy of the praise they have received, and of association with the old Iron Brigade."[78]

As nightfall approached, Doubleday sent a staff officer to order Meredith to retire. But the aide garbled the instructions, and Meredith held his position. When Doubleday discovered that the brigadier had not complied, he relieved Meredith of command, believing that he had disobeyed orders. Colonel Lysander Cutler assumed command and withdrew the brigade. A member of the Michigan regiment wrote four days later about their initiation into combat: "taking the thing all around it was a pretty big one—or seemed so at least to us greenhorns. If *ever* boys were glad to get out of a scrape it was us. Not that we felt licked!"[79]

The Iron Brigade lost a reported nine killed, forty wounded, and sixteen captured or missing. The men spent the night in line along Bowling Green Road, expecting a renewal of the fighting on the 14th. Burnside considered another assault, but his ranking subordinates convinced him of the futility and the needless sacrifice that would result. The army's casualties exceeded twelve thousand; its enemy's, slightly more than five thousand. The Federals began retreating across the river after nightfall on the 15th. By the next morning, the entire force lay north of the Rappahannock. The Iron Brigade was one of the last units across the pontoons on the morning of the 16th. A Wisconsin sergeant summarized the four-day ordeal: "I thought that we were marching to defeat, and this feeling was shared with me by the whole army."[80]

Two days later, on the night of December 17–18, a small group of Confederates crossed the Rappahannock and met pickets from the Twenty-fourth Michigan. The Federals, who were veterans now like their guests, shared coffee and hardtack with the gray-clad visitors. These Americans talked about the war and probably about their homes. The Southerners then returned to the opposite bank and became enemies again. "The most perfect feeling exists between the privates of the two armies," wrote one of the hosts. "They are quite as sick of this inhuman, wholesale manslaughter as we."[81]

11

✠

RIVER CROSSINGS

CHRISTMAS 1862 cheered few in the Army of the Potomac. Hospitals teemed with the broken bodies of comrades, and the memories of the dead before the stone wall at Marye's Heights were too fresh for celebration. An officer likened Fredericksburg to "foul murder," adding that "the *whole army* is almost mutinous." Around campfires, the most discussed question among the men was "What are we fighting for?"[1]

The letters of members of the Iron Brigade reflected the discontent throughout the army. A Wisconsin soldier asserted that they "are all discouraged. . . . The paper's all say that the soldiers are aching to fight," he explained, "but the papers are notorious liars. We were never so fast to have the war brought to a close." A sergeant believed that "the end is farther off now than it was last Christmas." Corporal Abel G. Peck, who carried the flag of the Twenty-fourth Michigan during the battle, admitted to home folks that he liked army life "as well as I expected to" until Fredericksburg, but now "I have lost all of my patriotism since I see how the thing works, and taking us across the river as they did right before such works, and not a leaf to hide us."[2]

To a man, it seemed, the Westerners blamed Ambrose Burnside and the administration in Washington. "This army seems to be overburdened with second rate men in high position," Major Rufus Dawes charged, "from General Burnside down. Common place and whisky are too much in power for the most hopeful future." A Hoosier lieutenant contended that the army's ranking officers had committed "criminal blunders" in the battle. Wisconsin Sergeant George H. Legate spoke for many when he wrote that "the army has long since lost all confidence in all the officials at Washington, and unless they change their tactics, the country will soon follow suit."[3]

A Seventh Wisconsin man who served in the Battery B, Fourth U.S. Artillery echoed a common refrain, stating "that if Mc [McClellan] had had command of this armey insted of Burnsid that we would have whiped them (insted of getting whiped) & been on our way to Richmond." But Sergeant John St. Clair of the Sixth Wisconsin spoke to a reality of Fredericksburg, telling his father: "the south never will give up they air hard boys they fite well."[4]

With the new year approaching, Fredericksburg stuck in the army's craw, a bitter memory less than a fortnight in the past. In their camps at Falmouth, the Federals prepared for winter, erecting wood cabins which measured roughly five feet by twelve feet, with fireplaces. The Yankees scoured the countryside for timber, and as a Westerner noted, the surrounding land soon appeared as if "it has been run to death and skinned in the bargain." They made the quarters as comfortable as they could, but a Michigander confessed that it would take a few days before "our eyes will be smoke proof."[5]

The Iron Brigade members named their site Camp Isabella, only to change it to Camp Shearer within a few weeks. Through much of January, the men lived "very well" with ample rations of fresh beef, rice, sugar, coffee, beans, potatoes, and vegetables. When they received an issue of rancid bacon, a corporal joked that he and comrades wanted it "put under guard to keep the worms from carrying it off." On January 10, Lieutenant Colonel Mark Flanigan returned from a short leave in Michigan, bringing with him "more than a ton of stuff" in wagons. Although much of it had spoiled, "the day was a gay one for the regiment," exclaimed a member.[6]

Solomon Meredith, who had been reinstated to command after the army recrossed the river, ordered a resumption of drills, and in the Second Wisconsin, Colonel Lucius Fairchild required regimental officers to attend study sessions on army regulations and tactical manuals. A rumor circulated among the Westerners that they had been selected to receive new seven-shot Spencer rifles for their muzzle-loading Springfields. Sickness continued to stalk the camps, and although none of the Westerners wrote about deserters from their regiments, they noted that many men in the army had fled their units after the battle.[7]

Fredericksburg's seemingly inexplicable carnage gnawed at the men, eroding morale. When Private Henry Matrau learned that his brother was thinking about enlisting, the Sixth Wisconsin man counseled that "if he will take the advice of his luckless soldier brother he will steer clear of the army and stay at home with mother for take my word for it, though I'll own it aint romantic, a good soldier cares more for a good meal than he does for all the glory he can put in [a] bushel basket."[8]

Like Matrau, Michigander John Ryder had received similar news from home about a friend, who had already volunteered. Ryder had been in Virginia less than five months, had endured the artillery fire at Fredericksburg, and along the way had lost his youthful romantic notions about soldiering. To mutual friends, he described what a novice soldier could expect, writing: "He may imagine, some dark and stormy night, when it is cold, and the mud halfway to your knees, and the order to strike tents, and be ready to march in 10 minutes. And in that time you are ready, and a going, and it is dark, and you fall over rocks, and by morn, you are all wet through, and covered with mud from head to toe."[9]

A divisive topic debated around campfires during January was President Lincoln's Emancipation Proclamation, which had gone into effect on the first of the month. Issued five days after Antietam, Lincoln's executive action as commander-in-chief declared all slaves in areas of the South controlled by Confederate armies "are, and henceforward shall be free." Always an astute politician, Lincoln balanced the clamor of abolitionists for immediate freedom and the Northern majority's opposition to the African race. But the president's proclamation recast the conflict's meaning to both the reestablishment of the Union and human freedom. The trumpet's notes heralded a revolution as portentous as that embraced by the Confederacy in the spring of 1861.[10]

The reaction to the policy by the soldiers from the Old Northwest, where slavery had been banned since the 1780s, paralleled those of the majority of the army. The Nineteenth Indiana's Lieutenant William Orr declared: "I dont like it. I dont want to fight to free the darkeys." He considered resigning but did not, although arguing that they were not fighting for "what I enlisted for." But, he concluded, "I go for my country, *right* or *wrong*."[11]

An enlisted man in Orr's regiment believed "as a true republican" that "slavery to be a great evel and should be glad to see them immencipated." But, he thought, "the African race should be a separate nation," and the freed slaves should be colonized abroad. "Dont understand bye this," he explained, "that I look upon them as not being human beings yet I think they should not be intimate associates of ours."

To the Hoosier soldier, however, "the cause" overrode his misgivings toward emancipation. The cause was "just and right" and clear—if the South achieved "their indepenance other states would think they had the same right to seceed and consequently the United States would forever be fighting among them selves, why then not fight while the matter is provocked."[12]

Lincoln's proclamation also included an authorization to enlist free blacks and former slaves into the army. In time, the emancipation's impact upon the Confederacy's war effort and the performance of black troops allayed opposition to the policy. For the present, however, the Northern populace and the armies wrestled with the implications of the measure and with the disturbing question of future race relations. They would wait and watch if the road the president had taken led to victory for the cause that brought them forth in the spring of 1861.[13]

At Falmouth, meanwhile, the routine of winter quarters ended abruptly with marching orders on January 19. For weeks, Ambrose Burnside had contemplated and planned another offensive against the Confederates beyond the Rappahannock River. Since the Battle of Fredericksburg, the weather had been mild and clear, and if it held, Burnside saw an opportunity to strike the enemy by moving up the river and turning the Rebels' flank. Shortly after noon on the 19th, two grand divisions of the army lumbered out of their camps, angling northwest toward Banks's and United States fords.[14]

The movement proceeded well on that day, with the units closing on the crossing sites. Optimism prevailed on the 20th, as officers told their men that the impending battle would end the war. At army headquarters, however, Burnside hesitated, stalling the army in place. At nightfall, rain began to fall, increasing in intensity as a storm blew in with howling winds and sheets of rain. An Iron Brigade officer described it as "one of the most miserable nights I ever passed as a soldier." Without shelter, the men suffered terribly in the cold downpour.[15]

The winter storm lashed the Federals throughout the 21st, and with

Confederates alerted to the movement, Burnside abandoned the offensive. As the rain continued the next day, the army started back for its camps. The Yankees crawled through the mud, moving it seemed by inches. "Twelve mules could not pull a supply wagon," a Wisconsin soldier stated. "God alone knows how much I suffered," exclaimed a Hoosier, while a fellow brigade member asserted that "I was in a living Hell." Hundreds in the army deserted in "the great skedaddle," as a Michigander phrased it. Some army wit posted a sign along the trough of mud that read: "Burnside stuck in the mud."[16]

The muddy, soaked, and "thoroughly disgusted" Federals straggled into their camps on the 23rd and 24th. When the Twenty-fourth Michigan arrived at their quarters, the members found the huts occupied by an Ohio regiment. The Michiganders' ranks had been so reduced that they shared the cabins that night with the Ohioans. The men dubbed the ordeal the "Mud March." As far as they were concerned, Burnside was finished as their commander. The Wisconsin lieutenant who had found himself in "a living Hell" recalled that "I pacified myself that I would keep my vow with Govt (and Father Abraham) and do the right thing to the end. It was tough medicine tho."[17]

The army's morale plummeted to a depth worse than during Fredericksburg's aftermath. "An evidence of disaffection in this army," a Second Wisconsin lieutenant recorded in his diary on January 25, "is known by the no. of stragglers & deserters caught down by Potomac & brought in." In the history of the Iron Brigade, never had so many men abandoned the ranks. A Michigan soldier estimated ten days later that about one hundred members had been court-martialed, noting that "our guard house is full." Most of the accused were sentenced to loss of pay and to hard labor. Seven brigade members were found guilty of "misbehavior before the enemy," and on February 21, in front of their comrades, had their heads shaved and were drummed out of the service. Lieutenant Henry Kinney of Company I, Twenty-fourth Michigan was convicted of cowardice and received a dishonorable discharge. Kinney claimed that he had refused to fight because the Federals could not suppress the Southern rebellion.[18]

In Washington, Lincoln reacted to the Mud March and to the reports of mass discontent and desertions by relieving Burnside of command and replacing the general with Major General Joseph Hooker on January 25. The ambitious Hooker had openly expressed his scorn for Burnside's generalship and had undermined his leadership. The president knew of Hooker's actions, and on the 26th penned a frank letter to the new commander, in which he stated: "during Gen. Burnside's command of the Army, you have taken counsel of your ambition, and thwarted him as much as you could, in which you did a great wrong to the country, and to a most meritorious and honorable brother officer. I have heard, in such a way as to believe it, of your recently saying that both the Army and the Government needed a Dictator. Of course it was not *for* this, but in spite of it, that I have given you the command. Only those generals who gain successes, can set up dictators. What I now ask of you is military success, and I will risk the dictatorship."[19]

Lincoln chose Hooker because "Fighting Joe," as he was known, had a reputation for combativeness and possessed self-confidence and energy. He could perhaps galvanize the army, but it would take time. For the men in the ranks, the dismissal of Burnside was welcome news. A few days later, however, probably speaking for most of the army, Sergeant Horace Emerson wrote, "to tell the truth fighting is played out. The Army of the Potomac is demoralised to a great extent and will never show as good a front as they did while Mac was with us."[20]

For the Westerners and their army comrades, Hooker's appointment portended change as they settled back into winter quarters. As February lengthened, with its colder temperatures and the arrival of snow, the men huddled in their cabins and performed the routine duties of guard mounting and picketing. In the Iron Brigade, rations improved when some men built a bakery and provided "soft bread" for their fellow soldiers. Hardtack remained a staple, however, and they used it to prepare a concoction by frying it in water and pork fat until browned. They called the dish a "*Son of a bitch*."[21]

The black-hatted veterans amused themselves as well as they could. One soldier noted in his diary that there was "great rejoicing in camp" when "C. Ford changed his shirt" on February 14. The members of the Second Wisconsin evidently pilfered anything they could find, moving one of them to brag that "this Regt can beat the world stealing." About fifty of the men left the brigade, transferring to Battery B, Fourth U.S. Artillery, as its ranks had been depleted by the termination of service of two-year enlistees. Illness continued to bring death, or as the Westerners termed it, "going to their long home." For others, homesickness served as the constant enemy. One of them confessed to his brother that the lonely men sought the sexual favors of contraband women "with as good relish" as they had for women at home.[22]

"Our men," remembered an Irishman in the Sixth Wisconsin, "were not of the hymn-singing, testament-carrying kind who spent their time in camp in writing home letters of the 'Just Before The Battle Mother' variety." When the Westerners had finished their duties, "they were more interested in a stag dance or penny ante than what the newspapers were saying about them."[23]

A feeling seemed to pervade the ranks that the struggle had taken a new fork and that the whirlwind in which they found themselves had no end. They had learned from those sent to Wisconsin to recruit that the "war feeling is entirely played out." But from across the Rappahannock came a more ominous voice. As the Federals talked with Rebel pickets, they learned, as a Michigander described it: "You will not find a southern man but will say we are fighting for our rights and will fight till we die."[24]

In the Shenandoah Valley the whirlwind seldom ceased during 1862. Few weeks passed without the war's presence in the region. The patriotic exuberance of a year before had given way to a sobering reality. Although those in the Valley celebrated Confederate victories, many waited with anxious uncertainty after each engagement for word from loved ones in the army. Winchester diarist Cornelia McDonald termed the mounting list of battles "the catalogue." When she heard of Fredericksburg, she asked in her journal: "Where will it end? Can nothing stop the dreadful havoc?"[25]

McDonald's painful query was echoed undoubtedly across the length and the breadth of the region. For the relatives and friends of the Valley men in the Stonewall Brigade each new entry in "the catalogue" brought anguish to Shenandoah homes. Although spared from the worst of Fredericksburg's carnage, the brigade members had suffered much on some of the year's bloodiest fields. Too often, it seemed, they had leaned into the whirlwind.

The toll exacted from the brigade amounted to about one third of its numbers. At year's end, brigade commander Frank Paxton prepared an accounting of the command's casualties. According to the tabulation, the Virginians had incurred losses of 1,220 killed and wounded during the year, a figure greater than the numbers of officers and men Paxton had with him after Fredericksburg.[26]

The casualty figures alone did not indicate fully how the brigade's combat effectiveness and unit discipline had been affected by the campaigns and battles. Critical to the command's cohesion as a fighting force was the crippling loss of regimental field officers. Of the fifteen colonels, lieutenant colonels, and majors who held those ranks as a result of the April reorganization, only six remained with their regiments. Five had been either killed or mortally wounded—James Allen, Lawson Botts, Frank Jones, William Baylor, and John Neff; three had been disabled by wounds—Charles Ronald, Robert Gardner, and Frederick Holliday; and one had resigned—Andrew Grigsby. Another one, Major William Terry of the Fourth Virginia, had been wounded at Second Manassas but had rejoined the regiment before Fredericksburg.[27]

Capable subordinates replaced those field officers, but arguably the brigade never recovered from this depletion of talent. "In these losses," Paxton wrote, "are many whom we were always accustomed to regard as our best men." Baylor was one of the army's most outstanding colonels and seemed certain for promotion, while Grigsby deserved a brigadiership. Allen had redeemed himself at Kernstown, and like Baylor and Grigsby, possessed the attributes for higher rank. The youthful Neff required seasoning, but his performance until his death at Brawner's Farm held promise. Botts, Jones, Gardner, and Holliday appeared to be officers who could, if given an opportunity, lead a regiment. The whirlwind had harvested many of the brigade's finest officers.[28]

Paxton's command problems worsened in early January 1863, when Colonel Ned Lee resigned the colonelcy of the Thirty-third Virginia. He had been plagued with respiratory problems, which had been aggravated by an operation in December. With Lee's departure, his regiment and the Second Virginia had lost the entire complement of field officers who had been elected in April.[29]

While Confederate regimental records must be examined with caution, the evidence indicates that at least one thousand brigade members deserted during 1862, either permanently or for an extended period of time. Many returned to the regiments voluntarily; others joined different units, particularly cavalry commands; but many left the ranks for the war's duration. Undoubtedly, the closeness to home lured hundreds, if not most, of them away from the army. Families provided security and daily needs. With the brigade spending seven months in the Valley, opportunities to desert were plentiful.[30]

The number of deserters also reflected the hardships of the campaigns and discipline problems within the command. The Valley men began deserting soon after First Manassas, but during 1862, the rate accelerated to more than twenty-five percent, a crippling proportion. As discussed previously, the Valley Campaign's demands upon men's bodies and souls caused two thousand brigade members to abandon the ranks for a period of time. Eventually, hundreds of them came back, but for the remainder of the year, the regiments' numbers never approached the figure of 3,681 present on May 3.[31]

Officers could not staunch the flow. Casualties among field- and company-level commanders surely contributed to a weakening of discipline. The regiments with the largest number of deserters, for instance, were the Second and Thirty-third Virginia, the two units which lost all their field officers. In the end, however, the individuals who deserted chose for various reasons to forsake their comrades and the cause during a year when Confederate fortunes in Virginia were in the ascendancy.[32]

For some of the deserters their acts incurred a price. During winter quarters, at least twenty-nine Valley men were convicted by courts-martial of either desertion or absence without leave. The guilty received sentences of months of hard labor, thirty-nine lashes, the branding of the letter D on hips, or death. While the records are incomplete, it appears that eleven received the death penalty, and of that number, eight were executed during February and March 1863.[33]

Paxton requested leniency, suggesting that only one man, chosen by lot, be shot. Stonewall Jackson and Robert E. Lee opposed the commutation of the sentences. Lee wrote that the sentences must be enforced, "however painful it may be to inflict the severe punishment which the good of the service requires." But President Davis intervened and pardoned three of them. After witnessing the execution of four soldiers, Paxton asserted: "It is a sad spectacle, and I sincerely wish that their lives might have been spared."[34]

The Stonewall Brigade by then was "a mere skeleton," in Paxton's words, as its members began building their winter huts during the last week of 1862. Camp Winder, as they named their rows of log cabins, was located three miles from Guiney Station, near Moss Neck, the home of Richard Corbin. Jackson established corps headquarters on the 1,600-acre estate, using a small wooden office near the manor house. Here, at Moss Neck, the Confederacy's most famous soldier and his old brigade of fellow Valley men would spend the next three months.[35]

Although the Virginians would have preferred to be stationed among their own in the Valley, the winter at Moss Neck was marked by relative quiet. They still lacked an adequate number of blankets and shoes, but duties proved to be routine. The five regiments alternated picket duty along the river. Regiments served a two-day stint. One soldier complained about the region downstream from Fredericksburg, grumbling that "I thought it was bad at (Romney) last winter, there was some bottom in the mountains but there don't appear to be any here, there is nothing but sand here."[36]

Boxes of foodstuffs and clothing from home enlivened the men's spirits. In late January, however, Colonel John Funk issued an order to the Fifth Virginia, reminding the soldiers to live by the "golden rule" with goods. The members apparently were gouging their comrades by selling articles and food to them at exorbitant prices. When whiskey could be purchased, a quart sold at fifteen dollars, more than the monthly pay of a private.[37]

Religious members of the brigade constructed a log chapel, with seating for more than four hundred worshippers. The officers and men dedicated it on February 1, and chaplains then used it for regular Sunday services, Bible classes, and prayer meetings. Jackson joined his fellow worshippers for the Sabbath a week after the dedication. In the Fifth Virginia, two companies built a log theater with private boxes. The "Stonewall Minstrels" performed three nights a week, netting about sixty dollars a night and using the proceeds to purchase clothing for themselves. The Fifth's band held concerts, and along with Union musicians, serenaded pickets from both armies along the Rappahannock.[38]

The enemy's presence beyond the river kept the Confederates on a constant alert. A Virginian noted that "we are under marching orders all the time," and were required to have a day's rations cooked ahead of time. Few of them, however, expected a Federal crossing during the winter because of Burnside's ill-fated Mud March. If Hooker dared to advance, argued a captain of the Thirty-third Virginia, "he comes to his destruction and he knows it."[39]

Like their opponents, the Valley men understood that the stakes had increased with the Republican administration's commitment to emancipation. Captain John P. Welsh of the Twenty-seventh Virginia perceived that there could be no turning back for either side. Although he hoped that "this dreadful war" would end, Welsh knew that "unless we can maintain our independence peace will do us no good." The struggle for states' rights had been recast into a conflict for the preservation of the Southern way of life. Welsh avowed, "any man that wouldent fight to the last ought to be hung as high as haman."[40]

As spring warmed the ground and dried the roads, Lee's army prepared for the renewal of a war whose meaning had been reshaped by the words of one man. The Confederates had passed the winter still cursed by supply shortages, but thousands of absentees, recruits, and conscripts had joined the ranks. While Lee could never expect to match his opponent's numbers, he counted 65,000 in the army along the Rappahannock by the end of April.[41]

At Camp Winder, the ranks of Paxton's five regiments had swelled to approximately two thousand. A member of the general's staff crowed that "the old Stonewall is larger than it has ever been since last April when re-organized." The men, he said, "are in fine state of drill and discipline." Except for the Fourth Virginia, with Major William Terry at its head, the regiments were commanded by colonels. Furloughs had been suspended, and around the campfires there was "a heap of talk about fighting."[42]

Bull Paxton was not so certain that the signs pointed to a battle. "The future, ever a mystery," the brigadier wrote during the final week of April, "is more mysterious now than ever before. Our destiny is in the hands of God, infinite in his justice, goodness and mercy; and I feel that in such time as he may appoint he will give us the blessings of independence and peace." Surely, Paxton believed, the Lord favored the Confederates because "we have a just cause."[43]

Solomon Meredith must have savored the moment. Although he wore the uniform of a Union general, Long Sol embraced politics with the fervor of an evangelist at war with Lucifer's minions. The time had come for a speech, and before him stood his fellow Westerners of the Iron Brigade. John Gibbon would have railed against such a gathering, but the old Regular was not a politician.

At home, Meredith began, sedition stalked the land. Opponents of the administration, Copperheads, were deceiving the public with falsehoods about demoralization in the army and about a plan to settle the conflict on dishonorable terms. He knew that if he could take the brigade home with him, they would silence the critics at the point of a bayonet. Instead, he wanted to make them citizens again for fifteen minutes to adopt a set of resolutions that, according to a listener, supported "a vigorous prosecution of the war, the conscript law, & expressing confidence in General Hooker." The men cheered their general and gave a unanimous approval to the resolutions.[44]

The Westerners' response to Meredith's proposal reflected the restoration of morale in the brigade and throughout the entire Union army. Since his appointment to command after the Mud March, Joseph Hooker had rejuvenated the demoralized ranks by attending to the men's needs, changing the army's command structure, and infusing it with his own self-confidence. The commanding general unsnarled supply problems, saw that the troops were better fed and clothed, granted furloughs, and adopted the idea of chief of staff Daniel Butterfield to give each of the seven corps a distinctive badge. While Butterfield argued that it could give commanders better control of units on a battlefield, the badges became a source of pride to corps's members. Within each corps, the badges were colored red, white, and blue for the First, Second, and Third divisions, respectively.[45]

Hooker abandoned Burnside's bulky grand division structure, eliminating another command layer within the army. He also appointed new corps commanders and created a cavalry corps to match the Confederates' superb horsemen. Unfortunately, in a clash of strong-willed men, Hooker reduced the authority of Henry J. Hunt, the army's highly capable artillery chief. Overall, however, the commanding general streamlined the organizational structure and created a mounted force which would, in time, rival Jeb Stuart's Southern cavalry.[46]

Beyond the changes, Fighting Joe exuded confidence as he rode through the camps and spoke to subordinate officers. According to a Michigander, when Hooker conversed with Colonel Henry Morrow, the general swore "that he was just as sure that he was a going to whip the rebs as he was a living man. He said all he was afraid of was that they would run before he got a chance to fight." Such words were repeated to the rank and file. They encouraged men who had been searching for another George McClellan, but such boastfulness had to be followed by victories.[47]

Military pageantry had always appealed to Hooker's personal showmanship. When the weather permitted, he massed the army for reviews. A member of the Iron Brigade believed that the one held on April 2 was "the finest military show I have ever seen since the day that we crossed the river at Fredericksburg." Trailed by fifty staff officers and subordinate commanders, Hooker dashed along the ranks, riding "as though the old Nick himself was after him." Each unit, "all being out in their best dress," then passed before the commanding general, emitting three cheers in his honor. A week later, when President Lincoln visited the army, Hooker repeated the spectacle for the commander-in-chief.[48]

No man could erase Fredericksburg's memories, but Hooker healed some of its scars. On Monday, April 27, as blossoms colored peach trees, the massive Union army, numbering over 100,000 troops, began leaving its winter camps. Hooker and his senior generals had been planning a spring offensive for weeks. With accurate estimates of Lee's strength, the Federal commanders settled upon a flanking movement up the Rappahannock, similar to Burnside's January debacle. This time, however, Hooker would pass farther upriver with a three-corps column to Kelly's Ford, cross there, and then over the Rapidan River, well beyond and around the Confederate left flank and rear. Downstream, two corps would join the column, crossing at Banks's and United States fords, while the final two corps demonstrated against Lee's right at Fredericksburg. If the Yankees could steal some marches on the Rebels, Lee would either have to give battle against a superior opponent on his flank or abandon the Rappahannock line.[49]

Across the river from Fredericksburg, Hooker left behind the First and Sixth corps, commanded by Major Generals John Reynolds and John Sedgwick, respectively. The Fourth Brigade, First Division of the First Corps, wearing the badge of a red disc on their hats, was Solomon Meredith's Westerners. They had been ready for weeks, as one of them put it, "to go down, and whisper a kind word in the rebs ears." The winter's sickness had abated, and the afflicted men had returned to the ranks. Deserters and those charged with cowardice at Fredericksburg and during the Mud March had been publicly humiliated and dishonorably discharged from the brigade, or in a private's words, it was "disposing of its cowards pretty fast." There was now a tempered hardness to the men of the Iron Brigade, and as they prepared for a renewal of what Colonel Lucius Fairchild called "this holy war," the army needed hard men.[50]

New men stood at the head of some of the Western regiments. In Meredith's former regiment, the Nineteenth Indiana, a majority of officers and men had endorsed Lieutenant Colonel Samuel Williams and Major William Dudley for promotion. Governor Oliver Morton preferred Captain Luther E. Wilson of Company E for the colonelcy, but Meredith wrote to his political ally "that it will not do to appoint Capt. Wilson colonel of the 19th." The governor heeded the advice, and Williams and Dudley were appointed, to rank from October 7, 1862.[51]

A "big-hearted man with a loud laugh," Williams had been a cattle breeder from Selma, and the former captain of Company K. Like Williams, Dudley had organized a company in 1861, and served as its original captain until appointed major after Antietam. Only twenty years old, Dudley was a member of a distinguished New England family who had relocated to Indiana less than a year before the war.[52]

Lieutenant Colonel Edward Bragg ascended to the colonelcy of the Sixth Wisconsin when Lysander Cutler, who had held the post since the regiment's organization, was promoted to brigadier general. The relationship between the two officers had always been strained. Both men possessed inordinate ambition, and frequently in his letters to his wife, Bragg grumbled about Cutler and his handling of the regiment. Bragg merited promotion as he had demonstrated at Second Manassas and Antietam, leading the unit because of Cutler's wounding at Brawner's Farm. To his wife in January, the Fond du Lac man boasted that he and the troops were connected to each other with "coils of steel." In his estimation, the Sixth was "the best Regiment in Uncle Sam's service" and its reputation "is dear to me."[53]

Major Rufus Dawes, perhaps the Sixth's finest officer, replaced Bragg as lieutenant colonel. Unlike Cutler and Bragg, Dawes seemed to keep a check on his ambition, but he complained often in letters home about his superiors. Dawes's successor as major was forty-five-year-old John F. Hauser, captain of Company H. A native of Germany and a soldier by trade, Hauser was, in Dawes's view, "a character," who possessed, however, a "commanding figure" and a "voice like a trumpet." He was also renowned throughout the regiment for his difficulties with the English language.[54]

In the other three regiments, colonels Lucius Fairchild, William Robinson, and Henry Morrow continued in command. Fairchild's Second Wisconsin and Robinson's Seventh Wisconsin both lost their lieutenant colonels, one to promotion in another regiment and the other to resignation. Lieutenant Colonel Charles Hamilton of the Seventh had tried to serve, but his Brawner's Farm wound would not heal, and he resigned. The grandson of Alexander Hamilton, he had been a popular officer with the rank and file and had honored his lineage as a soldier.[55]

A year's gleaning had brought these officers into their current positions, and now as Fighting Joe Hooker marched the army toward the Rappahannock's fords, the Westerners knew that another harvest waited. Orders for an advance came to the Iron Brigade and the units of the First Corps on the morning of April 28. Before Meredith's troops left their camp, division commander Brigadier General James Wadsworth dispatched the Sixth and Seventh Wisconsin with loaded rifles to quell a mutiny in the Twenty-fourth New York. The New Yorkers claimed that their two-year term of enlistment dated from when they signed their papers, not from their acceptance into Federal service. They had no intention of fighting Rebels beyond their term and refused to march. Backed by the black-hatted veterans, Wadsworth convinced them to pick up their arms and rejoin their comrades.[56]

Shortly after noon, the Iron Brigade marched toward the river below Fredericksburg. Hooker wanted the First and Sixth corps to make a lodgment on the river's southern bank and to threaten the Confederate right flank. Sedgwick's divisions had orders to lay pontoon bridges two miles below the town at Franklin's Crossing, where the Yankees had crossed in December. Farther downstream, Reynolds's troops were to force a passage at Fitzhugh's Crossing. Both commands were to construct the bridges at first light on the 29th.[57]

The Federals moved to within a mile or so of the stream on the 28th, and then bivouacked. Sometime during the day, Rufus Dawes took time to write to Mary Beman Gates, his future wife, who lived in Marietta, Ohio. "We are advancing upon the enemy," Dawes began. "I doubt not that we must have a bloody, desperate battle. I leave this where I have perfect confidence it will be sent to you in case I am killed, and only in that event." Assuring her of his love, he concluded, "I dont believe you will ever think lightly of the love of a man, who if he had few other merits, gave his life freely for his country and the *right*."[58]

With the pontoons, Wadsworth's troops filed toward the river before midnight of the 29th. Halting short of the stream, the men lay down until dawn. With the morning's light, engineers and a gang of freedmen, assisted by members of the Twenty-second New York, rushed down the slope to the river's edge. From the opposite bank, Confederate skirmishers opened fire, causing a "panic" among the bridge builders, who fled precipitately toward shelter. Wadsworth hurried forward the Fourteenth Brooklyn to dislodge the enemy, and then added the Sixth Wisconsin to the action. The Wisconsinites took cover behind a stone wall and began shooting while Union artillery crews to the rear shelled the southern bank.[59]

The tenacity of the Rebels stalled the operation for hours, until about nine o'clock, when Wadsworth ordered the Sixth Wisconsin and Twenty-fourth Michigan to load into the boats and paddle across the water. Colonels Bragg and Morrow explained the situation to their men, direct-ing each company to man two boats. Bragg tried to reassure his troops by reminding them of the Westerners' renowned skill as oarsmen. One of the listeners was not so sure, writing later that "I confess I never saw anything that appeared so much like certain death as this movement did."[60]

The men removed knapsacks, haversacks, and canteens before officers aligned them four abreast in each column. Bragg and Morrow stepped to the front and signaled them forward. "With yells like demons or some-thing else," the Westerners plunged down the slope to the river. The Southern rifle pits on a hill exploded, and the bullets came "flying like hail stones." At the riverbank, a "scene of wild excitement" ensued as the Fed-erals piled into the boats. Some men grabbed oars; others returned the fire. In one vessel, a soldier shouted, "The first man up the bank shall be a Gen-eral." Dawes bragged two days later that "it was the finest regatta ever ran in this country."[61]

The Yankees crossed "so quick" that few were hit by enemy fire, al-though Lieutenant Colonel Mark Flanigan of the Twenty-fourth counted afterward ten holes in his coat. When they reached the opposite bank, they spilled from the boats into waist-deep water. Rufus Dawes, carrying the Sixth's national flag, was the second man on the riverbank. Officers shouted for the men to charge, and the Westerners raced up the hillside, routing the Southerners and capturing about two hundred of them. "It was the most brilliant and exciting affair I ever seen," exclaimed an on-looker in the Seventh Wisconsin.[62]

Behind the cheering troops in the enemy rifle pits, the crews resumed the construction of the bridge. By noon, they had finished the task. When Wadsworth crossed, he joined the attackers and thanked them for their performance. By nightfall, Hooker had his lodgment on the Fredericks-burg side of the river. Rain began to fall after midnight as the Federals slept.[63]

Confederate artillerists welcomed the Yankees on the morning of April 30. The Federals dug fieldworks and huddled in them as the enemy gun crews fired sporadically throughout the day. The Rebels ceased their fire during May 1. Late in the day, the opponents heard the low rumble of distant cannonading from the west. Early the next day, Southern gunners resumed the bombardment. At mid-morning, however, Wadsworth's division filed out of the works and recrossed the river. John Reynolds's entire First Corps had been ordered upstream to Hooker's main force. An Iron Brigade member estimated later that they marched thirteen miles, before halting short of United States Ford. As they pitched camp, the sounds of battle, heavier than the day before, rolled toward them from beyond the Rappahannock.[64]

Locals called it the Wilderness, a forsaken swath of Virginia that sprawled across roughly seventy square miles of countryside north and west of Fredericksburg. For decades residents had felled its trees for charcoal to fuel iron furnaces and foundries. Stunted stands of scrub oak, pine, cedar, and hickory choked the land, while dense snarls of undergrowth grew beneath the branches.[65]

Few dwellings and clearings broke up the thickets. Most houses were along Orange Turnpike and Orange Plank Road, the two main roads that passed through the region, connecting Fredericksburg to the Virginia Piedmont. The Turnpike and Plank Road joined at Chancellorsville, a seventy-acre clearing where the Chancellor family's large brick house sat near the intersection with Ely's Ford Road. A handful of small farms, a tavern, and a church dotted the landscape. Small streams or runs, dignified with names, coursed though the Wilderness, creating ravines, bogs, and gnarled ground. It was a difficult place for men to earn a living, an awful place for men to fight a battle. But here on May 1, 1863, Joseph Hooker and the bulk of the Army of the Potomac found themselves.[66]

For four days the Union offensive unfolded as well as Hooker had planned it. He had outflanked the Confederates, seized the initiative from his opponent, Robert E. Lee, and brought five corps to or near Chancellorsville. Hooker's intelligence network had kept him informed of Lee's numbers and dispositions. With another day's march on May 1, he expected to clear the Wilderness into open terrain, where his superior numbers and artillery could be decisive. He also expected the combative Lee to give battle.[67]

Lee excelled at the interpretation of conflicting information, but it was not until the afternoon of April 30 that he told a staff officer "the main attack will come from above" or from the Chancellorsville area. To meet the threat, Lee had to divide his outnumbered army. As he explained to Richmond, "I determined to hold our lines in rear of Fredericksburg with part of the force and endeavor with the rest to drive the enemy back to the Rapidan." Late in the day, orders went to subordinates for the troops to cook two days' rations and for the wagons to be sent to the rear. Lee would meet Hooker with four fifths of his army, leaving only Jubal Early's division and an additional brigade to watch the Yankees at Fredericksburg. It was a bold gamble even for the audacious Confederate commander.[68]

Lee and Stonewall Jackson rode at the head of three divisions of the Second Corps on the morning of May 1, following Orange Turnpike west toward the Wilderness. Among the marchers were Frank Paxton's Stonewall Brigade. During the previous night, the Valley men had been serenaded by the brigade band with such favorite songs as "Annie Laurie" and "The Swallows Are Homeward Flying." To an officer on Jackson's staff, "the Old Brigade is a noble set of men." A morning's fog soon gave way to a splendid spring day in Virginia.[69]

About 8:30 A.M., riding ahead of his troops, Jackson reined up at Zoan Church, four miles east of Chancellorsville, where the divisions of Richard Anderson and Lafayette McLaws of the First Corps were deployed. The corps's other two divisions were in southeastern Virginia with corps commander Longstreet, gathering supplies. Although Lee had alerted Longstreet to Hooker's advance, the troops could not rejoin the army in time.[70]

Jackson took two hours to familiarize himself with the terrain and to prepare for an advance. At 10:30 A.M., the Confederates stepped off, covering the Turnpike and Orange Plank Road, which diverged east of Chancellorsville before combining again at Chancellorsville. Jackson pressed the action, and when Hooker learned that he confronted two divisions, backed by Jackson's troops, the Union commander ordered a withdrawal into the Wilderness. Although he assured a subordinate that "I have got Lee just where I want him; he must fight me on my own ground," Hooker had relinquished the tactical initiative to a dangerous, aggressive foe.[71]

Lee seized the opportunity. Establishing headquarters at the intersection of Plank Road and Catharine Furnace Road later in the day, Lee conferred with Jackson at dusk. The Chancellor house lay a mile to the northwest, its clearing ringed by the Federals. The pair of generals studied a map and discussed options until Jeb Stuart rode up and joined them. The cavalryman reported that Hooker's right flank along the Turnpike, west of Chancellorsville, dangled, unanchored by any terrain feature. Lee pored over the map again and before long proposed a wide, sweeping march around the Union army. Jackson, said Lee, would execute it, but the details could be left until the next morning. In a clearing amid pine trees, Lee and Jackson lay down for a few hours of sleep.[72]

Jackson rose well before dawn on May 2, and walked to a campfire for warmth in the morning chill. He awakened aides, sending them for more information about roads and a guide. After some time, Lee joined him by the fire, where they discussed the march while sitting on cracker boxes. When Lee asked how many troops Jackson would take with him, the subordinate answered his three infantry divisions and artillery—28,000 men—leaving Lee with Anderson's and McLaws's divisions of 14,000 troops. "Well," said Lee, "go on."[73]

The soldiers started at 7:30 A.M., down Catharine Furnace Road. The march demanded secrecy and celerity, but within an hour Federal troops sighted the column, sending a few artillery rounds toward the Rebels. When the intelligence reached Union headquarters, Hooker concluded that Lee was in retreat. Late in the morning, a blue-clad unit clashed with a Georgia regiment near the furnace, but did not halt the movement. A member of the Stonewall Brigade described the ordeal in a letter a week later: "it was through brushes swamps and hills we marched in the heat of the day I thought that he [Jackson] would kill all of us before we would get to the enemy. Men laid by the bushey rode side." At the junction of Plank Road and Germanna Ford Road, Paxton's Virginians filed out of the column and moved east on Plank Road to guard the crossroads.[74]

It was not until late afternoon before the column turned east on Orange Turnpike, proceeded a mile to a low, wooded ridge, and halted. More time was consumed in aligning the brigades into a battle line, which would, when completed, stretch for a mile on both sides of the turnpike. Less than a half mile to the east, the unsuspecting Yankees were preparing evening meals. When Major General Robert Rodes, whose division manned the front line, told Jackson he was ready, the corps commander said: "You can go forward, then." Officers scurried to relay the attack orders, and within minutes, bugles blared. An acoustical shadow deadened the sound to the east.[75]

The Confederates swept forward through the forest in one of the great infantry assaults of the war. The stunned Northerners fled in an initial panic, but as the attackers drove ahead, blue-clad troops rallied and fought. The Rebels overlapped the islands of resistance, wrecking one enemy unit after another. As darkness ended the assault, Hooker's right flank had been crushed. Southern officers worked to untangle the regiments and brigades in the blackness. Jackson, A. P. Hill, and a coterie of staff officers and couriers rode beyond their lines to reconnoiter. Clusters of opposing troops still fired at each other. When Jackson's party turned to reenter their lines, some Federals stumbled toward the Confederates, and suddenly musketry flashed along the front of a North Carolina brigade. Jackson reeled in the saddle, struck by three bullets. The volley also wounded three aides and killed four other members of the party.[76]

A pair of aides assisted Jackson from his mount, and Hill soon joined them, their past differences forgotten with the tragedy. They managed to get Jackson to Plank Road, where a litter party met them. The bearers carried the wounded general to an ambulance, which bore him four miles west to the Second Corps field hospital in a field near Wilderness Tavern. Here, in the morning hours of May 3, a team of surgeons amputated Jackson's left arm near the shoulder.[77]

Like the other Confederate troops, the Stonewall Brigade learned of their old commander's fall during the night. The Virginians had been on the right flank of the attack force, astride the Plank Road, and were not engaged in the combat. In the nighttime confusion, they were shifted twice, finally bedding down with their right on the roadbed. A brigade staff officer never forgot "the disturbing cry of the whip-poor-will" that long night in the Wilderness.[78]

Frank Paxton was leaning against a tree, reading his Bible, when orders came to advance at 6:30 A.M. on May 3. Before his promotion to brigade command, Paxton had been, in the words of a staff officer, "a rather profane and godless man." Since then he had had a religious conversion and was "a new man." He read the scriptures often and kept his Bible in a pocket. During the night of May 2–3, Paxton expressed to a staff member his conviction that he would be killed during the next day's combat. When he arose on the 3rd, he prepared himself for that eventuality.[79]

The Stonewall Brigade and the other units of Brigadier General Raleigh E. Colston's division formed the second line of the Second Corps. Ahead of them, Hill's six brigades had advanced at first light against Federal log

fieldworks that extended on both sides of Plank Road. Lee had ordered
the assault to maintain the tactical initiative. On this morning, the flam-
boyant Stuart commanded the infantry of Jackson's corps. Lee had selected the cavalry officer when Hill suffered a wound during the confusion
and firing after Jackson's fall. Senior brigadier Henry Heth led Hill's division.[80]

Heth's troops ran into a cauldron of Union resistance. Charge and
countercharge marked the struggle as the Rebels seized the works only to
be repulsed. The casualties were fearful on both sides. By the time Colston's division entered the fighting, some of Heth's units had retired to log
breastworks farther west. Colston was inexperienced, and his advance
was disjointed and slow. The Stonewall Brigade had been shifted to south
of Plank Road, and reaching the first line of works, found a brigade of
South Carolinians of "whom fear had taken the most absolute possession," reported Colonel John Funk of the Second Virginia. The Valley men
passed over the huddled troops, "saying, with not very pleasant levity,"
remembered a South Carolinian, "that they could show us how to clear
away a Federal line."[81]

Paxton adjusted the line after the regiments cleared the works. On their
right, Colonel Thomas Garnett's brigade formed. Color-bearers stepped
to the front, and the Confederates advanced through the woods. Waiting
for them behind the second line of works were five Union regiments of
Brigadier General Thomas Ruger's Twelfth Corps brigade. When the
Southerners closed to within seventy yards, the Yankees blasted them with
"a terrible volley." The attackers responded, and both sides gripped the
fury as if it were a precious thing.[82]

"It seemed as if nothing but the hand of God could save a man," exclaimed Captain John Welsh of the Twenty-seventh Virginia. Welsh's commander, Colonel James Edmondson, mounted on a horse, was knocked to
the ground by a piece of a shell that mangled his left arm. Later that day, a
surgeon amputated the limb with a penknife. Ordnance Sergeant William
Scanlon, who had served in the Mexican War and was described as a
"good soldier," was killed. In the Fifth Virginia, Private Andrew Long
held the head of his brother, Frank, in his lap until he died. "This only in-
terrupted my fighting a few minutes," Andrew wrote.[83]

The Second Virginia held the brigade's right. In the smoke and roar of
gunfire, the regiment drifted farther right, creating a gap between itself
and the Fourth Virginia. Federal reinforcements raked the Fourth's flank,

forcing back the Virginians. Paxton's entire line began to become un-hinged, and the brigade withdrew under a punishing fire. A private admit-ted that "how I made the escape without being hurt I cannot say." Paxton was standing among the men when a bullet sliced through his left arm into his heart. Falling to the ground, the brigadier gasped to an aide, "Tie up my arm," and died.[84]

The Valley men halted and re-formed at the first line of works, where Colonel Funk assumed command of the brigade. Here they remained as the third Confederate line of battle, Major General Robert Rodes's divi-sion, entered the combat. Later, a brigadier, Stephen Dodson Ramseur, claimed that his North Carolinians passed over troops, including the Stonewall Brigade, who refused to advance. When the Virginians heard of Ramseur's assertion, they vigorously disputed it. Colonel Funk wrote to Ramseur a week later. Funk argued that no troops passed over his men, and it would appear that the evidence supported the Virginians.[85]

Before long, ironically, Stuart ordered Funk to move to Ramseur's sup-port. The Virginians scrambled over the logs, charging toward the second line of fieldworks. Union resistance was fierce for several minutes, but the Confederates seized the breastworks. A private stated that "men fell on both sides of me and if it had not been that God was with me I believe I'd fell too." Another private declared, however, that "I became unconscious of danger," while a lieutenant contended that "nothing but the love of one's country would cause men to undergo what we have done." Casual-ties in the brigade approached one third of its numbers.[86]

Ramseur's assault had created a breach in the Union lines; the attack of the Stonewall Brigade secured the North Carolinians' flank. Other Con-federate units widened the breach and swarmed over Fairview, a plateau that overlooked Chancellorsville. Behind them, Southern gunners hurried cannon on to Hazel Grove, an elevation that dominated the field, and un-leashed their rounds. By ten o'clock, Anderson's brigades had linked up with Stuart's on Fairview, uniting the two wings of Lee's army. The attack-ers stormed off the heights into the clearing around the Chancellor house. The triumph, according to a historian, "was the greatest moment Robert E. Lee had experienced in his military life."[87]

For two more days the Federals clung to their lines north of Chancel-lorsville. John Sedgwick lumbered out of Fredericksburg after swatting aside Jubal Early's Confederates, but Lee met this threat on the afternoon of the 3rd, at Salem Church, and again the next day. Lee contemplated an assault on the main enemy force during the 5th, but a rainstorm post-poned it until the next morning. When the Rebels probed forward on May 6, however, they discovered empty Union works. The Yankees had re-treated during the night.[88]

Among the Federals who filed across pontoons at United States Ford were the Westerners of the Iron Brigade. Since their arrival on the field around Chancellorsville, they had held a section of the works on the army's right, subjected only to artillery fire from the enemy. "It is almost incredible," noted a Wisconsin soldier, "that we who had been engaged in the battle knew almost nothing of it." They received a whiskey ration on the 5th, which enlivened their morale. Orders came later that day for the withdrawal, prompting Rufus Dawes to note in his journal, "We cannot understand it in any other way than as a great disaster." The campaign had cost them eleven killed, forty-five wounded, and three missing, all of which had been incurred at Fitzhugh's Crossing.[89]

Once across the river, the Wisconsin, Indiana, and Michigan troops slogged through mud toward their camps. A member of Horace Berdan's renowned Sharpshooters watched them file by and later recorded the scene:

> As the great Western or Iron Brigade passed, looking like giants with their tall black hats, they were greeted with hearty cheers. . . . And giants they were, in action. . . . I look back and see that famed body of troops marching up that long muddy hill unmindful of the pouring rain, but full of life and spirit, with steady step, filling the entire roadway, their big black hats and feathers conspicuous.[90]

The victory at Chancellorsville had cost Lee about thirteen thousand offi-cers and men, nearly one fifth of his army. Hooker's losses exceeded seven-teen thousand, although the Federals fought primarily a defensive battle. In the Stonewall Brigade, the toll amounted to 55 killed, 430 wounded, and 9 missing, an even higher proportion than for the army as a whole. The Valley men had lost another brigade commander, Frank Paxton, and another regimental commander, the Twenty-seventh's James Edmondson, whose amputation ended his service. Lieutenant Colonel Hazael Williams of the Fifth summarized well his regiment's performance and that of the other four units when he wrote in his report: "Never did our brave men behave with more gallantry, coolness, and deliberation than on this occasion." A lieutenant in Edmondson's command put it more simply: "Braver men cannot live."[91]

To the Virginians and to the entire army, the gravest casualty was Stonewall Jackson. After the amputation of his arm, the general was transported to Guiney Station to the nearby home of Thomas Coleman Chandler. Placed in the estate's small office near the mansion, he appeared to be recovering well. He asked for details of the battle, and when a surgeon mentioned his old brigade, Jackson stated: "The men of that command will be proud one day to say to their children: 'I was one of the Stonewall Brigade.' I have no right to the name 'Stonewall.' It belongs to the brigade and not at all to me."[92]

Anna Jackson, with their daughter, joined her husband at his bedside on May 7. By then, however, he was weakening. That morning he had awakened with a severe pain in his side. Dr. Hunter McGuire, his friend and surgeon, prescribed treatment for pneumonia. But McGuire's efforts could not stay the illness that was drowning the warrior's lungs. By Sunday, May 10, the soldier no longer had the strength to stay the darkness. With Anna at his side, he fought the unseen enemy. Delirium returned him to battlefields as he called out orders to subordinates. Finally, in the afternoon, Jackson said, "Let us cross over the river and rest under the shade of the trees." Then, he died.[93]

12

+

"THIS CURSED WAR"

THE news of Stonewall Jackson's death reached the Shenandoah Valley on Monday, May 11, 1863. In Staunton, a diarist recorded the reaction: "There is universal lamentation in this community. It is like the mourning in the 'Valley of Megiddon,' when King Josiah was slain." Down the Valley, in Winchester, Cornelia McDonald turned to her diary: "The shadows are darkening around us in the devoted town. . . . No loss could be felt as his will be." In Jackson's adopted hometown, Lexington, the residents mourned and prepared to welcome him back to where he belonged.[1]

On the day the Valley learned of the loss, Jackson's remains were placed on a train for the journey to Richmond, where the body would lie in state in the Capitol until May 13. The Stonewall Brigade petitioned Robert E. Lee to serve as official escort. Lee, who had confided to his son that "I do not know how to replace him," denied the request in a letter to the command. The Virginians could not be spared at this time, wrote Lee, because he expected another movement by the enemy. He would allow a detail from each regiment to march with the remains from the Chandler house to the railroad at Guiney Station. More than that he could not permit. "I can fully appreciate the feelings of the members of the Brigade," Lee assured them. "They have reason to be proud of him, as he was proud of them. To the tried men of the Brigade, he was not only a General but a friend. They have been with him and true to him from the beginning of the war."[2]

Unfortunately for the Virginians, the detail arrived at the station an hour after the train with the coffin had departed for Richmond. Several brigade members somehow arranged another ride into the city and marched in the procession that took the general's remains from the governor's mansion to the Capitol. The next day, a train bore the casket, Anna Jackson, the general's staff officers, and dignitaries to Lynchburg, where on the 14th a packet boat finished the journey on the James River Canal. At Lexington, cadets from the Virginia Military Institute took the body from the boat and placed it in Jackson's former lecture room at the school.[3]

Valley residents came forth on Friday, May 15, to honor and to bury the Confederacy's most famous warrior and one of their own, who had come to live among them a dozen years before. A long procession of VMI cadets, veterans of the Stonewall Brigade who were at home, carrying the original flag of the Liberty Hall Volunteers, cavalry companies, military officers, government officials, friends, and family joined the general on his final march. Early in the afternoon, under a pine tree in the Lexington town cemetery, Jackson was buried. He was laid to rest beside his and Anna's first child and near his first wife, Elinor Junkin Jackson, and their stillborn son. Not far away, close enough for a general to shout orders to a subordinate, lay Frank Paxton, a fellow commander of the Stonewall Brigade, who had been interred three days earlier.[4]

At Fredericksburg, on May 16, the officers and men of the Stonewall Brigade adopted a set of resolutions that praised their old commander and "resolved . . . that in accordance with General Jackson's wish and the desire of this brigade to honor its first great commander, the Secretary of War be requested to order that it be known and designated as the 'Stonewall Brigade.'" All of the regimental commanders signed the document and forwarded it to Richmond. President Jefferson Davis and Secretary of War James Seddon approved it, and on May 30, Special Orders No. 129 announced it officially. The Virginians noted in the resolutions, "we will strive to render ourselves more worthy of it, by emulating his virtues, and like him, devote all our energies to the great work before us of securing to our beloved country the blessings of peace and independence."[5]

The War Department, meanwhile, had promoted Colonel James Walker to brigadier general and assigned him to command of the Stonewall Brigade, filling the post left vacant by Paxton's death at Chancellorsville. Lee had recommended the appointment of Walker, who had served formerly in the brigade. Walker joined his old comrades within days of Jackson's funeral.[6]

Thirty years old, Walker was a native of the Valley, born on a farm near Mt. Sidney in Augusta County. He had attended VMI until expelled three weeks before graduation in 1852, when he challenged an instructor, Thomas J. Jackson, to a duel after a classroom argument. Following his expulsion, Walker studied law at the University of Virginia and then opened a practice in Pulaski County. When the war began, he was elected captain of the Pulaski Guards, which became Company C, Fourth Virginia. He served with the company less than a month before obtaining the lieutenant colonelcy of the Thirteenth Virginia. His conduct and fearlessness on the battlefield earned him accolades from superiors and the nickname "Old Bull Dog" from his troops.[7]

As his sobriquet suggests, Walker was a gruff-mannered, pugnacious man. A staff member who came to know the general described him as "bold in battle and everywhere else." Although his demeanor appeared to be rough-hewn, a quality that endeared him to enlisted men, Walker was regarded as "an accomplished gentleman and gallant officer," who possessed "fight in his eyes." Another staff officer called him simply "that doughty man and soldier."[8]

Walker's appointment, however, caused another outburst of protest from the brigade. Despite his origins and brief association with the command, the officers and men did not want him. When the Virginians learned of his assignment to the brigade, the five regimental commanders tendered their resignations, asserting that only Jackson's chief of staff, Sandie Pendleton, or one of three of themselves—most likely Colonel John Nadenbousch, Colonel John Funk, or Major William Terry—would be acceptable. When Lee received their letters, he rejected the resignations. But like Charles Winder, Walker encountered an icy reception when he joined the brigade.[9]

Walker was but one of several officers who were promoted and reassigned in a major overhaul of the Army of Northern Virginia during the weeks after Chancellorsville. For months Lee had been deliberating a reorganization of the army. Jackson's death on May 10 convinced the commander that the time had come. On the 20th, Lee explained his decision to Jefferson Davis: "I have for the past year felt that the corps of this army were too large for one commander. Nothing prevented my proposing to you to reduce their size and increase their number but my inability to recommend commanders." Each of the two corps contained approximately thirty thousand troops, and "these are more than one man can properly handle and keep under his eye in battle in the country that we have to operate in. They are always beyond the range of his vision, and frequently beyond his reach."[10]

While Lee had James Longstreet at the head of the First Corps, he knew that no one could handle the Second Corps as Jackson had done. Consequently, Lee proposed the creation of a third corps and recommended Richard Ewell and A. P. Hill as corps commanders. Ewell would succeed Jackson, and Hill would get the new Third Corps. Both men were Virginians, and both of them had been fine divisional commanders. Ewell, however, had been away from the army for nine months, recovering from his wound at Brawner's Farm, which necessitated the amputation of his left leg. Questions about the capabilities of each man for higher command and more responsibility would linger until they were tested.[11]

The creation of a new corps necessitated a reshuffling of divisions and brigades. Hill received a division from Longstreet, and his own so-called Light Division was divided and brigades added to form two divisions. Ewell retained three divisions from Jackson's old corps, with Jubal Early, Robert Rodes, and Edward Johnson as commanders. The forty-seven-year-old Johnson replaced Raleigh Colston at the head of the Stonewall Division to which the Stonewall Brigade belonged. A West Pointer and Virginian, Johnson had been convalescing from a wound suffered at McDowell in May 1862, and like Ewell, returned to the army upon his promotion. Known throughout the army as "Allegheny" Johnson, he had been a solid brigade commander and redoubtable fighter.[12]

Lee completed the reorganization of the army as plans for a second offensive beyond the Potomac River matured. The victory at Chancellorsville gave Lee the strategic initiative in Virginia. He decided, once again, to seize it. On May 14, the commanding general traveled to Richmond, where he conferred with Davis and cabinet officials until the 18th. Lee argued before the civilian authorities that an invasion of Union soil would garner a harvest of supplies, bring relief from the war's ravages to the Old Dominion for weeks, and disrupt his opponent's plans for the summer. The proposal for an offensive generated debate, with one cabinet member opposing the idea. In the end, Lee had the approval of Davis and five department heads.[13]

Returning to Fredericksburg on the 18th, Lee spent the next fortnight finalizing the details for the movement. On June 3, while Hill's Third Corps held the works along the Rappahannock, Longstreet's and Ewell's divisions began the march that would carry the Rebels beyond the Potomac. Except for the leadership void created by Jackson's death, Lee perhaps never commanded a finer, more powerful weapon. A few weeks earlier, he had declared in a letter that "the country cannot overestimate its [the army's] worth. There were never such men in any army before & never can be again. If properly led they will go anywhere & never fail at the work before them."[14]

By June 8, units of the two corps had reached Culpeper Court House, where Lee halted them in a brief pause. Ahead of them towered the Blue Ridge—"to look at them when the sky is clear is a beautiful sight never to be forgotten," exclaimed a Confederate. When the Valley men of the Stonewall Brigade saw the mountains for the first time since the previous November, they cheered. On the 9th, Union cavalry crossed the Rappahannock, clashing with Jeb Stuart's horsemen at Brandy Station, a few miles east of Culpeper. The Southerners repulsed the attackers in some fierce mounted fighting, with the Yankees unable to confirm the presence of enemy infantry in the region.[15]

The engagement at Brandy Station delayed the resumption of the northward movement for only a day. On June 10, Jackson's old foot cavalry, with Ewell at the head, resumed the march, heading for the Blue Ridge and the Shenandoah Valley beyond. The Second Corps crossed the mountains two days later. When the Stonewall Brigade entered Front Royal, the members shifted from route step to "close order, march," as their band played music. It was a homecoming, and the Virginians responded as if on review.[16]

The Confederates' target in the Valley was a seven-thousand-man Union force at Winchester, under Major General Robert H. Milroy, who had been discounting the warnings of the approaching storm. On June 13, Ewell closed on the Federals, sending Rodes's division north toward Charlestown and Early's and Johnson's units toward Winchester. While Early marched west to the Valley Pike to approach the town from the south, Johnson followed Front Royal Road, coming in from the southeast.

The Stonewall Brigade led Johnson's division, with the Second Virginia skirmishing with enemy troops. Although supported by batteries, the Virginians' advance stalled before Milroy's cannon. By nightfall, Early had shoved troops beyond Kernstown, near Winchester's southern outskirts. Milroy, however, refused to abandon the town.[17]

On the morning of June 14, from a hill south of Winchester, Ewell and Early plotted the end of Milroy's hold on the town. While one brigade demonstrated against the Yankees from the eminence, Early would take three brigades and batteries and march west by a concealed route to assault West Fort, situated on a rise north and west of Winchester. Johnson's troops, meanwhile, would press forward from the east, engaging enemy skirmishers until Early launched the attack. The tactics were similar to those used by Jackson at First Winchester in May 1862.[18]

Early's circuitous march took several hours to complete. During the late morning and early afternoon, Ewell's other units engaged the enemy with skirmishers and artillery along Winchester's southern and eastern edges. Johnson assigned the duty to the Stonewall Brigade, whose regiments advanced between the Millwood and Berryville roads. The Fifth Virginia manned the skirmish line five hundred yards in front of their comrades. Occupying a house along the Berryville road, the Fifth's members became ensnared in a nasty engagement with the Eighteenth Connecticut. The Yankees charged the house, routing the Virginians and capturing ten of them. In the action, the Fifth's Lieutenant Colonel Hazael Williams fell with a severe wound in a thigh. The Virginians rallied and shoved back the Federals into a local cemetery.[19]

Finally, at four o'clock, Early's troops attacked West Fort. Richard Taylor's old command of Louisianans, who had spearheaded Jackson's assaults at First Winchester and Port Republic, led the charge, overwhelming the fort's defenders. Milroy's troops, however, maintained their hold on two other forts, backed by Union batteries. At nine o'clock, as darkness smothered the day, Milroy ordered a retreat north to Harper's Ferry. It required three hours for the Northerners to form ranks, and shortly after midnight the column disappeared into the night.[20]

Ewell had anticipated the possibility of a retreat, and as Milroy ordered a withdrawal, the Confederate commander directed Johnson to march north and seal the route beyond the town. Allegheny Johnson started at once with two brigades and eight cannon, leaving one brigade east of Winchester and sent instructions to Walker to follow with the Stonewall

Brigade. The Rebels stumbled across the countryside through the early morning hours but were posted two hundred yards east of the Valley Pike near Stephenson's Depot before dawn. When Johnson discovered the Union column on the road, he ordered his troops to open fire.[21]

The explosion of musketry and artillery fire in the darkness stunned the Federals. Blue-coated officers tried to restore order, but many of the men fled to the north and west. Ohio troops rallied and attacked the Southerners, who held a ridge behind a railroad track. A narrow stone bridge spanned the rails, and on it the Rebels had placed two cannon. Three times the Northerners drove for the pair of guns, and three times were repulsed. Canister tore into the attackers' ranks, blasting them apart.[22]

The Stonewall Brigade arrived, and the Second and Fifth Virginia crossed the tracks north of the bridge, pushing ahead to the pike. In the Union rear, teamsters panicked in a stampede of wagons and teams. Hundreds of Federals surrendered as the Rebels swarmed among them. Walker's Virginians bagged nearly eight hundred men and three flags. The Southerners captured more than three thousand prisoners, twenty-three cannon, hundreds of wagons, and piles of quartermaster and commissary stores. At a loss of less than three hundred, Ewell achieved a victory that exceeded Jackson's a year before.[23]

The Confederates spent the 15th and 16th gathering up the spoils and herding away the prisoners. Rodes's infantrymen and Southern horsemen, meanwhile, had forded the Potomac and entered Maryland. Ewell followed on the 17th. Within a few days, the entire Second Corps occupied western Maryland, with advanced contingents roaming into southern Pennsylvania. Behind them, their comrades in the First and Third corps were descending into the Valley. Jeb Stuart's troopers had shielded the movement by holding the gaps of the Blue Ridge against sorties by Union cavalrymen. On June 25, Longstreet's and Hill's units began the fording of the Potomac as Ewell's men, like a stain in gray and butternut, roamed across southern Pennsylvania. The Rebels found the Keystone State a rich larder of foodstuffs. A Stonewall Brigade member wrote that the civilians "treated us very kindly but I think it was only from the teeth out."[24]

Lee entered Chambersburg, Pennsylvania, on Saturday, June 27, accompanied by Longstreet, their staffs, and thousands of troops. The two generals pitched their headquarters tent outside the strongly pro-Union town in a grove of trees used by locals as a picnic area, and here they would stay until the 30th. The Confederate offensive had proceeded well, except for the lack of information about the movements of the Union Army of the Potomac. Lee's cavalry commander, Jeb Stuart, and three brigades had separated from the army while in Virginia, undertaking a ride around the Federal units, and had disappeared seemingly from the campaign. It was not until late on the night of the 28th that Lee learned from one of Longstreet's spies, an actor named Henry Harrison, that the entire enemy army was in Maryland. Confronted with the prospects of his scattered divisions being overtaken by the Northerners, Lee ordered a concentration, contingent upon Federal movements, either at Cashtown or at Gettysburg, east of Chambersburg and South Mountain.[25]

Ewell's Second Corps, meanwhile, had carried the vanguard of the Confederate invasion to the Susquehanna River below Harrisburg, the state capital. Early's division led the march east, occupying York, where the general obtained $28,000 as a levy upon its residents, but failed to se-cure a covered railroad bridge across the river at Wrightsville when militia troops burned the structure. Rodes's brigades and cavalry had moved upon the capital, the horsemen skirmishing with local defense troops. Throughout the marches, the Rebels cleaned the countryside of supplies and livestock. When Lee countermanded the movement, Ewell recalled his troops. By nightfall of June 30, Rodes and Early were within three miles of each other, bivouacked near Heidlersburg, about ten miles north of Get-tysburg. Johnson and the Stonewall Division were camped near Scotland, a few miles northeast of Chambersburg.[26]

South and west of Ewell's campsites, the fires of Longstreet's and Hill's troops glowed along Chambersburg Pike on both sides of South Moun-tain. Farther south in Maryland, blue-clad troops gathered around their campfires. The Yankees had filled roads for days in pursuit of their foes. As the embers died and men slept in both armies, the residents of Gettys-burg snuffed out lamps and retired for the night.[27]

A month after the Battle of Chancellorsville, Lieutenant Lucius Shattuck of the Twenty-fourth Michigan offered an explanation for the death of a comrade. Private Forest Brown of Company C had been killed at Fitzhugh's Crossing on April 29. The enlisted man had been struck down either during the passage of the river or in the assault on the Rebel works. Shattuck knew that friends and family members at home had read the newspaper accounts of the battle and undoubtedly had paled at the casualty figures. Like Brown, hundreds of others had sacrificed their lives in the bitter defeat, but as the lieutenant believed, their deaths required meaning that probably had escaped those in Michigan.

"When men stand up and face death," Shattuck argued to his kinfolk, "or rush enthusiastically to its embrace, in defense of *principle*, it shows the triumph of the *man* over the *animal*. It shows that they hold life not as the animal, a mere existence but as a price to be paid in the cause of human weal." Private Brown and his fallen comrades had suffered death for something more than themselves.[28]

If the young officer found sense in Chancellorsville's cost, other Westerners in the Iron Brigade were not as certain. Even Shattuck, however, earlier had expressed discontent with the outcome, writing: "I have often thought it impossible for me ever to *desire* a fight. But hoping to make *that battle* a decisive one I wanted to see our entire force exerted." To Rufus Dawes, the defeat had resulted from the simple fact that Fighting Joe Hooker had been "out-generaled." Chancellorsville had convinced Dawes that the "Rebellion" could not "be crushed here, unless we may *annihilate* the great army in front of us." Brigade commander Solomon Meredith confided to his wife that "if they had let McClellan alone the rebellion would of been put down before this time." But the army, Meredith thought, must stand by the administration because "anything else is fatal to success."[29]

Hooker's confident, if not boastful, pronouncements before the campaign now echoed with hollowness. He had deserved credit for restoring morale and for reorganizing the army in the wake of Ambrose Burnside's tenure. When the army crossed the Rappahannock and Rapidan rivers, Hooker marched with a weapon that sought redemption. But in the demonic confines of the Wilderness, Hooker and key subordinates faltered. As Dawes claimed, Lee "out-generaled" Hooker, sending the Union army once again in retreat across the Rappahannock. The Federals' optimism evaporated amid Chancellorsville's realities.

The ten-day campaign returned the Northerners to their camps opposite Fredericksburg. As May lengthened, they resumed the routine of an army locked in place, watching for signs of a movement by their opponents. Pickets roamed the riverbanks while units conducted drills and the troops grumbled about another general defeated by "Bobby" Lee.

The Iron Brigade was stationed upstream from Fredericksburg, sharing picket duties at Banks's Ford. Chancellorsville's carnage gave way to camaraderie among soldiers in both armies. Corporal Horace Currier of the Seventh Wisconsin reported that "the Rebs are first rate friends with the Iron Brigade at present." The Westerners swapped coffee for tobacco with the Southerners, and on one warm day, the opponents swam together in the river. The Confederates agreed not to fire on the "Black Hats" but refused to extend the truce to New Englanders when the latter troops patrolled the banks. "The Rebs have respect for us," explained Currier. "They say that they would rather fight one whole division of New Eng. troops than our Brigade. They say so in earnest."[30]

In camp, the Wisconsin, Indiana, and Michigan men listened to temperance speakers—"Intemperance is a great evil in the army," complained a Hoosier—and gathered in small knots for card playing. "Gambling has become fashionable," declared a soldier. Some players seemed consumed by the cards, refusing to quit games and willing to pay five cents for a glass of water. One private earned $6.50 in a day, one half of a month's pay, selling drinks to gamblers.[31]

On May 21, the routine ended for the brigade when officers awoke the troops at 3:00 A.M. to prepare for a march. Army headquarters had received a report that the Eighth Illinois Cavalry had been trapped by Confederates while on a raid in the "Northern Neck," the region between the Potomac and Rappahannock rivers. Headquarters selected the Westerners for the relief operation, and within an hour of being roused and without breakfast, four of the regiments, all except the Seventh Wisconsin, were on the march.[32]

The first day proved to be the worst as dozens of men straggled in the heat and the dust. The infantrymen did not halt until noon, when they boiled coffee and cooked a meal. Resuming the march, the Westerners covered roughly thirty miles that day before camping for the night. On the 22nd, the pace slowed as the troops had to rebuild a bridge over a stream. Late on the afternoon of the 23rd, the weary marchers met the Illinois horsemen, who were burdened by wagons, livestock, and runaway slaves. The Federals encountered no enemy troops during the expedition, returning to the army on the 26th, after marching one hundred miles by their estimates.[33]

The next day, May 27, the members of the Twenty-fourth Michigan received their black hats. At Fredericksburg and at Fitzhugh's Crossing, they had proved themselves worthy of membership in the Iron Brigade, and their Wisconsin and Indiana comrades bestowed the unit's distinctive badge of honor upon them. It was done without ceremony—the issuance of the hats was enough, for it symbolized their acceptance into the renowned unit.[34]

At month's end, Major General John Reynolds reviewed the First Corps. A member of the Second Wisconsin admitted afterward that "I think our regt. never did poorer marching on review than this time." Reynolds also reorganized Brigadier General James Wadsworth's First Division into two brigades, reducing the number of regiments from nineteen to eleven. With the change, the Iron Brigade became the First Brigade, First Division of the First Corps, a designation they would remember later with pride, believing that it signified their stature as the army's finest brigade.[35]

On the day after the review, Rufus Dawes wrote a letter to Mary Beman Gates. She had been in his thoughts often during the previous week as he had sent her an earlier letter, pledging "myself to *you* for life" and proposing marriage. As he waited for a reply, he turned to military matters. "We have great rumors about our destiny this summer," he noted, with the prevailing opinion among the officers and men that "General Lee is going to attack this army." "Well," he added, "this most unfortunate Army of the Potomac is yet a power, and when thrown upon its defense can not be defeated by the whole force of the rebellion. I am not sure that an offensive campaign by the enemy is not to be hoped for by the country."[36]

When Dawes finished the letter, he left camp for picket duty along the Rappahannock. Little had changed along the stream since the Westerners' previous assignment to the duty. But before long—in fact, within days of Dawes's "hoped for" offensive—the Confederates began the march toward the Potomac River. Although Southern pickets still prowled along the river, screening the movement, Hooker received indications of enemy activity. He shifted some units farther up the Rappahannock, but hesitated to commit the army to a countermove. When a report placed Southern cavalry at Culpeper Court House, the Union commander ordered his mounted units to "disperse and destroy" the Rebel force.[37]

For Hooker, the clash at Brandy Station on June 9 resulted in neither the destruction of Stuart's horsemen nor in solid intelligence about the numbers and composition of enemy units in the area. Two more days passed before Hooker was convinced that the bulk of Lee's army had abandoned the Fredericksburg line. Although he had continued to move more troops upstream on the 10th and 11th, the march in pursuit of the

Rebels accelerated on June 12. All camp followers and surplus baggage were sent to the rear.[38]

The Iron Brigade marched on the 11th, and by nightfall of the 12th camped near Hartwood Church. During the second day's march, the Westerners were assembled to witness the execution of Private John P. Woods, a Nineteenth Indiana soldier who had been sentenced to death for desertion and misbehavior before the enemy. A chaplain spoke privately with Woods before guards led the condemned man to a coffin in the center of the formation. Woods sat on the coffin with his hands and legs bound and his eyes blindfolded. An officer dropped his hat, and a squad of twelve men fired a volley. The blast knocked Woods off the coffin but did not kill him. Two soldiers walked forward and shot him in the heart. "We left the men digging his grave," wrote an eyewitness, "and resumed the march as if nothing had happened."[39]

The march continued the next day as the army followed the Orange & Alexandria Railroad north. On the morning of the 14th, the Westerners reached Warrenton Junction, where they ate a noonday meal before proceeding toward Manassas. All afternoon and through the night the brigade tramped. The black-hatted veterans arrived at Centreville about sunrise on the 15th, and were, in the words of Dawes, "tired, sore, sleepy, hungry, dusty and dirty as pigs." They spent that day and the next in camp, resting "blistered feet" and washing shirts. The respite ended on the 17th, when the regiments started toward Leesburg to the northwest.[40]

The men described the march of the 17th as the worst of all of them. "The blazing sun of Virginia poured down upon us like fire," reported a brigade member. Three men in the Twenty-fourth Michigan died from sunstroke, and another one became "crazy in the heat." The dust hung in the air, suffocating the men. Dawes likened the march to a passage through a "furnace." They halted finally in mid-afternoon at Hamilton, west of Leesburg in Loudoun County, having marched twenty miles. "It is amazing how much *men* can endure," thought a Michigander.[41]

Hooker halted the army for the next several days with most of its units concentrated in the Centreville area. While the infantry corps rested, Union cavalrymen probed west toward the gaps of the Blue Ridge. At Aldie, Middleburg, and Upperville, the blue-jacketed troopers collided with Stuart's mounted Rebels. In some fierce clashes, the Confederates prevented the Federals from reaching the mountain defiles. On June 25, as Ewell's Southerners advanced through southern Pennsylvania and

Longstreet's and Hill's corps began the passage of the Potomac, Union foot soldiers in columns that stretched for miles resumed their northward trek.[42]

During this week-long interlude the Iron Brigade had remained in Loudoun County. "We know really nothing of what is going on," Captain William Speed of the Twenty-fourth Michigan told his wife on June 21, "or where the rest of the army is, where the Enemy is or what is to be done." The members welcomed back Solomon Meredith, who had been absent on leave in Indiana. Meredith reassumed command from Colonel Henry Morrow, and when his troops started toward the Potomac on the 25th Long Sol led the march.[43]

The Westerners crossed the river on a pontoon bridge at Edwards Ferry. Soon after they entered Maryland, they passed a schoolhouse to the accompaniment of cheers from the students. "The thoughts of my dear wife and children rushed to my mind," wrote one soldier to his family, "and I could hardly cheer because my heart was drowned with tears." He added that "I hope that not one Rebel will get out of Maryland. I am anxious to see the end of this cursed war." Before nightfall, the brigade reached Barnesville and bivouacked.[44]

The Federals awoke to rain on the 26th, but they plodded on farther into Maryland. Hooker had assigned John Reynolds to command of the army's advanced wing, which consisted of the First, Third, and Eleventh corps. Consequently, the Iron Brigade and other units of the First Corps led the advance through Maryland during the 26th, 27th, and 28th. Rumors mounted each day about the location of the Rebels. During one halt, Meredith gathered the regiments together and told the troops, as one listener recounted his words, that "we was about to meet our enemies again and said he did not ask us to do better than we had, but to do as well." By the evening of June 28, the Westerners were camped nine miles south of Frederick.[45]

In Washington, meanwhile, President Lincoln had accepted the resignation of Hooker as army commander. For days, Hooker had been embroiled in a dispute with General-in-Chief Henry Halleck about the garrison at Harper's Ferry. Hooker opposed Halleck's proposal to hold the post. The pair of officers exchanged telegrams in a controversy which was exacerbated by their dislike of each other. When Hooker demanded that either the troops abandon Harper's Ferry or he would resign, the administration accepted his resignation, appointing Major General George G. Meade, commander of the Fifth Corps, as his successor. Meade was a forty-seven-year-old West Pointer who was regarded as a capable, no-nonsense officer with a fearsome temper when angered. As the two armies neared a collision, Meade faced one of the greatest burdens of command ever given to an American soldier.[46]

Meade pushed the army toward Pennsylvania on June 29. Union cavalrymen roamed ahead of the infantry and artillery units, probing into the Keystone State. Reynolds's three-corps wing trailed the horsemen, closing on Emmitsburg, located just south of the Pennsylvania line. An Iron Brigade member described the day in his dairy as "a long & tiresome march in mud." By sunset, Reynolds's own First Corps was in the forefront of the infantry, bivouacked closest to the Keystone State.[47]

June 30 dawned overcast, and rain fell "by spells" throughout the day. Reynolds started his corps north about eight o'clock. As the column entered Pennsylvania, the residents greeted the soldiers in their "holiday attire." A Sixth Wisconsin man claimed that "it seems almost like going home to go into some of these farmhouses." Another brigade member related that he and his comrades were heartened by the reception given them, "knowing that there were people to defend who appreciated their sacrifices." At noon, the Westerners and their comrades in Wadsworth's other brigade halted at a bridge across Marsh Creek, roughly five miles south of Gettysburg on Emmitsburg Road. During the afternoon, the regiments mustered for pay.[48]

Reynolds had halted the movement because of reports from Brigadier General John Buford, the commander of a cavalry division, that indicated a possible Confederate advance either on Gettysburg or Fairfield to the south and west. In turn, Reynolds decided to block the roads from the two directions. Buford had two of his brigades at Gettysburg and would remain there to keep Reynolds alerted to any Confederate movement.

In the fields by Marsh Creek, the veterans in Wadsworth's division bedded down for the night. Meredith's brigade and that of Brigadier General Lysander Cutler, the former commander of the Sixth Wisconsin, numbered slightly over four thousand officers and men. Up the road toward Gettysburg, the Nineteenth Indiana manned the picket line. No Union infantrymen in the army were closer to the crossroads town than the Hoosiers. The soldiers had spent part of the day discussing the prospects of a battle and concluded, as one of them noted in his diary, that "we think they [the Rebels] will not stand this side of York." Many of them had probably never before heard of Gettysburg.[49]

1 3

✠

GETTYSBURG

RUFUS DAWES awoke on the morning of July 1, 1863, as an overnight rain continued to fall. In three more days the native Ohioan would be twenty-five years old. When he left Mauston, Wisconsin, to enlist in the army, he knew nothing about soldiering. But his fellow volunteers from Juneau County elected him captain of the Lemonweir Minute Men. Since those jubilant, innocent days in 1861, he had earned promotion to major and then lieutenant colonel of the Sixth Wisconsin. Now, on this wet morning in southern Pennsylvania, the regiment belonged to Rufus Dawes.[1]

Dawes had held temporary command of the Sixth during the past month after a horse kicked Colonel Edward Bragg in the foot. The injury resulted in erysipelas, requiring Bragg to obtain medical treatment in Washington. Dawes succeeded the colonel and marched with the regiment every mile from Fredericksburg to its present bivouac site north of Marsh Creek along Emmitsburg Road. Although the northward pursuit of the Confederates had been grueling on some days, Dawes had welcomed the entry into Maryland and Pennsylvania. "We have marched through some of the most beautiful country I ever saw," he wrote on June 30. "It is very refreshing to get out of the barren desert of Virginia into this land of thrift and beauty."[2]

The Westerners of the Iron Brigade seemed to share Dawes's views. Their morale was high on the morning of July 1 as they enjoyed breakfast and packed bedrolls. Although they anticipated another day of marching, they ate their hardtack, drank their coffee, and finished the preparations rather leisurely. Ordnance wagons, however, soon rolled into camp, and each man was issued sixty rounds of ammunition. To veterans, this number of cartridges indicated trouble. About seven o'clock, Dawes and the other regimental commanders received orders to "pack up, be ready to march immediately."[3]

Major General John Reynolds, commander of the army's left wing, had spent the night near the camp of the Iron Brigade at Moritz Tavern, where a staff officer had awakened him before dawn with an order from army commander George Meade to march to Gettysburg that day. Reynolds then relayed instructions to the commanders of the First, Third, and Eleventh corps. While Reynolds's own First Corps, under the temporary command of Major General Abner Doubleday, moved to Gettysburg, the other two corps would follow, with priority on the roads given to the troops, not to the wagon trains. Since Brigadier General James Wadsworth's division of the First Corps held the advance at Marsh Creek, it would lead the march.[4]

When James Wadsworth received the instructions, he notified brigade commanders Solomon Meredith and Lysander Cutler. At fifty-five years old, Wadsworth was the second oldest divisional commander in the army, having held a brigadiership since the summer of 1861. He owed the commission to his stature as a leading New York Republican—he had lost the gubernatorial election in the fall of 1862—but his troops liked his unpretentious manners and his concern for their welfare. He was, in a fellow officer's opinion, "always busy at something and with a good allowance of common sense." He had performed capably at Chancellorsville, but the division's role had been limited. Whether he could handle units in a fiercely contested struggle remained unknown.[5]

The First Division numbered slightly over four thousand officers and men on this morning. The day's march rotation gave Cutler's five regiments of New York and Pennsylvania troops—the Seventh Indiana was detached, guarding wagons—the front of the column. Between seven and eight o'clock, they started north on Emmitsburg Road. To their rear came Captain James Hall's Battery B, Second Maine Light Artillery. When Cutler's brigade and the battery crossed the bridge over Marsh Creek and passed the Iron Brigade bivouac site, the black-hatted veterans began to form ranks. It was probably another fifteen minutes or more until Meredith turned his column into the road.[6]

The Second Wisconsin led the brigade's march, followed by the Seventh Wisconsin. When the column reached the picket line of the Nineteenth Indiana, the Hoosiers filed into place behind the Seventh and ahead of the Twenty-fourth Michigan. Dawes and the Sixth Wisconsin trailed the Michiganders, while a brigade guard, which consisted of twenty men drawn from each regiment and two officers, completed the column.[7]

The Federals tramped unhurriedly—one officer said cautiously—on Emmitsburg Road. The overcast skies had broken, revealing a summer's sun that had begun to heat the day. They passed through a countryside much like the one that had impressed Dawes, with stone and brick farmhouses and large, sturdy barns set amid fields of ripening grain. The slow pace allowed the men to joke and to chat with each other. The Germans in Company F, Sixth Wisconsin sang a song in their native language, prompting the native-born Americans in the regiment to respond with other songs in English. At one point during the march, a staff officer rode along the column and shouted erroneously that McClellan now commanded the army. The troops cheered.[8]

As Meredith's column approached Gettysburg, Dawes decided that he wanted "to make a show" when the regiment passed through the town. He ordered the colors unfurled and summoned the drum corps to the front of the Sixth. The musicians began playing "The Campbells Are Coming," enlivening even more the marchers' spirits. Suddenly, however, from the north and west rolled the sound of cannon fire. The drummers stopped as the mood changed along the column.[9]

Ahead of the Sixth Wisconsin, the brigade's other regiments were already filing through a gap in the post-and-rail fence that bordered the roadway near the Nicholas Codori farmstead. When the Westerners turned into fields west of the road, officers sent noncombatants to the rear, and "the men stripped for action." There was no time for the men to load their rifles; only the Hoosiers of the Nineteenth Indiana had rounds in their weapons because of the previous night's picket duty. At the double quick, the nearly nineteen hundred Westerners hurried to the sounds of a familiar reckoning.[10]

On this July morning, these men with their famous black hats were arguably the best combat infantrymen in the army. During the past year they had honed their skills and efficiency in some of the war's worst fighting. Their ranks had been reduced until an average of 380 officers and men remained in each regiment, a core, as one officer believed, which characterized a regiment at its best. Their enthusiasm for combat had faded amid its realities, replaced by an acceptance of duty's call. They wanted to survive the terribleness, to return home, but honor and devotion to something beyond themselves kept them in the ranks, rushing across unknown fields toward another rendezvous of the brotherhood.[11]

John Reynolds had preceded his First Corps veterans to Gettysburg. The time of his arrival has been the subject of historical debate, but the time frame of events indicates that the popular general met John Buford probably fifteen or twenty minutes after nine o'clock. When he reined up west of the town, Reynolds encountered a billowing fight between Buford's horse soldiers and Confederate infantry. The initial contact between the opponents had occurred about seven o'clock. Slowly, Buford's men had retired, skirmishing, before the Third Corps division of Major General Henry Heth, backed by Confederate artillery. Ordered by Lee "to ascertain what force was at Gettysburg . . . without forcing an engagement" if he met Union infantry, Heth was preparing to advance against Buford's troopers with two of his four brigades when Reynolds appeared on the field.[12]

Buford apprised Reynolds of the tactical situation, telling the superior officer that "the devil's to pay!" The best defensible ground around Gettysburg, which Reynolds had passed and taken notice of, lay south and east of the village, but Buford had decided to delay the Southerners on ridges west of the community of 2,400 residents. Tradition has it that Reynolds and Buford met on Seminary Ridge, named for the Lutheran Seminary situated on it, and together rode west a half mile to double-crested McPherson's Ridge, where they viewed Heth's oncoming infantry. Reynolds told Buford to hold the ridge while he went back to hurry forward his troops. The major general also sent aides to his three corps commanders to accelerate their marches to Gettysburg.[13]

Returning through the town, Reynolds rode to the Codori farm, where he had staff officers level a section of the fence along Emmitsburg Road. Wadsworth and the head of the division's column soon arrived. By now, the rumble of artillery fire was audible to the troops. Reynolds ordered Wadsworth to detour the two brigades through the fields at the double quick. The Union commander then spurred ahead as pioneers, wielding axes, rushed forward, ripping gaps for the infantrymen in the numerous fences that divided the fields.[14]

Wadsworth's leading brigade, Cutler's five regiments, passed over Seminary Ridge about ten o'clock, trailed by Captain James A. Hall's Battery B, Second Maine Light Artillery. Reynolds directed the six-gun battery to the western crest of McPherson's Ridge beside Chambersburg Pike and ordered three of Cutler's regiments into the fields north of the road and the other two into position south of the Maine artillerists around the house and barn of Edward McPherson, for whom the ridge was named. To the west, Heth's two brigades, one on each side of the pike, were approaching. As the Rebels closed, volleys of musketry exploded.[15]

Perhaps fifteen to thirty minutes behind Cutler's troops came the Iron Brigade. Crossing the ridge south and west of the Seminary buildings, Meredith's men angled northwest toward McPherson's Ridge. Lieutenant Colonel John A. Kress of Wadsworth's staff met Colonel Lucius Fairchild at the head of the Second Wisconsin and ordered the regimental commander to lead his men into a woodlot south of the McPherson farm and to attack the enemy. Acting First Corps commander Abner Doubleday was on the field, having ridden ahead of the other two divisions, and claimed in his report that he pointed the black-hatted veterans toward the woods, urging them to hold it to the "last extremity." In response, the men exclaimed: "If we can't hold it, where will you find men who can?"[16]

Fairchild shifted his 302 officers and men into battle ranks. A soldier in a trailing regiment thought that the Second Wisconsin looked like "a dark line of worn and ragged blue." The regiment ascended the ridge, and Reynolds met them, shouting: "Forward men, forward, for God's sake, and drive those fellows out of those woods." The Wisconsinites entered the woodlot, a five-acre stand known locally as Herbst Woods, with Reynolds trailing behind the line, encouraging the troops.[17]

The Federals neared a rail fence, strung among the trees, on the eastern crest of McPherson's Ridge. Ahead of them, at some places only forty paces in the distance, Tennesseeans and Alabamians of Brigadier General James Archer's brigade leveled their rifles. When the Westerners topped the ridge, the Confederates fired. The gale of musketry blew through the trees into the Second Wisconsin, knocking down dozens of the blue-coated troops. The Union ranks staggered, with perhaps seventy-five or more men killed or maimed, including a mortally wounded Lieutenant Colonel George Stevens.[18]

At the edge of the woods, behind Fairchild's men, John Reynolds lay on the ground. He had watched the Second Wisconsin plunge into the woods and then turned his head to see how close the brigade's other regiments were from the ridge. A bullet from the volley struck him in the back of the head. He lurched in the saddle and fell off his mount, his life ebbing away on the limestone soil of his native Pennsylvania. Aides rushed to him, picked him up, and carried the unconscious general to the rear. Eventually, his devoted staff officers lay him in the small stone house of a stranger along Emmitsburg Road in town.[19]

Many of the members of the Second Wisconsin had been unable to load their rifles during the rapid march across the fields. The few with loaded weapons fired at the Rebels. Fairchild's orders were to attack the enemy, and although the casualties had been frightful and their muskets were empty, the colonel shouted for a bayonet charge. The Federals drove deeper into the woods, loading their firearms as they advanced. Their opponents raked them with another volley.[20]

On the Yankees' left, however, the Seventh Wisconsin arrived on the ridge, followed by the Nineteenth Indiana and the Twenty-fourth Michigan. Like their comrades in the Second, the Seventh's men held unloaded rifles and were lashed by a blast from the Southerners. They staggered momentarily, but then charged. Beside them, the Hoosiers, with loaded weapons, extended the line. One of them wrote that the enemy was coming up the ridge, flags in front, and "howling like demons." When "we could see their heads and shoulders," the Indianans fired. The Confederates teetered to a halt. "We discovered," declared an Alabamian, "that we had tackled a hard proposition."[21]

One of the enduring stories of Gettysburg relates that the Confederates had expected to encounter Pennsylvania militiamen on July 1. When Archer's men saw the headgear of the Iron Brigade, one of them allegedly exclaimed: "There are those damned black-hatted fellows again. 'Taint no militia. Its the Army of the Potomac." Unfortunately for history, the tale is almost certainly apocryphal.[22]

Before long, the Twenty-fourth Michigan came into line on the Hoosiers' left. With a shout, the three regiments joined the Second Wisconsin in the counterattack. The Michiganders overlapped the Confederate right flank, and the Westerners along the entire brigade front hammered back the Rebels. The Second Wisconsin's Colonel Fairchild described the fighting as "most desperate." Fairchild soon fell with a shat-

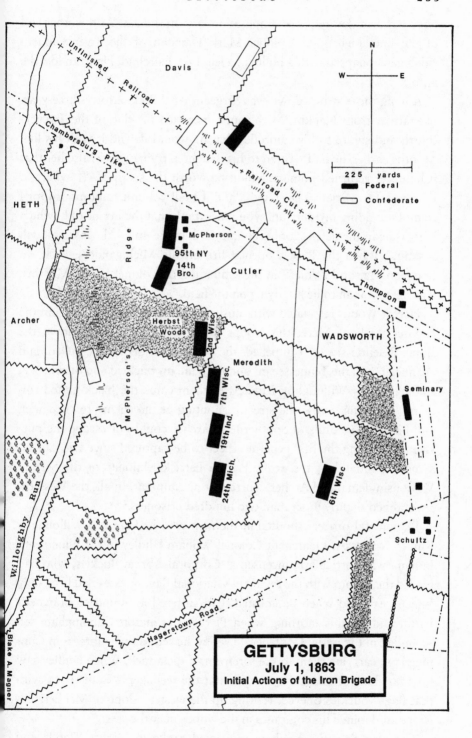

GETTYSBURG
July 1, 1863
Initial Actions of the Iron Brigade

tered left arm that required amputation later in the day. At the other end of the line, Lieutenant Colonel Mark Flanigan of the Twenty-fourth Michigan collapsed with a bullet in a leg. Like Fairchild, Flanigan lost the limb.[23]

Among those struck down was Sergeant Abel Peck, a forty-three-year-old farmer from Nankin, Michigan. He carried the flag of the Twenty-fourth and swore to his comrades that he would defend it with his life. Months earlier, he had written to his daughter, trying to reassure her that if he never returned home it would be worth the sacrifice. "I expect to have to take my part," he stated, "and if I fall you must not mourn for I think I am doing my duty and you must think that the honor of having a Father die in the defense of his country will make up for the loss you will sustain." When the Rebels opened fire on the Michiganders, Peck, "a brave and faithful soldier" in the estimation of Colonel Henry Morrow, was the first man to be hit, dying on the field.[24]

Herbst Woods resonated with musketry and filled with smoke, but the counterattack of Meredith's troops drove the Confederates down the slope. Relentlessly, as if impelled, the Federals loaded, fired, yelled, and advanced until the Tennesseeans and Alabamians buckled and then broke, spilling across Willoughby Run. After them came the black-hatted soldiers, swarming across the stream, shouting at the enemy to surrender, and bagging handfuls of Southerners. Archer could not escape the pursuers, becoming the first general officer to be captured since Lee had assumed command of the army. Private Patrick Maloney of the Second Wisconsin demanded Archer's surrender at gunpoint. In all, the Westerners grabbed slightly more than two hundred prisoners.[25]

Regimental officers shouted at the men who had crossed Willoughby Run to withdraw. Lieutenant Colonel William Dudley of the Nineteenth Indiana was particularly incensed at Corporal Abram Buckles, who had waded the stream with the regiment's national flag. Buckles had been only fifteen years old when he enlisted, had suffered a wound at Brawner's Farm, and on this morning when Private Burlington Cunningham fell wounded in the initial Confederate volley, he seized the colors from Cunningham, carrying them to the forefront of the attack. When Dudley saw how far Buckles had gone, he yelled at the teenager: "Come back with that flag!" Buckles obeyed, retiring up the western slope of McPherson's Ridge, and joined his comrades in the woods near the crest.[26]

The Iron Brigade members re-formed ranks in Herbst Woods and guarded the prisoners. From their right and rear they heard musketry, the familiar noise sounding like the ripping of canvas cloth. While they had repulsed Archer's troops, Heth's second brigade, Mississippians and North Carolinians under Brigadier General Joseph Davis, had scoured the fields north of Chambersburg Pike of Cutler's three blue-clad regiments. The Yankees had fought tenaciously and valiantly, but the Southerners had overlapped their flanks, enfilading the ranks, and were now rolling toward the pike. South of the roadway, Cutler's two remaining regiments, the Fourteenth Brooklyn and Ninety-fifth New York, wheeled to face the gray-clad attackers. To their right stood the Sixth Wisconsin and the Iron Brigade guard.[27]

When the four regiments of Westerners had rushed to McPherson's Ridge, Doubleday had halted the Sixth Wisconsin and the brigade guard in the swale west of Seminary Ridge. Here the roughly 430 black-hatted troops waited as Davis's Confederates assailed Cutler's line north of Chambersburg Pike. Shortly, Lieutenant Benjamin Martin of Doubleday's staff reported to Rufus Dawes with orders to move toward the road as support for the right flank of the Union line. Dawes divided the brigade guard into two companies and assigned them to the regimental flanks. The veterans faced right, shifting from a battle line into a column, and Dawes on horseback led his men north between the ridges. They marched at a "steady double quick" until one of Wadsworth's staff officers met the column, shouting: "Go like hell! It looks as though they are driving Cutler!" Dawes accelerated the pace as the broken ranks of Cutler's men fled across the fields, pursued by gray-coated Rebels.[28]

When the Sixth neared the post and rail fence along the southern edge of the pike, Dawes swung the column back into a battle line. Probably no one in the ranks recalled at that moment the endless times John Gibbon had demanded such an execution of the movement on a parade ground, but now it mattered, and they reacted as battle-wise Regulars. Beyond the road, less than two hundred yards away, the Rebels saw them. "We were feeling that the day at that point, at least, was ours," remembered a Mississippi captain, when "a cloud of blue coats, fresh & eager for the fray, confronted us."[29]

The Confederates, however, were prepared, unleashing a volley. A private in the Sixth recalled that when the enemy fired, he and his comrades bowed their "heads to the leaden storm and dashed forward." The musketry killed Dawes's horse, sprawling the officer on the ground. He jumped to his feet, assuring the men that he was unharmed, and shouted for them to "fire by file." The Federals lay their rifles on the fence rails and squeezed the triggers. On their left, the Ninety-fifth New York and Fourteenth Brooklyn added to the flaming musketry.[30]

The Southerners sought shelter in a six-hundred-foot long cut that had been carved through eastern McPherson's Ridge for the bed of an unfinished railroad. In the center of the defile, the depth measured ten to fifteen feet, preventing the Confederates who had scrambled down into it at that point from firing at the enemy. Along the other sections, the Rebels had a natural breastworks and used it. A member of the Sixth Wisconsin asserted that the enemy were "kowardly sons of bitches" for seeking protection in it.[31]

The rifle fire from the cut was described by Dawes as "murderous." He decided that his men could not withstand a pounding without suffering grievous casualties, so he ordered an attack, bellowing: "Over the fence boys and Charge. Charge!" The soldiers began shouting: "Charge! Charge! Charge!" They scrambled over the rails. The Confederate musketry intensified, slamming into the Federals as the latter exposed themselves. "We never hesitated," declared a Westerner.[32]

The flank companies of the regiment never heard Dawes's order, and only reacted to it when they witnessed their comrades in the center scale the fence. Consequently, the Sixth's formation resembled an inverted V, with the flag at the apex. On the Westerners' left, the Ninety-fifth New York and Fourteenth Brooklyn joined in the assault as soon as they saw the black-hatted soldiers advance. The Yankees had about 175 yards of open ground to cover, and the Southerners turned it into a slaughter pit.[33]

The gunfire sounded like an "unbroken roar." Captain Loyd Harris, commanding the brigade guard company on the Sixth's left, believed that "the fire was the worst I ever experienced." Harris had men with him from each of the brigade's five regiments and claimed later that "there was no difference in the fighting qualities" of the troops. In the center, the Sixth's national flag went down three times. Captain John Ticknor, one of the regiment's finest company commanders, was killed after crossing the pike. Corporal James Kelly of Company B stopped Dawes in the midst of the attack and opened his blouse to reveal a chest wound. "Colonel," said the Prescott, Wisconsin, volunteer, "won't you write to my folks that I died a soldier." Kelly succumbed to the wound three weeks later.[34]

When the Northerners closed to within ten paces, the Mississippians and North Carolinians triggered a final volley. The blast, in the opinion of a sergeant in the Sixth, "had been so fatal that it seemed half our men had fallen." Another soldier claimed, however, that the Federals "seemed all unconscious to the terrible situation; they were mad and fought with a desperation seldom witnessed." When they reached the cut, a hand-to-hand melee ensued, punctuated by shouts from the Federals to surrender.[35]

The men's faces were "black and grimy with powder and heat." A frenzy overtook some at the edge of the cut, seemingly at its worst in the struggle for the flag of the Second Mississippi. Several Wisconsinites tried to seize the colors, including Private John Harland, who was killed as he grabbed for it. Harland's friend, Private Levi Tongue, saw him fall and rushed at the Rebel who had killed him. The Mississippian pleaded: "Don't shoot! Don't kill me!"

"All hell can't save you now," retorted Tongue, who lowered his rifle toward the man's chest and shot him.[36]

Private Samuel Wallar and Sergeant Francis A. Wallar, two Company I brothers from DeSoto, Wisconsin, rushed toward the gray-clad color bearer. While Samuel flattened an enemy soldier, Francis wrestled with Corporal W. B. Murphy of the Second Mississippi. Francis had been a farmer, robust and strong, whom Murphy remembered as "a large man," and he overpowered the Southerner, capturing the flag and Murphy. The Mississippi corporal had carried the standard since April 1861.[37]

The hand-to-hand combat ended within minutes as scores of Confederates, trapped in the deepest section of cut, threw down their muskets and surrendered. A Union soldier told his brother at home afterward that "the rebels fought bravely, for they thought we were the militia, but when they found their mistake, they soon slackened their fire." Some of the Westerners claimed that a number of Rebels continued to fire until Major John Blair of the Second Mississippi relinquished his sword. The black-hatted veterans captured over two hundred officers and men. The Confederates who had been along the railroad bed where the banks were low escaped the attackers, fleeing north and west across the fields. The Fifty-fifth North Carolina, positioned on the left of Davis's line, covered the retreat.[38]

Dawes assigned the prisoners to Major John Hauser and a detail. When Sergeant Wallar presented the Confederate flag to the lieutenant colonel, Dawes handed it to Sergeant William Evans, who had been wounded in both thighs and was using a pair of rifles for crutches. Evans was en route to the rear for medical treatment, and Dawes believed it would be safe with the sergeant.[39]

In his report, Dawes declared: "I can only say the men of the Sixth most nobly vindicated their history in this desperate struggle." The regiment and the brigade guard had lost over one third of their numbers, including two company commanders killed and five wounded. But their charge on the railroad cut, supported by Cutler's two New York regiments, had saved abandoned Union cannon and the right flank of the line. The troops in Wadsworth's division had given their generals time until other Federal units reached Gettysburg. To the north and to the west, additional Confederate forces were converging on the town. An interlude followed the struggle for the railroad cut, but it would be only a pause in a battle neither side had expected on this Wednesday morning.[40]

The lull extended into mid-afternoon. During the midday hours, additional units arrived on the battlefield. From the north, Richard Ewell and two divisions of the Confederate Second Corps, numbering over fourteen thousand troops and advancing along the Carlisle and Harrisburg roads, approached Gettysburg and deployed. From the west, A. P. Hill's second division, under Major General William D. Pender, aligned its seven thousand officers and men behind Heth's four brigades on Herr Ridge, one mile from McPherson's Ridge, bringing Southern numbers to upward of 28,000.[41]

While the gray-coated forces grew, the roads south of Gettysburg were filled with the ranks of oncoming Federals. Reynolds's messages to subordinates to hurry the march brought the remaining two divisions of the First Corps and Major General Oliver O. Howard's three divisions of the Eleventh Corps on to the field between noon and 2:00 P.M. These units increased Union strength to approximately twenty-four thousand. The First Corps troops filed into position on the morning's battleground, supporting Meredith's Iron Brigade on McPherson's Ridge and extending the line beyond Chambersburg Pike on to Oak Ridge, as locals called Seminary Ridge north of the road. Howard, who assumed command as senior officer on the field, placed two of his divisions on the plain north of town and east of Oak Ridge to cover the Carlisle and Harrisburg roads. His final division was held in reserve on Cemetery Hill, a dominant heights south of Gettysburg.[42]

In Herbst Woods on McPherson Ridge, Solomon Meredith fashioned a new line during the lull. The ranks of the four regiments—the Sixth Wisconsin was on Seminary Ridge serving as infantry support for their old comrades in Battery B, Fourth U.S. Artillery—curved through the trees from the southwest corner of the woods to beyond their northern edge in the field just west of the McPherson farm buildings. The Nineteenth Indiana held the left, at the edge of the trees behind Willoughby Run, with the Twenty-fourth Michigan in a concave line on its right. The Second and Seventh Wisconsin then extended the line in a straight north–south direction through the woods. On the Westerners' right, and about one hundred yards to the rear, Colonel Roy Stone's three Pennsylvania regiments formed an inverted L around the McPherson house and barn and along the pike. Two hundred yards to the left and rear of the Nineteenth Indiana, Colonel Chapman Biddle's brigade covered the fields toward Fairfield Road between the ridges.[43]

The position of Meredith's and Stone's troops was a half-mile beyond Seminary Ridge and exposed to enfilading artillery fire from Oak Hill, a six-hundred-foot high eminence at the northern terminus of Oak Ridge. Meredith and his regimental commanders recognized the isolation of Herbst Woods and requested a withdrawal to Seminary Ridge. Colonel Samuel Williams of the Nineteenth Indiana also expressed his concern about the brigade's left flank. Corps commander Abner Doubleday, however, repeated his orders to hold the position "at all hazards."[44]

Confederate infantry renewed the struggle about two o'clock with the advance of three brigades from Major General Robert Rodes's division into the fields first north of and then west of Oak Ridge against troops of the Union First Corps. Southern artillery crews from Oak Hill and Herr Ridge pounded the Federals, including Meredith's men in Herbst Woods. About thirty minutes later, Henry Heth sent forward his final two brigades, commanded by Colonel John M. Brockenbrough and Brigadier General J. Johnston Pettigrew, roughly twenty-five hundred Virginians and North Carolinians. Heth's officers and men descended Herr Ridge south of the pike, moving directly toward Meredith's four regiments and the One Hundred Fiftieth Pennsylvania of Stone's brigade on McPherson's Ridge.[45]

The Virginians and North Carolinians "advanced in perfect alignment," in the words of one of them, with color-bearers and guards four paces to the front. To a Pennsylvania officer, watching the advance, the Rebels were "grey treason." The Twenty-sixth North Carolina, a huge regiment of nearly 850 officers and men, led Pettigrew's en echelon assault, marching straight for Herbst Woods and the Twenty-fourth Michigan. Within the trees, Colonel Henry Morrow braced his men. Before the Confederate regiment reached Willoughby Run, Morrow shouted: "Give 'em hell boys."[46]

Herbst Woods flashed with a volley from the Michiganders, the musketry slamming into the North Carolinians. The Yankees reloaded, fired a second, and a third, and a fourth time. In the Rebel ranks, it was as if a giant, swinging a scythe, had harvested men. Four color-bearers were hit before the regiment crossed the stream. The Southerners leaned into the fury, waded the run, swatting aside the briers and underbrush, and as if on drill, stopped and re-formed their alignment. Two more color-bearers fell before twenty-one-year-old Colonel Henry Burgwyn waved them forward. The North Carolinians "came on with rapid strides, yelling like demons," according to Colonel Morrow.[47]

When the Confederates closed, they triggered a volley that leveled Michiganders in clots. In both regiments men grabbed fallen flags and died for their valor. The gunfire from both regiments was withering, the casualties staggering. Neither regiment had ever experienced such a desperate, nightmarish struggle. The North Carolinians pressed the Federals through the woods to a second, third, and fourth position. At one point, the lines were only twenty paces apart, and at that point-blank range, many men hit their mark. The orders of officers could be heard in the opposing ranks.[48]

Casualties among color-bearers defied belief. When Colonel Burgwyn of the North Carolinians grabbed the flag to lead the advance, he was the eleventh man to hold the standard. But as he turned to hand it to another man, Burgwyn was cut down with a mortal wound in the lungs. Up the slope, Colonel Morrow picked up his regiment's flag when its fourth holder was struck by a bullet. Before Morrow could wave it, however, Private William Kelly grasped it and said: "The colonel of the Twenty-fourth shall never carry the flag while I am alive." Kelly had barely taken it in his hands when he was killed. Private Lilburn A. Spaulding then stepped forward and took the colors.[49]

The ranks of both regiments almost seemed to disappear. The carnage was not the usual thinning away but a wholesale decimation as seven out of every ten men in the ranks on each side fell killed or wounded. For the Michiganders, however, the valiant stand ended when additional Confederate troops overlapped their left flank, and opened a withering crossfire upon the Westerners' line.[50]

The Michiganders' comrades in the Nineteenth Indiana had held the brigade's left near Willoughby Run. As the Confederates prepared to advance during the afternoon, Colonel Samuel Williams asked to withdraw farther up the western slope of McPherson's Ridge, but Meredith directed that the position must be held. After the morning's fight, the Hoosiers numbered less than three hundred. When the Southerners came on about 2:30 P.M., moving "in a perfect line," Williams ordered the men to fire.[51]

The Hoosiers concentrated their musketry on the Twenty-sixth North Carolina until Pettigrew's second regiment, the Eleventh North Carolina, advanced on the Twenty-sixth's right, swinging their ranks toward the Indianans' left flank. Volleys from the Eleventh "almost annihilated" the Union regiment, according to Lieutenant Colonel William Dudley. "The line was held as long as there were men left to hold it," avowed Dudley. The North Carolinians drove ahead to the stream and raked the Hoosiers with gunfire, shoving the Northerners up the slope. Dudley claimed that eight color-bearers fell in succession, including Private Burlington Cunningham, who had rejoined the regiment after receiving medical treatment for his morning's wound.[52]

Like the Michiganders on their right, the Indianans withdrew fighting. But the fire from the enemy was relentless, scalding the ground and knocking down the Yankees. "The slaughter in our ranks now became frightful, beyond description," declared Captain William Orr. "The dead lay piled up on the ground, and the shrieks and groans of the wounded was too horrible for contemplation." One of Meredith's staff officers witnessed the combat and wrote later that "like dew before the morning sun our men wilted away."[53]

At last, Williams ordered a retreat. "We soon got into confusion," wrote Orr, "no soldiers on earth could stand such terrible fire from both front and flank." The Confederates were within twenty yards of the Hoosiers when the Federals withdrew, and in the words of a North Carolina officer, "we just mowed them down." The Indianans retired over the crest of McPherson's Ridge. Nearby, the Nineteenth's first commander, Solomon Meredith, lay unconscious on the ground, grazed in the head by a piece of an artillery shell.[54]

When the Indianans retired, they exposed the flank of the Michiganders to the fire of the Eleventh North Carolina. Captain William Speed rushed two companies of the Twenty-fourth to the left. The Southerners squeezed a volley, killing Speed with a bullet in the heart. In his report,

Colonel Morrow asserted that the officer's "death was a severe loss to the service and an almost irreparable one to his regiment." The Westerners could endure the punishment no longer, and Morrow ordered a retreat. What was left of the regiment, however, withdrew "step-by-step" to Seminary Ridge, trying to slow the Rebel pursuit. When they reached the latter heights, Morrow was wounded in the face, forcing him to relinquish command to Captain Albert Edwards.[55]

On the right of the Twenty-fourth Michigan, the Second and Seventh Wisconsin followed their comrades to Seminary Ridge. They had opposed Brockenbrough's Virginians, but in the view of Colonel Robinson of the Seventh, they had fired on the enemy "without doing him much injury." The Virginians subjected the Westerners to a "galling fire" before the two regiments fell back, joining Stone's Pennsylvanians and the Michiganders and Indianans. Among the dead on McPherson's Ridge was the Second's Sergeant Major George Legate, who earlier in the day had told a friend that "I will not come out alive." His fellow soldier replied that the sergeant could avoid the fighting, but Legate had refused.[56]

Herbst Woods and McPherson's Ridge belonged to the Confederates. The casualties, particularly among Pettigrew's regiments, had been "appalling." One officer claimed later that "too few were left for a successful bayonet charge" on Seminary Ridge. The losses in the Twenty-sixth North Carolina attested to the ferocity of the struggle for Herbst Woods. The regiment had suffered a staggering total of 86 killed and 502 wounded, a casualty rate of seventy percent. Fourteen color-bearers, including Colonel Burgwyn, had fallen. Its percentage of loss ranks it third among Confederate regiments for a single engagement during the war.[57]

On Seminary Ridge, meanwhile, the survivors in Meredith's, Stone's, and Biddle's brigades re-formed behind breastworks of logs and fence rails, supported by Union artillery crews. The orders had not changed— hold the position "at all hazards." About four o'clock, the Yankees saw the advance of three additional Confederate brigades, approximately five thousand unscathed troops in Pender's division. Their ranks stretched from Chambersburg Road to beyond Fairfield Road. Where pious young men prepared themselves for the Lord's work, other men now prepared themselves for the furies that could possess souls.[58]

Brigadier General Alfred M. Scales's North Carolinians spearheaded Pender's assault, moving through the fields directly south of the pike. Rufus Dawes, whose Sixth Wisconsin had rejoined its fellow Westerners on

Seminary Ridge, watched the oncoming ranks and remembered: "Their bearing was magnificent. They maintained their alignment with great precision." But then Union cannon opened with canister, and blue-coated infantrymen triggered volleys. The North Carolinians "went down like grass before the scythe," reported Colonel Robinson. The gray-coated soldiers staggered and then halted before the wall of artillery and rifle fire, seeking shelter in a shallow ravine. Four hundred of them were casualties, including every officer in the brigade, except one lieutenant.[59]

On the North Carolinians' right, Colonel Abner Perrin's four regiments of South Carolinians passed over McPherson's Ridge into the open fields, directly toward Biddle's Union brigade, which held the left of the Federal infantry line. Along Fairfield Road, three regiments of blue-jacketed cavalrymen added their firepower. The Northerners raked the ranks of the South Carolinians, causing Perrin's left flank regiment to waver. The Confederate colonel rode to the front of his troops, steadied them, and waved the line forward. The Rebels surged up the slope of Seminary Ridge, pouring through a gap between Biddle's troops and the horse soldiers. The Union line unraveled, and once again the black-hatted Westerners were caught in a fearful cauldron of death and maiming.[60]

For the third time on this hot July day—a "Memorable Wednesday" to one Michigander—the Iron Brigade gave more of its own: Lieutenant Colonel Dudley, while holding the flag of the Nineteenth Indiana, fell with a wound that would cost him a leg; Sergeant Major Asa W. Blanchard collapsed with a mortal wound when he took the flag from Dudley; the three remaining members of the Twenty-fourth Michigan color guard were either killed or wounded; privates John W. Welsh and Edward B. Harrison died together as Welsh assisted his close friend from the field; and, Lieutenant Colonel John B. Callis of the Seventh Wisconsin was wounded in the chest and fated to lie on the ground for forty-three hours until a North Carolina officer had him removed to the Seminary when he learned Callis had been born in Fayetteville, North Carolina.[61]

Lieutenant William Orr, writing three weeks later, remembered vividly the death of a soldier who was standing near Orr. "He fell like a log of wood," Orr recounted, "and the blood spurted from the bullet hole in his forehead in a stream as large as your finger."[62]

When the Westerners finally abandoned Seminary Ridge, the Confederates "were so close that we could hear them yelling at us to halt and surrender," according to a Seventh Wisconsin soldier whose comrades covered the brigade's retreat. Officers managed to maintain some order in the ranks until they entered Gettysburg. As the Seminary Ridge defenders stumbled into the town, they encountered streets filled with panic-stricken troops from other units of the First Corps and from the Eleventh Corps, who had been routed by Rodes's and Early's divisions on Oak Ridge and on the plain north of town. "There was no more discipline or semblence of ranks," asserted a Sixth Wisconsin sergeant, "than would be found in a herd of cattle."[63]

The victorious Southerners raced in pursuit, their gunfire sweeping the streets. A number of Federal troops ducked into cellars and were subsequently taken prisoner. A Pennsylvanian remembered one Sixth Wisconsin soldier, identified by the numeral 6 on his black hat, who did not escape the enemy fire. As three of them ran down a side street, according to the Keystone State man, Rebel pursuers shouted: "Halt, you Yankee sons of bitches." When the Northerners refused, the gray-clad soldiers shot at them, and one bullet smashed into the head of the Wisconsinite. "It cracked like a pistol shot," wrote the eyewitness of the sound as the minié ball hit the skull. "He fell sprawling in the street. I looked down and saw his brains oozing out, and then stepped over him and hurried away."[64]

The blue-coated fugitives who eluded the captors eventually halted on Cemetery Hill south of Gettysburg. Here, Union reserves had formed a line, buttressed by cannon. It was the ground Buford and Reynolds had noticed, and now the heights provided a good defensive position for the Federals. Meade had sent Major General Winfield Scott Hancock, commander of the Second Corps, to Gettysburg to assume command of the troops. Hancock restored order, fashioned a battle line, and prepared for an anticipated assault. Although Lee, who was on the field, hoped to secure the heights with an attack, the daylight hours passed without a movement.[65]

The sacrifice of the officers and men of the First and Eleventh corps had been for this high ground—Cemetery Hill, Culp's Hill, and Cemetery Ridge. Many of the units, particularly in the First Corps, had bled more than they ever had on a battlefield. An officer on Abner Doubleday's staff, when he saw the survivors, described them as "a miserable remnant" and a "pitiable sight." Casualties in the three divisions of the corps approached 6,000 out of approximately 9,500 engaged. Rufus Dawes described it as "the horrid butchery of the 1st Corps."[66]

No unit paid a dearer price on this "Memorable Wednesday" than the Iron Brigade. A Wisconsin corporal had it right when he wrote a couple of weeks later that "it seems almost a miracle how any of us escaped." Nearly every survivor of the nearly nineteen hundred who went into the fight could count at least one bullet hole in his uniform. The unparalleled losses for the brigade amounted to 189 killed or mortally wounded, 774 wounded, and 249 captured or missing, for a total of 1,212.[67]

The numbers testified to the valor of the Westerners. Twelve of fifteen field officers had been killed, wounded, or captured; over two dozen color-bearers had fallen; casualty rates in the Second Wisconsin and Twenty-fourth Michigan approached or exceeded, respectively, sixty percent; and the total losses in the latter regiment were the highest of any Union regiment during the three-day battle. Casualties among officers at the regimental level had been devastating. A chaplain, writing about the Michigan regiment, could have spoken for the entire brigade when he described it as *"utterly decimated."*[68]

"Our Brig. never did better," boasted an Indiana soldier with justification. In time, Doubleday cited thirty-seven officers and men for their conduct. But as night came to Gettysburg on July 1, the Westerners sought food and sleep. They knew that they would never see many of their comrades again and could only hope that they would recover the wounded who lay among enemy troops. Perhaps some thought of Sergeant William Evans, to whom Dawes had given the flag of the Second Mississippi, or of Private Jefferson Coates, whose bravery on this day would earn the Seventh Wisconsin volunteer a Medal of Honor. As their comrades slept, Evans rested in a bed in town, having given the captured standard to the household members for safekeeping, and Coates looked into an eternal darkness, blinded by a bullet that had struck both of his eyes.[69]

The Stonewall Brigade and the three other brigades of Edward Johnson's division arrived at Gettysburg as their comrades in Richard Ewell's and A. P. Hill's corps celebrated their victory of July 1. Johnson's troops had been on the march all day, plodding along for twenty-five miles, their progress impeded by James Longstreet's First Corps wagons, which had clogged Chambersburg Pike. When Johnson reached Gettysburg, he was ordered to the east. As his troops passed through the town, some Valley men discovered a barrel of whiskey in a cellar, and the Virginians in a "constant stream" entered the dwelling, filling canteens until a lieutenant protested to superior officers.[70]

The Virginians numbered fourteen hundred. Like the majority of troops in the army, they were confident. In a typical view, one of them had written home earlier: "I think we will clear the Yankees out this summer and whip them." Earlier on the 1st, a British army officer who had joined the Southerners as an observer had watched "the celebrated 'Stonewall' Brigade" pass on the pike. "In appearance," he wrote later, "the men differ little from other Confederate soldiers, except, perhaps, that the brigade contains more elderly men and fewer boys."[71]

Soldiers in both armies and Gettysburg's civilians awoke to a summer's warmth and to silence on the morning of July 2. In time, controversies would stalk the day's events. But as the sun rose, Robert E. Lee was planning a resumption of the battle, choosing to retain the initiative by attacking the Federals. As he had affirmed to Longstreet late on the afternoon of the 1st: "If the enemy is there tomorrow, we must attack him." Lee had intended not to engage the Union army unless assailed by it, but the first day's success had made a battle "unavoidable" in his word. "It was thought advisable," he stated in his report, "to renew the attack."[72]

Lee had on the field that morning eight of nine infantry divisions and most of his artillery batteries to use in the offensive. The commanding general wanted a strike as soon as possible, settling upon an assault on the Union left flank. Delays ensued, however—Longstreet objected to an offensive; Lee conferred with subordinates; they waited upon the arrival of a brigade; and the movement to the attack point necessitated a countermarch to avoid detection.[73]

It was not until four o'clock in the afternoon when two of Longstreet's divisions rolled forward into a landscape destined to be christened with proper names because of the subsequent three hours of slaughter—Peach Orchard, Wheatfield, Devil's Den, Big Round Top, and Little Round Top. Eventually, Lee's en echelon attack moved against Cemetery Ridge, and after nightfall, Cemetery Hill and Culp's Hill. George Meade's blue-coated defenders withstood the successive blows, but the Southerners had nearly achieved a victory. During the fierce combat, it seemed to one of Longstreet's men that the Yankees never ran out of troops, causing him to exclaim to his comrades: "Great God! Have we got the universe to whip?"[74]

On the Confederate left, where Ewell's three Second Corps divisions held the town and guarded the eastern approaches to Gettysburg, meanwhile, the day had passed quietly, allowing Meade to shuttle units from that sector of the battlefield to the southern end where the Federals battled Longstreet's troops. Lee's instructions to Ewell were discretionary—when the corps commander heard Longstreet's attack, he should "make a simultaneous demonstration upon the enemy's right, to be converted into a real attack should opportunity offer." Ewell opened with artillery at four o'-clock, but more than two hours passed before Johnson advanced with three brigades against Culp's Hill, a rock-strewn, wooded elevation southeast of Cemetery Hill.[75]

Culp's Hill anchored Meade's right flank, its rugged terrain favoring defenders. Rock Creek edged its eastern base. Two peaks, rising 180 feet and 80 feet, respectively, above the stream and 400 yards apart, capped the hill's crest. Any attack force would have to negotiate Rock Creek and then scale the heights. The Federals had strengthened the hill's natural features with earthen and log breastworks. When Johnson moved against the position, however, the defending force had been reduced by Meade's need for reinforcements on the Union left.[76]

Johnson's attack floundered at the outset as the troops groped across Rock Creek. Once the Confederates became engaged, Brigadier General George Steuart's brigade occupied abandoned works on the Union right, wheeled left, and struck the enemy. Blue-clad reinforcements stopped Steuart's thrust, but the Rebels held the works east of the lower peak. When additional Federal units returned to Culp's Hill, they were surprised to discover the enemy in the works. Darkness ended the struggle, and the Confederates bedded down where they were at the combat's conclusion.[77]

James Walker and the Stonewall Brigade had spent July 2 guarding Ewell's left flank on Brinkerhoff Ridge along Hanover Road, east of Gettysburg. Late in the afternoon, Union cavalrymen approached on foot, and Walker sent the Second Virginia against the enemy. The Virginians shoved the Yankees back through a wheatfield and woods before rejoining the brigade. Walker then received orders from Johnson to protect the division's flank as it advanced upon Culp's Hill. The fighting had ceased before the Virginians could become engaged, and they halted for the night in the rear of Steuart's brigade.[78]

Sometime late in the day, Sergeant David Hunter of the Second Virginia wrote a letter to his mother. "We are in all probability on [the] eve of a terrible battle," he thought. "The two contending armies lie close together and at any moment may commense the work of death. Great results hang upon the issue of the battle. If we are victorious peace may follow if not

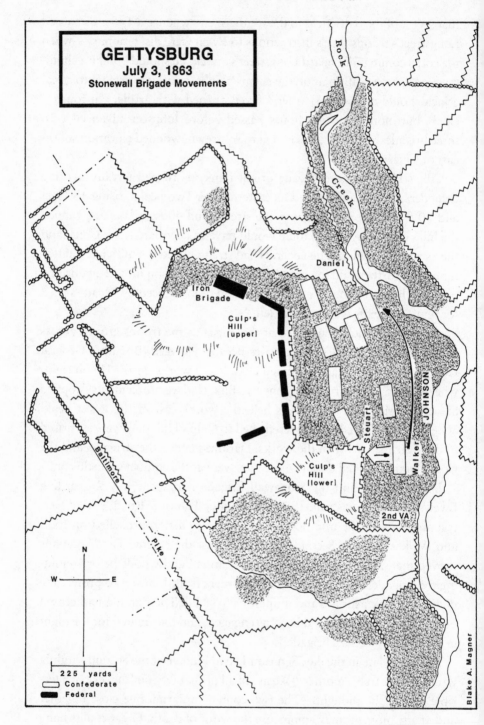

GETTYSBURG
July 3, 1863
Stonewall Brigade Movements

Iron
Brigade

Culp's
Hill
[upper]

Culp's
Hill
[lower]

Daniel

JOHNSON

Steuart

Walker

2nd VA

Rock

Creek

Baltimore

Pike

N
W   E
S

225 yards
☐ Confederate
■ Federal

Blake A. Magner

we may look for a long and fierce war. We trust in the wisdom of our Gens. and the goodness of our Father in Heaven who doeth all things well."[79]

The "terrible battle" that Hunter predicted began about daybreak on July 3. Ewell had been instructed by Lee to attack at first light with Johnson's division and brigades from Rodes's and Early's commands. At the designated hour, Johnson's troops moved through the woods and up the slope of Culp's Hill. The Stonewall Brigade advanced behind and in support of Steuart's men. To protect their left flank, Steuart detached the First North Carolina and Walker, the Second Virginia.[80]

On the crest, the Federals waited until the shadowy figures closed within range and then fired. The Southerners responded in kind, igniting a struggle that would last for roughly the next seven hours. The musketry rolled back and forth, up and down the hillside, in sheets of flame and in bitter, acrid clouds of smoke. The Confederates shielded themselves behind trees and boulders when officers were not urging them to press forward. Battle lines fragmented amid the trees and rocks as groups of Rebels scrambled up the slope only to be blasted back down.[81]

Like their gray-coated comrades, the Virginians of the Stonewall Brigade made little progress even in support of Steuart's regiments. When the Valley men had expended their ammunition in what Walker described as "incessant firing," he withdrew them to replenish their cartridge boxes. Johnson soon encountered them in the rear and directed them to the right of the line to replace another brigade at the front. Walker complied, bringing his regiments into position on the right of Brigadier General Junius Daniel's brigade of Rodes's division. The Virginians and Daniel's North Carolinians, who had assisted in the defeat of the Union First Corps on July 1, ascended the hillside.[82]

The earlier fighting had been only a prelude to the broiling fury these Old Dominion and Old North State volunteers now encountered. The Union gunfire pinned down the Virginians. Clusters of men tried to claw their way forward, but could advance only so far—beyond certain points no man could survive. "I think it was the hardest battle we ever had," avowed a member of the Thirty-third Virginia. In that regiment, Captain George R. Bedinger, a popular officer who jokingly called his Irishmen of Company E "Greeks," died while urging them up the slope. A fellow officer believed that Bedinger fell closer to the enemy works than any other Confederate.[83]

In the Twenty-seventh Virginia, Captain John Welsh of Company B suffered "a severe flesh wound in my right hip," as he would inform his wife a few days later. A farmer from Rockbridge County, Welsh had not enlisted in the regiment until March 1862. He had a brother, James, who had relocated to Illinois in 1853. When the secession of Southern states began in the winter of 1861, the brothers exchanged letters, each arguing the rightness of their causes. James tried to dissuade John from embracing the Confederacy while John replied that he did not "intend to submit to Black Republican rule any longer." They chose their separate paths—John into the Twenty-seventh, James into an Illinois regiment. Now, on the soil his brother had volunteered to defend, John received a wound that would take his life on July 15. James would survive the war.[84]

During some of the worst musketry, a member of the Fourth Virginia raised a white flag. The Confederates were trapped by the gunfire; they could neither advance nor retreat. When Private John McKee of Company I, a Liberty Hall Volunteer who had been captured at Kernstown and exchanged, saw it, he asked his captain if he could shoot the soldier. The officer refused, suggesting that McKee throw rocks at him. McKee did, and the white cloth came down.[85]

The enemy musketry had become "so destructive," Walker reported, "that I suffered the brigade to fall back to a more secure position, as it was a useless sacrifice of life to keep them longer under so galling a fire." For nearly a quarter of the Fourth Virginia, however, Walker's order came too late. The Fourteenth Connecticut rushed the Virginians, capturing the regimental flag and sixty-one men, including Private McKee. Another two dozen in the other three regiments either were captured or surrendered, unwilling to risk their lives running the gauntlet of gunfire.[86]

The Confederate assault on Culp's Hill ended in a bloody failure. Casualties in the Second Corps units exceeded two thousand. In the Stonewall Brigade, the losses amounted to 62 killed or mortally wounded, 169 wounded, and 87 captured or missing— a total of 318, or nearly one fourth of the command. The Second Virginia incurred the fewest losses, having engaged only in a brisk skirmish south of the hill. Ironically, the only member of the Second killed in the action was twenty-four-year-old Private John Wesley Culp of Company B. Culp had been born in Gettysburg but moved to Shepherdstown, Virginia, when his employer, a carriage maker, relocated his business to that community. Culp had enlisted in the Second in 1861. Now, two years later, he returned home to die near the farm and hill owned by and named for his great-grandfather.[87]

About two hours after the combat subsided on Culp's Hill, Confederate artillery, upward of 170 cannon, opened a bombardment on the center of the Union line on Cemetery Ridge. Lee had decided, again over the objections of Longstreet, to launch a frontal assault across nearly a mile of open ground against the Federals. When the guns ceased, fifty Confederate regiments from eleven brigades, numbering perhaps fourteen thousand, advanced in the most renowned infantry charge of the war. But Lee's final gamble at Gettysburg ended in a repulse. The three-day battle had exacted a price from both armies of more than fifty thousand casualties.[88]

Rain began falling late in the day on July 4 at Gettysburg, increasing during the night to a downpour. After nightfall, the Confederate army abandoned its lines around the town, turned south, and marched for home beyond the Potomac River. It would not be until the 14th, however, before the Southerners returned to Virginia. Their passage would be delayed by the swollen river, forcing them to build fieldworks near Williamsport, Maryland, to defend the crossing sites from Meade's pursuing army. With their withdrawal across the Potomac, the Gettysburg Campaign ended.[89]

Within days of the return to Virginia, a Confederate surgeon visited his former command, the Fourth Virginia. He was shocked by how few remained. He believed that "the whole regt. is about 1/3 larger" than the company of men which had marched out of Blacksburg in the spring of 1861. The "contrast," he told his wife, "almost makes me sad."[90]

A day earlier, Sergeant Daniel Sheetz of the Second Virginia wrote a letter home. "I can not say that I am enjoying myself at all at this time," the Valley man stated. "I am too much woried down from the march that we had in the yankee states . . . it was the hardest times that we had since the war. I was in good hopes that the war would soon be over, but it don't look much like it at this time."[91]

A member of the Iron Brigade thought that the Fourth of July at Gettysburg "was a day like a funeral." Another Westerner believed that the stench that seemed to envelop the entire battlefield "was so strong that it would drive a dog out of the tanyard." For Rufus Dawes, the day marked his twenty-fifth birthday, but his mood, as he described it to his future wife, was "solemn." So few remained in his Sixth Wisconsin and in the brigade. "Oh Mary," he wrote, "it is awful to look now at my shattered band of devoted men," explaining that "the fighting has been the most desperate I ever saw."[92]

Although the Southerners remained in visible battle lines, the Federals began the sad and gruesome task of burying the dead. Rain came in the afternoon, soaking the survivors and slowing the work as the ground turned to mud. On the 5th, when the black-hatted veterans learned of the Confederate retreat, many of them walked from their position near Culp's Hill to the scene of the first day's fighting, searching for comrades still alive. Orders for a march, however, prevented them from burying their own.[93]

One of Dawes's soldiers, after crossing the ground, told his family in a letter that "the battle field of Gettysburg was one vast slaughter pen. Dead & wounded lay in all directions. A man that went through the carnage unhurt may call himself a lucky man." The killing and maiming had convinced him that "I would as soon throw my old musket down & take a turn at farming as not."[94]

To a man, it would seem, the soldier's comrades shared his sentiments. A Hoosier officer admitted to his wife: "Oh Maggie, I pray God that I may never witness such another slaughter." Similarly, Dawes asserted to his Mary: "May God save me and my men from any more such trials. Our bravest and best are cold in the ground or suffering on beds of anguish." The three days of battle, Dawes believed, "seem more like a horrible dream than the reality."[95]

But it was the reality of it that overwhelmed them. Perhaps they sensed or knew, as they walked among their fallen comrades on McPherson's Ridge, in Herbst Woods, beside the railroad cut, and on Seminary Ridge, that the Iron Brigade would never be the same. Too many black hats, some in knots, some in ragged lines, like distinctive headstones, lay upon the ground.

Their sacrifice and that of other Yankees on July 1, however, had given the Union army the heights south of town from which the Confederates could not dislodge it on the 2nd and 3rd. While they had suffered grievous casualties, they had inflicted crippling losses on some of the attacking units. Except for the Sixth Wisconsin's brief involvement in the action on Culp's Hill on the evening of the 2nd, the Westerners were spared from the carnage on the final two days. When Lee's final assault failed on the afternoon of the 3rd, the Iron Brigade members reacted with "great jubilation." Like other units, their role had been instrumental in the Union victory. But no brigade had paid such a price in blood for that victory.[96]

The Iron Brigade, or "all there is left of it," marched away from Gettysburg on Monday, July 6, in pursuit of the retreating Confederates. Thousands in the Union army were barefooted, with many wearing the same clothing for the past three weeks. The heavy rains that swelled the Potomac and stalled Lee's army in Maryland slowed the Union efforts to overtake the Rebels. Although Meade and his ranking generals discussed an assault on the enemy works around Williamsport, the Southerners escaped before the Federals attacked. When the Yankees discovered the empty lines, a Michigander grumbled in his diary that "the hog has got away & we the whippet run up to the fence and bark."[97]

On July 17, three days after the enemy returned to Virginia, a Second Wisconsin man wrote home. Although he referred only to his regiment, his words applied to all the units in the Iron Brigade. The soldier was convinced that a time would come again, as it had on July 1, when some generals would "just shove them ahead like a lot of cattle going to the slaughter." The generals knew, he complained, "that the Wis. Boys will fight and not run." But "one more shove," he concluded, and "then the 'jig is up.'"[98]

14

✠

Two Rivers

A silence came to Virginia after Gettysburg. When the Army of Northern Virginia recrossed the Potomac River on July 14, 1863, the war in the Old Dominion entered a period of relative quiet that would continue through the fall and winter months into the spring of 1864. Only twice during this nine-month lull—in mid-October and at the end of November—would either the Confederates or their opponent, the Army of the Potomac, undertake an offensive operation. In both instances, little resulted except to lengthen the casualty lists.

Since his accession to army command on June 1, 1862, General Robert E. Lee had seized and retained the strategic initiative in the East. He and his army had forged the conflict's course for thirteen months. Only in May 1863, during the Chancellorsville Campaign, had an opponent, Major General Joseph Hooker, determined the battleground. Gettysburg had been an unwanted collision, but the engagement had resulted from Lee's second thrust into the North. In the aftermath of the Confederate defeat and the unparalleled losses, the war in the East paused, as if two antagonists could give no more.

During this interlude a divided nation would watch the recoursing of the conflict in the West, beyond the Appalachian Mountains. The events in the region heralded the rise of a different warrior, Union Major General Ulysses S. Grant, and the decline of Southern fortunes. The reshaping of the war began on July 4, with the surrender of Vicksburg, Mississippi, and its garrison to Grant. It would turn suddenly with a Confederate victory at the Battle of Chickamauga in Georgia, on September 19–20, only to culminate in a Union victory at Chattanooga, Tennessee, on November 23–25. The victor at Chattanooga would again be Grant, and before another winter released its hold, he would be summoned east to confront the man who had governed the war from Seven Days through Gettysburg.

For the present in Virginia, however, Lee brought his army to familiar ground, the region drained by the Rappahannock and Rapidan rivers. By July's final week, the Confederates were positioned south of the streams, their camps and picket posts strewn behind the rivers from Gordonsville and Orange Court House in the Piedmont to Fredericksburg on the Rappahannock. Here, in a region that had witnessed much of the war in 1862, the Southerners stopped and would stay for the next nine months. North of the Rappahannock, their old nemesis settled into camps.[1]

Major General Richard Ewell's Second Corps manned the lines along the Rapidan River southeast of Culpeper Court House. From this location a year ago, Stonewall Jackson had marched forth to give battle at Cedar Mountain, where the Stonewall Brigade had lost its commander, Charles Winder. Now, both Winder and Jackson were gone as the Virginians and their fellow Second Corps members guarded familiar fords and attended to the duties of camp life.[2]

To a man, most likely, the Virginians welcomed the return to their native state and the weeks of rest. Gettysburg had not been forgotten, but the defeat had not caused a breakdown of morale. Although hundreds of men deserted after the army crossed the Potomac, Lee and the troops believed that the campaign had achieved most of its objectives despite the battle's outcome. They had been beaten because the Federals had held a formidable position and had fought tenaciously. To them, Gettysburg had been a setback, not a turning point. The war remained at hand, an easy day's march across a river.[3]

They were, however, weary of the conflict and of the carnage. While "the general belief" held that the war would be over by next spring, they wanted to be home with family and friends. "I would be glad," wrote Private John Garibaldi of the Twenty-seventh Virginia to his wife in a typical letter during August, "if this war was to stop so that we might all come and mind our business at home. I think if fighting will settle this matter there has been fighting enough now, and if fighting wouldn't settle it, there is no use of any more bloodshed."[4]

For Garibaldi and his comrades, however, duty along the Rapidan offered a reprieve. The Valley men rotated picket duty at the fords with the other brigades in Major General Edward Johnson's division during August and September. While not assigned to guard the shallows or to camp, details from the division constructed fieldworks along the river. Private Garibaldi believed that such efforts would not "do much good," explaining that "the yankees never did attack us in our fortifications yet. Wherever we fortify in one place, they go and attack us in another."[5]

While in camp, the troops groused about the restrictions imposed by their commander, Brigadier General James Walker. The discontent with Walker's orders was so deep that one brigade member headed a letter with "Camp Stonewall Penetentiary," explaining that "we are not alloud any privilidges at all." When the officers held a picnic and the guard found Walker drunk, sprawled in a road, the enlisted men were incensed. "The Brigade," asserted one of them, "hates him worse than they did Winder." If it had been a private instead of Walker who had been inebriated, the brigadier "would have had him put in the guard house and linched," contended the soldier. "Such a man is not worth living."[6]

Temporary relief from the routine of picket duty and Walker's strictures came on October 9, when the Confederates forded the Rapidan, marching north. Although the army's strength had been reduced a month earlier with the detachment of two infantry divisions and an artillery battalion, under James Longstreet, to Tennessee, Lee undertook an offensive movement to turn the Union army's right flank and to operate against its main supply line, the Orange & Alexandria Railroad.[7]

The resulting Bristoe Campaign lasted for a dozen days. The Federals retreated north before the Confederates, halting eventually behind Bull Run. The only bloody clash of the operations occurred on October 14, at Bristoe Station. In a badly managed action, A. P. Hill's Third Corps units were repulsed in attacks upon enemy troops sheltered by the railroad embankment at Bristoe Station. Three days later, Lee abandoned the offensive, and on the 20th, the final contingent of his army recrossed the Rappahannock. Total casualties in the campaign exceeded three thousand.[8]

The Stonewall Brigade participated in the operations but suffered few, if any, casualties. Within days of the campaign's conclusion, the Virginians and their comrades in other units had resumed picket duty at the fords. During November, they built additional fieldworks along the river, held an inspection and review for President Davis, and received "a whole lot" of shoes, shirts, pants, jackets, and underdrawers from the people in the Valley. "This was far the best clothing for winter," declared a private, "we drew for a long time." The entire brigade had "good warm clothing."[9]

Rations, however, were "very scanty," according to a soldier. During the month, a religious revival swept through the army, harvesting a new batch of believers, including many Valley men. The renewal of faith was coupled with the fervor of romance. "There seems to be a great marrying fever in the Brigade at present," claimed a member in a letter. As for the prospects of peace, a soldier in the Fourth Virginia thought that "our independence is mighty hard to get, but we are not discouraged. I do not believe it ever will be settled that is by fighting."[10]

The fighting resumed during the final week of November. Prodded by the administration in Washington to assail the Confederates before winter, Major General George Meade sent his army across the Rapidan in an offensive on November 26. Like Lee the month before, Meade attempted to move around his opponent's right flank in what became known as the Mine Run Campaign.[11]

This time the Stonewall Brigade was not spared. On the afternoon of the 27th, the Virginians and two other brigades of Johnson's division encountered a Union force near the farm of Madison Payne. The ground was heavily wooded, except around the farm buildings. The combat ignited when the Second Virginia, posted in front as skirmishers, clashed with enemy skirmishers. For two hours, the regiment dueled with the Yankees, losing its commander, Lieutenant Colonel Raleigh T. Colston, with a leg wound. The injury necessitated amputation, and Colston would succumb to pneumonia on December 23. In his report, Johnson described Colston as "chivalric."[12]

About four o'clock, the combat intensified when the Yankees pushed ahead against the Second Virginia. Walker reacted by advancing the rest of the brigade, repulsing the enemy thrust and advancing toward the farm. On the Virginians' left, however, a supporting brigade failed to keep pace, exposing Walker's ranks to an enfilade fire. Some of the Confederates wheeled to face the enemy, but the Union musketry lashed the Valley men, who withdrew into the shelter of the trees. Here, the two other brigades joined them, and the combat frittered away.[13]

The Battle of Payne's Farm cost the Stonewall Brigade about 150 officers and men. The Second and Fourth Virginia incurred more than half of the casualties. One member of the Second called the engagement "the Battle of the Georges" as four of the five enlisted men killed or mortally wounded in the regiment had the first name of George.[14]

The opposing armies confronted each other along Mine Run for another three days after Payne's Farm. The Confederates manned a strong defensive position behind fieldworks, and Meade hesitated to assault Lee's troops. When Union probes uncovered no weak sectors of the enemy line, Meade ordered a withdrawal that commenced on December 1. With the Federals back across the Rapidan on the 2nd, active campaigning in Virginia ended for the year. On both sides on the rivers, soldiers prepared for winter.[15]

The Valley men's camp was situated outside Orange Court House. The Virginians built their cabins that served as their homes for the next five months. Just before Christmas, the brigade was assigned on a rotating basis to picket duty at Morton's Ford on the Rapidan. As winter settled in, life simplified, its rhythms governed by the weather and by the duties of camp and of picketing.[16]

With the approach of a new year, barely a thousand Virginians remained in the five regiments. Chancellorsville, Second Winchester, Gettysburg, Payne's Farm, and nameless skirmishes had taken almost an equal number of their comrades during the previous months. While desertions slowed as compared to 1862, approximately 425 men abandoned the ranks during the year. Dozens of deserters were arrested, court-martialed, and received sentences of death, hard labor, loss of pay, or imprisonment. Several were ordered to be executed, but only one man, Private Layton B. Morris of the Second Virginia, faced a firing squad. Authorities spared the others on a technicality that less than two-thirds of the officers on the courts-martial had approved the sentences.[17]

The year's final week along the Rapidan was wet as rain fell for three days. The men ate their meager fare of bacon and bread for Christmas and finished building their huts. They thought of home, waited for the mail, and watched for Yankees beyond the stream. "An armistice," noted one of them, had been declared, not by man but by nature.[18]

✠

Corporal Horace Currier had stood in the ranks of Company I, Seventh Wisconsin nearly two years from his enlistment on July 10, 1861, until his capture at Gettysburg on July 1, 1863. Throughout the months, he had chronicled his service and that of the regiment in letters home to Oasis, Wisconsin. His soldiering had ended on the afternoon of July 1, when Confederate troops overtook the corporal during the Union flight through Gettysburg. He was herded with other captives south and eventually imprisoned in Richmond, Virginia. His confinement was brief, however, as he became ill, was exchanged, and admitted to a hospital in Annapolis, Maryland. Currier died there on August 15 of an unspecified disease. Gettysburg had taken another black-hatted Westerner.[19]

Currier's Iron Brigade comrades probably learned of his death sometime around the one-year anniversary of Brawner's Farm. The loss of another of them only added to the fearful gleaning of their ranks that had begun on the late afternoon of August 28, 1862. Nearly three thousand members of the brigade had been killed, wounded, or captured during the past year. Hundreds more had been sent home, discharged for various reasons. When they had left Wisconsin, Indiana, and Michigan, their ranks swelled, pulsating with youthful idealism, and now the regiments appeared to be no larger than an oversized company. They had embraced the fury on that August afternoon at John Brawner's, and it began to consume them at a terrible rate.[20]

But nothing had compared to Gettysburg. Forty percent of the brigade's losses had come during this battle. So many of the most experienced officers and best men had been struck down that the unit's combat effectiveness would never again be as good. While an officer could rightfully assert that "we claim to be as good fighting material as this country affords," the brigade that rushed across the fields south of the Seminary buildings on the morning of July 1 soon disappeared, ripped apart on McPherson's Ridge, in Herbst Woods, and before the railroad cut.[21]

Gettysburg, in fact, had reached into the soul of the brigade. The survivors had seen hell on that July day and wanted no part of it again. Rufus Dawes saw Gettysburg's toll in the men's faces, heard it in their words, and described the passage they had been through together in a letter to his fiancée. "The Iron Brigade has a *record* beyond reproach and a record it will vindicate," he wrote, "but the Iron Brigade terribly *dreads* a battle. There is no man talking any other way, Mary. A battle to *veterans* is an awful thing."[22]

Never again would they answer combat's summons with "headlong recklessness." They now believed, according to Dawes, that *"safety"* was the "best securer of victory." The Westerners also were convinced that when the time came again they would not be spared. "We may have to fight some hard battles this fall yet but I think not," stated a Hoosier. "I hope not any ways if there is any fighting we will be sure to get in on it for they could not leave out the Iron Brigade."[23]

The war was not far away, beyond the Rapidan and Rappahannock rivers. Like their opponents, the Federals guarded the shallows and established camps back from the streams. By the first week of August, the Westerners were posted in the vicinity of Rappahannock Station on the Orange & Alexandria Railroad and Beverly Ford on the river. Colonel William Robinson of the Seventh Wisconsin commanded the brigade in the absence of Solomon Meredith, who was recuperating from his Gettysburg wound.[24]

Routine marked the hot days of August and September along the Rappahannock. One of the Westerners claimed that "the army is in the best of spirits." A rumor persisted in the brigade for weeks that they were to be sent home to recruit. Strings of conscripts or drafted men, dressed in new uniforms and escorted by guard details, arrived. Dawes described them as "a sorry looking set," and grumbled that "what a contrast between such hounds and the enthusiastic and eager volunteers of 1861. Our men thoroughly despise these cattle." When an inspector passed through the bivouac site of the Twenty-fourth Michigan, he pronounced it to be, in a diarist's entry, "the d-d-t nastiest camp in the Army of the Potomac."[25]

The highlight of these weeks for the Westerners occurred on September 17. Citizens from the men's home states had raised $1,000 and had commissioned Tiffany's in New York City to make a flag for the brigade. When the company finished it, preparations were completed for a ceremony with the anniversary of Antietam designated as the date. On the 17th, a delegation of citizens and government officials, bearing the flag, arrived by railroad from Washington.[26]

The Second Wisconsin met the train and escorted the guests to the ceremonial site. At 5:00 P.M., Colonel Robinson accepted the flag on behalf of the brigade before the black-hatted veterans, invited generals and officers, and the delegation. Robinson expressed the command's gratitude and then presented the banner to the troops. The standard was, crowed a soldier, *"the most beautiful flag the country ever saw!"*[27]

Tiffany's had used the finest dark blue silk for the flag, with a fringe of deep, rich gold. In the center an eagle, perched on a United States shield, its wings spread, soared above a bank of clouds. Its talons held eight scrolls, one with "E Pluribus Unum," another with "Iron Brigade" on it, and six with the names of the brigade's engagements. The names of the five regiments completed the design. Unwilling to carry the flag into battle, the brigade sent it to Wisconsin for safekeeping, and today it rests in the War Museum at the state capitol.[28]

With the ceremony ended, Robinson invited officers and guests to a banquet. Champagne flowed at the tables set in a grove of trees. An enlisted man noted in his diary that "the officers had a big drunk proposing toast, drinking health & feeling good generally." Dawes complained that by the end of the meal the revelers were "almost unanimously drunk" and "conferred little honor on the brigade as gentlemen." The next morning regimental officers allowed the rank and file to drain the bottles, and in the words of a soldier, "they had a grand brigade drunk." Several brawls between the men concluded the two-day festivities.[29]

Three weeks later the tactical stalemate along the rivers ended when the Confederates marched north, initiating the Bristoe Campaign. The Iron Brigade and the other units of the Union army withdrew in reaction and followed the tracks of the Orange & Alexandria Railroad. On the night of October 19–20, Rebel cavalry bagged thirty-four members of the Seventh Wisconsin who were on picket duty. When Lee abandoned the offensive and retreated south, the Federals remained near Centreville until the last week of the month. During this interlude, details from the Iron Brigade returned to Brawner's Farm and reburied the exposed corpses of their comrades who had fallen there. On October 25, in a cold rain, the Westerners headed south, arriving at the front along the Rapidan and Rappahannock by November 1.[30]

During the return march, some Federal troops had killed livestock and stolen property that belonged to a Union-sympathizing family. Acting division commander Lysander Cutler, former colonel of the Sixth Wisconsin, accused members of the Iron Brigade and demanded that the Westerners pay for the damages, which had been assessed at $150. Cutler's accusation created "a considerable stir in our Brigade," wrote a Hoosier. Dawes dubbed it a "strange demand" that soon was "all blown over" when Cutler learned that the Fourteenth Brooklyn had committed the depredations.[31]

On November 3, the members of the Wisconsin regiments voted in their state's election. The troops cast their ballots overwhelmingly for Republican candidates, in one soldier's count, 602 to 17. They wanted to assure that Wisconsin would remain steadfast in support of the war effort and the administration in Washington. They believed, as a brigade officer put it in an earlier letter, that the North "will eventually reestablish the Government," although it might "take time, *perhaps a long time.*"[32]

The brigade's thinned ranks still testified to the command's losses at Gettysburg. Earlier, the First New York Battalion of Sharpshooters had been assigned to the brigade to augment its numbers. But if the regiments were to be strengthened, recruits were required. During the first week of November, an officer and two enlisted men from the Wisconsin and Indiana regiments departed for their respective states to enlist new men. For the veterans, the government offered bounties and thirty-day furloughs if they reenlisted.[33]

Two weeks later, the Westerners welcomed back Solomon Meredith. The brigadier had returned from leave in October and had spent a day with the brigade while it was at Centreville. Now he had come to say farewell. He still suffered physically and mentally from the effects of his Gettysburg wound and believed he could not resume active service in the field. He had been popular with the rank and file and had proven to be a better commander than John Gibbon had predicted. As a testimony to the man and to the soldier, brigade officers prepared a resolution in which they expressed their "esteem" for and "warm sentiments" to Meredith.[34]

On Saturday, November 21, Meredith "said good-by to us," according to a diarist. What he said went unrecorded, but if he had been brief, it would have been uncharacteristic of the politician-turned-soldier. No longer would his giant hulk be a familiar sight in camp or at the head of the column. With the departure of Long Sol, the brigade lost one of its most colorful individuals.[35]

While Meredith remained in the army, eventually assuming command of the garrison at Cairo, Illinois, other brigade officers who had been wounded at Gettysburg either resigned or were discharged because of their injuries. In the Second Wisconsin, Colonel Lucius Fairchild tendered his resignation after promotion to brigadier general and returned to Wisconsin, where the one-armed veteran would forge a political career that culminated with the governorship. In the Twenty-fourth Michigan, Lieutenant Colonel Mark Flanigan, Major Edwin B. Wight, and two captains resumed their civilian lives. For his conduct at Gettysburg, Flanigan would be promoted to the brevet or temporary rank of brigadier general on March 13, 1865.[36]

Colonel Robinson of the Seventh Wisconsin, meanwhile, retained command of the brigade and led it during the Mine Run Campaign. The Union army advanced across the rivers on November 26, and as noted previously, confronted its opponents along Mine Run until December 2. The Westerners lost two men to wounds during the operations. According to a lieutenant, they "had a very rough time of it" because of the cold weather and the lack of tents.[37]

Upon its return from Mine Run, the Union army began the construction of winter quarters. Robinson's troops were assigned to a campsite about four miles downstream from Rappahannock Station. They finished the cabins a week before Christmas and were never "more comfortably situated than at present," remarked an officer. The Westerners celebrated Christmas as "grog flowed free." Before year's end, however, orders came for the brigade to relocate to the Culpeper Court House area. The men reacted to the change with "some considerable swearing," but they abandoned the cabins, marched across the Rappahannock, and were quartered temporarily in houses in the town.[38]

But few orders could dampen the spirits of the Wisconsin and Indiana men. After more than two months of speeches by officers, serenades of "patriotic music," and debates around campfires, enough officers and men in the Sixth and Seventh Wisconsin and Nineteenth Indiana were signing papers of enlistment as "veteran volunteers." The "ever lasting veteran question" had been the topic of ceaseless discussion for weeks. The army would grant to each enrolled man in a regiment a thirty-day furlough when three-fourths of its aggregate strength—the number of officers and men present and absent—reenlisted.[39]

The efforts to secure the required figures in each regiment intensified as the new year approached. A bounty of $400 was offered as an inducement to enlisted men. To qualify for the leave and the money, the members' original term of enlistment had to expire by September 1, 1864. For a while, the rank and file of the Twenty-fourth Michigan believed that they were eligible, but on December 21 they learned otherwise. "The final bursting of the Veteran Volunteer bubble, the little 24th played out, forgotten" was how a member described their reaction. In the Second Wisconsin, officers failed to secure a sufficient number of men.[40]

The Seventh Wisconsin met the requirement first, followed by the Sixth Wisconsin and then the Nineteenth Indiana. By January 10, 1864, the "veteran volunteers" from the three regiments had boarded trains for home. Many of them had not seen family and friends in more than two years. For thirty days, at least, the war would not be beyond a river.[41]

Winter came to Virginia, roaring and snowing, during the first week of 1864. In the Confederate camps south of the Rappahannock and Rapidan rivers, the soldiers huddled in their huts, warming themselves before the smoky fires. The cold weather portended weeks of suffering and shortages, a slow gnawing at body and soul.[42]

By the second week of the new year, the daily meat ration had been reduced to either a quarter of a pound of bacon or three quarters of a pound of beef. Frequently, however, lard was substituted for the meat. When they received cornmeal, it was, wrote a Valley man, "as corse as hominy." Although one member of the Stonewall Brigade contended that "we all are living very well," most of his comrades complained about the rations. Regular issues of sugar and coffee, supplemented by rice and dried fruit, eased some of the hunger and silenced some of the grumbling.[43]

Shortages of winter clothing, socks, and shoes compounded the suffering. By February, two hundred men in the Stonewall Brigade had neither socks nor shoes. For the others, the footwear required constant repair. Private John Casler of the Thirty-third Virginia, seeing an opportunity to earn money, opened a repair shop with a messmate from the Fourteenth Louisiana. The Louisianan stole the leather, and Casler patched the shoes, charging five dollars for each pair. One day, Casler's bold partner even cut off the saddle skirts of an officer, but another soldier pilfered them before Casler could use the fine leather.[44]

As they had the winter before, the Virginians provided amusement for soldiers from other units. The Valley men and the Louisianans built a log theater, more spacious than the one constructed in 1863, and staged nightly theatricals. The Stonewall Brigade band provided the music for a troupe who performed as black minstrels. They also staged a burlesque of army surgeons that they dubbed the "Medical Board." Performing every night to a full audience, they donated one dollar of the admission charge to a fund for Confederate widows and orphans.[45]

The war remained a constant companion. On February 6, a lieutenant and fifteen men of the Fifth Virginia were captured while on picket duty at Morton's Ford on the Rapidan by a Union detachment. In the Twenty-seventh Virginia, fifteen of the officers petitioned army headquarters for the transfer of the regiment to southwestern Virginia. The Twenty-seventh numbered barely 150 members, and the officers argued that a return to their homes would aid recruiting efforts. Although six Confederate congressmen from the region endorsed the request, Robert E. Lee refused to approve it unless a regiment stationed there would agree to transfer to the Stonewall Brigade. When none evidently did, the Twenty-seventh remained with their Valley comrades.[46]

Within the Stonewall Brigade, two regiments received new commanders. Twenty-seven-year-old Captain William W. Randolph was promoted to lieutenant colonel and succeeded Colonel John Nadenbousch, who had resigned because of disability. A graduate of the University of Virginia, Randolph had enlisted originally as a private but had been elected unanimously as captain of Company C in April 1862. He had spent the fall of 1863 and most of the winter of 1864 as Clarke County's delegate in the Virginia legislature. His appointment to command was a popular choice among the rank and file.[47]

In the Thirty-third Virginia, Major George W. Huston received his lieutenant colonelcy and command of the regiment. In 1862, Huston had been placed under arrest for a lengthy absence during the summer, but Stonewall Jackson remitted the sentence because of the officer's conduct at Cedar Mountain, Second Manassas, and Sharpsburg. Huston replaced Colonel Frederick Holliday, who, like Nadenbousch, had resigned because of the effects of a wound. Holliday had been serving in the "Invalid Corps" since the amputation of his right arm in December 1862.[48]

Both Randolph and Huston assumed their new posts as spring heralded the approach of the fourth year of fighting. Winter released its hold grudgingly with a snowfall, heavy and wet, near the end of March. The Virginians and Louisianans used the foot of snow to launch a spirited attack on the camp of Robert Rodes's troops. The snowballs flew in volleys, but Rodes's men received reinforcements and routed the attackers. Later in the day, with James Walker at their head, the two brigades renewed their assault, and according to one of them, "we gained a grate Victory." During the melee, one of the Virginians or Louisianans, throwing a rock encased in snow, hit Brigadier General George Doles of Rodes's division in the head and knocked him off his horse.[49]

The snowfall delayed the resumption of drills, but once it melted and the ground hardened, officers renewed the familiar training. On April 8, the Confederates paused for a day of fasting, thanksgiving, and church services. In the Second Corps, Reverend Beverly Tucker Lacy eulogized his old friend and commander, Stonewall Jackson, before three thousand listeners. Lacy's words, remarked a Valley man, "appealed to the old brigade in language which was calculated to move the hardest heart."[50]

As the month lengthened and the air warmed, the drills, inspections, and dress parades increased. Their portent was lost on few, if any. An officer in the Stonewall Brigade wrote home that "the sweet bright days are gone, and now the stern work of war is about to begin." A private, writing during the last week of April, stated that "it can not be much longer until we are ingaged in the deadly strife wich will end the days of many here on Earth."[51]

The Fourth Virginia's Lieutenant Ted Barclay shared the private's concern about the impending sacrifice. "I would like to survive the conflict," Barclay informed his sister on May 2. "I would like to see our land free from tyrants' grasp and established as one of the stars in the galaxy of nations, but if I am to fall, God help me to say, 'Thy will be done.'"[52]

The "veteran volunteers" of the Nineteenth Indiana spilled from cars of the Orange & Alexandria Railroad to "a splendid reception" by their comrades in the Iron Brigade. Fellow soldiers, visiting civilians, and a band welcomed the Hoosiers back from their thirty-day furlough. They had been feted in Indianapolis by Governor Oliver Morton, Solomon Meredith, and other state dignitaries. "The boys were in excellent spirits," according to a city newspaper, when they boarded the train for Virginia. Home had never been far away, but the journey back had narrowed the distance. Thoughts of families and friends undoubtedly lingered.[53]

The reenlisted members of the Sixth and Seventh Wisconsin had preceded the Hoosiers. Members of the Seventh returned first from leave with "a good many of them minus all the bounty they had received, and in debt besides." The Sixth followed about a week later. Although he had not reenlisted, Rufus Dawes had been granted a furlough and traveled to Marietta, Ohio, where on January 18 he and Mary Beman Gates were married in her family's home.[54]

Dozens of recruits accompanied the veterans back to the army and more would follow during March and April. Upon the new men's arrival, training began, conducted by noncommissioned officers and some of the veteran privates. When the weather permitted, the recruits drilled for six hours each day. According to a sergeant, whenever "the boys" who had been at Brawner's Farm and Gettysburg had the opportunity, they told the novices "big bear and bull stories, which they listen to with eyes & ears open, and believe as implicitly as if they read them out of the Bible."[55]

Although the Westerners had "better quarters" than the year before and "more than we can eat," illness stalked the camps. Mumps, measles, and smallpox placed many men in hospitals. "There is considerable sickness throughout the army," wrote Elmer Wallace, a hospital steward in the Twenty-fourth Michigan. From his experience, Wallace believed that for every man killed or mortally wounded in battle three succumbed to disease. The number of smallpox patients forced the brigade to establish a separate hospital. The surgeons also outfitted a medical wagon with instruments and supplies to accompany the ambulance train when active field operations resumed.[56]

At the end of March as the sick mended and the weather improved, a brigade member wrote that "the boys are always hoping that the fighting may be done by someone else. That something may happen to prevent a battle & but never express a wish showing any impatience—have all learned to be very patient upon that point." They recognized the signs that before long something would be astir.[57]

The signs were everywhere. Sunday morning inspections had resumed. Each man had to appear with a clean weapon and a neatly packed knapsack. Drills for all the troops, not just recruits, increased. Generals held reviews. To Rufus Dawes, the situation seemed evident. "There is a desperate struggle before us," he told Mary. "Both sections seem to have chosen this as the ground for the last grand conflict. If we gain it, in my opinion, the rebellion will be crushed."[58]

Before the army advanced, however, its commander, George Meade, had ordered a reorganization. He reduced the five infantry corps to three—the Eleventh and Twelfth corps had been sent to Tennessee in September 1863—by eliminating the First and Third corps and consolidating their units into the Second, Fifth, and Sixth. Meade wanted to streamline the army's organization, and because of the losses incurred by the First and Third at Gettysburg, he selected them for disbandment. The decision was not welcomed in either command.[59]

For the Iron Brigade, its proud designation as the First Brigade, First Division, First Corps ended with the consolidation. "We do not like the change a bit," was how Captain William Orr of the Nineteenth Indiana described the Westerners' reaction. Their division, still under James Wadsworth, was assigned to the Fifth Corps, commanded by Major General Gouverneur K. Warren. A green Maltese Cross, badge of the Fourth Division, Fifth Corps, replaced the red disc on the black hats.[60]

The reorganization also brought other changes to the brigade. The former colonel of the Sixth Wisconsin, Lyander Cutler, was assigned to command of his former comrades. Army headquarters also transferred the Seventh Indiana into the brigade. Commanded by Colonel Ira B. Grover, the Seventh was, in Dawes's description, "a large and remarkably fortunate regiment." It had, claimed Dawes, sustained fewer casualties in more than a dozen engagements than the Sixth Wisconsin had at Gettysburg. Finally, a contingent of recruits—fourteen Chippewa Indians—joined the Seventh Wisconsin near the end of April. On the night after their arrival, the Chippewas staged a war dance for the regiment.[61]

By May 1, the Army of the Potomac, including the recently assigned Ninth Corps, numbered nearly 120,000 troops. Well armed and well supplied, it was a powerful weapon, readying itself to march. On that same day, Rufus Dawes confided to his wife that "I cannot deny that I never dreaded the battlefield as I do this spring."[62]

At last, after nine months of stalemate along two rivers, the Federals marched after midnight of May 3–4. Across the Rapidan at Ely's and Germanna fords the Yankees came, moving southeast toward an old landscape of slaughter, the Wilderness near Chancellorsville. By mid-afternoon, the army's right wing, Warren's Fifth Corps, had halted, covering one of the main roads that led west toward the Army of Northern Virginia. Before he slept, Colonel Samuel Williams, the popular commander of the Nineteenth Indiana, wrote a letter to his wife: "whether we shall be permitted to meet again in this world or not, my earnest prayer is that you may live long and happily and that we may at least meet in our Father's home, where there is no war to separate his children. May God bless you, and mother and our little children."[63]

"The last grand conflict" that Dawes had predicted six weeks earlier might be at hand. For those who had been with Fighting Joe Hooker a year before, memories surely rushed back of the Wilderness's demonic confines. Would the new man, who had come to them from "way down beyond the sunset," be another Hooker? They did not know, nor could they know that with another day's sun they and their old nemeses would enter a long corridor to hell.

15

✠

"PLAYED OUT"

ULYSSES S. GRANT turned forty-two years old on April 27, 1864, a week before he directed the Army of the Potomac toward the Wilderness. For a number of those years, life had rubbed hard against Grant. A native Ohioan, West Pointer, Mexican War veteran, he had been struggling to provide for his family in Galena, Illinois, when the war came and rescued him. His successes in the West at forts Henry and Donelson, Shiloh, Vicksburg, and Chattanooga had culminated in his appointment as general-in-chief with the reauthorized rank of lieutenant general, the highest rank in the U.S. Army, in March 1864.[1]

Grant possessed the inner steel of a warrior. He eschewed military pomp, wore a plain uniform, and approached warfare with a levelheaded reality. He was a tenacious, even relentless, foe. He allowed few individuals to know him well, and if he revealed part of himself, it seemed to percolate slowly out of the man. Confederate general James Longstreet had been Grant's best friend at the academy and in the Regular Army and knew him better than most Union officers. When Longstreet learned of his old friend's appointment, the Southerner warned his comrades, "That man will fight us every day and every hour till the end of the war."[2]

For Grant personally, the chosen battleground was Virginia and a direct confrontation with Robert E. Lee. As commander of all Union forces, Grant could have established his headquarters anywhere but decided to accompany George Meade's army. Although Meade retained command of the army, it moved under Grant's overall direction. For the next eleven months the war in Virginia centered upon the contest between Grant and Lee. It began initially in the Wilderness, inaugurating a forty-day nightmare known as the Overland Campaign.[3]

In the Wilderness, the killing and maiming followed the few roads. Where clearings broke the carpet of trees, the slaughter was fearful. For the men, clad in blue and gray, it was a landscape of terror—of blinding, smoke-choked woods, of ambushes, of flames fed by underbrush, and of dying. Chancellorsville did not compare; nothing seemed to compare.[4]

The fury exploded at 1:00 P.M., on May 5, with the attack of Major General Gouverneur Warren's Fifth Corps along Orange Turnpike. With three divisions in front and one in reserve, Warren's command advanced against Lieutenant General Richard Ewell's Confederate Second Corps posted in the woods west of Saunders' Field. In the center of the Union force marched Brigadier General James Wadsworth's division, its right flank skirting the field's southern edge. There Wadsworth had placed his best unit, the Iron Brigade, which numbered upward of two thousand officers and men.[5]

The Westerners advanced on a four-regiment front with the Seventh Indiana and Sixth Wisconsin stacked behind the brigade's right flank. Officers tried vainly to keep an alignment as the men struggled through the dense shrubs and thickets. Unknowingly, the line began drifting to the left away from the left-flank brigade of Brigadier General Charles Griffin's division in Saunders' Field. The Iron Brigade passed beyond the field, stumbling ahead as if blindfolded. Before they saw the Confederate line, a brigade of Georgians rose from the ground and blasted the right front and flank of the Federals.[6]

The volley slammed into the Second and Seventh Wisconsin, the Seventh Indiana, and the Sixth Wisconsin. Rufus Dawes estimated that the Confederate fire knocked down dozens in the Sixth. The Iron Brigade line staggered under the gunfire. In the Nineteenth Indiana, Sergeant Abram Buckles, regimental color-bearer, unfurled the flag. He had received permission from the regimental surgeon to remain in the rear because of his unhealed Gettysburg wound but had refused. Now, Buckles waved the flag and shouted for his comrades to follow him. The Hoosiers lurched forward into a scythe of gunfire. Buckles fell with a bullet that passed through his body. He handed the flag to another man, who was soon killed. For his bravery, Buckles would earn the Medal of Honor.[7]

Isolated, with both flanks exposed—the brigade on their left had been mired in a marsh—raked by volleys from two enemy brigades, the Westerners reeled under the hammer blows. When a third Confederate brigade attacked, the Iron Brigade broke and fled in confusion for the first time in its history. Colonel Henry Morrow of the Twenty-fourth Michigan, struck by a bullet in the right leg, hobbled away with his men. Where the Sixth Wisconsin stood, Major Philip Plummer lay dead. Casualties in the brigade probably approached five hundred, with scores of officers and men overtaken by the Rebels and captured.[8]

The Confederate counterattack wrecked Wadsworth's entire line and a brigade from another division. Colonel Roy Stone's Pennsylvanians, who had stood with the black-hatted troops on McPherson's Ridge, were savaged by the Southerners as they tried to close on the Iron Brigade's left. A Pennsylvanian described their and the Westerners' position as a "hell hole" and claimed that Stone was drunk.[9]

Wadsworth's shattered ranks eventually halted and began to re-form at the Lacy House, roughly two miles to the rear. The troops constructed fieldworks of dirt and logs as the fighting along the turnpike and Orange Plank Road to the south pulled in additional units from both armies. The worst of the butchery occurred in the woods on both sides of the Plank Road, finally shuttering to an end about nine o'clock.[10]

Private James McCown of the Fifth Virginia had been a soldier for barely ten months on May 4, 1864. Most of that time he had served on provost duty until his recent assignment to the Stonewall Brigade. He had never seen an army shake itself to life as it prepared for a march. He watched, found a place in the column, and later recorded what he had been a part of in his diary: "We are on the march. The morning is bright and pleasant; all nature seems smiling on the spring morn. What a grand sight is the Army of Lee in motion. The whole brigade is all life, seems as though they are never to be conquered."[11]

Behind the Confederates lay their abandoned winter huts, appearing to McCown "like a deserted city." Ahead of them rode Brigadier General James Walker, looking "brave and gallant" to the private. "Well he may be," wrote McCown, "to command the Stonewall is no small honor."[12]

Private McCown, his fellow Valley men, and their comrades in the Second Corps were on the move east on Orange Turnpike because of reports that placed Union columns south of the Rapidan River. For days, General Robert E. Lee had expected an enemy movement from that direction. When he learned of it on this day, he ordered forward Richard Ewell's divisions on the turnpike and Lieutenant General A. P. Hill's Third Corps on Orange Plank Road. Their roles were to pin down the Yankees in the Wilderness until Lieutenant General James Longstreet's First Corps divisions, stationed near Gordonsville, could join them. By nightfall on the 4th, Ewell's and Hill's units were strung out along the pair of roads within a few miles of the Federals bivouacked in the Wilderness.[13]

Not all of Walker's Virginians shared the exuberance of Private Mc-Cown, who had never even been on a skirmish line. The veterans understood what lay ahead, down the turnpike, and what it might mean for them and their country. Two weeks earlier, Sergeant John Garibaldi of the Twenty-seventh Virginia, a soldier who had seen combat's terrible countenance, had written to his wife. His words to her could have been written by probably all the veterans in the brigade. "I am pretty tire[d] of this war by this time," Garibaldi declared, "but there is no chance for us unless the war stops, for we all have [to] keep fighting untill the Yankees gives up or untill we shall be subjugated."[14]

Ewell had his troops astir early on May 5. Major General Edward Johnson's division, including Walker's Virginians, led the march on the turnpike. By six o'clock, the four brigades were filing off the road into the woods at the western edge of Saunders' Field. Brigadier General John Jones's Virginians covered the southern portion of the field while Brigadier General George Steuart's Virginians and North Carolinians faced the open ground north of the road. On Steuart's left flank, Brigadier General Leroy A. Stafford's Louisianans and Walker's Valley men extended the line north through the woods. These latter two commands had to struggle through an almost impenetrable thicket to align on Steuart's ranks. "A more difficult and disagreeable field of battle could not well be imagined," asserted a Confederate.[15]

Johnson's troops dug shallow trenches, topped by logs, and waited. Skirmishers ranged ahead, but only occasional rifle shots characterized the action. Behind the fieldworks, where the men lay, "there is an awful silence," in McCown's words. The private noticed that many of his comrades were either reading their Bibles or praying. "All nature," he thought, "seems to expect some awful shock."[16]

The shock came at 1:00 P.M., when units of the Union Fifth Corps charged across Saunders' Field. Volleys of musketry rolled over the trees from the southeast toward Walker's and Stafford's men. Their lines were spared from the combat as the struggle centered upon the fields and the woods to their south. Steuart's, Jones's, and brigades from Major General Robert Rodes's divisions repulsed the enemy attacks, routing some of the blue-coated units, including "those damned black hats." Two hours later, however, additional Union troops renewed the offensive north of the turnpike.[17]

During the initial Federal attack, Stafford and Walker evidently shifted their brigades south as support. When the enemy was hammered to the rear, they returned to their sector of the works but with Walker next to Steuart and Stafford on the left of the Stonewall Brigade. The Virginians and Louisianans had barely redeployed when reports came back of a second enemy advance.[18]

The Louisianans scrambled over the logs and plunged into the woods, searching for the flank of the Union line. One fourth of a mile to the east, they found the Yankees and charged. Walker's Virginians, however, had lagged behind, creating a gap between the two brigades. Walker ordered a leftward shift to close the breach. As the Virginians responded to the command, disaster struck. Forty yards away, concealed by the trees and thickets, a Union brigade unleashed a "staggering volley" into the Confederates.[19]

The blast of gunfire tore apart the ranks of the Fourth, Fifth, and Twenty-seventh Virginia. Many of the Rebels scrambled for safety in the rear, but Colonel William Terry of the Fourth and other officers rallied the men and restored the line. On the Virginians' left, enemy troops poured into the gap and lashed the Stonewall Brigade's flank, their volleys raking the Second and Thirty-third Virginia. A lieutenant in the latter regiment wrote later that combat "raged with inconceivable violence along the whole front of the brigade." Walker stood behind the line, shouting, "Remember your name."[20]

Lieutenant Colonel William Randolph, who had been in command of the Second Virginia for only ten days, lay on the ground, his life flowing away from a bullet wound in the head. Captain William Shuler of the Thirty-third and nineteen-year-old Major Philip Frazer of the Fourth were both dead, struck down early in the fighting. One of Frazer's fellow regi-

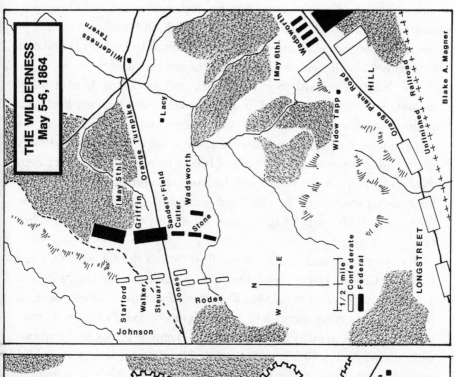

THE WILDERNESS
May 5-6, 1864

Wilderness Tavern

Orange Turnpike

Lacy

May 5th.

Griffin

Sanders' Field

Cutler

Wadsworth

Stone

Stafford

Walker

Steuart

Jones

Rodes

Johnson

May 6th.

Wadsworth

Widow Tapp

Orange Plank Road

HILL

Unfinished Railroad

LONGSTREET

Blake A. Magner

N
E
W
S

1/2 mile

Confederate
Federal

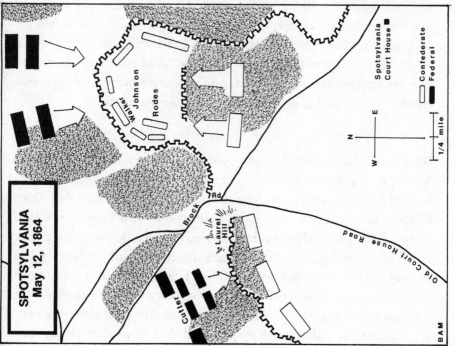

SPOTSYLVANIA
May 12, 1864

Walker

Johnson

Rodes

Brock Rd

Laurel Hill

Cutler

Old Court House Road

Spotsylvania
Court House

N
E
W
S

1/4 mile

Confederate
Federal

BAM

mental officers, Captain James Bosang, had tried unsuccessfully to persuade his eighteen-year-old brother, Sergeant John Bosang, to remain in the rear. John was sick and barefoot but wanted to be with his men in Company C. With them and at his post, the teenager died.[21]

The Yankees pressed their advantage, and Walker ordered a withdrawal. The Virginians retired in order "under a most galling fire" to a position seventy-five yards to the rear. Within minutes, the Louisianans came running through the woods. Caught in a vise of musketry, Stafford's ranks had disintegrated into a mob of fleeing men. Stafford tried to stem the flood when a bullet ripped into his body, severing his spine. Some of his troops gathered up the paralyzed general and carried him over the fieldworks. He lingered in agony until the 8th, dying in a Richmond hotel.[22]

The Virginians and Louisianans rallied behind the log works. When Brigadier General Harry Hays's Louisiana brigade came to their support, a counterattack was ordered. But Walker misunderstood the instructions, believing that his regiments had been relieved by Hays's troops. Consequently, the Louisianans encountered two enemy brigades in the woods and suffered the fate of Stafford's men. As Hays's Confederates scrambled toward the fieldworks, the Virginians leveled their rifles and lashed the oncoming Yankees. The Louisianans added their firepower. The Federals staggered, halted, and then disappeared. The "dead and dying" seemed to lie everywhere to Private McCown, who was now a member of the brotherhood. "The Lord has delivered me," he wrote that night.[23]

Wilderness's hell resumed shortly before five o'clock on the morning of May 6, with a massive Union assault along Orange Plank Road. Thirteen Federal brigades, stacked in four lines, wrecked A. P. Hill's two Third Corps divisions. Lee's army faced destruction when Longstreet's First Corps veterans arrived on the field, hurried into a battle line, and charged. Powerful, relentless, the counterattack rolled forward, reclaiming lost ground and harvesting hundreds of Union killed, wounded, and captured. For most of the day, the Plank Road served as an axis of slaughter. Charges and countercharges took hundreds more on both sides. The musketry ignited the undergrowth in spots, and fed by a wind, the flames carried a new horror to those caught within them.[24]

In this charnel house was Lysander Cutler's Iron Brigade. One of its of-

ficers described it as only "our remnant" on this day. The Westerners and
their comrades in Wadsworth's division were posted north of the Plank
Road when some of Longstreet's troops smashed into the Federals' flank.
The brigade in front of Cutler's ranks dissolved under the onslaught.
More Rebel units rushed into the fighting. It was more than the Northerners could withstand, and they streamed rearward. For the second time in
as many days, the veterans of Brawner's Farm and Herbst Woods fled in
disorder.[25]

Among the Iron Brigade dead was Colonel Samuel Williams of the
Nineteenth Indiana. An artillery round had smashed into his chest, killing
the popular officer instantly. One of his men stated in his diary under this
date that "the loss of Col. Williams will not soon be forgotten in the Regt.
He was beloved by all who knew him." In their home in Selma, Indiana,
his wife was left with the hope and "earnest prayer," as he had expressed it
to her in his letter of May 4, that they would "at least meet in our Father's
home."[26]

Later in the day, the Westerners learned that their division commander,
James Wadsworth, had been mortally wounded while rallying troops. A
natural leader of men, although unschooled in warfare, Wadsworth had
earned the soldiers' respect and affection. He died on the 8th, adminis-
tered to in his final hours by Confederate surgeons. Cutler assumed command of the division, and Colonel William Robinson of the Seventh
Wisconsin replaced Cutler at the head of the Iron Brigade.[27]

Nightfall on the 6th ended the Battle of the Wilderness. It had cost
nearly eighteen thousand Federals and eleven thousand Confederates. In
the Iron Brigade, the losses amounted to a reported 86 killed, 456
wounded, and 182 captured or missing. The total of 724 comprised one
third of the command. The casualties included those sustained by the Seventh Indiana and First New York Battalion of Sharpshooters. In the five
original regiments of the brigade, the losses were 526. Only Brawner's
Farm and Gettysburg had taken more of the black-hatted Westerners.[28]

But the Wilderness was only a beginning. On the night of May 7, the
battered Union army, instead of withdrawing across the Rapidan River as
it had the year before, turned south. Led by the Fifth Corps, the Federals
marched all night toward Spotsylvania Court House and open ground.
Lee had anticipated such a move by Grant, and the Confederates, moving
on a parallel, but shorter, route, won the race for the crossroads village.
The collision came on the morning of the 8th at Laurel Hill, west of the in-

tersection of Brock Road and Old Court House Road. The Southerners held the hill, and the Northerners attacked. The twelve-day Battle of Spotsylvania had begun.[29]

For members of the Iron Brigade, Laurel Hill became another place to die. Three times—on the 8th, 10th, and 12th—they formed ranks, stepped out, and charged. Three times they failed. Ironically, two years ago, not far from here, at Fredericksburg, they had complained that the war might elude them. Instead the war had all but destroyed them. The Wilderness had exposed a terrible truth; Laurel Hill magnified it. The Westerners no longer possessed the superb combat discipline and willingness to enter battle that had made them perhaps the finest infantry brigade in the army for more than ten months.

Their own words attested to the reality. Rufus Dawes reported that during the assault on the 8th the "line broke in disorder." A lieutenant in the Seventh Wisconsin confessed that "men got sort of panicky (for the first time in our Brigade's history.)." Two days later when hit by "a terribly destructive fire," the Westerners recoiled as "temporary confusion ensued" and sought safety in a ravine. Pinned down by Confederate musketry and artillery fire, the Federals began digging "glory holes" with canteens. The underbrush in front of them ignited into a fire whose "red mantle of flames" charred the bodies of the dead. A few soldiers braved enemy gunfire to drag wounded comrades to safety. Later in the afternoon, they received orders to prepare to join in an attack on another sector of the Southern lines. When the directive was canceled, the men "felt glad," recalled an officer, "we didn't have to go into that Hell."[30]

The assault of May 12 was, argued Dawes, "manifestly hopeless at the outset." The Iron Brigade and other units in two divisions advanced only a short distance before seeking shelter in another ravine. There the Federals remained until Cutler's division was withdrawn and sent into a wretched slaughter that had been engulfing a portion of the Confederate works known as the Mule Shoe since first light on May 12. Before the fighting had ceased, the day was, in Dawes's opinion, the "most terrible twenty-four hours of our service in the war."[31]

All night the gray-coated defenders heard the sounds, the muffled rumble of a billowing storm. The darkness and fog added to the concern of the men. They had labored hard during the past three days to strengthen the extensive bulge or salient in the army's line. Its configuration made it vulnerable to attack on three sides. "Our men did not like it [at] all," declared a defender. "It was so liable to be enfiladed by artillery and would be a dangerous trap to be caught in should the line be broken on the right or left." Because of its shape, it was dubbed the Mule Shoe.[32]

The apex of the Mule Shoe was held by the 4,500-man division of Edward Johnson. The roughly nine hundred Virginians of the Stonewall Brigade covered the northwestern face of the salient where the works bent south. On their left was the division of Robert Rodes. Late on May 10, a Union force, advancing on a narrow front in a compact mass, like a lance in blue, had pierced the works. The fighting spread to the sector manned by the Stonewall Brigade, resulting in the rout of the Second and Thirty-third Virginia. Confederate reinforcements, including the Valley men, sealed the breach. But the initially successful Federal attack revealed the salient's weakness.[33]

Although Johnson's command had missed the worst of the combat on May 6 in the Wilderness, the losses it had incurred on the previous day had seriously crippled its combat effectiveness. Johnson's four brigades constituted the weakest division in the Second Corps at the same time that it held the apex of the salient. It was a prescription for disaster.[34]

The temporary breakthrough on the 10th had convinced Grant that another assault in a similar formation but with many more units might crush the salient and divide Lee's army in half. Grant committed the entire Union Second Corps, almost twenty thousand troops, to the massive attack. The army's other three corps were directed to support the attackers either by demonstrating against the Rebel lines or by charging sections of the works. By ten o'clock on the night of May 11, Major General Winfield Hancock's Second Corps was marching toward the tip of the Mule Shoe. It was their movement, sounding to a Confederate staff officer like "distant falling water or machinery," that worried and alerted Johnson's men in the trenches. Aides hurried through the darkness with warnings. But the salient's defenders had run out of time.[35]

Minutes after 4:30 A.M., on May 12, the Federals emerged from the fog. The Confederates saw them, leveled their rifles and most likely prayed. From beyond the works, thousands of men cheered, a thunderous clap of voices whose sound rolled over and passed beyond the waiting Southerners. The mass of attackers began to double-quick, the ranks fusing into a swarm of onrushing men. Along the salient's northwestern face, the Valley men squeezed their triggers only to discover that the night's rain had dampened the powder in many of their rifles, causing misfires. The Rebels braced themselves for an avalanche of blue-clad warriors.[36]

Within minutes, the Mule Shoe became the scene of fearful, almost unimaginable, violence. The impetus of the assault carried many Federals over the works and into the trenches. "For a time, every soldier was a fiend," declared a Yankee. "The attack was fierce—the resistance fanatical." A lieutenant in the Stonewall Brigade avowed that the struggle was the "most desperate of the war."[37]

Volleys scorched the ground; men grappled with each other in hand-to-hand combat, wielding muskets as clubs. "It was terrific beyond any description," remembered Private James McCown of the Fifth Virginia. "Every twig seemed cut down." The Stonewall Brigade fought Yankees in the front and on both flanks. "No sooner would a flag fall than another carrier who picked it up would be shot or bayoneted," recounted a comrade of McCown. "Men were so close their heads were at the end of gun muzzles as they shot each other. When ammunition ran out or got wet they crushed each other's skulls with gun butts."[38]

The Federal numbers, however, were overwhelming. "All that human courage and endurance would effect was done by these men on this frightful morning," declared a lieutenant in the Thirty-third Virginia, "but all was to no avail." Brigade commander James Walker strode in the midst of the fury, fighting "like a tiger." An enemy soldier at point-blank range fired at the general. The bullet smashed into one of Walker's arms, shattering the elbow. Afterward, when the doughty officer refused amputation, a surgeon was able to save the limb.[39]

The Virginians fought with a desperation "until we were completely surrounded," wrote Private McCown. Hundreds of Virginians surrendered, trapped in the trenches. The Federals seized the flags of the Fourth and Thirty-third Virginia and would have captured the Fifth's colors, but its bearer ripped it from the staff and concealed it in his shirt. Within thirty minutes, the Stonewall Division virtually ceased to exist as a command. The Yankees had bagged upward of two thousand prisoners, including the commander, Allegheny Johnson. Private McCown, who had been in combat for the first time a week ago, was among the herd of captives.[40]

The swift destruction of Johnson's division jeopardized Lee's army. The jubilant Yankees penetrated deeper into the salient but soon encountered oncoming Confederate brigades. The Southern counterattack slammed into the jumbled Union ranks, driving the Northerners back toward the salient's apex, which would become known as the Bloody Angle. The battle for the Mule Shoe raged all day and into the evening. More units were fed into the maelstrom, whose ferocity surpassed anything that many of the troops had ever experienced. The killing abated at darkness, but did not end. It was not until 3:00 A.M. on May 13 before the Confederate defenders received orders to withdraw to a new line along the Mule Shoe's base. Casualties in both armies amounted to nearly seventeen thousand officers and men.[41]

When the survivors of the Stonewall Brigade gathered on May 13, barely two hundred Valley men answered the roll call. The next day, authorities combined the remnants of the Virginia regiments in Johnson's division into one brigade. Colonel John Funk of the Fifth Virginia assumed command of the contingent of Valley men, and the Stonewall Brigade ceased to exist officially as an independent unit.[42]

A week later, Colonel William Terry of the Fourth Virginia was promoted to brigadier general and assigned to command of the consolidated brigades. Thirty-nine years old, reticent and modest, Terry had served with distinction in the Fourth since the beginning of the war, when he abandoned his law practice in Wytheville to volunteer. He had suffered a slight wound at the Mule Shoe, the third of the war for him. Ironically, when so few of the Valley men remained and were no longer a separate command, one of their own led them.[43]

On May 21, Lee's Army of Northern Virginia abandoned its lines at Spotsylvania, marching south. As he had after the Wilderness, Grant ordered the Army of the Potomac toward Richmond. The Confederates again moved in response to interdict the Federal advance. Before they departed from Spotsylvania, a Georgia soldier saw the shreds of the five Valley regiments that once had been led by Stonewall Jackson, Richard Garnett, and Charles Winder. "The Stonewall Brigade," the Georgian wrote, "is played out—not worth a cent."[44]

"By the blessing of God I am still alive," Rufus Dawes began his letter to his wife Mary on May 14. He and his fellow Westerners had spent much of the previous two days and nights in the awful slaughter of the Mule Shoe. Withdrawn from the lines before Laurel Hill on the afternoon of the 12th, they had been sent into the combat at the salient, standing "in mud over my boot tops, firing all night." Throughout the 13th, the Wisconsin, Indiana, and Michigan men huddled in the trenches under musketry and artillery fire. "Do not give me up if you see me reported killed," Dawes informed Mary. "Such things are often mistakes." If they could "only finish this horrible business here," he concluded, "our lives are of poor moment in comparison."[45]

On the night of May 13, the Iron Brigade was relieved from the Mule Shoe trenches and marched much of the night to the rear. For the next week, the Westerners held a reserve position. Spotsylvania had taken another three hundred men, bringing the brigade's total casualties to more than one thousand since May 5. Dawes described the combat in the Wilderness and at Spotsylvania as a "scene of horrid butchery." To Mary, he confessed on the 15th that "I am almost prostrated with over exertion and with fighting." Four days later, he asserted that "this campaign has been by far the most trying I have known."[46]

The horror extended far behind the lines. Lieutenant Amos D. Rood was wounded at the Mule Shoe, hit by a bullet in the left shoulder and lung. In his postwar memoirs, Rood recounted the experience of wounded men once they had been removed from the battlefield. Placed in an ambulance, the lieutenant endured a fifteen-mile "jolt" to Fredericksburg. The trip *"was Hell,"* recalled Rood. He was carried to a hospital, where the beds were infested with fleas. "Great big black, blue, and green flies were scouting about after carrion," he wrote. A surgeon examined the wound and bandaged it, but another five days passed before a doctor changed the dressing.

On May 25, thirteen days after his wounding, Rood boarded a steamer for Washington. In a city hospital a nurse discovered on June 3 "a nest of *maggots,* an inch long" in Rood's shoulder socket. Six days later, a surgeon removed the bullet. The doctor reexamined the wound each of the next two days, extracting more splinters of lead. It would be more than three months before Rood could return to duty. Granted a leave, the officer returned to Wisconsin, where he resigned from the army.[47]

While Rood underwent the ordeal so common to wounded soldiers, his comrades in the Iron Brigade marched with the army away from Spotsylvania. For four days the opponents confronted each other along the North Anna River before Grant ordered another southward sidle that shifted the operations to the Peninsula, east of Richmond. At Cold Harbor, on June 3, Grant launched a frontal assault on Lee's well-entrenched troops, who erased the Federal lines in a bloodbath that cost Grant approximately seven thousand men in less than an hour. A deadly duel between sharpshooters and skirmishers characterized the killing and maiming for the next eight days.[48]

The Iron Brigade lost an additional 178 men during these weeks. Most of the casualties had been incurred in an action at Jericho Ford on the North Anna. Others seemed less explicable. On June 2, Private Lanson D. Finton of the Sixth Wisconsin, while visiting with former schoolmates in another regiment, was killed by a sharpshooter or stray bullet. Finton was, wrote a comrade, "intensely loyal." Except for Colonel Edward Bragg, who had been assigned to temporary command of a Pennsylvania brigade, every regimental commander had been either killed, wounded, or captured since the army had crossed the Rapidan River.[49]

In letters home, many of the men settled for a simple assurance to family and friends, "I am alive and well." A captain told his wife that "I never knew how much I could stand before," adding in a subsequent letter to his father that "there is scarcely a man in the co. but what has been hit." Exhaustion numbed all of them. Colonel Bragg admitted to Rufus Dawes that he could "not write an intelligent account" of the campaign to his wife because "I am too stupid for any use." To his wife, Dawes pleaded, "God grant it soon over."[50]

On June 11, the "terrible campaign" ended for the original members of the "Ragged Ass" Second Wisconsin. Their three-year term of enlistment expired on this day, and they prepared to leave for home. They had bled first on the slope of Henry House Hill, had answered first John Gibbon's call at Brawner's Farm, and had crossed first McPherson's Ridge at Gettysburg. "What is left of them," in the words of a Michigander, marched away from their comrades and the war on the 11th, boarded a steamer the next day for Washington, and arrived in Madison on the 18th. City residents welcomed them with a dinner, and by June 30, the men had been mustered out of the service.[51]

Less than a company remained in the Second Wisconsin, comprised of officers and men who had joined at later dates. Lysander Cutler assigned the Wisconsinites to provost duty at divisional headquarters. In the Twenty-fourth Michigan, the survivors, 130 officers and men, were reorganized into four companies. A fortnight later, the Sixth Wisconsin underwent a similar consolidation. The Seventh Wisconsin counted about the same number in the ranks as did the Twenty-fourth Michigan, while an officer in the Nineteenth Indiana claimed that fewer than one hundred Hoosiers remained. The Westerners still wore the black hats and carried the name Iron Brigade, but they appeared on the march and in a battle line to be only a regiment with many flags.[52]

In the weeks ahead, wounded men who had healed, reenlisted veterans, and recruits increased the numbers in the ranks. But remorselessly, the war continued to use up the Westerners. In the end, it was a new type of warfare, a harbinger of future conflicts, that would finish the famous unit. It came at Petersburg before the chill of autumn had settled over Virginia.

On June 12, the Union army began a withdrawal from the lines at Cold Harbor and marched toward the James River. Grant had targeted Petersburg, the railroad center located roughly twenty miles south of Richmond. If the Federals could seize it before Lee's army arrived, they could sever the Confederates' supply lines to the capital and its gray-clad defenders. It was a brilliant strategic maneuver by Grant, but Petersburg's garrison repulsed disjointed Union assaults until Lee's veterans filled the earthworks and secured the city.[53]

The failure of the Union attacks on June 16–18 convinced Grant that Petersburg would have to be invested and the railroad lines cut. Consequently, the Federals began siege operations, digging miles of trenches and bombproofs that scarred the landscape. The work became a constant process as both armies created a complex of earthworks that would in time extend from south and west of Petersburg to the east of Richmond. Periodic assaults on the Confederate lines and raids upon the network of rails marked the campaign. But most of the time for the men in the trenches, death came from either disease, a sharpshooter's bullet, or a piece of artillery shell. It was a withering away that favored the numerically superior Union army.[54]

The Iron Brigade had participated in the June 18 assaults on the Confederate works east of the city. The attack was, in Dawes's words, "another horrid massacre of our corps." The Yankees crossed *"half a mile"* of open ground. "For about 15 minutes," declared a captain in the Nineteenth Indiana, "the Bullets flew as thick as I ever seen them." The attackers never had a chance and were forced to scramble for cover in a ravine. The Confederate gunfire seared the ground. "I never want to get into a place like it again," wrote a Hoosier soldier. "We had to lay and take it." Darkness covered their withdrawal. Afterward, Dawes remarked bitterly that "our brigade was simply food for powder."[55]

Casualties in the brigade approached two hundred. Among the dead in the Sixth Wisconsin was Private Jesse Pearson of Company A. His brother William had been killed at Gettysburg on July 1, 1863, and three days after Jesse's death a Confederate soldier mortally wounded the third brother, Levi, who died on July 21, 1864.[56]

With their fellow soldiers in the army, the Westerners began, as one of them put it, *"diging diging diging"* on fortifications. The work was constant and dangerous as they soon learned. If a man ventured to expose his head above the trenches, he frequently lost his life. Dawes compared life in the sweltering trenches to "the Calcutta black hole." Another officer told his father that "I am heartily tired and sick of the Service."[57]

By August 1, nearly 120 veterans of the Sixth Wisconsin and Nineteenth Indiana, with their enlistments expired, had departed for home. A Hoosier sergeant who was still with the regiment noted in his diary, "I am glad to see them go, they deserve it." Within another two weeks, eight officers of the Sixth Wisconsin, including Rufus Dawes, were mustered out. Dawes had been the regiment's finest field officer, perhaps the finest in the brigade, but with his term of service completed, he wanted out of the war and at home with Mary. Eventually, the couple would have children, one of whom would become a vice president of the United States.[58]

A month later, the Iron Brigade ceased to exist as an independent command. Another two hundred members of the brigade had been lost during a raid on the Weldon Railroad on August 18–21. The men had fought well, capturing two flags and many Confederates. In the Sixth Wisconsin, a captain, the regimental adjutant, and Lieutenant John Timmons were killed. Timmons was waiting for his mustering-out paperwork to be completed when he fell in the fighting.[59]

Army headquarters dissolved the Fourth Division, Fifth Corps and assigned its units to the Third Division. The Iron Brigade was combined with the Pennsylvania brigade or "Bucktails," which had fought with the Westerners on McPherson's Ridge. Edward Bragg, who had been promoted to brigadier general, assumed command of the consolidated brigades. Like the Stonewall Brigade, the Iron Brigade has lost its distinctive identity.[60]

The withering away of the renowned unit continued. On September 23, the Seventh and Nineteenth Indiana were dissolved and transferred to the Twentieth Indiana. The officers and men of the Nineteenth tried to have the order rescinded but failed. On October 12, the Hoosiers held a "regular party." The next morning, with "many of them pretty drunk," the Indianans marched away from their Wisconsin and Michigan comrades, "with arms reversed & tears in their eyes." A Wisconsin officer, watching the column depart, noted that "the friendships that are formed in camp and on the field of danger are Stronger than they are in civil life." He then added: "Thus they go. There will Soon be nothing of our once Splendid Brigade left together."[61]

For the Westerners left behind, sharing campfires with the Pennsylvanians, life in Petersburg's trenches governed their existence as autumn passed into winter. They welcomed recruits and conscripts; participated in raids upon the railroads, wrecking the rails, burning ties, barns, mills, and even residences; voted overwhelmingly for Abraham Lincoln in the November presidential election; foraged for food behind the lines; consumed alcohol; brawled among themselves; wrote letters home; and passed another Christmas and New Year's away from family and friends. The battalion of the Second Wisconsin rejoined their comrades, merging with the Sixth Wisconsin. "Soldiering," wrote one of them during these months, "teaches one hard lessons, but they will last a man his life time."[62]

During the first week of February 1865, Bragg's Westerners and Pennsylvanians joined in another raid upon a railroad. At Hatcher's Run, south and west of Petersburg, the Federals collided with Confederate troops. For two days, on the 6th and 7th, the opponents fought in a series of charges and countercharges. With a final repulse, the Northerners withdrew and constructed fieldworks. During the raid, members of the One Hundred Fiftieth Pennsylvania and Sixth Wisconsin "had a row" over fence rails for campfires.[63]

On the morning of February 11, orders reached Bragg's headquarters directing the brigade commander to march his troops to City Point on the James River for transportation north. Authorities had selected the command for special assignments. The men undoubtedly cheered the news. By nightfall, the Westerners and Pennsylvanians were on board steamers, waiting for their departure on the 12th. Bragg celebrated by becoming "beastly intoxicated."[64]

During the night, however, the drunken brigadier received instructions to return the Sixth and Seventh Wisconsin to the army. One officer alleged that if Bragg had been sober he would have opposed the order and might have been able to have it canceled. Instead, the Wisconsin troops unloaded and marched back into the war. The Michiganders and Pennsylvanians left later in the day, bound for Baltimore and new duties away from the dying. "This is the last of the famous Iron Brigade," wrote an officer.[65]

The Twenty-fourth Michigan had been assigned to garrison duty at Camp Butler near Springfield, Illinois. Camp Butler was an assembly point for recruits and conscripts. Daily, however, dozens of the new soldiers deserted before they could be put on trains for assignments to regiments. The Michiganders' duty was to guard the camp and to prevent desertion.[66]

The Michiganders spent the next four months at Camp Butler. They performed their duties well, frequently visited Springfield on passes, celebrated the surrender of Lee's army by cheering and throwing their hats into the air, and performed the somber duty of escorts for the body of Abraham Lincoln after he was slain by an assassin's bullet and returned home for burial. On June 19, the regiment boarded a train for Detroit. Less than two hundred of its original members were in the ranks when they marched through the city to the accompaniment of a band and hundreds of onlookers. They held a final dress parade on June 28, and two days later received their discharges. Many of them could walk home.[67]

At Petersburg, meanwhile, the Sixth and Seventh Wisconsin had been organized into a provisional brigade under the command of Colonel John A. Kellogg of the Sixth. In early March, the Ninety-first New York Heavy Artillery with eighteen hundred members joined the Wisconsinites. Kellogg's troops participated in the final reduction of the Confederate lines at Petersburg and marched with the army in pursuit of Lee's retreating forces. They were with the victorious Union army when Lee surrendered to Grant at Appomattox Court House, on April 9. Elsewhere in the Union ranks, the Hoosiers of the former Nineteenth Indiana stood.[68]

From Appomattox, the Army of the Potomac slowly followed the roads north to Washington. The government had decided to hold a "grand review" of George Meade's and William T. Sherman's armies. On May 23, the Army of the Potomac passed down Pennsylvania Avenue to the cheers of thousands of spectators, followed the next day by Sherman's veterans of Chattanooga, Atlanta, and the March to the Sea.[69]

At the head of the Sixth and Seventh Wisconsin, whose column included the battalion of the Second Wisconsin, rode Henry Morrow, the former colonel of the Twenty-fourth Michigan who now wore a general's star. Morrow had been seriously wounded at Hatcher's Run and had been at Camp Butler until ordered East to lead the final contingent of the Iron

Brigade. Also in the ranks of the Fifth Corps on this day were the knot of men of the Nineteenth Indiana and Battery B, Fourth U.S. Artillery. Their presence harkened back to a seemingly long ago past when John Gibbon had ridden into the camps of the Westerners.[70]

Railroads carried Gibbon's former soldiers home. The Hoosiers returned to Indianapolis and their official muster out as the Twentieth Indiana on July 12. Their Wisconsin comrades, meanwhile, had arrived in Madison for their disbandment on July 2. They spent their final days as soldiers together in Camp Randall. The "camp is much changed," thought one veteran. So were they, and so was the nation.[71]

A group of Confederate soldiers lay in a field next to a road that had brought them west, away from Petersburg, Virginia. They had stacked their rifles and were resting when General Robert E. Lee and his staff halted in the road beside them. "I dont reckon," one of the soldiers wrote later, recalling the scene, "he knew the remnant of the Stonewall Brigade was by him. Everything looked & felt dead it was so quiet." Lee leaned forward in the saddle, placed a hand upon his forehead, and said nothing. "I reckon," concluded the private, "he thought it was all over."[72]

If Lee had known who they were, perhaps he would have spoken to them. There were so few of them left, barely one hundred, from the old brigade. Although they still referred to themselves as the Stonewall Brigade, it had been nearly a year since the Mule Shoe at Spotsylvania and their dissolution as an independent unit. They had refused, however, to relinquish the proud name and had fought for Lee and the Confederacy until only this "remnant" remained.

Ironically, during most of the previous summer and fall, they had defended their beloved Shenandoah Valley. Sent by Lee with their comrades in the Second Corps to the region in mid-June 1864, to repel a Union force that was threatening the railroad center of Lynchburg, they spent the next five months in the Valley. Led by Lieutenant General Jubal Early, Jackson's old foot cavalry saved Lynchburg, chased the Yankees into the Allegheny Mountains, and then turned north, descending into the Valley. Lee had given Early instructions that if circumstances allowed he should cross the Potomac and threaten Washington. Early seized the opportunity. By the end of July he had returned to Virginia after defeating an enemy force at the Battle of the Monocacy, near Frederick, Maryland, demonstrating before the capital's defenses, routing another Federal command in the Second Battle of Kernstown, and sending his cavalry to burn Chambersburg, Pennsylvania. Early's raid recalled memories of Jackson's 1862 campaign.[73]

Lee's bold gamble and Early's execution of the operations compelled Grant to react. Pressured by the Lincoln administration, Grant dispatched units to Harper's Ferry, and appointed his cavalry commander, Major General Philip H. Sheridan, to command of the newly created Army of the Shenandoah. During the first week of August, Sheridan advanced south against the Rebels. When Lee dispatched additional units to the Valley, Sheridan withdrew to Harper's Ferry. For the next month the opponents engaged in what a Northerner termed derisively a "mimic war" of marches and countermarches. But when Sherman's army captured Atlanta, Georgia, on September 2, Grant decided the time had come to unleash Sheridan, whose army outnumbered Early's by nearly three to one.[74]

Sheridan's powerful command came seeking battle on September 19. The final struggle for the Valley began that day at the Third Battle of Winchester and ended thirty days later at the Battle of Cedar Creek. In one month, the Federals inflicted four battlefield defeats upon the Confederates and implemented Grant's instructions to ravage the region by burning mills and barns and collecting livestock. The destruction was systematic, thorough, and devastating. Residents of the Valley paid a dear price for their allegiance to the Confederacy.[75]

The campaign also cost them more of their own as the Valley men of the old Stonewall Brigade fought at Third Winchester, Fisher's Hill, and Cedar Creek. Colonel John Funk, whom the men called "Stover Fink," fell mortally wounded at Winchester, dying in his family home on Market Street in the town on September 21. He had led the Virginians since the Mule Shoe. In the same battle, Major Matthew D. Bennett of the Fourth Virginia fell wounded, and Major James Newton of the Fifth Virginia suffered a leg wound that necessitated amputation. The Second Virginia had its flag captured.[76]

A month later at Cedar Creek, Lieutenant Colonel Hazael Williams of the Fifth Virginia received his second wound of the war, and the capable officer was gone from the service. Casualties among the Valley men in all of the battles surpassed one hundred or about one third of their numbers.[77]

In a postwar memoir, Private George Mooney of the Fifth Virginia summarized his and his comrades' views about the campaign, writing: "In the Valley in Jacksons life time we seldom were hungry but when with Early in the Valley we seldom had a full belly. Oh what a difference between Jackson's army & the fire he put into us & the will to fight & burn. It all dried up under Early."[78]

Following the defeat at Cedar Creek, Lee recalled the Second Corps to Petersburg, leaving Early behind with a skeleton command. Lee's orders brought the corps's members into Petersburg's trenches for the first time. They soon learned the dangers of such warfare. Like other units in the army, they suffered from lack of clothing and rations and saw their numbers wither away from disease, enemy fire, and desertion. Private Mooney claimed later that "the trenches in front of Petersburg were the roughest part of the war." When men deserted, he claimed, they did so with the "greatest regret and under irresistible pressure."[79]

From the Valley, residents sent what they could spare in food and clothing to their men at Petersburg. Except for a "great dinner" on Christmas, Lee's men subsisted on scanty rations. A member of the Second Virginia, writing in January 1865, professed, "If the south can hold out I believe the boys think it will be a life time business, as it appears to go on like usial." He thought the war could last another four years.[80]

But the Confederacy could not "hold out," and Lee's army was dwindling daily. The commander tried to retrieve the inevitable on March 25, by attacking Fort Stedman in the Union lines. The Valley men joined in the charge, losing dozens of men. One of those killed was Private John Dull. The night before he had written a letter to his wife, ending it with, "The Lord bless you and take care of you is the humble prare of your affectionate husband." Also struck down, but only wounded, was Brigadier General William Terry, their brigade commander and former colonel of the Fourth Virginia.[81]

Lee's Fort Stedman gamble resulted in a bloody repulse. For him and his army the end at Petersburg came a week later, on April 2, when the Union army rolled forward, crushing the thin Confederate ranks. The Southerners resisted fiercely, giving Lee enough time to escape across the Appomattox River and to march west. It became a race for the next seven days, but Union cavalry overtook the Rebels at Appomattox Court House on the night of April 8. The next morning, the proud members of Lee's army tried to punch a hole in the blue-clad cordon and failed. Among those slain in the abortive attack was Private John P. Moore of the Liberty Hall Volunteers of the Fourth Virginia. Lee met with Grant that afternoon, Palm Sunday, April 9, and surrendered his army.[82]

Grant's terms were generous but he required each Confederate soldier to be paroled and for the army to surrender formally their weapons and flags. One hundred ten members of the old Stonewall Brigade were paroled at Appomattox. In none of the five regiments did an officer rank above captain. One of the Valley men in the ranks at the end was Sergeant John Francis Brooke of the Fifth Virginia. Brooke had enlisted on April 17, 1861, and had been with the regiment throughout the conflict. He would enjoy a long postwar life, dying on March 26, 1942, the last known survivor of his regiment.[83]

On April 12, for the last time in its history, the Army of Northern Virginia marched down a road. Federal troops saluted their passage as the Confederates lay down their arms and relinquished their flags. Then the former soldiers began the long walks to home. All of them, including the Valley men, would have to rebuild lives from the ashes of a cause in a new nation.

16

✝

A BROTHERHOOD
OF VALOR

B Y the end of the Civil War, approximately 8,100 Virginians had served in the Stonewall Brigade, and approximately 8,200 Wisconsinites, Indianans, and Michiganders had stood in the ranks of the Iron Brigade. They were mostly native-born Americans of rural backgrounds—farmers, laborers, clerks, craftsmen, and merchants. They had shared similar beliefs and a common national heritage. The overwhelming majority of them had been volunteers, men who had enlisted for more than any other reason because of a commitment to a cause and from a sense of honor and duty. When their country divided, each group had answered a different summons.[1]

In time, the war itself became their common enemy. It imposed common hardships whether a soldier wore a blue or a gray uniform. The conflict consumed men on battlefields, in hospitals, and behind prison walls in numbers unmatched in the nation's annals. As the struggle lengthened, the nature of warfare changed, exacting a horrific price. How men or units reacted to or withstood the fury measured them. The reputations of individual soldiers and units were forged in terrible places.

The war gripped the Stonewall Brigade at the outset. By nightfall on July 21, 1861, on the battlefield of First Bull Run or Manassas, the Virginians had become Confederate heroes, men who had turned the battle's tide on Henry House Hill. Their defense of the ground and their capture of Union cannon had won for themselves and their commander, Thomas J. Jackson, an imperishable nickname. They earned a distinctive identity and a reputation as warriors.

As Jackson's renown grew, their association with him enhanced their stature as one of the army's best combat units. "They achieved a reputation for invincibility accepted by North and South alike," a historian of the brigade has written. "Confederate troops seemed to grow in confidence if they knew the Stonewall Brigade was charging in an assault with them." During the war and since then, their name has come to be identified with the elite units in the Army of Northern Virginia.[2]

At one point, probably in 1862, Jackson offered his judgment upon his fellow Valley men, telling a staff member, "You cannot praise these men of my brigade too much; they have fought, marched and endured more than I even thought they would." Years later, a former Louisiana officer who had served in the same division as the Virginians argued that "for a fast, rough and tumble, desperate fight I would take Hays Louisianans, the Stonewall Brigade and Hoods Texans."[3]

During the four years of war, slightly more than one thousand Virginians were either killed, mortally wounded, or died from disease, prison confinement, or by accident. Roughly one half of those deaths resulted from combat. Of seventy Confederate regiments ranked in a study according to percentage of casualties in a single engagement, only the Fourth Virginia is listed, ranked thirty-eighth for Second Manassas and fifty-eighth for Chancellorsville. The Stonewall Brigade does not rank among the top eighteen Confederate brigades in this category. While Confederate troops as a whole sustained a combat-related death rate of eleven to twelve percent, the Virginians' rate was roughly six percent.[4]

Combat casualties can be attributed to a number of factors. Perhaps nothing dictated a unit's losses more than the circumstances of a battle. Who were their opponents? Were they on the attack or defending a position? Did they oppose superior numbers? Had their commander committed a grievous mistake? Were they selected for a particularly deadly assignment? Although these battlefield conditions contributed to a regiment's or a brigade's losses, a unit's casualty rate reflected its discipline and prowess in the terribleness of combat. Training, leadership, experience, and a willingness to incur sacrifices affected a command's performance and its numbers of killed, wounded, and captured. Nevertheless, casualty figures provide only one measure of a unit's record.

The Stonewall Brigade's desertion rate reflected upon its members' discipline and commitment to the cause. As noted previously, desertion began to drain away men within weeks of First Manassas. It reached a floodtide during the 1862 Shenandoah Valley Campaign when more than fifty percent of the Virginians abandoned the ranks. Regardless of Confederate fortunes, the Valley men deserted at a crippling rate through much of the war. To be sure, many of them returned after a period of absence, some enlisted in other units, and others rejoined the regiments after being arrested and punished.

A number of factors impelled men to desert—the physical and mental exhaustion that marked some campaigns, the reality of combat, the pleas from family members at home, the course of the war, and individual circumstances. While not typical, the case of Private John F. Lackey of the Twenty-seventh Virginia offers a tragic example. He fled homeward in October 1862, probably after learning that his wife and children had been stricken with diphtheria. Whether he arrived in time to give comfort before all of them died is unknown. Lackey returned to the army but as a member of a cavalry regiment.[5]

With the Virginians, however, no reason seems more compelling than their proximity to their homes. When they campaigned in or were stationed in the Valley, the desertion rate accelerated. During 1862, they spent at least eight months in the region, and more of them deserted during these months than at any other time in the conflict. They knew the roads and the places of concealment, had relatives or friends who would assist them, and were only a few days away from their homes. Each regiment of the brigade lost more men to desertion in 1862 than in any other year. In all the brigade's regiments, except the Second Virginia, the numbers for that year exceeded the combined totals for the other three years.[6]

The numbers of permanent deserters from the brigade amounted to no fewer than thirteen hundred—more than the deaths in the brigade. It was a rate of sixteen percent, a staggering figure. Deaths from either disease or combat and permanent deserters removed twenty-eight percent of the unit's membership from the ranks. The Second Virginia lost the greatest number to permanent desertion, slightly more than four hundred, while the Fourth Virginia the fewest at about eighty. The Thirty-third rivaled the Second with a figure of at least 350.[7]

After 1862, however, the numbers of temporary and permanent deserters abated. Men continued to leave the ranks for the remainder of the war, but the rigors of campaigns and combat accounted for most of the brigade's losses in 1863 and 1864. Hundreds of veterans in each regiment, comprising the core of the unit, stayed, bleeding and dying from Malvern Hill to Spotsylvania. They believed in the cause despite shortages of food and clothing, battlefield defeats, and the destruction that was visited upon families and friends in the Valley during the autumn of 1864.

The Louisiana officer who ranked the Stonewall Brigade among the army's finest also contended that the troops in the Army of Northern Virginia "were all good when they had a good commander." Leadership at company, regimental, and brigade levels was an essential element in the combat quality of a unit. At its organization, the Stonewall Brigade benefited from the number of officers who either had received a military education, had served in militia companies, or had gained experience during the Mexican War. Their presence in the regiments had expedited training during the initial weeks of the conflict and had inspired their novice soldiers on Henry House Hill. Few, if any, Confederate brigades entered the service with a similar contingent of field and company commanders.[8]

The reorganization of the regiments in April 1862 brought forth a group of promising field officers. By year's end, however, James W. Allen, William S. H. Baylor, Lawson Botts, Andrew J. Grigsby, Frederick W. M. Holliday, and John F. Neff had either fallen killed or been wounded in battle or resigned. Had Baylor not been killed at Second Manassas he seemed destined for command of the brigade, while Grigsby deserved promotion despite Jackson's opposition. Capable replacements emerged, such as James K. Edmondson, John H. S. Funk, John Q. A. Nadenbousch, and William Terry, but the losses of so many good officers crippled the brigade's discipline and combat efficiency. The Seven Days, Cedar Mountain, Second Manassas, and Sharpsburg campaigns ravaged the field officer ranks of the brigade. This void was never adequately filled.

Ultimately, however, the Stonewall Brigade belonged to one man— Thomas J. Jackson. He knew the manner of men who filled its ranks, tempered them in the furnace of duty and discipline, and led them on to Henry House Hill. For a year, from that July Sunday, through Romney and Kernstown, to Port Republic at the end of the Shenandoah Valley Campaign, he demanded more of them than of any other troops under his command. At First Manassas he and the Virginians saved the Confederate army, and during the Valley Campaign, the brigade formed the bedrock of Jackson's army. For the war's first year, no unit in the Confederacy rendered more valuable service than the Stonewall Brigade. It was the best brigade in the armies of the Confederacy. Wherever the Valley men marched and fought, Jackson was nearby.

Richard B. Garnett, Charles S. Winder, Frank Paxton, and James A. Walker followed Old Jack at the head of the Virginians. Winder was the best of the group and the one most disliked by the rank and file. The Marylander led them through the Valley Campaign, Seven Days, and at Cedar Mountain, where he was killed. When they returned to the Valley after Sharpsburg, where only 250 of them had stood in the ranks on that September day, they would never again be the premier brigade in the army. Other units, such as Richard Taylor's Louisianans, John B. Hood's Texans, Georgians, and South Carolinians, and Stephen D. Ramseur's North Carolinians, supplanted the Virginians until these units had little left to give. The war took from them as it had earlier from the Stonewall Brigade. It was the cost of valor.

Unlike the Virginians, the Westerners had their reckoning with the fury delayed for a year. Although the Second Wisconsin had learned some of combat's lessons on Henry House Hill, it was not until Brawner's Farm at Second Manassas when the Westerners stood together and fought as a brigade. Until then, they had known only the monotony of drill, the strictures of discipline, the exhaustion of marches, and the hardships of soldiering. But those months seasoned them. By most accounts, they were among the army's best-drilled and best-disciplined commands. When their time came at last in the twilight of an August day, those qualities counted.

From Brawner's Farm until the night of July 1, 1863, at Gettysburg, the Iron Brigade was the best combat unit in the Army of the Potomac. In fact, no other brigade in the army during the course of the war had a comparable record. Numbers testify to its unmatched stature. Nearly 1,750 brigade members lost their lives to disease or in combat. Of that figure, 1,150 were either killed or mortally wounded. "In proportion to its numbers," according to a historian who analyzed Civil War casualty rates and figures, "this brigade sustained the heaviest loss of any in the war."[9]

Five percent of all Union soldiers were either killed or mortally wounded in combat. By comparison, the rate of battle deaths among the five regiments of the Iron Brigade slightly exceeded fourteen percent. In the brigade, the Twenty-fourth Michigan sustained the lowest rate at slightly more than eleven percent, and the Second Wisconsin, the highest at nearly twenty percent. Three of the brigade's regiments—the Second and Seventh Wisconsin and the Nineteenth Indiana—rank among the twelve Union regiments that suffered the highest percentage of combat deaths. The Second Wisconsin stands at the top of the list.[10]

In total numbers, only two Union regiments lost more men in battle than did the Seventh Wisconsin, which had 281 members killed or mortally wounded. With 244 deaths, the Sixth Wisconsin ranks tenth. Compounding the losses due to deaths in battle were the hundreds of men who died from disease or in prison, were disabled by wounds, were discharged for various reasons, or deserted. These figures exceeded, if not doubled, the numbers who fell in combat. The attrition rate in the brigade amounted to more than one half its membership.[11]

Most of these combat fatalities were incurred during a span of ten months at Brawner's Farm, South Mountain, Antietam, and Gettysburg. The fighting at each of the engagements was some of the war's fiercest. At Brawner's Farm and Gettysburg, the opposing lines stood only paces apart, and few places in the conflict compared to the slaughter in the Cornfield at Antietam. When the Westerners dragged themselves off the field at Antietam, "those damned black hats" were known throughout both armies.

Several factors contributed to the brigade's unmatched record as warriors. A former member of the black hats offered one explanation to his comrades at a postwar reunion. He stated:

> When we went down to the Potomac in '61, we were the only Western soldiers in the entire army, and we would have died rather than dishonor the West. We felt that the eyes of the East were upon us, and that we were the test of the West. What made us good soldiers? Was it because we were gritty and didn't blanch, or because amid the zip zip of the bullets we didn't feel a peculiar corkscrew sensation, when we felt some Johnnie had the drop on us? No, it was our pride! We had rather have died than been branded as cowards! We stood when commanded to stand, and when ordered to go, we got![12]

Individual pride was braced by a devotion to duty, honor, and the cause. In their letters and diary entries, the Westerners espoused an intense patriotism and idealism. Although they complained frequently about generals and their lot, and questioned the administration's policies in regard to commanders and abolition, they did not waver in their allegiance to the restoration of the Union. They saw beyond themselves to the greater good, and accepted the sacrifices. About two hundred Westerners deserted permanently. This low number reflected, in part, the brigade members' adherence to the cause and the distance from their homes. In the end, when enthusiasm for battle had been bled from them, the cause remained, nourished by the commitment to duty, honor, and their comrades.[13]

A third factor was leadership. Like the Virginians, the Westerners bore the indelible imprint of one man. When John Gibbon joined the brigade as its commander in May 1862 at Fredericksburg, he fused four regiments into a cohesive unit. With unrelenting drill and with strict discipline, he made them soldiers. He also gave them a tangible symbol of identification—the black Hardee hats—that separated the Westerners from other troops in the army. The hats became their badge of honor and pride. Gibbon had prepared them better than they understood until Brawner's Farm. By the time he left them in November 1862, they had stood "like iron" amid the terribleness of the brotherhood.

None of Gibbon's successors—Solomon Meredith, Lysander Cutler, and Edward S. Bragg—compared to the West Pointer and Regular Army officer in ability or in the estimation of the rank and file. All three of them, however, proved to be capable, if not distinguished, brigade commanders. With other officers in the brigade, men such as Lucius Fairchild, John Mansfield, Rufus R. Dawes, John A. Kellogg, William W. Robinson, Charles A. Hamilton, Samuel J. Williams, Alois O. Bachman, Henry A. Morrow, and Mark Flanigan, they embodied the finest attributes of citizen soldiers. They had been given time to learn the rudiments of their new trade before being tested as leaders in combat. A total of 347 men served as officers in the brigade, and 56 of them lost their lives. Only one of them, a lieutenant, was cashiered for misconduct. They had been men worthy of the rank and file they had commanded.[14]

One member of the Iron Brigade calculated that he and his comrades had marched more than 1,430 miles during the war. If a Virginian in the Stonewall Brigade had made a similar estimate, the figure would have probably been within a handful of miles. Both of their journeys had been long, many times on the same or parallel roads. Three times they had fought each other directly across a bloody landscape. When the war ended, they came home, stored away their uniforms, and retrieved their lives.[15]

They never forgot, however. In time, they gathered for reunions in Virginia, Wisconsin, Indiana, and Michigan. They walked with ghosts for a day or so, and it pleased them. Some traveled back to battlefields to dedicate monuments or to remember. In 1880, the black-hatted veterans formed the Iron Brigade Association, welcoming into its membership their former comrades in Battery B, Fourth U.S. Artillery. They elected John Gibbon as their first president. Earlier at a reunion of Wisconsin soldiers, he had told the gathering that "at the judgment day I want to be with Wisconsin soldiers." They all possessed, as a former officer in the Second Wisconsin wrote, "bonds which cannot be explained and perhaps cannot be understood" except by those who had been by each other's side in a brotherhood of valor.[16]

APPENDIX

The organization of regiments is given according to their original musters unless designated otherwise.

STONEWALL BRIGADE

COMMANDERS

Brig. Gen. Thomas J. Jackson
Brig. Gen. Richard B. Garnett
Brig. Gen. Charles S. Winder
Col. William S. H. Baylor*
Col. Andrew J. Grigsby*
Brig. Gen. Elisha F. Paxton
Brig. Gen. James A. Walker
Brig. Gen. William Terry**

*Held temporary command
**Commanded consolidated Virginia regiments of Maj. Gen. Edward Johnson's division, including Stonewall Brigade regiments.

Second Virginia Infantry

COMMANDERS

Col. James W. Allen
Col. Lawson Botts
Col. John Q. A. Nadenbousch
Lt. Col. Raleigh T. Colston
Lt. Col. William W. Randolph

COMPANY	NICKNAME	COUNTY
A	*Jefferson Guards*	*Jefferson*
B	*Hamtramck Guards*	*Jefferson*
C	*Nelson Rifles*	*Clarke*

COMPANY	NICKNAME	COUNTY
D	Berkeley Border Guards	Berkeley
E	Hedgesville Blues	Berkeley
F	Winchester Riflemen	Frederick
G	Botts Greys	Jefferson
H	Letcher Riflemen	Jefferson
I	Clarke Rifles	Clarke
K	Floyd Guards	Jefferson

Fourth Virginia Infantry

COMMANDERS

Col. James F. Preston
Col. Charles A. Ronald
Lt. Col. Robert D. Gardner
Col. William Terry

COMPANY	NICKNAME	COUNTY
A	Wythe Grays	Wythe
B	Fort Lewis Volunteers	Montgomery
C	Pulaski Guards	Pulaski
D	Smyth Blues	Smyth
E	Montgomery Highlanders	Montgomery
F	Grayson Dare Devils	Grayson
G	Montgomery Fencibles	Montgomery
H	Rockbridge Grays	Rockbridge
I	Liberty Hall Volunteers	Rockbridge
K*	Rockbridge Rifles	Rockbridge

*Transferred to Fifth Virginia and then to Twenty-seventh Virginia. Replaced by company from Montgomery County that was designated Company L.

Fifth Virginia Infantry

COMMANDERS

Col. Kenton Harper
Col. William H. Harman
Col. William S. H. Baylor
Col. John H. S. Funk

COMPANY	NICKNAME	COUNTY
A	Marion Rifles	Frederick
B	Rockbridge Rifles	Rockbridge
C	Mountain Guard	Augusta
D	Southern Guard	Augusta
E	Augusta Greys	Augusta
F	West View Infantry	Augusta
G	Staunton Rifles	Augusta
H	Augusta Rifles	Augusta
I	Ready Rifles	Augusta
K	Continental Morgan Guards	Frederick
L	West Augusta Guard	Augusta

Twenty-seventh Virginia Infantry

COMMANDERS

Col. William W. Gordon

Col. John Echols

Col. Andrew J. Grigsby

Col. James K. Edmondson

Lt. Col. Daniel M. Shriver

Lt. Col. Charles L. Haynes

COMPANY	NICKNAME	COUNTY
A	Alleghany Roughs	Alleghany
B	Virginia Hibernians	Alleghany
C	Alleghany Rifles	Alleghany
D	Monroe Guards	Monroe
E	Greenbrier Rifles	Greenbrier
F	Greenbrier Sharp Shooters	Greenbrier
G	Shriver Grays	Wheeling
H*	Rockbridge Rifles	Rockbridge

*Transferred from Fifth Virginia after First Manassas.

Thirty-third Virginia Infantry

COMMANDERS

Col. Arthur C. Cummings

Col. John F. Neff
Col. Edwin G. Lee
Col. Frederick W. M. Holliday
Lt. Col. George W. Huston

COMPANY	NICKNAME	COUNTY
A	*Potomac Guards*	*Hampshire*
B	*Toms Brook Guards*	*Shenandoah*
C	*Tenth Legion Minute Men*	*Shenandoah*
D	*Mountain Rangers*	*Frederick*
E	*Emerald Guard*	*Shenandoah*
F	*Independent Greys*	*Hardy*
G	*Mt. Jackson Rifles*	*Shenandoah*
H	*Page Grays*	*Page*
I	*Rockingham Confederates*	*Rockingham*
K	*Shenandoah Sharpshooters*	*Shenandoah*

Rockbridge Artillery
COMMANDERS
Capt. William N. Pendleton
Capt. William McLaughlin
Capt. William T. Poague

Battery detached from Stonewall Brigade in October 1862 in artillery reorganization.

IRON BRIGADE

COMMANDERS

Brig. Gen. Rufus King

Brig. Gen. John Gibbon

Brig. Gen. Solomon Meredith

Col. William W. Robinson*

Brig. Gen. Lysander Cutler

Brig. Gen. Edward S. Bragg

Col. John A. Kellogg*

Brig. Gen. Henry A. Morrow*

*Held temporary command

Second Wisconsin Infantry

COMMANDERS

Col. S. Park S. Coon

Col. Edgar O'Connor

Col. Lucius Fairchild

Col. John Mansfield

COMPANY	NICKNAME	COUNTY
A	Citizens' Guard	Dodge
B	La Crosse Light Guards	La Crosse
C	Grant County Guards	Grant
D	Janesville Volunteers	Rock
E	Oshkosh Volunteers	Winnebago
F	Belle City Rifles	Racine
G	Portage City Guards	Columbia
H	Randall Guards	Dane
I	Miner's Guards	Iowa
K*	Wisconsin Rifles	Milwaukee

*Detached and converted to heavy artillery unit and replaced by a new Company K from Dane and Milwaukee counties.

Sixth Wisconsin Infantry

COMMANDERS

Col. Lysander Cutler

Col. Edward S. Bragg
Lt. Col. Rufus R. Dawes
Col. John A. Kellogg
Lt. Col. Thomas Kerr

COMPANY	NICKNAME	COUNTY
A	*Sauk County Riflemen*	*Sauk*
B	*Prescott Guards*	*Pierce*
C	*Prairie du Chien Volunteers*	*Crawford*
D	*Montgomery Guards*	*Milwaukee*
E	*Bragg's Rifles*	*Fond du Lac*
F	*Citizens' Corps*	*Milwaukee*
G	*Beloit Star Rifles*	*Rock*
H	*Buffalo County Rifles*	*Buffalo*
I	*Anderson Guards*	*Juneau and Dane*
K	*Lemonweir Minute Men*	*Juneau*

Seventh Wisconsin Infantry

COMMANDERS
Col. Joseph Van Dor
Col. William W. Robinson
Lt. Col. Mark Finnicum
Lt. Col. Hollon Richardson

COMPANY	NICKNAME	COUNTY
A	*Lodi Guards*	*Chippewa and Columbia*
B	*Columbia County Cadets*	*Columbia*
C	*Platteville Guards*	*Grant*
D	*Stoughton Light Guard*	*Dane*
E	*Marquette County Sharp Shooters*	*Marquette*
F	*Lancaster Union Guards*	*Grant*
G	*Grand Rapids Union Guards*	*Wood*
H	*Badger State Guards*	*Grant*
I	*Northwestern Tigers*	*Dodge and Waushara*
K	*Badger Rifles*	*Rock*

Nineteenth Indiana Infantry
COMMANDERS
Col. Solomon Meredith
Col. Samuel J. Williams
Lt. Col. John M. Lindley

COMPANY	NICKNAME	COUNTY
A	Union Guards	Madison
B	City Greys	Wayne
C	Winchester Greys	Randolph
D	Invincibles	Marion
E	Delaware Greys	Delaware
F	Meredith Guards	Marion
G	Elkhart County Guards	Elkhart
H	Edinburgh Guards	Johnson
I	Spencer Greys	Owen
K	Selma Legion	Delaware

Twenty-fourth Michigan Infantry
COMMANDERS
Col. Henry A. Morrow
Lt. Col. Albert M. Edwards

The companies of the Twenty-fourth Michigan adopted no nicknames. The majority of recruits came from Detroit and Wayne County. Other counties represented were Monroe, Washtenaw, Oakland, and Clinton.

Battery B, Fourth U.S. Artillery
COMMANDERS
Capt. Joseph B. Campbell
Lt. James Stewart

Battery was detached from Iron Brigade in fall of 1862.

ABBREVIATIONS

Works cited by author and short titles will be found in full in the Bibliography. The following abbreviations are used in the notes:

ACHS	Augusta County Historical Society
ANB	Antietam National Battlefield
B & G	*Blue & Gray Magazine*
B & L	*Battles and Leaders*
CHS	Chicago Historical Society
CR	Compiled Records
CSR	Compiled Service Records
CV	*Confederate Veteran*
DPL	Detroit Public Library
DU	Duke University
FSNMP	Fredericksburg-Spotsylvania National Military Park
GNMP	Gettysburg National Military Park
HL	Handley Library
HSP	Historical Society of Pennsylvania
IHS	Indiana Historical Society
ISL	Indiana State Library
IU	Indiana University
LC	Library of Congress
MC	Museum of the Confederacy
MHS	Maryland Historical Society
MNBP	Manassas National Battlefield Park
MOLLUS	Military Order Loyal Legion of the United States
MSU	Michigan State University
NA	National Archives
NCSA	North Carolina State Archives
NYHS	New-York Historical Society
OR	*War of the Rebellion: Official Records of Union and Confederate Armies*
ORS	*Supplement to the Official Records of the Union and Confederate Armies*
RHSP	*Rockbridge Historical Society Proceedings*
SAM	State Archives of Michigan
SHSP	*Southern Historical Society Papers*
SHSW	State Historical Society of Wisconsin

UM	University of Michigan
UNC	University of North Carolina
USAMHI	United States Army Military History Institute
UVA	University of Virginia
UWLC	University of Wisconsin—La Crosse
UWRF	University of Wisconsin—River Falls
VHS	Virginia Historical Society
VMHB	*Virginia Magazine of History and Biography*
VMI	Virginia Military Institute
VSL	Virginia State Library
VT	Virginia Tech University
WL	Washington and Lee University
WM	College of William and Mary
WMH	*Wisconsin Magazine of History*

NOTES

CHAPTER 1: GATHERINGS

1. Phillips, *Lower Shenandoah Valley*, p. 7; Unknown author–Martha, April 17, 1861, McCutchan Correspondence, WL.
2. Wallace, *Guide*, p. i; Robertson, *Stonewall Brigade*, p. 5; Albaugh and Simmons, *Confederate Arms*, p. 81; Samuel J. C. Moore–My Dearest Ellen, April 21, 1861, Moore Papers, UNC.
3. OR, 2, p. 775; Wallace, *5th Virginia Infantry*, p. 5; Staunton *Vindicator*, April 26, 1861; Turner, *My Dear Emma*, pp. 3–5.
4. Lyle, "Stonewall Jackson's Guard," p. 34, WL; Staunton *Vindicator*, April 26, 1861.
5. Staunton *Vindicator*, April 26, 1861; R. Henry Campbell–Father, [April 19, 1861], Campbell Letters, VMI.
6. Waddell, *Annals*, pp. 454–56, 485; Lyle, "Stonewall Jackson's Guards," p. 29; Wayland, *History of Rockingham County*, p. 131.
7. Waddell, *Annals*, pp. 1, 10, 18, 21, 22, 36, 343; Wayland, *History of Shenandoah County*, p. 35; Wert, *From Winchester*, pp. 27–28.
8. Driver, *Lexington*, p. 9; Waddell, *Annals*, p. 456; Unknown author–Martha, April 17, 1861, McCutchan Correspondence, WL; Wallace, *5th Virginia Infantry*, p. 5.
9. Wallace, *Guide*, p. i; Robertson, *Stonewall Brigade*, pp. 5, 16, 17; Robertson, *4th Virginia Infantry*, p. 1; Reidenbaugh, *33rd Virginia Infantry*, p. 2.
10. Frye, *2nd Virginia Infantry*, p. 6; Robertson, *4th Virginia Infantry*, p. 4; Wallace, *5th Virginia Infantry*, pp. 12, 13; Reidenbaugh, *27th Virginia Infantry*, pp. 2–7; Reidenbaugh, *33rd Virginia Infantry*, pp. 1–4; McDonald, *A Woman's Civil War*, p. 35.
11. Robertson, *Stonewall Brigade*, pp. viii, 13, 240; CV, 7, p. 506.
12. Bean, *Liberty Hall Volunteers*, p. 22; CV, 23, p. 57; Robertson, *Stonewall Brigade*, p. 21.
13. Robertson, *Stonewall Brigade*, pp. 14, 15; Frye, *2nd Virginia Infantry*, p. 10; Wallace, *5th Virginia Infantry*, p. 72; Reidenbaugh, *33rd Virginia Infantry*, pp. 4, 106; Casler, *Four Years*, p. 12.
14. Robertson, *Stonewall Brigade*, pp. 16, 17; Frye, *2nd Virginia Infantry*, p. 7; Wallace, *5th Virginia Infantry*, p. 73; Reidenbaugh, *27th Virginia Infantry*, pp. 20–21; Reidenbaugh, *33rd Virginia Infantry*, p. 26; Robinson, Confederate Company List, VT.
15. Robertson, *Stonewall Brigade*, p. 240; Bean, *Liberty Hall Volunteers*, p. 9; Robertson, *4th Virginia Infantry*, p. 1; Shields, "Recollections," RHSP, 9, p.

12; Mann, *They Were Heard From*, pp. 5–6; Johnson, *University Memorial*, pp. 31–36, 61–63, 222, 346, 477–78, 653, 751, 754.

16. Wallace, *Guide*, pp. i–iii.

17. Coco, *Civil War Infantryman*, pp. 9–10.

18. Robertson, *Stonewall Brigade*, pp. v–vi.

19. Wallace, *Guide*, pp. 83–84, 87, 110, 116; Frye, *2nd Virginia Infantry*, p. 6; Robertson, *4th Virginia Infantry*, pp. 1, 2, 4; Wallace, *5th Virginia Infantry*, pp. 1, 6, 7, 12, 13; Waddell, *Annals*, pp. 502–5; Reidenbaugh, *27th Virginia Infantry*, pp. 2–7, 9; Reidenbaugh, *33rd Virginia Infantry*, pp. 1–4; Kleese, *Shenandoah County*, p. 8.

20. Krick, *Lee's Colonels*, pp. 28, 43, 54, 96, 144–45, 153, 163, 164, 204, 256, 284; Mann, *They Were Heard From*, p. 5; Phillips, *Lower Shenandoah Valley*, p. 8; Wallace, *5th Virginia Infantry*, p. 125.

21. Krick, *Lee's Colonels*, pp. 178, 263, 302, 330; Frye, *2nd Virginia Infantry*, p. 6; *CV*, 16, p. 236; Robertson, *4th Virginia Infantry*, p. 4; Robinson, Confederate Company List, VT; Bean, *Liberty Hall Volunteers*, p. 25; Wallace, *5th Virginia Infantry*, pp. 12, 13, 19, 92, 113, 119, 125, 136, 138, 147, 153, 168, 170; Reidenbaugh, *27th Virginia Infantry*, pp. 4, 9; Reidenbaugh, *33rd Virginia Infantry*, pp. 1–4.

22. McAllister, *Sketch*, pp. 8–12, 14, 15; Reidenbaugh, *27th Virginia Infantry*, pp. 1–2; Robertson, *Civil War Letters*, pp. 9–11, 156.

23. Driver, *1st and 2nd Rockbridge Artillery*, p. 1; Warner, *Generals in Gray*, p. 234.

24. Driver, *1st and 2nd Rockbridge Artillery*, pp. 1–3; Smith, *With Stonewall Jackson*, p. 7.

25. Robertson, *Stonewall Brigade*, p. 6.

26. Frank B. Jones–Sue, April 23, 1861, Jones Papers, HL; Turner, *My Dear Emma*, p. 6.

27. Samuel J. C. Moore–My Dear Little Boy, May 16, 1861, Moore Papers, UNC.

28. Staunton *Vindicator*, May 10, 1861.

29. Love, *Wisconsin*, pp. 28, 31; Harney, *History*, p. 129.

30. Love, *Wisconsin*, pp. 140–43.

31. Herdegen, *Men Stood*, pp. 20, 21; Harney, *History*, p. 146; Beaudot and Herdegen, *Irishman*, pp. 1, 11.

32. Gaff, *If This Is War*, pp. 21–22.

33. Ibid., pp. 21–22, 24; Otis, *Second Wisconsin*, p. 23.

34. Gaff, *If This Is War*, Chapters 2 and 3; Love, *Wisconsin*, p. 229.

35. Gaff, *If This Is War*, Chapters 2 and 3; Harney, *History*, pp. 146, 147; William G. Davis–Parents, July 10, 1862, Davis Letters, MNBP.

36. Gaff, *If This Is War*, pp. 39, 41, 74; Nolan, *Iron Brigade*, p. 4; William G. Davis–Parents and Friends, May 18, 1861, Davis Letters, MNBP.

37. Horace Emerson–Brother Irvey, May 10, 1861, Emerson Letters, UM; Gaff, *If This Is War*, pp. 41, 73, 75; Otis, *Second Wisconsin*, p. 24.

38. Horace Emerson–Brother Irvey, May 10, 1861, Emerson Letters, UM; Nolan, *Iron Brigade*, p. 6; Alured Larke–My dear Ethel, June 5, 1861, Larke Letters, SHSW; Gaff, *If This Is War*, pp. 79, 81.

39. William G. Davis–Parents, June 19, 1861, Davis Letters, MNBP; Nolan, *Iron Brigade*, pp. 5, 6; Otis, *Second Wisconsin*, p. 24.

40. Nolan, *Iron Brigade*, p. 5; Otis, *Second Wisconsin*, p. 27; Gaff, *If This Is War*, p. 24; Newspaper clipping, Monteith Papers, SHSW.

41. Nolan, *Iron Brigade*, p. 5; Otis, *Second Wisconsin*, pp. 27, 28; Gaff, *If This Is War*, pp. 24–26.

42. Otis, *Second Wisconsin*, pp. 28–31, 32n; Gaff, *If This Is War*, Chapters 2 and 3.

43. Nolan, *Iron Brigade*, p. 4; Gaff, *If This Is War*, pp. 82–84, 87; Langworthy, "Reminiscences," pp. 1–3, SHSW.

44. Gaff, *If This Is War*, pp. 107–8; Ross, *Empty Sleeve*, p. 35.

45. Otis, *Second Wisconsin*, p. 24; Nolan, *Iron Brigade*, p. 6; Gaff, *If This Is War*, pp. 117–18.

46. Nolan, *Iron Brigade*, p. 6; P. J. Arndt–Father, Mother and Friends, February 7, 1864, SHSW; Mead, Journal, SHSW; *War Papers*, MOLLUS, Wisconsin, 1, p. 375; Horace Emerson–Brother, April 24, 1861, Emerson Letters, UM.

47. Otis, *Second Wisconsin*, pp. 24–26; *War Papers*, MOLLUS, Wisconsin, 1, pp. 376, 377; Langworthy, "Reminiscences," pp. 3–4, SHSW; Gaff, *If This Is War*, pp. 119–29, 134.

48. *War Papers*, MOLLUS, Wisconsin, 1, p. 378; Horace Emerson–Brother, June 27, 1861, Emerson Letters, UM.

49. Horace Emerson–Brother Irvey, May 10, 1861, Emerson Letters, UM; Mead, "Journal," SHSW; Hughes, "Report," SHSW.

1. *OR*, 2, p. 784.

2. Ibid., p. 784; Robertson, *Stonewall Jackson*, pp. 222–24; Jackson, *Memoirs*, p. 151.

3. Warner, *Generals in Gray*, p. 151; Carson, Memoirs, p. 10, VHS; Robertson, *Stonewall Jackson*, p. x; Lyle, "Stonewall Jackson's Guard," p. 10, WL.

4. Lyle, "Stonewall Jackson's Guard," p. 9, WL; Wright, Memoir, VHS; Robertson, *Stonewall Jackson*, pp. x, 209–10.

5. *OR*, 2, pp. 784, 785, 793, 802, 861; Thomas J. Jackson–Sir, August 5, 1861, Baylor file, CSR, NA; R. Henry Campbell–Mother, May 4, 1861, Campbell Letters, VMI; Robertson, *Stonewall Brigade*, pp. 8, 9.

6. Fryer, *2nd Virginia Infantry*, p. 6; Samuel J. C. Moore–My Dear Ellen, May 1, 1861, Moore Papers, UNC; *OR*, 2, p. 814.

7. R. Henry Campbell–Mother, May 4, 1861, Campbell Letters, VMI; Hanger, Diary, MNBP; Coco, *Civil War Infantryman*, p. 19; Mann, *They Were Heard From*, p. 3; Robertson, *Stonewall Jackson*, p. 227.

8. Frye, *2nd Virginia Infantry*, p. 8; Hanger, Diary, MNBP; Paxton, *Civil War Letters*, p. 6; *OR*, 2, pp. 861–62.

9. *OR*, 2, p. 861; Reidenbaugh, *33rd Virginia Infantry*, pp. 2, 3; A. S. Pendleton–Captain James Bumgarten, June 26, 1861, Harper Papers, UNC; James J. White–My Dear Mary, June 15, 1861, White Letters, UNC; Frye, *2nd Virginia Infantry*, p. 8.

10. Samuel J. C. Moore–My Dearest Ellen, May 29, 1861, Moore Papers, UNC; Phillips, *Lower Shenandoah Valley*, pp. 32–33; Report of A. S. Pendleton, July 7, 1861, Pendleton Papers, UNC.

11. Albaugh and Simmons, *Confederate Arms,* p. 3; *OR,* 2, pp. 810, 822; Wallace, *5th Virginia Infantry,* p. 15.

12. *OR,* pp. 810, 822; Undated ordnance report, Second Virginia, Pendleton Papers, UNC; Wallace, *Fifth Virginia Infantry,* p. 15; Undated ordnance report, Company K, Fifth Virginia, Kurtz Papers, UNC; Reidenbaugh, *33rd Virginia Infantry,* p. 2.

13. John Q. Winfield–Sallie, May 10, 1861, Winfield Papers, UNC; Turner, *Old Zeus,* p. 52; Turner, *My Dear Emma,* p. 9; Lyle, "Stonewall Jackson's Guard," p. 172, WL; Reidenbaugh, *33rd Virginia Infantry,* p. 3; Paxton, *Civil War Letters,* p. 6; Robertson, *Stonewall Jackson,* pp. 238–39.

14. Robertson, *Stonewall Jackson,* pp. 237–39; Jackson, *Memoirs,* p. 159.

15. Jackson, *Memoirs,* pp. 56, 159; Robertson, *Stonewall Jackson,* pp. xiv, 239–40, 241; *SHSP,* 25, p. 103; Frye, *2nd Virginia Infantry,* p. 8.

16. Gratton, "Reminiscences," p. 6, USAMHI; Samuel J. C. Moore–My Dearest Ellen, June 10, 1861, Moore Papers, UNC; Casler, *Four Years,* p. 58; Frank B. Jones–Mother, June 3, 1861, Family Collection, HL; Robertson, *Stonewall Jackson,* p. 242.

17. Robertson, *Stonewall Jackson,* pp. 242–43.

18. Ibid., pp. 244–46; Jackson, *Memoirs,* pp. 161–62.

19. Jackson, *Memoirs,* p. 162; Robertson, *Stonewall Jackson,* pp. 244–45.

20. Henry Ruffner Morrison–Brother, June 22, 1861, Morrison Papers, USAMHI; James J. White–My Dear Mary, June 21, 1861, White Letters, UNC; Bean, *Liberty Hall Volunteers,* p. 31.

21. Turner, *Ted Barclay,* p. 17; John W. Daniel–Father, June 26, 1861, Daniel Papers, UVA; *OR,* 2, p. 187; Wallace, *5th Virginia Infantry,* p. 74; Robertson, *Stonewall Jackson,* p. 247.

22. Hanger, Diary, MNBP; *OR,* 2, pp. 185, 186; *ORS,* 1, pp. 127–28; Wallace, *5th Virginia Infantry,* p. 15.

23. *OR,* 2, pp. 185, 186; Wallace, *5th Virginia Infantry,* p. 15; Jackson, *Memoirs,* p. 166; Frye, *2nd Virginia Infantry,* p. 10.

24. Grabill, "Diary," p. 3, *Shenandoah Herald,* January 8–15, 1922, copy in author's possession; Samuel J. C. Moore–My Dearest Ellen, July 9, 1861, Moore Papers, UNC.

25. Samuel J. C. Moore–My Dearest Ellen, July 9, 1861, Moore Papers, UNC; Hanger, Diary, MNBP; Turner, *Old Zeus,* p. 66.

26. Hennessy, *First Battle,* pp. 1–4.

27. Ibid., pp. 4–11, 28.

28. Ibid., p. 28, Hanger, Diary, MNBP; Fishburne, Memoirs, p. 18, UVA; Jones, "Liberty Hall Volunteers," p. 5, WL.

29. Hanger, Diary, MNBP; Wayland, *Stonewall Jackson's Way,* p. 32; Hennessy, *First Battle,* p. 28; Shields, "Recollections," *RHSP,* 9, p. 13.

30. Hanger, Diary, MNBP; *SHSP,* 19, pp. 87, 88; Reidenbaugh, *33rd Virginia Infantry,* p. 6.

31. Gaff, *If This Is War,* pp. 180–82.

32. Otis, *Second Wisconsin,* pp. 107, 108.

33. *OR,* 2, p. 314; Nolan, *Iron Brigade,* pp. 7, 8; Gaff, *If This Is War,* p. 156; Warner, *Generals in Blue,* pp. 441–42.

34. Gaff, *If This Is War*, pp. 145, 156, 157, 161, 302; Woodhead, *Echoes of Glory (Union)*, p. 33.

35. Otis, *Second Wisconsin*, pp. 131, 132, 135, 136; *War Papers*, MOLLUS, Wisconsin, 1, p. 377.

36. *War Papers*, MOLLUS, Wisconsin, 1, pp. 379, 380, 382; Gaff, *If This Is War*, p. 164.

37. Hennessy, *First Battle*, pp. 12–16.

38. Mead, "Journal," SHSW; *War Papers*, MOLLUS, Wisconsin, 1, p. 383; Gaff, *If This Is War*, pp. 170–74.

39. Mead, "Journal," SHSW; *War Papers*, MOLLUS, Wisconsin, 1, p. 383, 384; Gaff, *If This Is War*, pp. 175–78; Hennessy, *First Battle*, pp. 17–25; William G. Davis–Parents, July 20, 1861, Davis Letters, MNBP.

40. William G. Davis–Parents, July 20, 1861, Davis Letters, MNBP.

41. Gaff, *If This Is War*, pp. 185–87; Milwaukee *Sentinel*, July 30, 1861; clipping from Racine *Advocate*, MNBP; *OR*, 2, pp. 368–69.

42. Shields, "Recollections," *RHSP*, 9, pp. 14, 15; John C. Carpenter–William M. McAllister, December 26, 1902, Carpenter Letter, MNBP; Samuel J. C. Moore–Dr. R. Kownilar, August 5, 1861, Moore Papers, UNC; *OR*, 2, p. 481; Hennessy, *First Battle*, p. 38.

43. Samuel J. C. Moore–Dr. R. Kownilar, August 5, 1861, Moore Papers, UNC; Douglas, *I Rode with Stonewall*, p. 9; *OR*, 2, p. 481; Hennessy, *First Battle*, p. 68.

44. *OR*, 2, p. 481; Hennessy, *First Battle*, p. 69; *SHSP*, 19, p. 89; Samuel J. C. Moore–Dr. R. Kownilar, August 5, 1861, Moore Papers, UNC.

45. Hennessy, *First Battle*, Chapters 5 and 6, p. 69.

46. Ibid., pp. 69, 70, 76.

47. Ibid., p. 70; Frye, *2nd Virginia Infantry*, p. 13; Fonerden, *Brief History*, p. 9; Casler, *Four Years*, p. 25.

48. Hennessy, *First Battle*, pp. 75, 76; Staunton *Spectator*, August 27, 1861.

49. *OR*, 2, p. 481; Hennessy, *First Battle*, pp. 77–79; Wallace, *5th Virginia Infantry*, p. 17.

50. Samuel J. C. Moore–Doctor and Mrs. Kownilar, July 25, 1861, Moore Papers, UNC; Bean, *Liberty Hall Volunteers*, p. 45; Jones, "Liberty Hall Volunteers," pp. 7–8, WL; *Rockbridge County News*, February 2, 1911; Robertson, *Stonewall Brigade*, p. 38; Bosang, *Memoirs*, pp. 5, 6; Casler, *Four Years*, p. 41.

51. William Meade, Biographical Sketch, McDowell Correspondence, WL; the best and most reliable version of Bee's immortal words is in Robertson, *Stonewall Jackson*, pp. 263, 264; Hennessy, *First Battle*, p. 83.

52. Hennessy, *First Battle*, pp. 80–84; Robertson, *Stonewall Brigade*, p. 40.

53. Hennessy, *First Battle*, pp. 84–86; Richmond *Times-Dispatch*, June 4, 1905; Casler, *Four Years*, p. 27; John O. Casler–Randolph Barton, April 9, 1906, Casler Letter, VSL; *SHSP*, 38, pp. 274, 275.

54. Reidenbaugh, *33rd Virginia Infantry*, pp. 7–8; Casler, *Four Years*, pp. 27–29; Frank B. Jones–Sue, July 25, 1861, Family Collection, HL; Richmond *Enquirer*, August 4, 1861; Hennessy, *First Battle*, p. 97.

55. Samuel J. C. Moore–Doctor and Mrs. Kownilar, July 25, 1861, August 5,

1861, to Colonel James W. Allen, July 25, 1861, to My Dearest Ellen, July 31, 1861, *Moore Papers,* UNC; Frye, *2nd Virginia Infantry,* pp. 6, 80; Krick, *Lee's Colonels,* p. 28; Bean, "Valley Campaign," *VMHB,* 73, 3, p. 336n.

56. Allen's report was not published in the *Official Records* but has recently appeared in *ORS,* 1, pp. 189–90.

57. McAllister, *Sketch,* p. 18; Reidenbaugh, *27th Virginia Infantry,* p. 14; Hennessy, *First Battle,* pp. 97–98.

58. *OR,* 2, p. 482; McAllister, *Sketchbook,* p. 18; Hennessy, *First Battle,* p. 98; John C. Carpenter–William M. McAllister, December 26, 1902, Carpenter Letter, MNBP.

59. Reidenbaugh, *27th Virginia Infantry,* pp. 15, 16; John C. Carpenter–William M. McAllister, December 26, 1902, Carpenter Letter, MNBP; R. Henry Campbell–Mother, July 21, 1861, Campbell Letters, VMI; Henry Shanklin–Parents, July 23, 1861, Shanklin Letters, VSL.

60. Hennessy, *First Battle,* pp. 99–101; Edwin G. Lee–Mother, July 22, 1861, Pendleton Papers, UNC; James M. Nihiser–Wife, July 24, 1861, Nihiser Letter, FSNMP; Henry Shanklin–Parents, July 23, 1861, Shanklin Letters, VSL.

61. Samuel J. C. Moore–Dr. R. Kownilar, August 5, 1861, Moore Papers, UNC.

62. *OR,* 2, p. 369; Gaff, *If This Is War,* pp. 190–196; *War Papers,* MOLLUS, Wisconsin, 1, pp. 385–86; Horace Emerson–My Dear Irvey, July 26, 1861, Emerson Letters, UM; Milwaukee *Sentinel,* July 30, 1861; Hennessy, *First Battle,* pp. 102, 105.

63. *War Papers,* MOLLUS, Wisconsin, 1, p. 386; Horace Emerson–My Dear Irvey, July 26, 1861, Emerson Letters, UM; Gaff, *If This Is War,* pp. 196–200; Otis, *Second Wisconsin,* p. 108; *National Tribune,* October 25, 1883, August 14, 1902.

64. Alured Larke–Tom and Ethel, August 13, 1861, Larke Letters, SHSW; Gaff, *If This Is War,* pp. 203–5, 224, 230; Hughes, "Report," SHSW.

65. Gaff, *If This Is War,* pp. 213, 220, 223; Horace Emerson–My Dear Irvey, July 26, 1861, Emerson Letters, UM.

66. *OR,* 2, pp. 369–70; Hennessy, *First Battle,* Chapters 8 and 9.

67. *War Papers,* MOLLUS, Wisconsin, 1, p. 391; Gaff, *If This Is War,* pp. 233–37; William G. Davis–Father, August 4, 1861, Davis Letters, MNBP.

68. Madaus, "Into the Fury," *WMH,* 69, 1, p. 8; Langworthy, "Reminiscences," p. 5; *National Tribune,* October 25, 1883, August 14, 1902; Quiner, Correspondence, 1, p. 105, SHSW.

69. The most recent casualty figures are in Gaff, *If This Is War,* p. 261; other numbers can be found in *OR,* 2, p. 351; *War Papers,* MOLLUS, Wisconsin, 1, p. 392; Noble, Diary, UWRF; P. J. Arndt–Father, Mother and Friends, February 7, 1864, Arndt Letter, SHSW; information about the barn is in Mead, "Journal," SHSW.

70. Edwin G. Lee–Mother, July 22, 1861, Pendleton Papers, UNC; Hanger, Diary, MNBP; Hunter McGuire–Father, July 24, 1861, McGuire Papers, VHS; Bean, *Liberty Hall Volunteers,* p. 43; Opie, *Rebel Cavalryman,* p. 39.

71. *OR,* 2, p. 570; Robertson, *Stonewall Brigade,* p. 44; Fox, *Regimental Losses,* p. 560; Reidenbaugh, *33rd Virginia Infantry,* p. 10; Kleese, *Shenandoah County,* pp. 21, 22.

72. Robertson, *4th Virginia Infantry,* p. 7; Confederate States Army Casualties, NA; Mann, *They Were Heard From,* p. 3; Virginia Bedinger–Ma, July 27, 1861, Bedinger Letters, DU; Johnson, *University Memorial,* pp. 32, 37; Crites, *Glimpses,* p. 42; Newspaper clipping, Hotchkiss Papers, LC.

73. Edwin G. Lee–Mother, July 22, 1861, Pendleton Papers, UNC; Robertson, *Stonewall Brigade,* p. 44; other expressions of the brigade's achievements from Jackson and other members can be found in *OR,* 2, p. 482; Jackson, *Memoirs,* pp. 177–80; Paxton, *Civil War Letters,* p. 11; Baylor, *Bull Run,* p. 21; Frank B. Jones–Sue, July 25, 1861, Family Collection, WL.

74. Grabill, "Diary," *Shenandoah Herald,* January 8–15, 1922, copy in author's possession.

CHAPTER 3: VIRGINIA AUTUMN

1. Long, *Civil War,* pp. 101–2; Warner, *Generals In Blue,* pp. 290–91.
2. William G. Davis–Parents, August 4, 1861, Davis Letters, MNBP.
3. Ibid.; Otis, *Second Wisconsin,* p. 39; Gaff, *If This Is War,* pp. 284, 286; Mead, "Journal," SHSW; Ross, *Empty Sleeve,* pp. 34, 35.
4. Otis, *Second Wisconsin,* pp. 40, 40n, 253; Madaus, "Into the Fray," *WMH,* 69, 1, pp. 8, 9; Nolan, *Iron Brigade,* p. 11; Quiner, Correspondence, 2, p. 288, SHSW; O'Connor file, CSR, NA; William G. Davis–Parents, August 4, 1861, Davis Letters, MNBP.
5. Ross, *Empty Sleeve,* pp. 3–7, 14–16, 18, 19, 20–24, 28–30, 34, 35; Fairchild file, CSR, NA; Nolan, *Iron Brigade,* pp. 11, 12.
6. Otis, *Second Wisconsin,* pp. 31, 40; Gaff, *If This Is War,* p. 295; Nolan, *Iron Brigade,* p. 12; Mead, "Journal," SHSW.
7. Dawes, *Service,* p. 21; Mead, "Journal," SHSW; Hughes, "Report," SHSW.
8. Love, *Wisconsin,* p. 291; Nolan, *Iron Brigade,* pp. 14–16; Cheek and Pointon, *History,* pp. 12, 18, 19.
9. Beaudot and Herdegen, *Irishman,* pp. 19, 22, 23; Cook, Memoir, p. 2, SHSW; Holford, Diary, LC; E. A. Brown–Wife, July 3, 10, 1861, Brown Letters, SHSW.
10. *Roster of Wisconsin Volunteers,* 1, p. 494; Cutler file, CSR, NA; Byrne and Weaver, *Haskell,* p. 16; Nolan, *Iron Brigade,* p. 16; James Converse–Wife and Children, July 4, 1862, Converse Letters, CHS; Dawes, *Service,* p. 20; McLean, *Cutler's Brigade,* pp. 1–3.
11. *Roster of Wisconsin Volunteers,* 1, p. 494; Nolan, *Iron Brigade,* p. 17; Byrne and Weaver, *Haskell,* pp. 10, 16; E. A. Brown–Wife, August 13, 1861, Brown Letters, SHSW.
12. *Roster of Wisconsin Volunteers,* 1, p. 494; Nolan, *Iron Brigade,* p. 17; Bragg file, CSR, NA; Julius A. Murray–My Dear Boy, June 22, 1861, Murray Family Papers, SHSW; Dawes, *Service,* p. 20; E. A. Brown–Wife, August 13, 1861, Brown Letters, SHSW.
13. *Roster of Wisconsin Volunteers,* 1, pp. 494–536; Nolan, *Iron Brigade,* pp. 14–16; Dawes, *Service,* pp. 5–7, 12, 13.
14. Dawes, *Service,* p. 15; *Roster of Wisconsin Volunteers,* 1, pp. 494–536; Madaus, "Into the Fray," *WMH,* 69, 1, p. 10; Reuben Huntley–My Dear Wife, July 23, 1861, Huntley Papers, SHSW.

15. E. A. Brown–Wife, 7-28-61, Brown Letters, SHSW; Julius A. Murray–John, July 25, 1861, Murray Family Papers, SHSW.

16. E. A. Brown–Wife, July 3, 10, 24, 1861, Brown Letters, SHSW.

17. James Converse–Wife and Children, July 31, 1861, Converse Letters, CHS; Albion Pratt Howe–Hank and Maria, July 28, 1861, Howe Papers, FSNMP; Reid-Green, *Letters Home*, p. 9.

18. James Converse–Wife and Children, August 6, 1861, Converse Letters, CHS; Dawes, *Service*, pp. 18–19; Holford, Diary, LC.

19. Gaff, *On Many a Bloody Field*, p. 34; Turner, *Chronology*, pp. 3, 4, 10; Nolan, *Iron Brigade*, p. 22; *Report of the Adjutant General*, 2, pp. 168–75.

20. *Report of the Adjutant General*, 2, pp. 390–410; Gaff, *On Many a Bloody Field*, Chapter 2.

21. W. R. Moore–Sister, July 5, 1861, Moore Papers, IHS; William Orr–Father and Mother, July 19, 1861, Orr Papers, IU; Gaff, *On Many a Bloody Field*, p. 18.

22. Nolan, *Iron Brigade*, p. 20; Meredith file, CSR, NA; Gaff, *On Many a Bloody Field*, pp. 19–21.

23. Dunn, *Iron Men*, p. 5; Nolan, *Iron Brigade*, p. 20; Gaff, *On Many a Bloody Field*, pp. 20–21.

24. Dunn, *Iron Men*, p. 21; Nolan, *Iron Brigade*, p. 21; Stevenson, *Indiana's Roll of Honor*, 1, pp. 381–82; Gaff, *On Many a Bloody Field*, Chapter 2; *Report of the Adjutant General*, 2, p. 168.

25. Joseph Slack–Julietta Starbuck, August 11, 1861, Starbuck Civil War Letters, IHS; Turner, *Chronology*, pp. 10, 11; Wilson, *Indiana Battle Flags*, p. 154; Dunn, *Iron Men*, p. 16; Gaff, *On Many a Bloody Field*, pp. 32–36.

26. Love, *Wisconsin*, pp. 293–94; Historical Table of the 7th Wis. Vet. Vols., Perry Papers, SHSW; *Roster of Wisconsin Volunteers*, 1, pp. 538–76; Longhenry, "Yankee Piper," pp. 1-1, 1-2, ANB.

27. George Mitchell–Friend Maria, August 27, September 4, 1861, Mitchell Papers, UWLC.

28. Nolan, *Iron Brigade*, p. 26; *Roster of Wisconsin Volunteers*, 1, p. 538.

29. Nolan, *Iron Brigade*, p. 27; *Roster of Wisconsin Volunteers*, 1, p. 538.

30. Nolan, *Iron Brigade*, p. 27; Hamilton file, CSR, NA; *Roster of Wisconsin Volunteers*, 1, p. 538.

31. Rood, Memoir, SHSW; D. Cooper Ayres–Dr. Edward P. Vullum, October 9, 1862, Adjutant General's Records, Series 1200, SHSW; Longhenry, "Yankee Piper," pp. 1-4, 1-7, 1-8, 1-10, ANB; Horace Currier–[?], September 29, 1861, Currier Papers, SHSW.

32. Warner, *Generals in Blue*, p. 269; Byrne and Weaver, *Haskell*, p. 19; *Echoes*, p. 13.

33. James Converse–Wife and Children, October 10, 1861, Converse Letters, CHS; Otis, *Second Wisconsin*, p. 44; Dawes, *Service*, p. 25; William G. Davis–Parents, October 9, 1861, Davis Letters, MNBP; Holford, Diary, LC.

34. George Mitchell–Friend Maria, September 30, 1861, Mitchell Papers, UWLC; William G. Davis–Parents, October 9, 1861, Davis Letters, MNBP.

35. McPherson, *For Cause and Comrades*, p. ix; Nolan, *Iron Brigade*, p. 32; Fox, *Regimental Losses*, pp. 62, 63.

36. McPherson, *For Cause and Comrades,* pp. 5, 16, 18, 23, 91, 94.

37. William G. Davis–Mother, August 9, 1861, Davis Letters, MNBP; Cook, Memoir, p. 1, SHSW.

38. E. A. Brown–Wife, September 8, 1861, Brown Letters, SHSW; Julius A. Murray–Mary, n.d., Murray Family Papers, SHSW; Dunn, *Iron Men,* pp. 1, 2.

39. Rood, Memoir, p. 5, SHSW.

40. Herdegen, *Men Stood,* p. 35; Cheek and Pointon, *History,* p. 38; E. A. Brown–Father, August 28, 1861, Brown Letters, SHSW; Horace Emerson–Brother Irvey, October 13, 1861, Emerson Letters, UM.

41. Herdegen, *Men Stood,* p. 34; Cheek and Pointon, *History,* p. 20.

42. E. A. Brown–Father and Mother, October 13, 19, 1861, Brown Letters, SHSW; General Orders, No. 19, Adjut. Gen.'s Office, October 23, 1861, Holloway Collection, IHS; James Converse–Wife and Children, November 3, 1861, Converse Letters, CHS; Longhenry, "Yankee Piper," p. 1-13, ANB; Cheek and Pointon, *History,* p. 21; D. Kilgore–James Orr, September 22, 1861, Orr Papers, IU.

43. E. A. Brown–Wife, October 22, 1861, Brown Letters, SHSW.

44. Grabill, "Diary," *Shenandoah Herald,* January 8–15, 1922, p. 7, copy in author's possession; James J. White–My Dear Mary, August 15, 21, 26, 27, 1861, White Letters, UNC; Robertson, *4th Virginia Infantry,* p. 8; A. C. Cummings–D. T. Williams, August 21, 1861, Cummings file, CSR, NA.

45. Reidenbaugh, *27th Virginia Infantry,* pp. 19–20; Hanger, Diary, MNBP; Barton, Recollections, 1, p. 43, VHS; Robertson, *Stonewall Jackson,* p. 272; Casler, *Four Years,* pp. 49, 51; Special Orders, No. 189, [July 1861], Pendleton Papers, UNC.

46. James F. Preston–Charles, August 6, 1861, Preston Letter, FSNMP; Jackson, *Memoirs,* p. 184; Douglas, *I Rode with Stonewall,* p. 13; James J. White–My Dear Mary, August 16, 1861, White Letters, UNC.

47. Reidenbaugh, *33rd Virginia Infantry,* p. 11; Samuel J. C. Moore–[Ellen Moore], September 9, 1861, Moore Papers, UNC.

48. Casler, *Four Years,* p. 49; Reidenbaugh, *27th Virginia Infantry,* pp. 21, 22; Samuel J. C. Moore–My Dearest Ellen, August 21, 1861, Moore Papers, UNC.

49. Kenton Harper–T. J. Jackson, September 3, 1861, Harper Papers, UNC; Krick, *Lee's Colonels,* pp. 163, 164; Frank B. Jones–Sue Jones, September 4, 1861, Family Collection, HL; William S. H. Baylor–Col. [William N. Pendleton], n.d., Pendleton Papers, UNC.

50. William S. H. Baylor–Col. [William N. Pendleton], n.d., Pendleton Papers, UNC; Wallace, *5th Virginia Infantry,* p. 19.

51. Samuel J. C. Moore–My Dearest Ellen, August 21, 22, September 4, 1861, Report of James W. Allen, Moore Papers, UNC; Allen's report has been published recently in *ORS,* 1, pp. 189–90.

52. Samuel J. C. Moore–My Dearest Ellen, September 4, 1861, Moore Papers, UNC; McPherson, *For Cause and Comrades,* pp. 23, 59.

53. Krick, *Lee's Colonels,* pp. 145, 153; Grigsby file, CSR, NA; Paxton, *Civil War Letters,* p. vii; Hanger, Diary, MNBP; Reidenbaugh, *27th Virginia Infantry,* pp. 7, 8, 20.

54. Krick, *Lee's Colonels*, pp. 145, 153; Grigsby file, CSR, NA; Paxton, *Civil War Letters*, p. vii; Hanger, Diary, MNBP; Reidenbaugh, *27th Virginia Infantry*, pp. 7, 8, 20.

55. Davis, *Confederate General*, 3, p. 206; Levin, "*This Awful Drama,*" pp. v, vii, 26, 31; Special Orders, No. 234, July 27, 1861, Lee Papers, VHS; Samuel J. C. Moore–[Ellen Moore], September 9, 1861, Moore Papers, UNC.

56. James J. White–My Darling Mary, August 27, 1861, White Letters, UNC; Frye, *2nd Virginia Infantry*, p. 16; Turner, *Old Zeus*, p. 87; Driver, *1st and 2nd Rockbridge Artillery*, p. 8; Krick, *Lee's Colonels*, p. 236.

57. James J. White–My Darling Mary, August 27, 1861, White Letters, UNC; Samuel J. C. Moore–My Dearest Ellen, August 30, 1861, Moore Papers, UNC; Hanger, Diary, MNBP.

58. Joseph F. Shaner–Sister, September 23, 1861, Shaner Correspondence, WL; Hanger, Diary, MNBP; Beard, Diary, FSNMP; James J. White–My Dear Mary, August 21, 1861, White Letters, UNC.

59. Kinzer, Diary, p. 4, VHS; Frank B. Jones–Mother, September 21, 1861, Family Collection, HL; Casler, *Four Years*, p. 298n; George Baylor–Sister, September 7, 30, 1861, McGuffin Family Papers, UVA; James R. McCutchan–My very dear Kate, September 22, 1861, McCutchan Letters, WL.

60. Frank B. Jones–Mother, September 21, 1861, Family Collection, HL; Samuel J. C. Moore–[Ellen Moore], September 29, 1861, Moore Papers, UNC.

61. Samuel J. C. Moore–[Ellen Moore], September 29, 1861, Moore Papers, UNC; Hite, Diary, HL.

62. James R. McCutchan–My very dear Kate, September 22, 1861, McCutchan Letters, WL; G. W. Smith–J. Q. A. Nadenbousch, October 19, 1861, Nadenbousch Papers, DU; Samuel J. C. Moore–My Dearest Ellen, September 4, October 18, 1861, Moore Papers, UNC.

63. Kinzer, Diary, VHS; Hite, Diary, HL; White, *Sketches*, p. 61; Ritter, "Battle Flag," FSNMP; George W. Baylor–Sister, October 31, 1861, McGuffin Family Papers, UVA; Henry Shanklin–Father, November 1, 1861, Shanklin Letters, VSL.

64. Robertson, *Stonewall Jackson*, pp. 279–82; Turner, *My Dear Emma*, p. 65.

65. Grabill, "Diary," *Shenandoah Herald*, January 8–15, 1922, copy in author's possession; Robertson, *Stonewall Jackson*, p. 282; Turner, *My Dear Emma*, p. 65; Newspaper clipping, Hotchkiss Papers, LC.

66. Robertson, *Stonewall Jackson*, pp. 282–83; Newspaper clipping, Hotchkiss Papers, LC; Turner, *My Dear Emma*, p. 65.

67. Newspaper clipping, Hotchkiss Papers, LC; White, *Sketches*, p. 61; Turner, *My Dear Emma*, p. 65.

CHAPTER 4: "DAMD HARD BUSINESS"

1. Samuel J. C. Moore–My Dearest Ellen, November 7, 1861, Moore Papers, UNC.

2. Ibid., *OR*, 5, p. 939; Kinzer, Diary, p. 8, VHS; Daniel Hileman–My Very Dear Kate, September 22, 1861, Hileman Civil War Letters, WL.

3. Kinzer, Diary, pp. 8, 9, LC; Hite, Diary, HL; Reidenbaugh, *33rd Virginia Infantry*, p. 14; *OR*, 5, p. 977.

4. Samuel J. C. Moore–My Dearest Ellen, November 11, 1861, Moore Papers, UNC; Tanner, *Stonewall in the Valley*, pp. xviii, xix; Turner, *My Dear Emma*, pp. 67, 68.

5. Samuel J. C. Moore–My Dearest Ellen, November 11, 1861, Moore Papers, UNC; Turner, *My Dear Emma*, pp. 67, 68; Robertson, *Stonewall Jackson*, p. 289; Sperry, "Diary," p. 79, HL; Opie, *Rebel Cavalryman*, pp. 48–50; Tanner, *Stonewall in the Valley*, p. xix.

6. Kinzer, Diary, pp. 10, 11, VHS; James P. Charlton–Oliver, November 18, 1861, Charlton Family Papers, VT; Ambrose Hite–Sister, November 6, 1861, Hite Papers, WM; Driver, *1st and 2nd Rockbridge Artillery*, p. 9; Randolph Fairfax–Jenny, November 21, 1861, Fairfax Letters, MC.

7. Chase, "War Time Diary," p. 19, HL; Kinzer, Diary, p. 10, VHS; Turner, *My Dear Emma*, pp. 69, 70; Beard, Diary, FSNMP; Paxton, *Civil War Letters*, p. 25.

8. T. J. Jackson–Maj. T. E. Rhett, November 11, 1861, copy in Krick Collection.

9. Davis, *Confederate General*, 2, pp. 168–69; Robertson, *Stonewall Jackson*, pp. 296, 297; Andrew J. Grigsby–William Garnett, July 12, 1862, Garnett Papers, MC.

10. Tanner, *Stonewall in the Valley*, p. 51; Robertson, *Stonewall Jackson*, p. 297.

11. Wallace, *5th Virginia Infantry*, p. 20; Hite, Diary, HL; James H. Langhorne–Aunt Nannie Kent, December 12, 1861, Langhorne Letters and Diary, VHS.

12. Samuel J. C. Moore–My Dearest Ellen, November 30, 1861, Moore Papers, UNC; Kinzer, Diary, p. 12, VHS; Tanner, *Stonewall in the Valley*, p. 60; Robertson, *Stonewall Jackson*, p. 297.

13. Kinzer, Diary, p. 12, 13, VHS; Samuel J. C. Moore–My Dearest Ellen, December 16, 1861, Moore Papers, UNC.

14. Kinzer, Diary, pp. 13–14, VHS; Tanner, *Stonewall in the Valley*, pp. 60–62; Cockrell, *Gunner with Stonewall*, p. 14; Grabill, "Diary," *Shenandoah Herald*, January 8–15, 1922, copy in author's possession.

15. Reidenbaugh, *27th Virginia Infantry*, p. 27; Samuel J. C. Moore–My Dearest Wife, December 27, 1861, Moore Papers, UNC.

16. Grabill, "Diary," *Shenandoah Herald*, January 8–15, 1922, copy in author's possession; Robertson, *4th Virginia Infantry*, p. 9.

17. Edward S. Bragg–My dear Wife, November 21, 1861, Bragg Papers, SHSW; James Converse–Wife, November 22, 1861, Converse Letters, CHS.

18. Reuben Huntley–Wife, November 21, 1861, Huntley Papers, SHSW; Longhenry, "Yankee Piper," p. 1-16, ANB; Edward S. Bragg–My dear Wife, November 21, 1861, Bragg Papers, SHSW.

19. E. A. Brown–Wife, November 23, 24, 1861, Brown Letters, SHSW; Orson Parker–Father, November 12, 30, 1861, Parker Letters, SHSW; Quiner Correspondence, 1, p. 155, SHSW; Gaff, *On Many a Bloody Field*, p. 56; W. R. Moore–Miss Lizzie Moore, September 15, 1861, Moore Papers, IHS.

20. E. A. Brown–Wife, October 22, 1861, Brown Letters, SHSW; William Orr–Father, November 15, 1861, Orr Papers, IU.

21. E. A. Brown–Father & Mother, November 24, 1861, Brown Letters, SHSW.

22. Ibid.

23. Ibid., December 15, 1861; C. C. Starbuck–Cousin, November 28, 1861, Starbuck Civil War Letters, IHS.
24. Horace Currier–[?], December 15, 16, 1861, Currier Papers, SHSW; Whitehouse, *Letters,* p. 11; E. A. Brown–Ruth, December 15, 1861, Brown Letters, SHSW.
25. Felton, "Iron Brigade Battery," *Gettysburg Magazine,* 11, p. 59; Gibbon, *Personal Recollections,* pp. 3–10; Lavery and Jordan, *Iron Brigade General,* p. 31, 38; Buell, *Cannoneer,* pp. 12, 13, 17.
26. Gibbon, *Personal Recollections,* pp. 10, 12, 13, 14; Nolan, *Iron Brigade,* p. 35; Second Wisconsin file, CR, NA.
27. Holford, Diary, LC; Longhenry, "Yankee Piper," p. 1-19, ANB.
28. Longhenry, "Yankee Piper," p. 1-20, ANB; E. A. Brown–Wife, December 31, 1861, Brown Letters, SHSW.
29. Newspaper clipping, Hotchkiss Papers, LC; Beard, Diary, FSNMP.
30. *OR,* 5, pp. 965–66; Rankin, *Stonewall Jackson's Romney Campaign,* pp. 2–4, 31, 44; Tanner, *Stonewall in the Valley,* pp. 79, 80.
31. *OR,* 5, p. 974; Robertson, *Stonewall Jackson,* pp. 294, 295, 300, 302; Allan, *History,* Chapter 1.
32. Beard, Diary, FSNMP; White, *Sketches,* pp. 71, 72; Kinzer, Diary, p. 15, VHS; Robertson, *Stonewall Jackson,* pp. 304–6.
33. Beard, Diary, FSNMP; Kinzer, Diary, pp. 15, 16, VHS; Tanner, *Stonewall in the Valley,* pp. 68, 69, 71, 72.
34. Beard, Diary, FSNMP; Kinzer, Diary, p. 16, VHS; White, *Sketches,* p. 71; Robertson, *Stonewall Jackson,* pp. 308, 309; Reidenbaugh, *27th Virginia Infantry,* p. 29; Joseph P. Shaner–Sister, January 12, 1862, Shaner Correspondence, WL.
35. Frank B. Jones–Sue, January 6, 1862, Family Collection, HL; Beard, Diary, FSNMP; Kinzer, Diary, pp. 16, 17, VHS; Randolph Fairfax–Mama, January 9, 1862, Fairfax Letters, MC; Bean, *Liberty Hall Volunteers,* pp. 84, 85.
36. Samuel J. C. Moore–My Dearest Wife, January 10, 1862, Moore Papers, UNC; Thomas M. Smiley–Sister, January 10, 1862, to Aunt, January 15, 1862, Smiley Family Papers, UVA; Daniel Hileman–Rachel A. McCutchan, February 13, 1862, Hileman Civil War Letters, WL; Turner, *My Dear Emma,* pp. 76, 77.
37. L. M. Blackford–My Dear Mother, January 16, 1862, Blackford Family Papers, UVA; Worsham, *One of Jackson's Foot Cavalry,* p. 29; Frank B. Jones–Sue, January 22, 1862, Family Collection, HL; Paxton, *Civil War Letters,* p. 37.
38. Kinzer, Diary, p. 17, VHS; Beard, Diary, FSNMP; Robertson, *Stonewall Jackson,* p. 313; Turner, *Ted Barclay,* p. 42.
39. Robertson, *Stonewall Jackson,* pp. 312, 313; Slaughter, *Sketch,* p. 21; Cockrell, *Gunner with Stonewall,* p. 18; Kinzer, Diary, p. 17, VHS; Frye, *2nd Virginia Infantry,* p. 19.
40. Kinzer, Diary, p. 17, VHS; Beard, Diary, FSNMP; Carson, Memoirs, p. 20, VHS; Harman, "Extracts," FSNMP; Lyle, *Sketches,* p. 362.
41. Robertson, *4th Virginia Infantry,* p. 10; Kinzer, Diary, p. 17, VHS; John Garibaldi–Wife, January 28, 1862, Garibaldi Collection, VMI; Banks Intelligence Reports, NA; Reidenbaugh, *33rd Virginia Infantry,* p. 21; William H.

Harman–My Dear Asher, February 19, 1862, Harman Letters, ACHS.

42. Robertson, *Stonewall Jackson*, pp. 315–17; *OR, 5*, p. 1053.

43. The best description of the events is in Robertson, *Stonewall Jackson*, pp. 317–21.

44. Henry Ruffner Morrison–Father, February 6, 1862, Morrison Papers, US-AMHI; Diary entry, Langhorne Letters and Diary, VHS; Frank B. Jones–Mother, February 4, 1862, Family Collection, HL.

45. Quarles, *Occupied Winchester*, p. 65; James R. McCutchan–Cousin, February 20, 1862, McCutchan Letters, WL; General Orders, No. 19, February 3, 1862, General Orders, No. 20, February 3, 1862, Orders and Circulars, NA; *OR, 5*, p. 1069; Haywood Hardy–Father, February 17, 1862, Hardy Papers, DU; Turner, *Ted Barclay*, p. 51.

46. Benjamin P. Ordway–Sister, January 20, 1862, Ordway Letter, SHSW; Reid-Green, *Letters Home*, p. 19.

47. James Converse–Affectionate Companion, January 15, 1862, Converse Letters, CHS; Orson Parker–Father, January 8, 1862, Parker Letters, SHSW.

48. Horace Emerson–Mother, February 12, 1862, Emerson Letters, UM; William G. Davis–Parents & Friends, January 30, 1862, Davis Letters, MNBP; Moore, "Reminiscences," IHS; Reid-Green, *Letters Home*, pp. 19, 43.

49. E. A. Brown–Wife, February 2, 1862, Brown Letters, SHSW; Gaff, *On Many a Bloody Field*, p. 104; Reid-Green, *Letters Home*, p. 19.

50. Ross, *Empty Sleeve*, pp. 38, 39; Nolan, *Iron Brigade*, pp. 36–37, 307n; *Roster of Wisconsin Volunteers*, 1, p. 538.

51. William G. Davis–Parents and Friends, January 30, 1862, Davis Letters, MNBP; Horace Emerson–Mother, February 12, 1862, Emerson Letters, UM; Reid-Green, *Letters Home*, p. 20.

52. Holford, Diary, LC; Herdegen and Beaudot, *In the Bloody Railroad Cut*, p. 364; Coco, *Civil War Infantryman*, pp. 65, 68; Wiley, *Life of Johnny Reb*, pp. 290, 291; Otis, *Second Wisconsin*, p. 141; Henry F. Young–Delia, February 15, 1862, Young Papers, SHSW.

53. *OR, 5*, pp. 713–20; Nolan, *Iron Brigade*, p. 35; E. A. Brown–Father and Mother, February 9, 1862, Brown Letters, SHSW.

54. Longhenry, "Yankee Piper," p. 1-24, ANB.

55. Horace Emerson–Mother, March 2, 1862, Emerson Letters, UM; Orson Parker–Sister, February 25, 1862, Parker Letters, SHSW.

56. Gaff, *Brave Men's Tears*, pp. 39–40.

CHAPTER 5: "IF THIS VALLEY IS LOST"

1. Kinzer, Diary, p. 22, VHS; Jones, "Diary," p. 5, HL; Henry Shanklin–Father, March 31, 1862, Shanklin Letters, VSL.

2. *OR, 12, 3*, p. 50; Harman, "Extracts," FSNMP; Robertson, *Stonewall Jackson*, p. 331.

3. Robertson, *Stonewall Jackson*, pp. 328–29.

4. Ibid., pp. 329–33; Diary, Moore Papers, UNC; Diary, Strickler and Jones Diary and Record Book, UVA; Jones, "Diary," p. 1, HL.

5. Kinzer, Diary, pp. 20, 21, VHS; Jones, "Diary," pp. 3, 4; Diary, Moore Papers, UNC; James R. McCutchan–Sister, March 13, 1862, McCutchan Letters, WL.

6. Robertson, *Stonewall Jackson*, pp. 336–38; *OR*, 12, 1, p. 380.

7. Kinzer, Diary, p. 22, VHS; Jones, "Diary," p. 5, HL; Waddell, *Annals*, p. 467; Henry Shanklin–Father, March 31, 1862, Shanklin Letters, VSL.

8. *OR*, 12, 1, p. 381; Tanner, *Stonewall in the Valley*, pp. 122, 124; Robertson, *Stonewall Jackson*, pp. 339–40; Jackson's testimony, Garnett Court-Martial Records, Garnett Papers, CM.

9. Jackson, *Memoirs*, p. 249.

10. *OR*, 12, 1, p. 381; Tanner, *Stonewall in the Valley*, pp. 122, 124; Robertson, *Stonewall Jackson*, p. 342; the best account of Kernstown is Ecelbarger, *"We Are in for It!,"* passim.

11. *OR*, 12, 1, pp. 381, 408; Jackson's testimony, Garnett Court-Martial Records, Garnett Papers, CM; Jones, "Diary," p. 6, HL; *SHSP*, 43, p. 156n; Confederate States Army Casualties, NA.

12. John Echols–Richard B. Garnett, July 30, 1862, Garnett Papers, CM; *OR*, 12, 1, pp. 393, 408, 409; David Bard–Kind Friend, March 28, [1862], Bard Correspondence, HL; *B&L*, 2, pp. 299, 307; Sawyer, *Military History*, p. 42; White, *Sketches*, p. 80.

13. *OR*, 12, 1, pp. 388, 395; Samuel J. C. Moore–My Dearest Wife, March 26, 1862, Moore Papers, UNC; Jones, "Diary," p. 6, HL; George K. Harlow–Father, Mother and Family, March 26, 1862, Harlow Letters, VHS.

14. *OR*, 12, 1, pp. 390, 391; Reidenbaugh, *27th Virginia Infantry*, p. 36; *CV*, 25, p. 175; Samuel J. C. Moore–My Dearest Wife, March 26, 1862, Moore Papers, UNC; David Bard–Kind Friend, March 28, [1862], Bard Correspondence, HL.

15. Robertson, *Stonewall Jackson*, pp. 342–43; Jackson testimony, Garnett Court-Martial Records, Garnett Papers, CM.

16. Richard B. Garnett–Samuel Cooper, June 2, 20, 1862, Statement of Elliott Johnston, July 25, 1862, Garnett Court-Martial Records, Garnett Papers, CM; *OR*, 12, 1, pp. 393; Ecelbarger, *"We Are in for It!,"* Chapter 7.

17. Samuel J. C. Moore–My Dearest Wife, March 26, 1862, Moore Papers, UNC; Jones, "Diary," p. 6, HL; Sawyer, *Military History*, p. 43; White, *Sketches*, p. 80; Robertson, *Stonewall Jackson*, pp. 344–45.

18. *OR*, 12, 1, pp. 382, 391, 392; Jackson testimony, Garnett Court-Martial Records, Garnett Papers, CM; Bean, "Valley Campaign," *VMHB*, 78, 3, p. 342; Robertson, *Stonewall Jackson*, p. 344.

19. *OR*, 12, 1, p. 392; Mooney, Memoir, p. 2, VHS.

20. *OR*, 12, 1, p. 397; Wallace, *5th Virginia Infantry*, p. 25; McDonald, *Make Me a Map*, p. 9.

21. *OR*, 12, 1, pp. 341, 384, 389, 394; Hugh A. White–Mrs. Brown, April 10, 1862, White Correspondence, MC; Frye, *2nd Virginia Infantry*, p. 23; Robertson, *4th Virginia Infantry*, pp. 11, 12; Reidenbaugh, *27th Virginia Infantry*, p. 36; Reidenbaugh, *33rd Virginia Infantry*, p. 24; Ecelbarger, *"We Are in for It!,"* pp. 274–77.

22. Clayton Coleman–My Darling Anna, March 25, 1862, Coleman Papers, MC; Samuel J. C. Moore–My Dearest Wife, March 26, 1862, Moore Papers, UNC; Randolph Fairfax–Jenny, April 3, 1862, Fairfax Letters, MC; White, *Sketches*, p. 81.

23. Garnett Court-Martial Records, Garnett Papers, MC; Bean, "Valley Campaign," *VMHB,* 78, 3, p. 344.

24. Bean, "Valley Campaign," *VMHB,* 78, 3, p. 344.

25. Jones, "Diary," p. 8, HL; Douglas, *I Rode with Stonewall,* p. 37; McMullen, *Surgeon,* p. 24; L. M. Blackford–My Dear Mother, April 3, 1862, Blackford Family Manuscripts, UVA.

26. Jones, "Diary," pp. 8, 9, HL; Garnett Court-Martial Records, Garnett Papers, CM; Colt, *Defend the Valley,* p. 130; Douglas, *I Rode with Stonewall,* p. 37.

27. Garnett Court-Martial Records, Garnett Papers, CM; Bean, "Valley Campaign, *VMHB,* 78, 3, p. 344.

28. Bean, "Valley Campaign," *VMHB,* 78, 3, p. 344.

29. Long, *Civil War,* pp. 179–82; Horace Currier–[?], March 12, 1862, Currier Papers, SHSW.

30. Long, *Civil War,* p. 182; Elkanah M. Gibson–Sylvester Jessup, March 25, 1862, Jessup Letters, IHS.

31. Elkanah M. Gibson–Sylvester Jessup, March 25, 1862, Jessup Letters, IHS; the best analysis of "hard war policy" is in Grimsley, *Hard Hand, passim.*

32. Horace Currier–[?], March 12, 1862, Currier Papers, SHSW; William G. Davis–Parents, March 17, 1862, Davis Letters, MBNP; Henry C. Marsh–Friend, March 24, 1862, Marsh Letters and Diary, ISL; Jesse M. Roberts–Mother and Sister, March 14, 1862, Roberts Letters, SHSW.

33. Long, *Civil War,* pp. 181–83.

34. Ibid., pp. 183–86; Mead, "Journal," SHSW; Muster roll, Sixth Wisconsin, CSR, NA.

35. Long, *Civil War,* p. 193; Charles W. Fuller–Brother, April 4, 1862, Fuller Papers, SHSW; Henry C. Marsh–Father, April 7, 1862, Marsh Letters and Diary, ISL.

36. Rood, Memoir, pp. 9, 10, SHSW; Holford, Diary, LC; Cheek and Pointon, *History,* pp. 24, 25.

37. Hughes, "Report," SHSW.

38. Dawes, *Service,* p. 42; E. A. Brown–Father, March 26, 1862, Brown Letters, SHSW.

39. Pohanka, "Notes"; Howard, *Recollections,* p. 77; Jones, "Diary," p. 9, HL.

40. Douglas, *I Rode with Stonewall,* p. 125; Casler, *Four Years,* p. 73.

41. Howard, *Recollections,* pp. 81, 83.

42. Ibid., p. 83; Casler, *Four Years,* p. 73; Douglas, *I Rode with Stonewall,* p. 37.

43. Tanner, *Stonewall in the Valley,* pp. 89, 90, 162; Harman, "Extracts," FS-NMP; McMullen, *Surgeon,* p. 24; Bean, "Valley Campaign," *VMHB,* 78, 3, pp. 344, 345; Frye, *2nd Virginia Infantry,* p. 24.

44. Allan, *History,* p. 60; Turner, *My Dear Emma,* pp. 87, 88, 90; Daniel Hileman–Rachel A. McCutchan, April 12, 1862, Hileman Civil War Letters, WL; Frye, *2nd Virginia Infantry,* pp. 24, 25; Reidenbaugh, *33rd Virginia Infantry,* pp. 25, 55.

45. Harman, "Extracts," FSNMP; Jones, "Diary," pp. 14–15, HL; Diary, Shaner Correspondence, WL.

46. McPherson, *For Cause and Comrades,* pp. 48, 53, 55, 57; Krick, *Lee's Colonels,* pp. xiii, xiv.

47. Samuel J. C. Moore–My Dearest Ellen, April 27, 1862, Moore Papers, UNC; Howard, *Recollections*, p. 87.

48. Krick, *Lee's Colonels*, pp. 135, 302; Robertson, *4th Virginia Infantry*, pp. 10, 12; McMullen, *Surgeon*, p. 26.

49. Thomas J. Jackson–J. P. Benjamin, October 5, 1861, A. T. Bledsoe–J. P. Benjamin, October 10, 1861, William S. H. Baylor–A. S. Bledsoe, October 15, 1861, Baylor file, CSR, NA; McDonald, *Make Me a Map*, p. 22; William S. H. Baylor–Wife, April 22, 1862, Baylor Correspondence, VT.

50. Krick, *Lee's Colonels*, p. 132; Wallace, *5th Virginia Infantry*, pp. 26, 119, 171.

51. Grigsby file, CSR, NA; *CV*, 4, p. 69; Reidenbaugh, *27th Virginia Infantry*, p. 147.

52. *SHSP*, 28, pp. 166, 167; *CV*, 13, p. 365; Fonerden, *Brief History*, p. 15; Robertson, *Stonewall Jackson*, p. 293; Krick, *Lee's Colonels*, p. 73.

53. Cummings file, CSR, NA; Reidenbaugh, *33rd Virginia Infantry*, p. 26.

54. Reidenbaugh, *33rd Virginia Infantry*, p. 26; Krick, *Lee's Colonels*, p. 264; L. M. Blackford–My Dear Mother, April 24, 1862, Blackford Family Manuscripts, UVA; Neff file, CSR, NA.

55. Reidenbaugh, *33rd Virginia Infantry*, pp. 26, 27; Appointment, lieutenant colonel, April 22, 1862, Lee Papers, VHS; John O. Casler–Randolph Barton, April 9, 1906, Casler Letter, VSL.

56. Krick, *Lee's Colonels*, p. 178; *CV*, 7, p. 465; L. M. Blackford–My Dear Mother, April 24, 1862, Blackford Family Manuscripts, UVA.

57. Driver, *1st and 2nd Rockbridge Artillery*, pp. 18, 72; Moore, *Story*, p. 45; L. M. Blackford–My Dear Mother, April 24, 1862, Blackford Family Manuscripts, UVA.

58. Thomas M. Smiley–Aunt, April 20, 1862, Smiley Family Papers, UVA; Jones, "Diary," pp. 14–18, HL; Bean, "Valley Campaign," *VMHB*, 78, 3, p. 353; Turner, *Ted Barclay*, p. 138; White, *Sketches*, p. 88.

59. Williams, *Rebel Brothers*, p. 54; Jackson, *Memoirs*, p. 248.

CHAPTER 6: WAR IN THE "DAUGHTER OF THE STARS"

1. Gaff, *On Many a Bloody Field*, p. 95; Warner, *Generals in Blue*, p. 171.

2. Warner, *Generals in Blue*, p. 171; Lowery and Jordan, *Iron Brigade General*, p. 43.

3. Lowery and Jordan, *Iron Brigade General*, p. 43; John Gibbon–My dear Mama, April 21, 1862, Gibbon Papers, HSP; Gibbon, *Personal Recollections*, p. 27.

4. Diary, Meredith Papers, IHS; Diary, Fairfield Papers, SHSW; John Gibbon–My dear Mama, May 15, 1862, Gibbon Papers, HSP.

5. Gibbon, *Personal Recollections*, pp. 36, 37; Nolan, *Iron Brigade*, p. 51.

6. Gibbon, *Personal Recollections*, p. 37.

7. Ibid., pp. 39, 40; Gaff, *Brave Men's Tears*, p. 38; Nolan, *Iron Brigade*, p. 52.

8. Gibbon, *Personal Recollections*, p. 40; Gaff, *Brave Men's Tears*, pp. 35, 38.

9. Moore, "Reminiscences," IHS.

10. Jesse M. Roberts–Brother and Sister, May 11, 1862, Roberts Letters, SHSW; Gibbon, *Personal Recollections*, p. 93; Nolan, *Iron Brigade*, pp. 292–95; Herdegen and Beaudot, *In the Bloody Railroad Cut*, pp. 340–45.

11. Nolan, *Iron Brigade,* pp. 292–95; Herdegen and Beaudot, *In the Bloody Railroad Cut,* pp. 331–33, 340–48; Cheek and Pointon, *History,* p. 27.

12. Herdegen and Beaudot, *In the Bloody Railroad Cut,* pp. 337, 340; Nolan, *Iron Brigade,* pp. 292–93.

13. Nolan, *Iron Brigade,* p. 293; Beecham, *Gettysburg,* p. 64; Dawes, *Service,* p. 132; Curtis, *History,* p. 117; Herdegen and Beaudot, *In the Bloody Railroad Cut,* p. 337.

14. Cheek and Pointon, *History,* p. 27; Solomon Meredith–J. P. Wood, June 26, 1862, Meredith Papers, IHS; Jesse M. Roberts–Brother and Sister, May 11, 1862, Roberts Letters, SHSW; Dawes, *Service,* pp. 44, 45; Henry C. Marsh–Father, May 23, 1862, Marsh Letters and Diary, ISL; William Orr–Father, May 26, 1862, Orr Papers, IU.

15. Gibbon, *Personal Recollections,* pp. 27–30.

16. Ibid., p. 28; Gaff, *On Many a Bloody Field,* pp. 132–35.

17. John Gibbon–My dear Mama, May 19, 23, 1862, Gibbon Papers, HSP; William G. Davis–Parents, May 18, 1862, Davis Letters, MNSP; Eugene Anderson–Parents, May 11, 1862, Anderson Papers, ANB; Jeremiah G. Burdick–To all at home, May 13, 1862, Burdick Papers, FSNMP.

18. Long, *Civil War,* pp. 191–215.

19. Ibid., pp. 215–16.

20. John Gibbon–My darling Mama, May 27, 1862, Gibbon Papers, HSP; *OR,* 12, 3, pp. 310–11; Diary, Fairfield Papers, SHSW; Eugene Anderson–Parents, June 5, 1862, Anderson Papers, ANB; Orson Parker–Father, May 26, 1862, Parker Letters, SHSW.

21. L. L. MacIntosh–Father, May 19, 1862, MacIntosh Letters, ANB; Horace Emerson–Sister Maria, May [?], 1862, Emerson Letters, UM.

22. John Gibbon–My darling Mama, May 29, 1862, Gibbon Papers, HSP; Diary, Fairfield Papers, SHSW; Rood, Memoir, p. 11, SHSW; Eugene Anderson–Parents, June 5, 1862, Anderson Papers, ANB.

23. Eugene Anderson–Parents, June 5, 1862, Anderson Papers, ANB; Rood, Memoir, p. 11, SHSW; *National Tribune,* December 11, 1902.

24. Diary, Fairfield Papers, SHSW; John Gibbon–My darling Mama, June 5, 9, 1862, Gibbon Papers, HSP; *Echoes,* pp. 22, 23.

25. E. A. Brown–Wife, June 11, 1862, Brown Letters, SHSW; William G. Davis–Parents, June 11, 1862, Davis Letters, MNBP; Dawes, *Service,* pp. 45–48; Ainsworth Saunders–Cousin David, June 17, 1862, Saunders Letter, UWRF.

26. Gibbon, *Personal Recollections,* pp. 34, 35; Brigade Order, No. 58, June 26, 1862, Meredith Papers, IHS; Dunn, *Iron Men,* p. 46.

27. D. Cooper Ayres–Dr. Edward P. Vullum, October 9, 1862, Adjutant General's Records, Series 1200, SHSW; Henry C. Marsh–Father, May 23, 1862, Marsh Letters and Diary, ISL; Diary, Fairfield Papers, SHSW.

28. Whitehouse, *Letters,* p. 35; E. A. Brown–Wife, June 11, 22, July 4, 1862, Brown Letters, SHSW.

29. William G. Davis–Parents, June 26, 1862, Davis Letters, MNBP.

30. Wert, "Valley Campaign," *Virginia Cavalcade,* 34, 4, p. 150; Jones, "Diary," pp. 18–21, HL; Harman, "Extracts," FSNMP.

31. Jones, "Diary," pp. 20–21, HL; Bean, "Valley Campaign," *VMHB*, 78, 3, p. 355; Diary, Shaner Correspondence, WL; Robertson, *Stonewall Jackson*, pp. 368, 369; Reidenbaugh, *27th Virginia Infantry*, p. 39.

32. Diary, Shaner Correspondence, WL; McDonald, *Make Me a Map*, pp. 35, 36.

33. Robertson, *Stonewall Jackson*, p. 366; Wert, "Valley Campaign," *Virginia Cavalcade*, 34, 4, p. 158.

34. *OR*, 12, 3, pp. 859, 860, 866; Wert, "Valley Campaign," *Virginia Cavalcade*, 34, 4, pp. 158, 159.

35. *OR*, 12, 3, p. 872; Wert, "Valley Campaign," *Virginia Cavalcade*, 34, 4, pp. 158, 159.

36. Robertson, *Stonewall Jackson*, pp. 369–70; Diary, Shaner Correspondence, WL; Waddell, Annals, pp. 469, 470; McDonald, *Make Me a Map*, pp. 36, 37.

37. Wert, "Valley Campaign," *Virginia Cavalcade*, 34, 4, pp. 159–60; Robertson, *Stonewall Jackson*, pp. 371–76; John H. Kiracofe–Wife and Daughter, May 12, 1862, Kiracofe Papers, DU; Jones, "Diary," p. 25, HL.

38. Jones, "Diary," pp. 28–29, HL; Robertson, *Stonewall Jackson*, pp. 378–81.

39. Jones, "Diary," pp. 28–29, HL; Robertson, *Stonewall Jackson*, pp. 381–85; Reidenbaugh, *27th Virginia Infantry*, pp. 42–43.

40. Wert, "Valley Campaign," *Virginia Cavalcade*, 35, 1, p. 39.

41. Ibid., p. 39; Taylor, *Destruction and Reconstruction*, p. 46.

42. McDonald, *Make Me a Map*, pp. 46, 47; Casler, *Four Years*, p. 76; Robertson, *Stonewall Jackson*, pp. 387–88.

43. *OR*, 12, 1, p. 701; Taylor, *Destruction and Reconstruction*, pp. 42–43; Colt, *Defend the Valley*, p. 140.

44. *OR*, 12, 1, p. 702; McDonald, *Make Me a Map*, p. 48.

45. Lawson Botts–J. F. O'Brien, May 22, 1862, Botts Collection, VMI.

46. *OR*, 12, 1, p. 702; Wert, "Valley Campaign," *Virginia Cavalcade*, 35, 1, pp. 40–41.

47. Wert, "Valley Campaign," *Virginia Cavalcade*, p. 41.

48. Ibid., p. 41; *OR*, 12, 1, pp. 702–3, 735.

49. *OR*, 12, 1, pp. 704, 735; Barton, Recollections, 1, p. 46, VHS; L. M. Blackford–My Dear Father, June 7, 1862, Blackford Family Papers, UVA; Colt, *Defend the Valley*, p. 143.

50. *OR*, 12, 1, pp. 735, 744, 751, 752, 756; pt. 3, p. 879.

51. Ibid., pt. 1, pp. 748, 749; White, *Sketches*, pp. 86, 87; Tanner, *Stonewall in the Valley*, pp. 275–77.

52. *OR*, 12, 1, pp. 705, 736, 737; Taylor, *Destruction and Reconstruction*, p. 63; L. M. Blackford–My Dear Father, June 7, 1862, Blackford Family Papers, UVA; William [?]–Brother, May 30, 1862, Chesson Collection, USAMHI; Wert, "Valley Campaign," *Virginia Cavalcade*, 35, 1, p. 42.

53. Taylor, *Destruction and Reconstruction*, pp. 62–64; *OR*, 12, 1, pp. 705–7; Wert, "Valley Campaign," *Virginia Cavalcade*, 35, 1, p. 42; Joseph F. Shaner–Father, May 25 or 26, 1862, Shaner Correspondence, WL.

54. Turner, *My Dear Emma*, p. 95; Letter of a member of Company H, Twenty-seventh Virginia, May 26, 1862, Smith Papers, NCSA; Randolph Fairfax–Bert, May 27, 1862, Fairfax Letters, MC; Jackson, *Memoirs*, p. 265.

55. Waddy C. Charlton–Oliver, May 26, 1862, Charlton Family Papers, VT; L. M. Blackford–My Dear Father, June 7, 1862, Blackford Family Papers, UVA; Letter of a member of Company H, Twenty-seventh Virginia, May 26, 1862, Smith Papers, NCSA.

56. General Orders, No. 52, May 25, 1862, Ewell Papers, NYHS; Turner, *Ted Barclay*, p. 72; *OR*, 12, 1, pp. 707, 708, 737.

57. *OR*, 12, 1, pp. 707, 738, 739; McDonald, *Make Me a Map*, p. 49.

58. *OR*, 12, 1, pp. 707–8; McDonald, *Make Me a Map*, p. 50; Jedediah Hotchkiss–A.C. Hopkins, September 2, 1896, Hotchkiss Papers, LC.

59. McDonald, *Make Me a Map*, p. 50; *OR*, 12, 1, p. 739; McKim, *Soldier's Recollections*, p. 107.

60. McKim, *Soldier's Recollections*, p. 107; McDonald, *Make Me a Map*, p. 50; Casler, *Four Years*, p. 81; L. M. Blackford–My Dear Father, June 13, 1862, Blackford Family Papers, UVA; Tanner, *Stonewall in the Valley*, pp. 338, 339.

61. McKim, *Soldier's Recollections*, pp. 107–8; Winder, Diary, MHS.

62. Robertson, *Stonewall Jackson*, pp. 421–22; Bean, "Valley Campaign," *VMHB*, 78, 3, p. 362; Beard, Diary, FSNMP.

63. L. M. Blackford–My Dear Mother, June 14, 1862, Blackford Family Papers, UVA; Robertson, *Stonewall Jackson*, p. 425; Turner, *My Dear Emma*, pp. 96–97; Harman, "Extracts," FSNMP.

64. A good description of Jackson's options and decision making on June 4 is in Robertson, *Stonewall Jackson*, pp. 426–27; Beard, Diary, FSNMP.

65. Beard, Diary, FSNMP; Winder, Diary, MHS; Bean, "Valley Campaign," *VMHB*, 78, 3, p. 364.

66. Winder, Diary, MHS; the best account of the Cross Keys engagement is in Krick, *Conquering the Valley*, Chapters 7–14.

67. Winder, Diary, MHS; Krick, *Conquering the Valley*, Chapters 4–5, pp. 127, 277, 278; Bean, "Valley Campaign," *VMHB*, 78, 3, p. 364.

68. Krick, *Conquering the Valley*, Chapter 14; Winder, Diary, MHS; *OR*, 12, 1, p. 747.

69. Winder, Diary, MHS; *OR*, 12, 1, pp. 742, 745, 747, 751, 753, 758; Randolph Fairfax–Jenny, June 7, 1862, Fairfax Letters, MC.

70. Krick, *Conquering the Valley*, pp. 127–30, 305.

71. Ibid., pp. 309, 311, 321, 326.

72. Ibid., pp. 318–21; *OR*, 12, 1, pp. 745, 747.

73. *OR*, 12, 1, pp. 745, 747; Mooney, Memoir, p. 3, VHS; Krick, *Conquering the Valley*, pp. 319, 328, 336.

74. *OR*, 12, 1, pp. 742, 750, 753; Krick, *Conquering the Valley*, pp. 340, 341, 345, 355, 358.

75. *OR*, 12, 1, pp. 741, 742, 750, 753; Krick, *Conquering the Valley*, pp. 360–64, 373, 377.

76. Krick, *Conquering the Valley*, Chapters 22 and 23.

77. Ibid., Chapters 24–26.

78. Ibid., pp. 507–12; *OR*, 12, 1, p. 717.

79. Krick, *Conquering the Valley*, pp. 470–75; Moore, *Story*, pp. 80, 81; *OR*, 12, 1, pp. 750–51; Winder, Diary, MHS.

80. L. M. Blackford–My Dear Father, June 7, 1862, Blackford Family Papers, UVA; Casler, *Four Years,* p. 86.

81. *OR,* 12, 1, p. 742; pt. 3, p. 879.

82. Ibid., 3, p. 879; Tanner, *Stonewall in the Valley,* pp. 427–28.

CHAPTER 7: VIRGINIA SUMMER

1. Wert, *General James Longstreet,* pp. 125–27.

2. Ibid., p. 127; Warner, *Generals in Gray,* pp. 180–81.

3. Wert, *General James Longstreet,* pp. 125, 126.

4. Ibid., pp. 127–29, 135.

5. Ibid., pp. 108, 126, 129, 130.

6. Ibid., pp. 132–34.

7. Winder, Diary, MHS; Robertson, *Stonewall Brigade,* p. 113.

8. Winder, Diary, MHS; Taylor, *Destruction and Reconstruction,* p. 76; Robertson, *Stonewall Jackson,* p. 452.

9. Robertson, *Stonewall Jackson,* pp. 450–57.

10. Ibid, pp. 458–69; Jones, "Diary," pp. 29, 30, HL; Casler, *Four Years,* p. 87.

11. Robertson, *Stonewall Jackson,* pp. 470–72.

12. Wert, *General James Longstreet,* Chapter 7.

13. Ibid.

14. Ibid., pp. 137–39; *OR,* 11, 2, p. 570.

15. *OR,* 11, 2, pp. 570, 575, 578; Frye, *2nd Virginia Infantry,* p. 32; William S. H. Baylor–John Peyton Clark, [August 1862], Baylor letter, HL; Wallace, *5th Virginia Infantry,* p. 33.

16. *OR,* 11, 2, pp. 570, 575, 580; Frye, *2nd Virginia Infantry,* p. 32; Samuel J. C. Moore–My Dearest Ellen, July 20, 1862, Moore Papers, UNC; Jones, "Diary," p. 30, HL; Colt, *Defend the Valley,* pp. 171, 172; William S. H. Baylor–John Peyton Clark, [August 1862], Baylor letter, HL.

17. *OR,* 11, 2, pp. 570, 575, 580; Wert, *General James Longstreet,* pp. 138–39.

18. *OR,* 11, 2, pp. 570, 573, 577, 578, 580, 581, 583, 585, 973.

19. Wallace, *5th Virginia Infantry,* p. 33.

20. Wert, *General James Longstreet,* pp. 139–46.

21. Ibid., pp. 147–49.

22. *OR,* 11, 2, pp. 571, 572, 573, 576, 578, 579, 583, 585, 586, 973; Grigsby file, CSR, NA; Andrew J. Grigsby–William Garnett, July 12, 1862, Garnett Papers, MC; John F. Neff–Parents, August 4, 1862, Neff Papers, USAMHI; Wallace, *5th Virginia Infantry,* p. 34.

23. Turner, *My Dear Emma,* pp. 99–100.

24. B. B. Weirman–Brother, August 31, 1862, Weirman Letters, FSNMP.

25. Robertson, *4th Virginia Infantry,* p. 16.

26. Diary, Fairfield Papers, SHSW; James Converse–Wife and Children, July 4, 1862, Converse Letters, CHS; John Gibbon–My darling Mama, July 5, 1862, Gibbon Papers, HSP; Eugene Anderson–Father and Mother, July 6, 1862, Anderson Papers, ANB.

27. James Converse–Wife and Children, July 4, 1862, Converse Letters, CHS.

28. Dawes, *Service,* pp. 51–52, 147.

29. Henry C. Marsh–Father, July 9, 1862, Marsh Letters and Diary, ISL; E. A.

Brown–Wife, July 12, 1862, Brown Letters, SHSW.

30. John Gibbon–My darling Mama, May 27, July 14, 1862, Gibbon Papers, HSP.

31. Diary, Fairfield Papers, SHSW; Diary, Meredith Papers, IHS; John Gibbon–My darling Mama, July 19, 1862, Gibbon Papers, HSP.

32. Charles W. Fuller–Sister, July 20, 1862, Fuller Papers, SHSW; Wolford, Diary, LC.

33. E. A. Brown–Ruth, August 3, 1862, Brown Letters, SHSW; Lavery and Jordan, *Iron Brigade General*, p. 45.

34. Dawes, *Service*, p. 48; Dawes file, CSR, NA; Byrne and Weaver, *Haskell*, pp. 20, 21.

35. Diary and Rufus King–Solomon Meredith, June 21, 1862, Meredith Papers, IHS.

36. Dawes, *Service*, p. 53; Diary, Fairfield Papers, SHSW.

37. Reidenbaugh, *27th Virginia Infantry*, p. 61.

38. Wert, *General James Longstreet*, pp. 155–56.

39. Ibid., pp. 156–57; Warner, *Generals in Gray*, pp. 376–77.

40. Wert, *General James Longstreet*, pp. 156–57.

41. Ibid., p. 157.

42. Shuler, Diary, LC; Robertson, *Stonewall Jackson*, pp. 513–14.

43. Casler, *Four Years*, pp. 101, 102.

44. John F. Neff–Parents, August 4, 1862, Neff Papers, USAMHI; Samuel J. C. Moore–My Dearest Ellen, August 13, 1862, Moore Papers, UNC; Turner, *My Dear Emma*, p. 101.

45. Robertson, *Stonewall Jackson*, pp. 519–22; Krick, *Stonewall Jackson*, Chapter 1; Samuel J. C. Moore–My Dear Sir, August 12, 1862, Moore Papers, UNC.

46. Robertson, *Stonewall Jackson*, pp. 523–25; Krick, *Stonewall Jackson*, Chapter 2; OR, 12, 2, p. 191; Samuel J. C. Moore–My Dear Sir, August 12, 1862, Moore Papers, UNC.

47. Krick, *Stonewall Jackson*, pp. 40, 48; OR, 12, 2, pp. 191, 194.

48. Krick, *Stonewall Jackson*, pp. 45–47.

49. Ibid., pp. 49, 51, 53, 57, 61, 63, 74; Samuel J. C. Moore–My Dear Sir, August 12, 1862, Moore Papers, UNC.

50. Pohanka, "Notes"; Krick, *Stonewall Jackson*, pp. 95, 96; White, *Sketches*, p. 113.

51. Samuel J. C. Moore–My Dear Sir, August 12, 1862, Moore Papers, UNC; White, *Sketches*, p. 113.

52. Krick, *Stonewall Jackson*, pp. 109, 112–16; OR, 12, 2, pp. 192, 197; ORS, 2, p. 708; CV, 27, p. 448.

53. Krick, *Stonewall Jackson*, pp. 115, 116, 142, 143, 145, 146, 151; OR, 12, 2, pp. 192, 197; Shuler, Diary, LC.

54. OR, 12, 2, pp. 197, 199; Krick, *Stonewall Jackson*, pp. 167, 170, 172–74.

55. Samuel J. C. Moore–My Dear Sir, August 12, 1862, Moore Papers, UNC; OR, 12, 2, pp. 192, 196; ORS, 2, pp. 708–9; H. J. Williams–Jedediah Hotchkiss, January 30, 1897, Hotchkiss Papers, LC; Krick, *Stonewall Jackson*, pp. 188, 203, 205, 212, 217, 218, 225.

56. *OR,* 12, 2, p. 196; *ORS,* 2, p. 709; Samuel J. C. Moore–My Dear Sir, August 12, 1862, Moore Papers, UNC; H. J. Williams–Jedediah Hotchkiss, January 30, 1897, Hotchkiss Papers, LC; Krick, *Stonewall Jackson,* pp. 243–45.

57. H. J. Williams–Jedediah Hotchkiss, January 30, 1897, Hotchkiss Papers, LC; Thomas Smiley–Sister, August 13, 1862, Smiley Correspondence, UVA; *ORS,* 2, p. 709; Krick, *Stonewall Jackson,* pp. 243–46; T. A. Brownlee–J. M. Quarles, June 3, 1896, Quarles Papers, MNBP.

58. Krick, *Stonewall Jackson,* Chapters 12 and 13; Mooney, Memoir, p. 5, VHS; Worsham, *One of Jackson's Foot Cavalry,* p. 103.

59. *OR,* 12, 2, p. 193; Samuel J. C. Moore–My Dearest Ellen, August 13, 1862, Moore Papers, UNC; Charles Byrne–Samuel Cooper, August 13, 1862, Byrne file, CSR, NA; Krick, *Stonewall Jackson,* pp. 174, 212.

60. Krick, *Stonewall Jackson,* pp. 367–74; Reidenbaugh, *33rd Virginia Infantry,* p. 41; *CV,* 7, p. 465; Samuel J. C. Moore–My Dear Sir, August 12, 1862, Moore Papers, UNC; Confederate States Army Casualties, NA.

61. Samuel J. C. Moore–My Dearest Ellen, August 13, 1862, Moore Papers, UNC; *OR,* 12, 2, pp. 183, 186.

62. Robertson, *Stonewall Jackson,* pp. 537–38; Long, *Stonewall's "Foot Cavalryman,"* pp. 9, 12.

63. John Gibbon–My darling Mama, August 8, 1862, Gibbon Papers, HSP; Diary, Fairfield Papers, SHSW.

64. Diary, Fairfield Papers, SHSW; John Gibbon–My darling Mama, August 8, 1862, Gibbon Papers, HSP; Rood, Memoir, p. 12, SHSW.

65. Diary, Fairfield Papers, SHSW; John Gibbon–My darling Mama, August 8, 1862, Gibbon Papers, HSP; *OR,* 12, 2, p. 122.

66. Diary, Fairfield Papers, SHSW; *OR,* 12, 2, p. 122.

67. Diary, Fairfield Papers, SHSW; *OR,* 12, 2, p. 124; John Gibbon–My darling Mama, August 8, 1862, Gibbon Papers, HSP; Hughes, "Report," SHSW.

68. Diary, Fairfield Papers, SHSW; *OR,* 12, 2, p. 123; John Gibbon–My darling Mama, August 8, 1862, Gibbon Papers, HSP; Hughes, "Report," SHSW.

69. *OR,* 12, 2, p. 123; Orson Parker–Father, August 9, 1862, Parker Letters, SHSW; Longhenry, "Yankee Piper," p. 2-2, ANB.

70. *War Papers,* MOLLUS, Wisconsin, 2, pp. 347–49; Diary, Fairfield Papers, SHSW; Longhenry, "Yankee Piper," p. 2-2, ANB; John Gibbon–My darling Mama, August 12, 1862, Gibbon Papers, HSP; Holford Diary, LC.

71. John Gibbon–My darling Mama, August 14, 1862, Gibbon Papers, HSP; Jeremiah G. Burdick–Mother, August 9, 1862, Burdick Papers, FSNMP; Longhenry, "Yankee Piper," p. 2-3, ANB.

72. Holford Diary, LC.

CHAPTER 8: INTO THE BROTHERHOOD

1. Hennessy, *Return to Bull Run,* p. 99; Robertson, *Stonewall Jackson,* p. 550.

2. Wert, *General James Longstreet,* pp. 157–60.

3. Ibid., pp. 160–62; *OR,* 12, 3, p. 941.

4. Wert, *General James Longstreet,* pp. 161–62; *OR,* 12, 2, p. 564; pt. 3, p. 941.

5. Hennessy, *Return to Bull Run,* p. 96; James Power Smith–My Dearest Sister,

August 19, 1862, Smith Correspondence, MC; Casler, *Four Years,* p. 106; Frye, *2nd Virginia Infantry,* p. 36.

6. Hennessy, *Return to Bull Run,* pp. 96, 99; Wert, *General James Longstreet,* p. 163.

7. Hennessy, *Return to Bull Run,* pp. 106, 107, 111–15; Wert, *General James Longstreet,* p. 163; Robertson, *Stonewall Jackson,* pp. 551–53.

8. Wert, *General James Longstreet,* p. 163; Robertson, *Stonewall Jackson,* pp. 549, 552, 553.

9. Robertson, *Stonewall Jackson,* pp. 555–56.

10. Ibid., pp. 557–58; Frye, *2nd Virginia Infantry,* p. 37; Thomas G. Pollock–Father, September 7, 1862, Pollock Papers, UVA.

11. Robertson, *Stonewall Jackson,* pp. 558–60; Hennessy, *Return to Bull Run,* pp. 130–52.

12. Diary, Fairfield Papers, SHSW; Holford, Diary, LC.

13. *National Tribune,* December 11, 1902; Hennessy, *Return to Bull Run,* pp. 135, 139–43.

14. Diary, Fairfield Papers, SHSW; John Gibbon–My darling Mama, August 20, 1862, Gibbon Papers, HSP; Longhenry, "Yankee Piper," pp. 2-3, 2-4, ANB; *National Tribune,* December 11, 1902; T. H. Benton–Sister, August 9, 1862, Benton Civil War Letters, IHS.

15. Diary, Fairfield Papers, SHSW; Gaff, *Brave Men's Tears,* pp. 69, 72, 73; OR, 12, 3, pp. 580, 780; Frank A. Haskell–Brother and Sister, August 31, 1862, Haskell Letters, SHSW; Hennessy, *Return to Bull Run,* pp. 161–63.

16. *War Papers,* MOLLUS, Wisconsin, 2, pp. 355–56; Diary, Fairfield Papers, SHSW; Hennessy, *Return to Bull Run,* pp. 163–64.

17. Herdegen, *Men Stood,* p. 89; Diary, Fairfield Papers, SHSW; Hennessy, *Return to Bull Run,* p. 164.

18. OR, 12, 2, pp. 377, 378; Hennessy, *Return to Bull Run,* pp. 169–70; Gibbon, *Personal Recollections,* pp. 51–52.

19. OR, 12, 2, p. 378; Reid-Green, *Letters Home,* p. 33; Gibbon, *Recollections,* pp. 51, 52.

20. Gibbon, *Personal Recollections,* p. 52; Gaff, *Brave Men's Tears,* p. 45; Nolan, *Iron Brigade,* pp. 81–83; Hennessy, *Return to Bull Run,* p. 178.

21. Hennessy, *Return to Bull Run,* pp. 168, 169, 172; *National Tribune,* July 14, 1892.

22. Gibbon, *Personal Recollections,* p. 52; Gaff, *Brave Men's Tears,* pp. 69, 70; Quiner, Correspondence, 2, p. 298, SHSW; Otis, *Second Wisconsin,* p. 56.

23. ORS, 2, p. 730; Gaff, *Brave Men's Tears,* p. 70; Herdegen, *Men Stood,* p. 93.

24. Hennessy, *Return to Bull Run,* p. 174; Blackford, *War Years,* pp. 120, 121; Robertson, *Stonewall Jackson,* p. 561.

25. Robertson, *Stonewall Jackson,* p. 561; OR, 12, 2, pp. 661, 662, 663; Confederate States Army Casualties, NA; Shuler, Diary, LC.

26. Krick, *Lee's Colonels,* p. 43; C. A. Ronald, et al–Gen. S. Cooper, August 15, 1862, Baylor file, CSR, NA.

27. William S. H. Baylor–Wife, August 18, 1862, Baylor Correspondence, VT; Edward Payson Walton–Jefferson Davis, August 16, 1862, Baylor file, CSR, NA.

28. Hennessy, *Return to Bull Run,* pp. 174–75; Shuler, Diary, LC.

29. Hennessy, *Return to Bull Run*, p. 175; Frye, *2nd Virginia Infantry*, p. 39; Moore, "Civil War Experiences," FSNMP.

30. *ORS*, 2, p. 730; Hughes, "Report," SHSW; Thomas G. Pollock–Father, September 9, 1862, Pollock Papers, UVA; Casler, *Four Years*, p. 109.

31. Moore, "Civil War Experiences," FSNMP; David H. Walton–Jno. Neff, September 2, 1862, Walton Letter, MNSP; *OR*, 12, 2, p. 663; B. B. Weirman–Brother, August 31, 1862, Weirman Letters, FSNMP; Wayland, *History of Shenandoah County*, pp. 311, 551; Gaff, *Brave Men's Tears*, p. 82; Casler, *Four Years*, pp. 109, 110.

32. Frye, *2nd Virginia Infantry*, pp. 39, 129; Gaff, *Brave Men's Tears*, pp. 82, 83.

33. Quiner, Correspondence, 2, pp. 298, 299, 312, SHSW; *National Tribune*, July 10, 1924; Racine *Advocate*, September 10, 1862; Gaff, *Brave Men's Tears*, pp. 80, 81; Otis, *Second Wisconsin*, p. 56.

34. Hennessy, *Return to Bull Run*, pp. 175, 176; Gaff, *On Many a Bloody Field*, p. 156.

35. Gaff, *Brave Men's Tears*, p. 72; Dunn, *Iron Men*, p. 80; Moore, "Reminiscences," IHS.

36. Dunn, *Iron Men*, p. 75; Gaff, *Brave Men's Tears*, pp. 79–80.

37. Gaff, *On Many a Bloody Field*, p. 161; Harden, *Those I Have Met*, pp. 90, 235; R. O. Dormer–Mr. Benton, September 2, 1862, Benton Civil War Letters, IHS.

38. Hennessy, *Return to Bull Run*, pp. 176–77.

39. Ibid., p. 177; Dawes, *Service*, pp. 60, 61; Gaff, *Brave Men's Tears*, p. 73.

40. Hennessy, *Return to Bull Run*, pp. 177, 179.

41. Henry F. Young–Father, September 9, 1862, Young Papers, SHSW; D. Cooper Ayres–Dr. Edward P. Vallum, October 9, 1862, Adjutant General Records, Series 1200, SHSW; Rood, Memoir, p. 16, SHSW; Hamilton file, CSR, NA.

42. Dawes, *Service*, p. 61; Beaudot and Herdegen, *Irishman*, p. 45; Diary, Fairfield Papers, SHSW; Holford, Diary, LC; *National Tribune*, December 11, 1902.

43. *ORS*, 2, p. 781; Thomas, *History*, p. 354; Diary, Fairfield Papers, SHSW; Dawes, *Service*, p. 61; Hennessy, *Return to Bull Run*, pp. 180, 181.

44. *ORS*, 2, p. 781; "A fairly good-looking young fellow," Watrous Papers, SHSW; Herdegen, *Men Stood*, pp. 99, 101; Rood, Memoir, p. 15, SHSW.

45. Thomas, *History*, p. 354; Hennessy, *Return to Bull Run*, pp. 184, 185; Gaff, *Brave Men's Tears*, pp. 83, 84, 85.

46. Edward S. Bragg–My Dear Wife, September 28, 1862, Bragg Papers, SHSW; *OR*, 12, 2, p. 382.

47. Cheek and Pointon, *History*, p. 39.

48. Hennessy, *Return to Bull Run*, pp. 183–84; Diary, Fairfield Papers, SHSW; Dawes, *Service*, p. 64; *OR*, 12, 2, p. 382; *ORS*, 2, pp. 781–82.

49. Herdegen, *Men Stood*, p. 101; Diary, Fairfield Papers, SHSW; Moore, "Reminiscences," IHS; Blackford, *War Years*, p. 122; *National Tribune*, July 10, 1924.

50. *National Tribune*, March 31, 1892; Coco, *Civil War Infantryman*, pp. 137–47.

51. Gaff, *Brave Men's Tears,* pp. 156–58; *OR,* 12, 2, pp. 337, 377, 382; *ORS,* 2, p. 731; Quiner, Correspondence, 2, pp. 287, 294, SHSW; Cutler file, CSR, NA; D. Cooper Ayres–Dr. Edward P. Vallum, October 9, 1862, Adjutant General Records, Series 1200, SHSW; Ross, *Empty Sleeve,* p. 45; William H. Church–Father, Mother and Sister, September 2, 1862, Church Papers, SHSW; Dunn, *Iron Men,* p. 79; McLean, *Cutler's Brigade,* p. 3; Solomon Meredith–O. P. Morton, August 31, 1862, Meredith Papers, IHS.

52. Gaff, *Brave Men's Tears,* p. 156; Gibbon, *Personal Recollections,* pp. 53, 55.

53. *OR,* 12, 2, pp. 377, 378, 380, 381; *ORS,* 2, p. 689; John Gibbon–My darling Mama, September 1, 1862, Gibbon Papers, HSP; Gaff, *Brave Men's Tears,* pp. 145–47.

54. *OR,* 12, 2, p. 382; Henry C. Marsh–Father, September 6, 1862, Marsh Letters and Diary, ISL; Dawes, *Service,* p. 68.

55. *OR,* 12, 2, pp. 661–63; Confederate States Army Casualties, NA; Gaff, *Brave Men's Tears,* pp. 159, 161; Hennessy, *Return to Bull Run,* p. 188; Robertson, *Stonewall Brigade,* p. 147.

56. B. B. Weirman–Brother, August 31, 1862, Weirman Letters, FSNMP; David H. Walton–Jno. Neff, September 2, 1862, Walton Letter, MNBP; *OR,* 12, 2, p. 657.

57. Hennessy, *Return to Bull Run,* p. 188; Fox, *Regimental Losses,* p. 556; "A fairly good-looking young fellow," Watrous Papers, SHSW.

58. Hennessy, *Return to Bull Run,* pp. 189–90.

59. Ibid., p. 340; Robertson, *Stonewall Jackson,* pp. 563, 564.

60. Robertson, *Stonewall Jackson,* p. 564.

61. Wert, *General James Longstreet,* pp. 167–68.

62. Ibid., pp. 169–71; Robertson, *Stonewall Jackson,* pp. 566–68.

63. Wert, *General James Longstreet,* pp. 174–75.

64. Ibid., pp. 175–76.

65. Ibid., p. 176.

66. Ibid.; the fullest and finest description of the battle is in Hennessy, *Return to Bull Run,* Chapters 18–20.

67. Hennessy, *Return to Bull Run,* pp. 347, 348; *SHSP,* 40, p. 226.

68. Johnson, *University Memorial,* p. 225; Cockrell, *Gunner with Stonewall,* pp. 38, 39; Edward P. Walton–My Dear Friend, October 1, 1862, Baylor Correspondence, VT; Wallace, *5th Virginia Infantry,* p. 39.

69. Hennessy, *Return to Bull Run,* pp. 347, 348; *OR,* 12, 2, p. 660; James Power Smith–My dearest Sister, August 31, 1862, Smith Correspondence, MC; Wallace, *5th Virginia Infantry,* p. 39; *Shenandoah Herald,* July 23, 1909; Jedediah Hotchkiss–Wife, September 21, 1862, Hotchkiss Papers, LC.

70. Hennessy, *Return to Bull Run,* pp. 348, 349; White, *Sketches,* pp. 1, 11, 12, 120; James Power Smith–My dearest Sister, August 31, 1862, Smith Correspondence, MC.

71. *CV,* 22, p. 231; *SHSP,* 40, p. 227; Hennessy, *Return to Bull Run,* p. 349; Wallace, *5th Virginia Infantry,* pp. 39, 40.

72. *OR,* 12, 2, p. 565; Wert, *General James Longstreet,* p. 177.

73. Fairfield Diary, Fairfield Papers, SHSW; Otis, *Second Wisconsin,* p. 69; Dawes, *Service,* p. 70.

74. *OR*, 12, 2, p. 379; Hughes, "Report," SHSW; Cheek and Pointon, *History*, p. 42; Hennessy, *Return to Bull Run*, pp. 336, 356, 358, 360.

75. *OR*, 12, 2, p. 379; Fairfield Diary, Fairfield Papers, SHSW; Hennessy, *Return to Bull Run*, p. 426; Cheek and Pointon, *History*, p. 43.

76. Fairfield Diary, Fairfield Papers, SHSW; Hennessy, *Return to Bull Run*, p. 426; Cheek and Pointon, *History*, pp. 43, 44; John Gibbon–My darling Mama, September 1, 1862, Gibbon Papers, HSP.

77. Gibbon, *Personal Recollections*, p. 65; Diary, Fairfield Papers, SHSW; Wert, *General James Longstreet*, pp. 177–78.

78. Hughes, "Report," SHSW; Wert, *General James Longstreet*, pp. 178–79; Robertson, *Stonewall Jackson*, pp. 578–79.

79. Henry F. Young–Father, September 9, 1862, Young Papers; Edward S. Bragg–My Dear Wife, September 28, 1862, Bragg Papers, SHSW.

80. *OR*, 12, 3, p. 795; Fox, *Regimental Losses*, pp. 33, 36, 117, 431; Table of Casualties, Second Wisconsin, Adjutant General Records, Series 1200, SHSW; William Orr–Father, August 31, 1862, Orr Papers, IU.

81. McMullen, *Surgeon*, p. 38; *OR*, 12, 2, p. 561.

82. *OR*, 12, 2, p. 561, 662–64; Fox, *Regimental Losses*, p. 567; Confederate States Army Casualties, NA.

83. B. B. Weirman–Brother, August 31, 1862, Weirman Letters, FSNMP.

CHAPTER 9: "CORN ACRES OF HELL"

1. Thomas G. Pollock–Father, September 7, 1862, Pollock Papers, UVA.

2. *OR*, 19, 1, p. 144; pt. 2, pp. 590, 591; Gallagher, *Antietam*, p. 37.

3. Wert, *General James Longstreet*, pp. 180–81; Gallagher, *Antietam*, pp. 39, 41, 42, 43.

4. Wert, *General James Longstreet*, pp. 181–82.

5. Ibid., pp. 182–84; Robertson, *Stonewall Jackson*, pp. 591–92.

6. Wert, *General James Longstreet*, pp. 183–84; *OR*, 19, 2, pp. 603, 604; Sears, *Landscape*, pp. 90, 91.

7. Sears, *Landscape*, Chapters 3 and 4; Robertson, *Stonewall Jackson*, p. 603.

8. Sears, *Landscape*, p. 17; John Gibbon–My darling Mama, September 3, 1862, Gibbon Papers, HSP.

9. Sears, *Landscape*, pp. 15, 17; John Gibbon–My darling Mama, September 3, 1862, Gibbon Papers, HSP.

10. Sears, *Landscape*, pp. 9–16.

11. Ibid., pp. 102–9.

12. Ibid., pp. 109–13.

13. Ibid., p. 113; Gibbon, *Personal Recollections*, p. 73.

14. James Converse–Wife and Children, September 5, 1862, Converse Letters, CHS; John Gibbon–My darling Mama, September 3, 1862, Gibbon Papers, HSP.

15. John Gibbon–My darling Mama, September 3, 1862, Gibbon Papers, HSP; Nolan, *Iron Brigade*, p. 117; Jackson, Diary, IHS; Longhenry, "Yankee Piper," p. 2-7, ANB; D. Cooper Ayres–Dr. Edward P. Vullum, October 9, 1862, Adjutant General Records, Series 1200, SHSW.

16. E. A. Brown–Ruth, September 13, 1862, Brown Letters, SHSW.

17. Fairfield Diary, Fairfield Papers, SHSW; Jackson, Diary, IHS; *OR,* 19, 1, pp. 247, 417.

18. Sears, *Landscape,* pp. 128–30.

19. Ibid., pp. 130–41; *OR,* 19, 1, p. 417.

20. *OR,* 19, 1, pp. 247, 249, 253; Hughes, "Report," SHSW.

21. *OR,* 19, 1, pp. 247, 249; Fairfield Diary, Fairfield Papers, SHSW; Gibbon, *Personal Recollections,* pp. 76, 79.

22. *OR,* 19, 1, pp. 249, 250, 252; Moore, "Reminiscences," IHS.

23. *OR,* 19, 1, p. 250; Sears, *Landscape,* pp. 141, 142.

24. *OR,* 19, 1, p. 250, 252; Mead, "Journal," SHSW.

25. *OR,* 19, 1, p. 256; *ORS,* 3, p. 581; Herdegen, *Men Stood,* p. 143.

26. *OR,* 19, 1, pp. 253, 256; *ORS,* 3, p. 581; Dawes, *Service,* pp. 81, 82.

27. *OR,* 19, 1, pp. 253, 254; Dawes, *Service,* pp. 82, 83.

28. *OR,* 19, 1, pp. 248, 250, 252, 254, 256; Holford Diary, LC; Whitehouse, *Letters,* p. 58; Fairfield Diary, Fairfield Papers, SHSW; Herdegen, *Men Stood,* p. 149.

29. *OR,* 19, 1, pp. 250, 252, 254, 256; Mead, "Journal," SHSW; Dawes, *Service,* p. 83.

30. *OR,* 19, 1, pp. 52, 184, 253; Frank A. Haskell–Brothers and Sisters, September 22, 1862, Haskell Letters, SHSW; Otis, *Second Wisconsin,* p. 29.

31. Cheek and Pointon, *History,* p. 47; *Roster of Wisconsin Volunteers,* 1, p. 499.

32. John Gibbon–My darling Mama, September 15, 1862, Gibbon Papers, HSP; *OR,* 19, 1, pp. 215, 248, 417.

33. John Gibbon–My darling Mama, October 5, 1862, Gibbon Papers, HSP.

34. Wert, *General James Longstreet,* p. 190.

35. Ibid., pp. 190–91; Robertson, *Stonewall Jackson,* pp. 602–6.

36. Robertson, *Stonewall Jackson,* pp. 606–7; *OR,* 19, 1, p. 1011; John R. Jones–E. A. Carman, February 25, 1896, Carman Papers, ANB.

37. Wert, *General James Longstreet,* p. 191; Sears, *Landscape,* pp. 180, 191; Gallagher, *Antietam,* p. 55.

38. Gallagher, *Antietam,* pp. 39–43; Wert, *General James Longstreet,* p. 186.

39. Gallagher, *Antietam,* pp. 43, 44.

40. Ibid., p. 44; *OR,* 19, 1, pp. 808, 1011, 1013.

41. John Garibaldi–Wife, October 24, 1862, Garibaldi Collection, VMI.

42. Wert, *General James Longstreet,* pp. 191, 201, 202.

43. Dawes, *Service,* p. 86; Sears, *Landscape,* pp. 127, 158, 159.

44. Dawes, *Service,* p. 86; Sears, *Landscape,* pp. 157–59; *OR,* 19, 2, p. 294.

45. Rood, Memoir, p. 19, SHSW; Sears, *Landscape,* pp. 160–61.

46. Wert, *General James Longstreet,* p. 194.

47. Ibid., pp. 194, 195; Sears, *Landscape,* p. 183.

48. Patterson, "Personal Recollections," p. 2, ISL.

49. *Sketches,* MOLLUS, Ohio, 3, pp. 252–53; Rood, Memoir, p. 20, SHSW.

50. Sears, *Landscape,* pp. 180, 181, 196; Gallagher, *Antietam,* p. 54; Wert, *General James Longstreet,* p. 195.

51. *OR,* 19, 1, p. 248; Otis, *Second Wisconsin,* p. 260; Jackson, Diary, IHS.

52. *OR,* 19, 1, pp. 254, 255; Dawes, *Service,* pp. 87, 88; Edward S. Bragg–E. A. Carman, December 26, 1894, Bragg Letter, ANB.

53. *Sketches*, MOLLUS, 3, pp. 254, 255; John P. Hart–Andrew Deacon, October 2, 1862, J. A. Watrous–Mrs. E. A. Brown, October 25, 1862, Brown Letters, SHSW.

54. *OR*, 19, 1, pp. 248, 255; Dawes, *Service*, pp. 88, 89; Typed reminiscence, pp. 12, 13, Rollins Papers, SHSW.

55. *OR*, 19, 1, p. 255; Holsworth, "Uncommon Valor," *B & G*, 13, 6, p. 16; *Sketches*, MOLLUS, Ohio, 3, pp. 256, 258.

56. *Sketches*, MOLLUS, Ohio, 3, p. 255; Horace Emerson–Mother and Sister, September 28, 1862, Emerson Letters, UM; Julius A. Murray–Daughters, September 27, 1862, Murray Family Papers, SHSW.

57. Edward S. Bragg–E. A. Carman, December 26, 1894, Bragg Letter, ANB; *OR*, 19, 1, pp. 255, 1012.

58. *CV*, 22, p. 66; John R. Jones–E. A. Carman, February 25, 1896, Carman Papers, ANB; *OR*, 19, 1, p. 1008; Davis, *Confederate General*, 3, p. 207.

59. *OR*, 19, 1, pp. 1008, 1012; A. J. Grigsby–E. A. Carman, May 7, 1895, Carman Papers, ANB.

60. *OR*, 19, 1, pp. 1008, 1012; Murfin, *Gleam*, p. 213; H. J. Williams–Jedediah Hotchkiss, January 30, 1897, Hotchkiss Papers, LC.

61. *OR*, 19, 1, p. 255; Edward S. Bragg–E. A. Carman, December 26, 1894, Bragg Letter, ANB; Dawes, *Service*, p. 84; Certificate, A. N. Preston, Surgeon, Sixth Wisconsin, October 16, 1862, Bragg file, CSR, NA; Edward S. Bragg–My dear Wife, September 21, 1862, Bragg Papers, SHSW.

62. *OR*, 19, 1, pp. 224, 227, 229, 233, 248; Holsworth, "Uncommon Valor," *B & G*, 13, 6, p. 16.

63. Shuler, Diary, LC; *OR*, 19, 1, pp. 1008, 1012, 1014; Dawes, *Service*, p. 84; A. J. Grigsby–E. A. Carman, May 7, 1895, John R. Jones–E. A. Carman, February 25, 1896, Carman Papers, ANB; H. J. Williams–Jedediah Hotchkiss, January 30, 1897, Hotchkiss Papers, LC.

64. *OR*, 19, 1, pp. 251, 257, 1008, 1012; Henry F. Young–Delia, October 4, 1862, Young Papers, SHSW; Worsham, *One of Jackson's Foot Cavalry*, p. 90.

65. Dawes, *Service*, p. 90; *OR*, 19, 1, p. 233; Edward S. Bragg–E. A. Carman, December 26, 1894, Carman Papers, ANB; Holsworth, "Uncommon Valor," *B & G*, 13, 6, p. 16.

66. Dawes, *Service*, p. 91; *Sketches*, MOLLUS, Ohio, 3, p. 259; Holsworth, "Uncommon Valor," *B & G*, 13, 6, p. 16.

67. *OR*, 19, 1, p. 256; Dawes, *Service*, p. 93; *Sketches*, MOLLUS, Ohio, 3, pp. 261–62; Frank A. Haskell–Brother and Sisters, September 22, 1862, Haskell Letters, SHSW.

68. *OR*, 19, 1, pp. 251, 257; Patterson, "Personal Recollections," p. 3, ISL; Holsworth, "Uncommon Valor," *B & G*, 13, 6, p. 20.

69. *OR*, 19, 1, pp. 251, 257; Jackson, Diary, IHS; Patterson, "Personal Recollections," p. 3, ISL; Dunn, *Iron Men*, p. 111; Rood, Memoir, p. 21, SHSW; Henry C. Marsh–Father, September 23, 1862, Marsh Letters and Diary, ISL; Harden, *Those I Have Met*, p. 235.

70. Whitehouse, *Letters*, p. 58.

71. Robbie–My dear, dear, wife, [December 1862], Robbie Letter, ANB; Horace Emerson–Mother and Sister, September 28, 1862, Emerson Letters,

UM; Eugene Anderson–Parents, September 22, 1862, Anderson Papers, ANB; Frank A. Haskell–Brother, September 19, 1862, to Brothers and Sisters, September 22, 1862, Haskell Letters, SHSW; Herdegen, *Men Stood,* p. 170.

72. Dawes, *Service,* p. 91; Edward S. Bragg–E. A. Carman, December 26, 1894, Bragg Letter, ANB; Holsworth, "Uncommon Valor," *B & G,* 13, 6, pp. 52, 53; Fox, *Regimental Losses,* p. 556.

73. *OR,* 19, 1, p. 229; *National Tribune,* May 8, 1890; Buell, *Cannoneer,* p. 33.

74. *OR,* 19, 1, p. 229; Buell, *Cannoneer,* pp. 33, 34; Jackson, Diary, IHS; *National Tribune,* May 8, 1890; Sears, *Landscape,* pp. 197–202.

75. Sears, *Landscape,* pp. 201, 202.

76. Ibid., Chapters 6–8.

77. Ibid., Chapter 9; Wert, *General James Longstreet,* pp. 201–2.

78. John R. Jones–E. A. Carman, February 25, 1896, Carman Papers, ANB; H. J. Williams–Jedediah Hotchkiss, January 30, 1897, Hotchkiss Papers, LC; *OR,* 19, 1, p. 812, lists losses as eleven killed and sixty-eight wounded; Robertson, *4th Virginia Infantry,* p. 22; Wallace, *5th Virginia Infantry,* p. 42.

79. Robbie–My dear, dear wife, [December 1862], Robbie Letter, ANB.

80. Horace Currier–[Edwin], October 10, 1862, Currier Papers, SHSW; Dawes, *Service,* p. 94; James Converse–Wife and Children, September 30, 1862, Converse Letters, CHS; Patterson, "Personal Recollections," p. 8, ISL.

81. John Gibbon–My darling Mama, September 21, October 5, 1862, Gibbon Papers, HSP.

82. Dawes, *Service,* p. 96; *OR,* 19, 1, p. 189; Fox, *Regimental Losses,* p. 463; John Gibbon–My darling Mama, September 21, 1862, Gibbon Papers, HSP.

83. John Gibbon–My darling Mama, October 5, 1862, Gibbon Papers, HSP; Elisha B. Odle-Miss Briant, September 23, 1862, Odle Papers, ANB; Henry C. Marsh–Father, September 23, 1862, Marsh Letters and Diary, ISL; Whitehouse, *Letters,* p. 55; Eugene Anderson–Parents, September 22, 1862, Anderson Papers, ANB.

CHAPTER 10: "THIS WAR IT SEEMS CANNOT END"

1. Dawes, *Service,* p. 96; Henry C. Marsh–Father, October 10, 11, 1862, Marsh Letters and Diary, ISL; Herdegen, *Men Stood,* p. 197.

2. Nolan, *Iron Brigade,* pp. 130, 336; Clemens, "'Black Hats,'" *Columbiad,* 1, 1, p. 48.

3. Herdegen, *Men Stood,* p. 197.

4. Clemens, "'Black Hats,'" *Columbiad,* 1, 1, pp. 48–49; Nolan, *Iron Brigade,* pp. 130, 336.

5. Gibbon, *Personal Recollections,* p. 93.

6. Clemens, "'Black Hats,'" *Columbiad,* 1, 1, pp. 51–54.

7. Sears, *Landscape,* pp. 323, 324; Henry C. Marsh–Father, October 10, 11, 1862, Marsh Letters and Diary, ISL; Jackson, Diary, IHS; Holford, Diary, LC; C. B. Clark–Father, October 3, 1862, Clark Letters, SHSW.

8. *OR,* 19, 2, pp. 197, 373, 374; Nolan, *Iron Brigade,* p. 149.

9. Nolan, *Iron Brigade,* pp. 149–50; Rosentreter, "Those Damned Black Hats," *Michigan History Magazine,* July/August 1991, p. 25.

10. Nolan, *Iron Brigade*, pp. 150–51; Rosentreter, "Those Damned Black Hats," *Michigan History Magazine*, July/August 1991, p. 25.

11. Nolan, *Iron Brigade*, pp. 151–53; A. W. Brindle–Aunt, August 23, 1862, Ward Papers, DPL.

12. Curtis, *History*, pp. 34–38; Nolan, *Iron Brigade*, pp. 152, 153; Smith, *Twenty-fourth Michigan*, p. 7.

13. Curtis, *History*, pp. 43, 44; Nolan, *Iron Brigade*, p. 155; Smith, *Twenty-fourth Michigan*, p. 9.

14. Curtis, *History*, pp. 43–46; John E. Ryder–Brother, October 23, 1862, Ryder Letters, UM; Nolan, *Iron Brigade*, pp. 155, 156; Hadden, "Deadly Embrace," *Gettysburg Magazine*, 5, p. 20; Smith, *Twenty-fourth Michigan*, pp. 9, 10, 18.

15. Curtis, *History*, p. 41; Nolan, *Iron Brigade*, p. 154.

16. Curtis, *History*, pp. 41, 42; Nolan, *Iron Brigade*, p. 154; Smith, *Twenty-fourth Michigan*, p. 9.

17. *Record of Service*, 24, pp. ix, 1; Nolan, *Iron Brigade*, p. 153; Elmer Wallace–Father and Mother, September 1, 1862, Wallace Papers, UM; Abel G. Peck–Child, September 2, 22, 1862, Peck Letters, MSU; Newspaper clipping, Green Papers, UM.

18. John E. Ryder–Friends, September 11, 14, 1862, Ryder Letters, UM; A. W. Brindle–Aunt, Ward Papers, DPL; Curtis, *History*, p. 52.

19. Curtis, *History*, p. 55; George A. Codwise–Aunt, September 24, 1862, Codwise Letters, USAMHI; John E. Ryder–Friends, September 11, 24, 1862, Ryder Letters, UM; Henry A. Morrow–D. P. Woodbury, September 29, 1862, Morrow file, CSR, NA.

20. A. W. Brindle–Aunt, September 7, 1862, Ward Papers, DPL; John E. Ryder–Sister, September 16, 1862, to Friends, September 20, 1862, Ryder Letters, UM; Lucius Shattuck–Gill, September 14, 27, 1862, Shattuck Letters, UM.

21. John E. Ryder–Friends, September 20, 27, 1862, Ryder Letters, UM; Elmer Wallace–Parents, September 13, 28, 1862, Wallace Papers, UM; George A. Codwise–Aunt, September 7, 1862, Codwise Letters, USAMHI.

22. John E. Ryder–Friends, September 24, 28, 1862, Ryder Letters, UM.

23. Curtis, *History*, pp. 46, 55, 61; Elmer Wallace–Father and Mother, October 10, 1862, Wallace Papers, UM; *OR*, 19, 2, p. 368.

24. Curtis, *History*, p. 65; John Gibbon–My dear dear *Wife*, October 16, 1862, Gibbon Papers, HSP; Longhenry, "Yankee Piper," p. 2–12, ANB; Smith, *Twenty-fourth Michigan*, p. 41; Rood, Memoir, p. 27, SHSW; George A. Codwise–Aunt, September 24, 1862, Codwise Letters, USAMHI.

25. Rood, Memoir, p. 27, SHSW; Curtis, *History*, p. 65.

26. Moore, "Reminiscences," IHS; Dawes, *Service*, p. 101; Nolan, *Iron Brigade*, p. 160.

27. John Gibbon–My dear dear *Wife*, October 16, 1862, Gibbon Papers, HSP.

28. Sears, *Landscape*, pp. 326–31.

29. John E. Ryder–Mother, October 29, 1862, Ryder Letters, UM; John Gibbon–My darling Mama, October 25, 1862, Gibbon Papers, HSP.

30. John E. Ryder–Mother, October 13, 22, 29, 1862, Ryder Letters, UM.

31. Ibid., October 29, 1862; Long, *Civil War*, pp. 281–84; George C. Gordon–My Dear Wife, November 2, 1862, Gordon Papers, SAM.

32. John Gibbon–My darling Mama, November 4, 1862, Gibbon Papers, HSP; Gibbon, *Personal Recollections*, pp. 95, 96.

33. John Gibbon–My darling Mama, November 4, 1862, Gibbon Papers, HSP.

34. Ibid.; Gibbon, *Personal Recollections*, p. 96; Jackson, Diary, IHS.

35. Jackson, Diary, IHS; Curtis, *History*, pp. 75, 76; *ORS*, 43, p. 463; Sears, *Landscape*, pp. 339–41.

36. Sears, *Landscape*, pp. 339–41.

37. Ibid., pp. 342–45; John Gibbon–My darling Mama, November 9, 1862, Gibbon Papers, HSP.

38. C. C. Starbuck–Cousin, November 13, 1862, Starbuck Civil War Letters, IHS; Otis, *Second Wisconsin*, p. 65n.

39. Wert, *General James Longstreet*, pp. 203–4.

40. *OR*, 19, 1, p. 143; pt. 2, pp. 618, 619, 621, 639, 660, 664.

41. Wert, *General James Longstreet*, p. 204; Moore, *Story*, p. 265; Driver, *1st and 2nd Rockbridge Artillery*, p. 33.

42. Wert, *General James Longstreet*, pp. 205–8.

43. Ibid., p. 204; Paxton, *Civil War Letters*, p. 57.

44. Waddy C. Charlton–Oliver, October 1, 1862, Charlton Family Papers, VT; John Garibaldi–Wife, October 24, 1862, Garibaldi Collection, VMI; General Orders, Nos. 113, 114, 116, 117, 123, Orders and Circulars, NA; Reidenbaugh, *33rd Virginia Infantry*, p. 57.

45. James R. McCutchan–Cousin, October 29, 1862, McCutchan Correspondence, WL; Robertson, *4th Virginia Infantry*, p. 22; *OR*, 19, 2, p. 89; B. B. Weirman–My Dear Kate, October 25, [1862], Weirman Letters, FSNMP.

46. Wert, *General James Longstreet*, p. 213.

47. Robertson, *4th Virginia Infantry*, pp. 22, 170, 171; E. G. Lee–Fred, November 15, 1862, Holliday Papers, DU; Frye, *2nd Virginia Infantry*, p. 44; Wallace, *5th Virginia Infantry*, p. 74; James P. Charlton–Oliver, November 11, 1862, Charlton Family Papers, VT; Shuler, Diary, LC.

48. Paxton, *Civil War Letters*, p. 63.

49. Turner, *My Dear Emma*, p. 111; J. Q. A. Nadenbousch et al.–[?], [c. March 16, 1863], Endorsement by A. P. Hill, March 16, 1863, Endorsement by E. F. Paxton, March 16, 1863, Grigsby file, CSR, NA.

50. E. G. Lee–Fred, November 15, 1862, Holliday Papers, DU; S. Bassett French–Custis Lee, December 20, 1863, Grigsby file, CSR, NA; Robertson, *Stonewall Jackson*, p. 626.

51. A. J. Grigsby–G. W. Randolph, November 12, 1862, Grigsby file, CSR, NA; Turner, *My Dear Emma*, p. 111; Reidenbaugh, *27th Virginia Infantry*, pp. 72–73.

52. Samuel J. C. Moore–My Dearest Ellen, February 17, 1863, Moore Papers, UNC.

53. Paxton, *Civil War Letters*, pp. 1, 2, 63; Reidenbaugh, *27th Virginia Infantry*, p. 72; Robertson, *Stonewall Brigade*, pp. 165, 166.

54. Wallace, *5th Virginia Infantry*, p. 44; Paxton, *Civil War Letters*, pp. 48, 49; Cockrell, *Gunner with Stonewall*, p. 60.

55. Bean, *Stonewall's Man*, p. 79.

56. Wallace, *5th Virginia Infantry*, p. 44; Paxton, *Civil War Letters*, p. 63; Robertson, *Stonewall Jackson*, p. 642.

57. Robertson, *Stonewall Jackson*, pp. 642–43; Casler, *Four Years*, pp. 119, 120.

58. Robertson, *Stonewall Jackson*, pp. 182–84, 642–47; Paxton, *Civil War Letters*, pp. 65, 66, 67.

59. Robertson, *Stonewall Jackson*, pp. 647, 651; Wert, *General James Longstreet*, pp. 215–18.

60. Robertson, *Stonewall Jackson*, p. 651; John P. Welsh–Becca, December 7, 1862, Welsh Family Papers, VSL; James P. Charlton–Oliver, December 7, 1862, Charlton Family Papers, VT.

61. Lucius Shattuck–Gill and Mary, November 14, 16, 1862, Shattuck Letters, UM; Wert, *General James Longstreet*, pp. 213, 214.

62. Lucius Shattuck–Gill and Mary, November 14, 16, 1862, Shattuck Letters, UM; Wert, *General James Longstreet*, pp. 213–15.

63. John E. Ryder–Father, November 23, 27, December 8, 1862, Ryder Letters, UM.

64. Edward S. Bragg–My Dear Wife, November 16, 1862, Bragg Papers, SHSW; Longhenry, "Yankee Piper," p. 2-14, ANB; Whitehouse, *Letters*, p. 65; *Roster of Wisconsin Volunteers*, 1, pp. 345, 494, 538; *Report of the Adjutant General*, 2, p. 168.

65. Jackson, Diary, IHS; Meredith's muster-out roll, October 23, 1862, Meredith file, CSR, NA; Dunn, *Iron Men*, p. 120.

66. Meredith, Diary, IHS; Dunn, *Iron Men*, pp. 120, 140.

67. Herdegen, *Men Stood*, p. 73; Jackson, Diary, IHS.

68. *OR*, 21, p. 87.

69. Wert, *General James Longstreet*, pp. 215, 216.

70. Ibid., pp. 217–18.

71. Ibid.; Robertson, *Stonewall Jackson*, pp. 650–53.

72. Wert, *General James Longstreet*, p. 219.

73. Ibid., pp. 219–20.

74. *OR*, 21, pp. 543, 562, 677, 678, 680, 681, 682; *CV*, 14, p. 419; Frye, *2nd Virginia Infantry*, p. 45; Wallace, *5th Virginia Infantry*, p. 44; Henry Kyd Douglas–My Dear Friend, December 22, 1862, Douglas Papers, DU; Confederate States Army Casualties, NA.

75. Wert, *General James Longstreet*, pp. 221–22.

76. *OR*, 21, pp. 476, 478; Curtis, *History*, p. 91; William Speed–Charlotte Speed, December 15, 1862, Speed Papers, UM.

77. Asa Brindle–My Dear Aunt, December 15, 1862, Brindle Letters, DPL; Jackson, Diary, IHS; George H. Legate–Sister, December 27, 1862, Legate Letter, FSNMP; Curtis, *History*, pp. 93–95.

78. Abel G. Peck–Lina, January 16, 1863, Peck Letter, FSNMP; Dawes, *Service*, p. 112; *OR*, 21, p. 476.

79. *OR*, 21, p. 478; Dunn, *Iron Men*, pp. 148, 149; William Speed–Charlotte Speed, December 15, 1862, Speed Papers, UM; Lucius Shattuck–Gill and Mary, December 17, 1862, Shattuck Letters, UM.

80. *OR*, 21, pp. 137, 138, 464, 478; Long, *Civil War*, pp. 296, 297; George H. Legate–Sister, December 27, 1862, Legate Letter, FSNMP.

81. Lucius Shattuck–Gill and Mary, December 17, 1862, Shattuck Letters, UM.

CHAPTER 11: RIVER CROSSINGS

1. William Orr–Mother, December 24, 1862, Orr Papers, IU; William Speed–Charlotte Speed, December 29, 1862, Speed Papers, UM.
2. Reid-Green, *Letters Home*, p. 39; George H. Legate–Sister, December 27, 1862, Legate Letter, FSNMP; Abel G. Peck–Lina, January 16, 1863, Peck Letter, FSNMP.
3. Dawes, *Service*, p. 115; William Orr–Mother, December 24, 1862, Orr Papers, IU; George H. Legate–Sister, December 27, 1862, Legate Letter, FSNMP.
4. Henry W. Beecham–Mother, December 19, 1862, Beecham Letters, SHSW; John W. St. Clair–Father, December 30, 1862, St. Clair Papers, SHSW.
5. John E. Ryder–Sister, January 4, 1863, Ryder Letters, UM; Lucius Shattuck–Gill, January 12, 1863, Shattuck Letters, UM.
6. Abel G. Peck–Lina, January 16, 1863, Peck Letter, FSNMP; Lucius Shattuck–Gill, January 12, 1863, Shattuck Letters, UM; Elmer Wallace–Mother and Father, January 11, 1863, Wallace Papers, UM.
7. Diary, Currier Papers, SHSW; Noble, Diary, UWRF; John E. Ryder–Sister, January 4, 6, 1863, Ryder Letters, UM; George C. Gordon–My Dear Wife, January 18, 1863, Gordon Papers, SAM.
8. Reid-Green, *Letters Home*, p. 41.
9. John E. Ryder–Friends, January 10, 1863, Ryder Letters, UM.
10. Long, *Civil War*, p. 306.
11. Grimsley, *Hard Hand*, pp. 136–39; William Orr–Father and Mother, January 5, 1863, Orr Papers, IU.
12. Elisha B. Odle–Friend, March 7, 1863, Odle Papers, ANB.
13. Grimsley, *Hard Hand*, pp. 136–37.
14. Long, *Civil War*, pp. 312–13.
15. Ibid., p. 313; Noble, Diary, UWRF.
16. Dunn, *Iron Men*, p. 155; Rood, Memoir, p. 39, SHSW; Longhenry, "Yankee Piper," p. 3-4, ANB; John E. Ryder–Father, January 28, 1863, Ryder Letters, UM; Edward S. Bragg–My Dear Wife, January 25, 1863, Bragg Papers, SHSW.
17. Henry F. Young–Father, February 7, 1863, Young Papers, SHSW; Noble, Diary, UWRF; John E. Ryder–Father, January 28, 1863, Ryder Letters, UM; Rood, Memoir, pp. 38, 39, SHSW.
18. John E. Ryder–Father, February 1, 5, 22, 1863, Ryder Letters, UM; Curtis, *History*, pp. 113, 114; Diary, Currier Papers, SHSW; Newspaper clipping, Green Papers, UM; Longhenry, "Yankee Piper," pp. 3–8, ANB; Noble, Diary, UWRF.
19. Long, *Civil War*, p. 315.
20. Horace Emerson–Brother Irvey, January 31, 1863, Emerson Letters, UM.
21. General Orders, No. 5, February 1, 1863, Meredith Papers, IHS; Lucius Shattuck–Gill, February 6, 1863, Shattuck Letters, UM; Horace Emerson–Irvey, February 23, 1863, Emerson Letters, UM.
22. Nolan, *Iron Brigade*, p. 191; John E. Ryder–Father, February 10, 1863, Ryder Letters, UM; Longhenry, "Yankee Piper," p. 3-6, ANB; Buell, *Cannoneer*, pp. 47, 48; Horace Emerson–Irvey, February 23, 1863, Emerson Letters, UM.

23. Beaudot and Herdegen, *Irishman*, p. 3.

24. Dawes, *Service*, p. 123; Henry F. Young–Father, February 7, 1863, Young Papers, SHSW; John E. Ryder–Father, February 22, 1863, Ryder Letters, UM.

25. McDonald, *A Woman's Civil War*, p. 101.

26. Paxton, *Civil War Letters*, p. 70; Reidenbaugh, *33rd Virginia Infantry*, p. 55.

27. Paxton, *Civil War Letters*, p. 70; Krick, *Lee's Colonels*, pp. 28, 43, 54, 86, 115, 132, 135, 153, 178, 195, 254, 263, 264, 266, 302, 318, 370; Warner, *Generals in Gray*, p. 302; *OR*, 21, p. 543.

28. Paxton, *Civil War Letters*, p. 70.

29. Krick, *Lee's Colonels*, pp. 28, 54, 178, 195, 264; Levin, *"This Awful Drama,"* pp. 55, 56.

30. Frye, *2nd Virginia Infantry*, pp. 80–142; Robertson, *4th Virginia Infantry*, pp. 37–84; Wallace, *5th Virginia Infantry*, p. 77; Reidenbaugh, *27th Virginia Infantry*, pp. 127–85; Reidenbaugh, *33rd Virginia Infantry*, p. 57.

31. The desertion rate was calculated upon the rosters contained in the sources cited above in footnote No. 30; *OR*, 12, 1, p. 742; pt. 3, p. 879.

32. Frye, *2nd Virginia Infantry*, pp. 80–142; Reidenbaugh, *33rd Virginia Infantry*, p. 57.

33. General Orders, No. 6, January 20, 1863, No. 28, February 27, 1863, No. 55, April 9, 1863, Orders and Circulars, NA; Krick, 33rd Virginia Infantry File, FSNMP; Paxton, *Civil War Letters*, pp. 74, 75; Staunton *Spectator*, March 21, 1863; Douglas, *I Rode with Stonewall*, p. 213.

34. Douglas, *I Rode with Stonewall*, pp. 213, 214; Paxton, *Civil War Letters*, pp. 74, 75.

35. Robertson, *Stonewall Brigade*, p. 175; Wallace, *5th Virginia Infantry*, p. 45; Robertson, *Stonewall Jackson*, p. 667.

36. John P. Welsh–Becky, December 7, 1862, January 11, 1863, Welsh Family Papers, WL; Wallace, *5th Virginia Infantry*, p. 45; James R. McCutchan–Cousin, February 23, 1863, McCutchan Letters, WL; Colt, *Defend the Valley*, p. 223.

37. Staunton *Spectator*, February 17, 1863; Wallace, *5th Virginia Infantry*, p. 45; Thomas M. Smiley–Sister, January 4, 1863, Smiley Correspondence, UVA.

38. John Welsh–Becky, January 11, 1863, Welsh Family Papers, WL; Douglas, *I Rode with Stonewall*, pp. 211, 212; Wallace, *5th Virginia Infantry*, pp. 45, 46.

39. John Garibaldi–Wife, January 27, 1863, Garibaldi Letters, VMI; George R. Bedinger–Diddy, February 8, 1863, Bedinger Letters, DU.

40. John P. Welsh–Mother and Wife, January 30, 1863, Welsh Family Papers, WL.

41. Sears, *Chancellorsville*, p. 112.

42. *OR*, 25, 1, pp. 793, 1018; Wallace, *5th Virginia Infantry*, p. 74; John P. Welsh–Mother and Wife, May 8, 1863, Welsh Family Papers, WL; John Garibaldi–Wife, March 29, May 11, 1863, Garbaldi Letters, VMI; Colt, *Defend the Valley*, pp. 239, 240; A. Baldwin–Cousin, April 12, 1863, Holliday Papers, DU.

43. Paxton, *Civil War Letters*, p. 82.

44. John E. Ryder–Sister, March 29, 1863, Ryder Letters, UM; Longhenry, *"Yankee Piper,"* p. 3-13, ANB; Curtis, *History*, pp. 115–16; Noble, *"Diary,"* UM.

45. Sears, *Chancellorsville*, pp. 70–74.

46. Ibid., pp. 62–68.

47. John E. Ryder–Mother, March 7, 1863, Ryder Letters, UM.

48. Elmer Wallace–Mother, April 5, 1863, Wallace Papers, UM; Noble, Diary, UWRF; Diary, Currier Papers, SHSW.

49. Sears, *Chancellorsville*, pp. 128–41; Abel G. Peck–My dear Child, April 19, 1863, Peck Letters, MSU.

50. Longhenry, "Yankee Piper," p. 3-15, ANB; John E. Ryder–Sister, March 5, 29, 1863, to Father, March 10, 1863, to Mother, March 25, 1863, to Friends, April 14, 1863, Ryder Letters, UM; Curtis, *History*, p. 119; William Orr–Father, March 9, 1863, Orr Papers, IU; Ross, *Empty Sleeve*, p. 47.

51. Nolan, *Iron Brigade*, pp. 173–75; *Report of the Adjutant General*, 2, p. 168.

52. Dunn, *Iron Men*, p. 3; Gaff, *On Many a Bloody Field*, p. 4; *Report of the Adjutant General*, 2, p. 168.

53. *Roster of Wisconsin Volunteers*, 1, p. 494; Nolan, *Iron Brigade*, p. 197; Bragg file, CSR, NA; Warner, *Generals in Blue*, p. 110; Edward S. Bragg–My Dear Wife, January 25, 1863, Bragg Papers, SHSW.

54. Rufus R. Dawes–Luce, January 27, March 25, 1863, Dawes Papers, SHSW; Dawes file, CSR, NA; Nolan, *Iron Brigade*, p. 197; Dawes, *Service*, p. 144.

55. Nolan, *Iron Brigade*, pp. 27, 197, 198; *Roster of Wisconsin Volunteers*, 1, pp. 345, 538.

56. Abel G. Peck–My dear Child, May 10, 1863, Peck Letters, MSU; Dawes, *Service*, p. 135; Sears, *Chancellorsville*, p. 150.

57. Sears, *Chancellorsville*, pp. 140–41.

58. Herdegen, *Men Stood*, pp. 7–9; Rufus R. Dawes–[Mary Gates], April 28, 1863, Dawes Papers, SHSW.

59. Noble, Diary, UWRF; Rufus R. Dawes–Luce, May 1, 1863, Dawes Papers, SHSW; Reid-Green, *Letters Home*, p. 53; Henry F. Young–Father, May 13, 1863, Young Papers, SHSW.

60. *OR*, 25, 1, p. 267; Rufus R. Dawes–Luce, May 1, 1863, Dawes Papers, SHSW; Beaudot and Herdegen, *Irishman*, p. 77; Cheek and Pointon, *History*, p. 63.

61. Henry F. Young–Father, May 13, 1863, Young Papers, SHSW; Beaudot and Herdegen, *Irishman*, p. 77; George C. Gordon–My dear Carrie, May 1, 1863, Gordon Papers, SAM; Cheek and Pointon, *History*, p. 64; Rufus R. Dawes–Luce, May 1, 1863, Dawes Papers, SHSW.

62. Edward S. Bragg–My Dear Wife, May 8, 1863, Bragg Papers, SHSW; Cheek and Pointon, *History*, p. 65; Flanigan, Diary, DPL; Rufus R. Dawes–Luce, April 30, May 1, 1863, Dawes Papers, SHSW; Reid-Green, *Letters Home*, p. 54; Henry F. Young–Father, May 13, 1863, Young Papers, SHSW.

63. Edward S. Bragg–My Dear Wife, May 8, 1863, Bragg Papers, SHSW; *OR*, 25, 1, p. 267; Noble, Diary, UWRF; Sears, *Chancellorsville*, p. 157.

64. Noble, Diary, UWRF; Diary, Currier Papers, SHSW; Abel G. Peck–My dear Child, May 10, 1863, Peck Letters, MSU.

65. Sears, *Chancellorsville*, p. 193.

66. Ibid., pp. 178, 193–94.

67. Ibid., Chapters 6 and 7.

68. Ibid., pp. 188, 189.

69. Ibid., pp. 197, 198; Wallace, *5th Virginia Infantry*, p. 46; McDonald, *Make Me a Map*, p. 119

70. Sears, *Chancellorsville*, p. 198; Wert, *General James Longstreet*, pp. 238–239.

71. Sears, *Chancellorsville*, pp. 202–4.

72. Robertson, *Stonewall Jackson*, pp. 709–12.

73. Ibid., pp. 712–14.

74. Ibid., pp. 715–16; George W. Slifer–Unkle, May 9, 1863, Slifer Letters, FS-NMP; *OR*, 25, 1, p. 1013.

75. Robertson, *Stonewall Jackson*, pp. 718–22.

76. Ibid., pp. 722–31.

77. Ibid., pp. 731–37.

78. *OR*, 25, 1, p. 1013; Report of Lt. Col. Daniel M. Shriver, Colston Papers, UNC; Colt, *Defend the Valley*, p. 242.

79. Paxton, *Civil War Letters*, p. 85; Sears, *Chancellorsville*, p. 330.

80. Sears, *Chancellorsville*, pp. 298, 313–14.

81. Ibid., pp. 314, 330; *OR*, 25, 1, p. 1013.

82. *OR*, 25, 1, pp. 1013, 1024; Sears, *Chancellorsville*, pp. 330, 331.

83. John P. Welsh–Mother and Wife, May 8, 1863, Welsh Family Papers, WL; *OR*, 25, 1, p. 1022; Turner, *My Dear Emma*, p. 125; Reidenbaugh, *27th Virginia Infantry*, pp. 80, 81; John Garibaldi–Wife, May 9, 1863, Garibaldi Letters, VMI; Long, *Stonewall's "Foot Cavalryman,"* p. 16.

84. *OR*, 25, 1, pp. 1017, 1018, 1020, 1024; *SHSP*, 14, p. 365; Robertson, *4th Virginia Infantry*, p. 25; Colt, *Defend the Valley*, p. 242; George W. Slifer–Unkle, May 3, 1863, Slifer Letters, FSNMP.

85. J. H. S. Funk–Stephen D. Ramseur, May 9, 1863, Stephen D. Ramseur–J. H. S. Funk, May 22, 1863, Ramseur Papers, NCSA; *SHSP*, 14, pp. 367, 369.

86. *OR*, 25, 1, pp. 944, 1013, 1014, 1017, 1019, 1024; *SHSP*, 14, p. 366; John Garibaldi–Wife, May 9, 1863, Garibaldi Letters, VMI; Turner, *Ted Barclay*, p. 79; Loudoun *Times Mirror*, March 15, 1928.

87. Sears, *Chancellorsville*, Chapter 12, quotation on p. 365.

88. Ibid., Chapters 14 and 15.

89. Noble, Diary, UWRF; Diary, Currier Papers, SHSW; Brown, Daily Journal, p. 56, USAMHI; Dawes, *Service*, p. 139; *OR*, 25, 1, p. 173.

90. Nolan, *Iron Brigade*, p. 219.

91. Sears, *Chancellorsville*, pp. 492, 498, 501; *OR*, 25, 1, p. 1021; Loudoun *Times Mirror*, March 15, 1928.

92. Robertson, *Stonewall Jackson*, p. 741.

93. Ibid., pp. 746–53.

CHAPTER 12: "THIS CURSED WAR"

1. Waddell, *Annals*, p. 481; McDonald, *A Woman's Civil War*, p. 147.

2. Robertson, *Stonewall Jackson*, pp. 754–58; Robertson, *Stonewall Brigade*, pp. 191–92.

3. Robertson, *Stonewall Jackson*, pp. 758–61; John Garibaldi–Wife, May 11, 1863, Garibaldi Letters, VMI; Lexington *Gazette*, May 20, 1863.

4. Robertson, *Stonewall Jackson*, pp. 760–61; Lexington *Gazette*, May 20, 1863; Driver, *Lexington*, p. 44.

5. Smith, *With Stonewall Jackson,* pp. 100–102; Wallace, *5th Virginia Infantry,* p. 48.

6. *OR,* 25, 2, pp. 809–10; Caldwell, *Stonewall Jim,* p. 84.

7. Caldwell, *Stonewall Jim,* pp. 3, 4, 5, 12, 34; Reidenbaugh, *27th Virginia Infantry,* p. 84; Davis, *Confederate General,* 6, pp. 86, 87.

8. Colt, *Defend the Valley,* p. 284; Robertson, *4th Virginia Infantry,* p. 26; CV, 10, p. 36; Davis, *Confederate General,* 6, p. 86.

9. Robertson, *Stonewall Brigade,* pp. 196, 197; Reidenbaugh, *27th Virginia Infantry,* p. 84.

10. *OR,* 25, 2, p. 810; Wert, *General James Longstreet,* pp. 247, 248.

11. *OR,* 25, 2, p. 810.

12. Ibid., pp. 811, 840; Davis, *Confederate General,* 3, pp. 186–87.

13. Wert, *General James Longstreet,* p. 247.

14. Ibid., pp. 248, 250.

15. Ibid., pp. 250–51; Thomas M. Smiley–Sister, June 9, 1863, Smiley Family Papers, UVA.

16. Long, *Civil War,* pp. 364–65; Bean, *Liberty Hall Volunteers,* p. 146; Worsham, *One of Jackson's Foot Cavalry,* p. 97.

17. Grunder and Beck, *Second Battle of Winchester,* pp. 8, 28–30.

18. Ibid., pp. 34–36.

19. Ibid., pp. 36, 37; *OR,* 27, 2, p. 500.

20. Grunder and Beck, *Second Battle of Winchester,* pp. 41–46.

21. Ibid., pp. 46–48.

22. Ibid., pp. 46–50.

23. Ibid., pp. 50–51; *OR,* 27, 2, pp. 502, 517; Long, *Civil War,* p. 366; John Garibaldi–Wife, June 16, 1863, Garibaldi Letters, VMI.

24. Long, *Civil War,* pp. 368–71; Wert, *General James Longstreet,* pp. 251–53; John Garibaldi–Wife, July 19, 1863, Garibaldi Letters, VMI.

25. Wert, *General James Longstreet,* pp. 253–55.

26. *OR,* 27, 2, pp. 443–44.

27. Wert, *General James Longstreet,* pp. 255–56.

28. Lucius Shattuck–Gill and Mary, June 5, 1863, Shattuck Letters, UM; *Record of Service,* 24, p. 19.

29. Lucius Shattuck–Gill and Mary, May 17, 1863, Shattuck Letters, UM; Rufus R. Dawes–My dear Mary, May 18, 1863, Dawes Papers, SHSW; Solomon Meredith–My Dear Mama, May 23, 1863, Meredith Papers, IHS.

30. Diary, Horace Currier–[?], May 29, 1863, Currier Papers, SHSW; Jeremiah G. Burdick–Father, June 5, 1863, Burdick Papers, FSNMP; John E. Ryder–Mother, May 18, 1863, Ryder Letters, UM.

31. Jackson, Diary, IHS; Longhenry, "Yankee Piper," p. 3-19, ANB.

32. Brown, Daily Journal, pp. 91, 92, 103, USAMHI; Jackson, Diary, IHS; Hughes, "Report," SHSW.

33. Brown, Daily Journal, pp. 103, 106, USAMHI; Jackson, Diary, IHS; Hughes, "Report," SHSW.

34. Curtis, *History,* p. 142; Herdegen and Beaudot, *In the Bloody Railroad Cut,* p. 336.

35. Smith, *Twenty-fourth Michigan,* p. 109; Brown, Daily Journal, pp. 112, 113, USAMHI.

36. Dawes, *Service*, p. 145; Rufus R. Dawes–My dear Mary, May 26, 1863, Dawes Papers, SHSW.
37. Dawes, *Service*, p. 145; Jeremiah G. Burdick–Father, June 5, 1863, Burdick Papers, FSNMP; Coddington, *Gettysburg Campaign*, pp. 52–54.
38. Coddington, *Gettysburg Campaign*, p. 69; Dawes, *Service*, p. 151.
39. Currier Diary, Currier Papers, SHSW; Dawes, *Service*, p. 150; Elmer Wallace–Parents, June 16, 1863, Wallace Papers, UM; Reid-Green, *Letters Home*, p. 58.
40. Currier Diary, Currier Papers, SHSW; Longhenry, "Yankee Piper," p. 3–23, ANB; Dawes, *Service*, p. 152; Lucius Shattuck–Gill, June 16, 1863, Shattuck Letters, UM.
41. John E. Ryder–Mother, June 20, 1863, Ryder Letters, UM; Currier Diary, Currier Papers, SHSW; Longhenry, "Yankee Piper," p. 3-23, ANB; Dawes, *Service*, p. 153; Lucius Shattuck–Gill, June 16, 1863, Shattuck Letters, UM.
42. Coddington, *Gettysburg Campaign*, pp. 74–80, 122–23.
43. Currier Diary, Currier Papers, SHSW; William Speed–Charlotte Speed, June 21, 1863, Speed Papers, UM; Jackson, Diary, IHS.
44. Currier Diary, Currier Papers, SHSW; Longhenry, "Yankee Piper," p. 3–24, ANB; Noble, "Diary," UM; Smith, *Twenty-fourth Michigan*, p. 117.
45. Longhenry, "Yankee Piper," pp. 3–24, ANB; Noble, Diary, UWRF; Coddington, *Gettysburg Campaign*, pp. 122–23; John E. Ryder–Father, June 28, 1863, Ryder Letters, UM; Mead, "Journal," SHSW.
46. Coddington, *Gettysburg Campaign*, pp. 127–33.
47. Ibid., pp. 180–81; Noble, Diary, UWRF; Meade, "Journal," SHSW.
48. Holford, Diary, LC; Flanigan, Diary, DPL; Coddington, *Gettysburg Campaign*, p. 233; Russell Root–Grand Father, August 23, 1863, Root Letter, US-AMHI.
49. Noble, "Diary," UM; *ORS*, 5, p. 123; Busey and Martin, *Regimental Strengths*, p. 21; Flanigan, Diary, DPL.

CHAPTER 13: GETTYSBURG

1. Diary, Marsh Letters and Diary, ISL; Beaudot and Herdegen, *Irishman*, p. 92; Herdegen, *Men Stood*, pp. 3, 18, 23.
2. Dawes, *Service*, pp. 146, 147, 149; Bragg file, CSR, NA; Rufus R. Dawes–My dear Mary, June 30, 1863, Dawes Papers, SHSW.
3. Martin, *Gettysburg*, pp. 89–93; Dawes, *Service*, p. 158.
4. Martin, *Gettysburg*, pp. 89–92.
5. Warner, *Generals in Blue*, pp. 532–33; Nevins, *Diary*, p. 127.
6. Martin, *Gettysburg*, pp. 93–94; William W. Dudley–E. D. Townsend, June 20, 1878, Nineteenth Indiana Infantry File, GNMP; *Sketches*, MOLLUS, Ohio, 3, p. 364.
7. Martin, *Gettysburg*, p. 94; William W. Dudley–E. D. Townsend, June 20, 1878, Nineteenth Indiana Infantry File, GNMP; *Sketches*, MOLLUS, Ohio, 3, p. 364; Buell, *Cannoneer*, pp. 63–64.
8. *Sketches*, MOLLUS, Ohio, 3, p. 364; Beaudot and Herdegen, *Irishman*, p. 93.
9. *Sketches*, MOLLUS, Ohio, 3, p. 364.
10. Mead, "Journal," SHSW; William W. Dudley–E. D. Townsend, June 20,

1878, Nineteenth Indiana Infantry File, GNMP; Charles H. Veil–D. Mc-Conaughy, April 7, 1864, Brake Collection, USAMHI; Detroit *Free Press,* July 14, 1863; *War Papers,* MOLLUS, Wisconsin, 2, p. 210.

11. Beecham, *Gettysburg,* p. 32; McPherson, *For Cause and Comrades,* pp. 44, 45.

12. Martin, *Gettysburg,* p. 96; Shue, *Morning,* pp. 88–89, 92–93; Coddington, *Gettysburg Campaign,* p. 267.

13. Shue, *Morning,* pp. 92–96; Martin, *Gettysburg,* pp. 96–100; *OR,* 27, 1, pp. 244, 701.

14. Charles H. Veil–D. McConaughy, April 7, 1864, Brake Collection, USAMHI; Martin, *Gettysburg,* p. 100; McLean, *Cutler's Brigade,* p. 54.

15. McLean, *Cutler's Brigade,* pp. 58–66; Martin, *Gettysburg,* p. 104.

16. Mead, "Journal," SHSW; *War Papers,* MOLLUS, Wisconsin, 2, p. 210; Ladd and Ladd, *Bachelder Papers,* 1, pp. 335, 336; Account of July 1, 1863, probably by E. P. Halstead, staff officer, First Corps, Wadsworth Papers, LC; *OR,* 27, 1, p. 244.

17. Second Wisconsin File, CR, NA; Busey and Martin, *Regimental Strengths,* p. 23; Otis, *Second Wisconsin,* p. 84; Charles H. Veil–D. McConaughy, April 7, 1864, Brake Collection, USAMHI; Beecham, *Gettysburg,* p. 65.

18. Otis, *Second Wisconsin,* p. 84; Hughes, "Report," SHSW; Ladd and Ladd, *Bachelder Papers,* 1, p. 386; *War Papers,* MOLLUS, Wisconsin, 2, p. 210; McLean, *Cutler's Brigade,* p. 212.

19. Charles H. Veil–D. McConaughy, April 7, 1864, Brake Collection, USAMHI; Otis, *Second Wisconsin,* pp. 290–91; Martin, *Gettysburg,* pp. 142–43.

20. Ladd and Ladd, *Bachelder Papers,* 1, p. 336; Mead, "Journal," SHSW; *War Papers,* MOLLUS, Wisconsin, 2, p. 210; Otis, *Second Wisconsin,* p. 85.

21. *OR,* 27, 1, p. 279; *ORS,* 5, p. 124; Ladd and Ladd, *Bachelder Papers,* 1, p. 140; Rood, Memoir, p. 60, SHSW; William Orr–Maggie, July 27, 1863, Orr Papers, IU; Shue, *Morning,* p. 133.

22. Martin, *Gettysburg,* p. 156; as he correctly notes, the origin of the story remains dubious.

23. *OR,* 27, 1, p. 267; Ladd and Ladd, *Bachelder Papers,* 1, p. 336; Smith, *Twenty-fourth Michigan,* p. 126; Russell Root–Grand Father, August 23, 1863, Root Letter, USAMHI; Fairchild file, CSR, NA.

24. Smith, *Twenty-fourth Michigan,* p. 126; *Record,* 24, p. 115; Abel G. Peck–Child, November 2, 1862, Peck Letters, MSU; *OR,* 27, 1, p. 267.

25. *OR,* 27, 1, pp. 268, 279; *ORS,* 5, p. 124; Otis, *Second Wisconsin,* p. 85; William W. Dudley–E. D. Townsend, June 20, 1878, Nineteenth Indiana Infantry File, GNMP; Ladd and Ladd, *Bachelder Papers,* 1, p. 642; Storch and Storch, "What a Deadly Trap," *Gettysburg Magazine,* 6, p. 26.

26. Ladd and Ladd, *Bachelder Papers,* 1, p. 140; Muncie *Press,* October 8, 1908; *National Tribune,* December 30, 1896; Gaff, *On Many a Bloody Field,* pp. 13, 170, 256; *Report of the Adjutant General,* 2, p. 406.

27. McLean, *Cutler's Brigade,* Chapters 5 and 6; Rufus R. Dawes–I. D. Wood, July 17, 1863, Adjutant General's Records, Series 1200, SHSW.

28. Rufus R. Dawes–I. D. Wood, July 17, 1863, Adjutant General's Records, Series 1200, SHSW; Noble, Diary," UM; Busey and Martin, *Regimental*

Strengths, p. 23; *Sketches,* MOLLUS, Ohio, 3, pp. 364, 365; Herdegen and Beaudot, *In the Bloody Railroad Cut,* p. 179.

29. Rufus R. Dawes–I. D. Wood, July 17, 1863, Adjutant General's Records, Series 1200, SHSW; Herdegen and Beaudot, *In the Bloody Railroad Cut,* p. 182; Long, "Mississippian," *Gettysburg Magazine,* 4, p. 23.

30. Rufus R. Dawes–My dear Mary, July 14, 1863, Dawes Papers, SHSW; Milwaukee *Sunday Telegraph,* April 27, 1890; Newspaper clipping, July 1, File, GNMP; Herdegen and Beaudot, *In the Bloody Railroad Cut,* p. 182.

31. Rufus R. Dawes–I. D. Wood, July 17, 1863, Adjutant General's Records, Series 1200, SHSW; *Sketches,* MOLLUS, Ohio, 3, p. 368; Martin, *Gettysburg,* pp. 125, 126.

32. Rufus R. Dawes–My dear Mary, July 14, 1863, Dawes Papers, SHSW; *Sketches,* MOLLUS, Ohio, 3, p. 368; Rufus R. Dawes–I. P. Wood, July 17, 1863, Adjutant General's Records, Series 1200, SHSW; Herdegen and Beaudot, *In the Bloody Railroad Cut,* pp. 185, 186.

33. Hartwig, "Guts," *Gettysburg Magazine,* 1, p. 13; Rufus R. Dawes–I. P. Wood, July 17, 1863, Adjutant General's Records, Series 1200, SHSW; McLean, *Cutler's Brigade,* pp. 106–8.

34. Herdegen and Beaudot, *In the Bloody Railroad Cut,* pp. 188, 190; Herdegen and Beaudot, "With the Iron Brigade," *Gettysburg Magazine,* 1, pp. 29, 32; *Sketches,* MOLLUS, Ohio, 3, p. 368; OR, 27, 1, p. 277; Rufus R. Dawes–My dear Mary, July 6, 1863, Dawes Papers, SHSW; *Roster of Wisconsin Volunteers,* 1, p. 502.

35. George Fairfield–J. A. Watrous, n.d., Earl M. Rogers–J. A. Watrous, n.d., Watrous Papers, SHSW; Beaudot, "Francis Asbury Waller," *Gettysburg Magazine,* 4, p. 18.

36. Earl M. Rogers–J. A. Watrous, n.d., Watrous Papers, SHSW; Herdegen and Beaudot, *In the Bloody Railroad Cut,* pp. 199, 200.

37. Herdegen and Beaudot, *In the Bloody Railroad Cut,* pp. 200, 202; *Roster of Wisconsin Volunteers,* 1, pp. 529, 532; Beaudot, "Francis Asbury Waller," *Gettysburg Magazine,* 4, pp. 18, 20; Dawes, *Service,* p. 161; W. B. Murphy–Rufus R. Dawes, June 20, 1892, W. B. Murphy–F. A. Dearborn, June 29, 1900, Dawes Papers, SHSW.

38. Milwaukee *Sentinel,* July 20, 1863; Rufus R. Dawes–I. P. Wood, July 17, 1863, Adjutant General's Records, Series 1200, SHSW; Bandy and Freeland, *Gettysburg Papers,* 1, p. 238; McLean, *Cutler's Brigade,* p. 115; Clark, *Histories,* 3, p. 298; Herdegen and Beaudot, *In the Bloody Railroad Cut,* pp. 202, 205.

39. Rufus R. Dawes–I. P. Wood, July 17, 1863, Adjutant General's Records, Series 1200, SHSW; *Sketches,* MOLLUS, Ohio, 3, pp. 371, 372.

40. Rufus R. Dawes–I. P. Wood, July 17, 1863, Adjutant General's Records, Series 1200, SHSW; Herdegen and Beaudot, *In the Bloody Railroad Cut,* p. 211.

41. Martin, *Gettysburg,* Chapters 5 and 6; Busey and Martin, *Regimental Strengths,* pp. 150, 172.

42. Martin, *Gettysburg,* Chapters 5 and 6; Busey and Martin, *Regimental Strengths,* pp. 20, 78.

43. Hartwig, "Defense," *Gettysburg Magazine,* 1, p. 17; Martin, *Gettysburg,* pp. 342, 343, 355.

44. Hartwig, "Defense," *Gettysburg Magazine,* 1, p. 17; William W. Dudley–E. D. Townsend, June 20, 1878, Nineteenth Indiana Infantry File, GNMP.

45. Martin, *Gettysburg,* pp. 220–47, 342–55; Busey and Martin, *Regimental Strengths,* p. 173.

46. Louis Young–William J. Baker, February 10, 1864, Winston Papers, NCSA; Clark, *Histories,* 2, pp. 344, 348; John Musser–[Friend], September 15, 1863, Musser Civil War Letters, USAMHI; Busey and Martin, *Regimental Strengths,* p. 174; Curtis, *History,* p. 160.

47. Louis Young–William J. Baker, February 10, 1864, Winston Papers, NCSA; Clark, *Histories,* 2, p. 351; Hadden, "Deadly Embrace," *Gettysburg Magazine,* 5, pp. 27, 28; *OR,* 27, 1, p. 268.

48. *OR,* 27, 1, p. 268; Louis Young–William J. Baker, February 10, 1864, Winston Papers, NCSA; Clark, *Histories,* 2, pp. 351, 352; Hadden, "Deadly Embrace," *Gettysburg Magazine,* 5, pp. 28, 29.

49. Clark, *Histories,* 2, p. 352; Hadden, "Deadly Embrace," *Gettysburg Magazine,* 5, p. 29; *OR,* 27, 1, pp. 268, 269; Transcript of a reunion address by Henry C. Marsh, August 1913, Marsh Letters and Diary, ISL.

50. *OR,* 27, 1, p. 269; Hadden, "Deadly Embrace," *Gettysburg Magazine,* 5, pp. 28, 29; Russell Root–Grand Father, August 23, 1863, Root Letter, USAMHI; Curtis, *History,* pp. 160, 167; Gettysburg Newspaper Clippings, 6, p. 199, GNMP.

51. William W. Dudley–E. D. Townsend, June 20, 1878, Nineteenth Indiana Infantry File, GNMP; Gaff, "Here Was Made," *Gettysburg Magazine,* 2, p. 29; Dunn, *Iron Men,* p. 189.

52. *ORS,* 5, p. 125; Hartwig, "Defense," *Gettysburg Magazine,* 1, pp. 23, 24; Gaff, *On Many a Bloody Field,* p. 260; Muncie *Press,* October 8, 1908.

53. *ORS,* 5, p. 125; Gaff, "Here Was Made," *Gettysburg Magazine,* 2, pp. 29, 30; William Orr–Maggie, July 27, 1863, Orr Papers, IU; Gaff, *On Many a Bloody Field,* p. 260.

54. *ORS,* 5, p. 125; Gaff, "Here Was Made," *Gettysburg Magazine,* 2, p. 30; William Orr–Maggie, July 27, 1863, Orr Papers, IU; W. B. Taylor–Mother, July 29, 1863, Eleventh North Carolina Infantry File, GNMP.

55. *OR,* 27, 1, pp. 269, 270; Curtis, *History,* p. 161; Sword, "Iron Brigade," *Gettysburg Magazine,* 7, pp. 7, 11; Smith, *Twenty-fourth Michigan,* p. 130; Morrow file, CSR, NA.

56. *OR,* 27, 1, pp. 279, 280; George H. Legate–Sister, December 27, 1862, Postscript, Legate Letter, FSNMP.

57. Clark, *Histories,* 2, p. 374; 3, p. 237; Curtis, *History,* p. 167; Louis Young–William J. Baker, February 10, 1864, Winston Papers, NCSA; Busey and Martin, *Regimental Strengths,* p. 174; Fox, *Regimental Losses,* pp. 556, 556n.

58. Martin, *Gettysburg,* pp. 398–400, 421; Busey and Martin, *Regimental Strengths,* p. 179.

59. Martin, *Gettysburg,* pp. 403–4, 406, 421; Dawes, *Service,* p. 175; *OR,* 27, 1, p. 280; Clark, *Histories,* 2, p. 692.

60. Miller, "Perrin's Brigade," *Gettysburg Magazine,* 13, p. 26; Martin, *Gettysburg,* pp. 412, 413, 421.

61. Russell Root–Grand Father, August 23, 1863, Root Letter, USAMHI; William W. Dudley–E. D. Townsend, June 20, 1878, Nineteenth Indiana Infantry File, GNMP; *National Tribune,* August 20, 1881; Hawkins, "Sergeant-Major," *Indiana Magazine of History,* 34, 2, pp. 215, 216; Smith, *Twenty-fourth Michigan,* p. 137; Curtis, *History,* pp. 181, 182; Clark, *Histories,* 5, pp. 611, 612, 615; Ladd and Ladd, *Bachelder Papers,* 1, p. 616.

62. William Orr–Maggie, July 27, 1863, Orr Papers, IU.

63. Herdegen, "Lieutenant," *Gettysburg Magazine,* 4, p. 28; George Fairfield–J. A. Watrous, n.d., Watrous Papers, SHSW.

64. George Fairfield–J. A. Watrous, n.d., Watrous Papers, SHSW; Hubler, "Narrative," p. 6, USAMHI.

65. Martin, *Gettysburg,* Chapter 9.

66. Ibid., p. 581; Jacob F. Slagle–Brother, September 13, 1863, Slagle Letter, USAMHI; *OR,* 27, 1, p. 174; Busey and Martin, *Regimental Strengths,* p. 20.

67. Charles W. Fuller–Brother, July 20, 1863, Fuller Papers, SHSW; *OR,* 27, 1, p. 173; Table of Casualties, Adjutant General's Records, Series 1200, SHSW; Herdegen, *Men Stood,* p. 4; Dunn, *Iron Men,* p. 200.

68. Rufus R. Dawes–My dear Mary, July 4, 1863, Dawes Papers, SHSW; *ORS,* 5, pp. 125, 126; Curtis, *History,* pp. 164, 165, 167, 180; *War Papers,* MOLLUS, Wisconsin, 2, pp. 210, 212; *OR,* 27, 1, p. 270; Fox, *Regimental Losses,* pp. 17, 29, 30, 33, 36, 439; Detroit *Advertiser and Tribune,* July 16, 1863.

69. Diary, Marsh Letters and Diary, ISL; *OR,* 27, 1, p. 254; Milwaukee *Sunday Telegraph,* April 27, 1890; Coco, *Civil War Infantryman,* p. 138.

70. *OR,* 27, 2, pp. 503, 504; J. Q. A. Nadenbousch's report, n.d., Nadenbousch Papers, DU; Lexington *Gazette and Citizen,* August 16, 1888.

71. Busey and Martin, *Regimental Strengths,* p. 154; Ferdinand J. Dunlap–Sister, June 22, 1863, Dunlap Letters, USAMHI; Lord, *Fremantle Diary,* p. 202.

72. Wert, *General James Longstreet,* pp. 257–59; *OR,* 27, 2, p. 308.

73. Wert, *General James Longstreet,* Chapter 13.

74. Ibid., quotation on p. 278.

75. *OR,* 27, 2, pp. 318–19, 446; Coddington, *Gettysburg Campaign,* pp. 367, 428; Pfanz, *Gettysburg: Culp's Hill and Cemetery Hill,* p. 111, 205–6.

76. Pfanz, *Gettysburg: Culp's Hill and Cemetery Hill,* pp. 111–12, 204.

77. Ibid., Chapter 13, pp. 287–88.

78. Ibid., pp. 163, 166, 167, 287, 288; J. Q. A. Nadenbousch's report, n.d., Nadenbousch Papers, DU.

79. David Hunter–Mother, July 2, 1863, Second Virginia Infantry File, GNMP.

80. Pfanz, *Gettysburg: Culp's Hill and Cemetery Hill,* pp. 287–90; *OR,* 27, 2, p. 519.

81. The best account of the struggle for Culp's Hill is in Pfanz, *Gettysburg: Culp's Hill and Cemetery Hill,* Chapters 16–18.

82. Ibid., p. 314; *OR,* 27, 2, p. 519.

83. *OR,* 27, 2, pp. 519, 530; B. H. Coffman–Wife, July 12, 1863, Coffman Letters, USAMHI; Moore, *Story,* p. 200.

84. James L. Welsh–Brother, May 26, June 2, 1861, John P. Welsh–Brother, May 23, 1861, Welsh Family Papers, WL; John P. Welsh–Wife, July 8, 1863, Welsh

Papers, VSL; Bean, "House Divided," *VMHB,* 59, 4, pp. 397, 398; Reidenbaugh, *33rd Virginia Infantry,* p. 183.

85. Givens B. Strickler, Biographical Sketch, McDowell Correspondence, WL.

86. *OR,* 27, 2, pp. 519, 523, 526, 527, 528, 531; Robertson, *4th Virginia Infantry,* p. 28; Pfanz, *Gettysburg: Culp's Hill and Cemetery Hill,* pp. 325, 326.

87. Pfanz, *Gettysburg: Culp's Hill and Cemetery Hill,* pp. 328, 352; *OR,* 27, 2, p. 341; Wallace, *5th Virginia Infantry,* p. 50; J. Q. A. Nadenbousch's report, n.d., Nadenbousch Papers, DU; Frye, *2nd Virginia Infantry,* p. 55.

88. Wert, *General James Longstreet,* pp. 283–93.

89. Ibid., p. 293.

90. McMullen, *Surgeon,* pp. 54–55.

91. Frye, *2nd Virginia Infantry,* p. 55.

92. Herdegen, *Men Stood,* pp. 5–6, 9; Rufus R. Dawes–My dear Mary, July 4, 1863, Dawes Papers, SHSW.

93. Rufus R. Dawes–My dear Mary, July 4, 1863, Dawes Papers, SHSW; Detroit *Free Press,* July 17, 1863.

94. Reid-Green, *Letters Home,* p. 60.

95. William Orr–Maggie, July 27, 1863, Orr Papers, IU; Rufus R. Dawes–My dear Mary, July 6, 1863, Dawes Papers, SHSW.

96. Longhenry, "Yankee Piper," p. 3-25, ANB; *OR,* 27, 1, pp. 173–87.

97. Detroit *Free Press,* July 14, 1863; Longhenry, "Yankee Piper," p. 3-26, ANB; Henry F. Young–Father, July 11, 1863, Young Papers, SHSW; Rufus R. Dawes–My dear Mary, July 14, 1863, Dawes Papers, SHSW; Noble, "Diary," UM.

98. Herdegen, *Men Stood,* p. 17.

CHAPTER 14: TWO RIVERS

1. Wert, *General James Longstreet,* pp. 298–99.

2. Robertson, *Stonewall Brigade,* p. 210.

3. The best analysis of Confederate morale after Gettysburg is in Gallagher, *Third Day,* pp. 1–22.

4. John Garibaldi–Wife, August 4, [15], 1862, Garibaldi Letters, VMI.

5. Ibid., September 25, 1863.

6. Waddy C. Charlton–Oliver, two letters dated August 31, 1863, Charlton Family Papers, VT.

7. Long, *Civil War,* pp. 419–20.

8. Ibid., pp. 420–24.

9. John N. Hull–My Dear Friend, November 22, 1863, Hull Letter, VT; Daniel Hileman–Rachel A. McCutchan, November 17, 1863, Hileman Civil War Letters, WL; John Garibaldi–Wife, November 21, 1863, Garibaldi Letters, VMI.

10. John Garibaldi–Wife, November 15, 1863, Garibaldi Letters, VMI; Robertson, *Stonewall Brigade,* p. 212; Turner, *Ted Barclay,* p. 116; John N. Hull–My Dear Friend, November 22, 1863, Hull Letter, VT.

11. Long, *Civil War,* pp. 438–39.

12. *OR,* 29, 1, pp. 847, 849; Frye, *2nd Virginia Infantry,* pp. 57, 60.

13. *OR,* 29, 1, pp. 849, 851, 853, 855.

14. Casualty figures in *OR,* 29, 1, p. 837, totaled 144; in a table in Confederate States Army Casualties, NA, reported losses were 153.
15. Long, *Civil War,* pp. 440–42.
16. Casler, *Four Years,* p. 204; Colt, *Defend the Valley,* p. 297.
17. Frye, *2nd Virginia Infantry,* pp. 80–142; Robertson, *4th Virginia Infantry,* pp. 37–84; Wallace, *5th Virginia Infantry,* p. 77; Reidenbaugh, *27th Virginia Infantry,* pp. 127–85; Reidenbaugh, *33rd Virginia Infantry,* p. 57; General Orders, January 20, October 7, 24, November 4, December 7, 1863, January 21, 27, 28, March 8, 1864, Orders and Circulars, NA.
18. Turner, *Ted Barclay,* pp. 118, 119, 120.
19. *Roster of Wisconsin Volunteers,* 1, p. 569; Diary and Edwin Currier–[?], August 15, 1863, Currier Papers, SHSW.
20. Gaff, *On Many a Bloody Field,* p. 287; James Converse–Mary, September 4, 1863, Converse Letters, CHS.
21. Gaff, *On Many a Bloody Field,* p. 288.
22. Rufus R. Dawes–My dear Mary, August 6, 1863, Dawes Papers, SHSW.
23. Ibid.; Dunn, *Iron Men,* p. 217.
24. Rood, Memoir, pp. 70–71, SHSW; Elmer Wallace–Parents and all at home, August 4, 1863, Wallace Papers, UM; Dunn, *Iron Men,* p. 191; *OR,* 29, 2, p. 119.
25. Elmer Wallace–Parents and all at home, August 4, 1863, Wallace Papers, UM; Longhenry, "Yankee Piper," p. 3-31, ANB; Dawes, *Service,* p. 202; Noble, "Diary," UM.
26. Gladstone, "A Flag for the Iron Brigade," *Military Images,* 9, 1, p. 26; Madaus, "Into the Fury," *WMH,* 69, 1, p. 29; Rood, Memoir, p. 73, SHSW.
27. Noble, "Diary," UM; Otis, *Second Wisconsin,* p. 91; Longhenry, "Yankee Piper," p. 3-32, ANB; Rood, Memoir, p. 73, SHSW.
28. Madaus, "Into the Fury," *WMH,* 69, 1, pp. 29, 30; Gladstone, "A Flag for the Iron Brigade," *Military Images,* 9, 1, p. 26.
29. Noble, "Diary," UM; Gladstone, "A Flag for the Iron Brigade," *Military Images,* 9, 1, p. 26; Dawes, *Services,* p. 205; Jackson, Diary, IHS; Rood, Memoir, p. 74, SHSW.
30. Noble, "Diary," UWRF; Dean, Diary, SHSW; Nevins, *Diary,* p. 295; Rood, Memoir, pp. 79–81, SHSW; Dawes, *Service,* pp. 208–20.
31. Jackson, Diary, IHS; Dawes, *Service,* pp. 221–23.
32. Noble, "Diary," UWRF; Cheek and Pointon, *History,* p. 82; William Orr–Father, September 28, 1863, Orr Papers, IU.
33. *OR,* 29, 1, p. 217; Jackson, Diary, IHS; Noble, "Diary," UWRF; Longhenry, "Yankee Piper," pp. 3-34, 3-37, ANB.
34. William Orr–Father, October 25, 1863, Orr Papers, IU; Noble, "Diary," UM; Resolution to Solomon Meredith, Officers of the Iron Brigade of the West, October 18, 1863, Meredith Papers, IHS.
35. Longhenry, "Yankee Piper," p. 3-38, ANB; Warner, *Generals in Blue,* p. 320.
36. *Roster of Wisconsin Volunteers,* 1, p. 345; Fairchild file, CSR, NA; Warner, *Generals in Blue,* p. 148; Curtis, *History,* p. 210; *Record,* 24, p. 53.
37. *OR,* 29, 1, pp. 678, 689, 690; Mead, "Journal," SHSW; James Converse–Wife and Children, December 7, 1863, Converse Letters, CHS.

38. Jesse M. Roberts–Brother, December 16, 1863, Roberts Letters, SHSW; Dawes, *Service,* pp. 234–38; James Converse–Affectionate Companion, December 19, 31, 1863, Converse Letters, CHS; Rood, Memoir, p. 91, SHSW.

39. *OR,* 29, 2, pp. 558, 560; Longhenry, "Yankee Piper," pp. 3-34, 3-40, ANB; Jackson, Diary, IHS; Gaff, *On Many a Bloody Field,* p. 312; Dawes, *Service,* p. 233.

40. *OR,* 29, 2, p. 558; Beaudot and Herdegen, *Irishman,* p. 119; Noble, "Diary," UM; Dawes, *Service,* p. 235.

41. Rood, Memoir, pp. 91, 92; Longhenry, "Yankee Piper," pp. 3–40, ANB; Dawes, *Service,* p. 236; *ORS,* 28, p. 461; Turner, *Chronology,* p. 93; Jackson, Diary, IHS; Wilson, *Indiana Battle Flags,* p. 156.

42. Kite, Diary, HL; John Garibaldi–Wife, January 9, 1864, Garibaldi Letters, VMI.

43. John Garibaldi–Wife, January 9, April 22, 1864, Garibaldi Letters, VMI; Waddy C. Charlton–Oliver, February 1, 1864, Charlton Family Papers, VT; Reidenbaugh, *27th Virginia Infantry,* p. 93.

44. Reidenbaugh, *27th Virginia Infantry,* p. 93; Casler, *Four Years,* pp. 205, 206.

45. Wallace, *5th Virginia Infantry,* p. 54; Casler, *Four Years,* p. 204.

46. Wallace, *5th Virginia Infantry,* p. 54; Reidenbaugh, *27th Virginia Infantry,* pp. 92, 93.

47. Frye, *2nd Virginia Infantry,* pp. 61–62, 125; Krick, *Lee's Colonels,* p. 263.

48. Reidenbaugh, *33rd Virginia Infantry,* pp. 81, 125, 126.

49. John Garibaldi–Wife, March 24, 1864, Garibaldi Letters, VMI; Turner, *Ted Barclay,* p. 137; Waddy C. Charlton–Oliver, March 27, 1864, Charlton Family Papers, VT.

50. Kite, Diary, HL; Turner, *Ted Barclay,* pp. 138–40.

51. Reidenbaugh, *27th Virginia Infantry,* p. 94.

52. Turner, *Ted Barclay,* p. 144.

53. William Orr–Father, March 5, 1864, Orr Papers, IU; Rood, Memoir, p. 97, SHSW; Turner, *Chronology,* pp. 93, 96; Wilson, *Indiana Battle Flags,* p. 156.

54. Elmer Wallace–Parents, February 15, 1864, Wallace Papers, UM; Rood, Memoir, p. 97, SHSW; Cheek and Pointon, *History,* pp. 88, 89; Dawes, *Service,* pp. 235–37.

55. Loring Winslow–Parents, March 10, 11, 1864, Winslow Letters, SHSW; Dawes, *Service,* p. 238; Curtis, *History,* p. 346; Reid-Green, *Letters Home,* p. 75.

56. William Orr–Maggie, January 24, 1864, Orr Papers, IU; William J. Ketner–[?], March 6, 1864, Ketner Papers, SHSW; Elmer Wallace–Parents, February 11, 1864, Friends at Home, March 8, 1864, Mother, Father, and Friends in General, March 17, 1864, Wallace Papers, UM; *ORS,* 43, p. 468.

57. Gaff, *On Many a Bloody Field,* p. 332.

58. Curtis, *History,* p. 221; Dawes, *Service,* p. 239.

59. Rhea, *Battle of the Wilderness,* pp. 37–41.

60. William Orr–Father, March 28, 1864, Orr Papers, IU; Elmer Wallace–Parents, April 5, 1864, Wallace Papers, UM; Rood, Memoir, p. 99, SHSW; Dawes, *Service,* p. 240.

61. *OR*, 36, 1, p. 110; Warner, *Generals in Blue*, p. 110; Dawes, *Service*, pp. 247–49.

62. Rhea, *Battle of the Wilderness*, p. 35; Rufus R. Dawes–My dear Wife, May 1, 1864, Dawes Papers, SHSW.

63. Rhea, *Battle of the Wilderness*, pp. 60–74; Dunn, *Iron Men*, p. 238.

CHAPTER 15: "PLAYED OUT"

1. Warner, *Generals in Blue*, pp. 183–85; Rhea, *Battle of the Wilderness*, pp. 41–42.

2. Rhea, *Battle of the Wilderness*, p. 41.

3. Ibid., Chapter 2.

4. The best study of the Wilderness is Rhea, *Battle of the Wilderness*, *passim*.

5. Ibid., pp. 138, 139, 142, 157; Curtis, *History*, p. 230; Dawes, *Service*, p. 259; Dunn, *Iron Men*, p. 236.

6. Buckles, "Battle," p. 1, ISL; Dawes, *Service*, pp. 259, 260; Rood, Memoir, p. 100, SHSW; Rhea, *Battle of the Wilderness*, p. 157.

7. Dawes, *Service*, p. 260; Buckles, "Battle," p. 2, ISL; Rood, Memoir, p. 100, SHSW; Muncie *Press*, October 8, 1908.

8. Rhea, *Battle of the Wilderness*, p. 160; Rood, Memoir, p. 100, SHSW; Curtis, *History*, pp. 232, 233; Cheek and Pointon, *History*, p. 91; Medical Certificate, Morrow file, CSR, NA; *Roster of Wisconsin Volunteers*, 1, p. 494; *OR*, 36, 1, p. 125.

9. Rhea, *Battle of the Wilderness*, pp. 160, 162–63.

10. Ibid., Chapters 4 and 5; Curtis, *History*, p. 233.

11. Wallace, *5th Virginia Infantry*, p. 141; McCown, Memoirs, HL.

12. McCown, Memoirs, HL.

13. Kite, Diary, HL; P. Key–Father, May 29, 1864, Key Family Papers, VT; Doyle, "Memoir," LC; Rhea, *Battle of the Wilderness*, pp. 25–26.

14. John Garibaldi–Wife, April 22, 1864, Garibaldi Letters, VMI.

15. Doyle, "Memoir," LC; Trudeau, *Bloody Roads South*, p. 54; Rhea, *Battle of the Wilderness*, pp. 124, 125.

16. Kite, Diary, HL; McCown, Memoirs, HL.

17. Rhea, *Battle of the Wilderness*, Chapter 4.

18. Ibid., p. 180n.

19. Ibid., pp. 181, 182; Doyle, "Memoir," LC.

20. Doyle, "Memoir," LC; McCown, Memoirs, HL.

21. Doyle, "Memoir," LC; Kite, Diary, HL; Reidenbaugh, *27th Virginia Infantry*, pp. 96, 144; Bosang, *Memoirs*, pp. 11–12; Krick, *Lee's Colonels*, p. 290.

22. Rhea, *Battle of the Wilderness*, p. 182; Warner, *Generals in Gray*, p. 288.

23. Doyle, "Memoir," LC; Rhea, *Battle of the Wilderness*, pp. 182, 183; McCown, Memoirs, HL.

24. Rhea, *Battle of the Wilderness*, Chapters 6–8.

25. Ibid., pp. 296, 304, 306, 308, 335; Rood, Memoir, pp. 101, 102, SHSW; Dawes, *Service*, pp. 261, 262; Gaff, *On Many a Bloody Field*, pp. 343–44.

26. Gaff, *On Many a Bloody Field*, p. 344; Jackson, Diary, IHS.

27. Rhea, *Battle of the Wilderness*, pp. 363, 448–50; Gaff, *On Many a Bloody Field*, pp. 345, 350.

28. Rhea, *Battle of the Wilderness*, pp. 436, 440; *OR*, 36, 1, p. 125.

29. Rhea, *Battles*, pp. 50–52; *OR*, 36, 1, p. 618.

30. *OR*, 36, 1, pp. 618–19; Rood, Memoir, pp. 104, 106, 107, SHSW; Dawes, *Service*, pp. 264, 265; Chamberlin, *History*, pp. 225, 226; Cheek and Pointon, *History*, pp. 95, 96; Rhea, *Battles*, pp. 145, 148.

31. Dawes, *Service*, p. 267; Rhea, *Battles*, pp. 286, 288, 289, 303.

32. Rhea, *Battles*, pp. 90–91, 226; Matter, *If It Takes All Summer*, pp. 103, 104.

33. Rhea, *Battles*, pp. 172, 219, 234; Matter, *If It Takes All Summer*, pp. 162, 164, 167; Doyle, "Memoir," LC; Richmond *Sentinel*, June 3, 1864.

34. Rhea, *Battles*, p. 220; Kite, Diary, HL; Doyle, "Memoir," LC.

35. Rhea, *Battles*, pp. 212–31.

36. Ibid., pp. 231–40; Caldwell, *Stonewall Jim*, p. 104; *SHSP*, 21, pp. 235, 236; Colt, *Defend the Valley*, p. 313.

37. Rhea, *Battles*, pp. 233, 235, 240; Kite, Diary, HL.

38. McCown, Memoirs, HL; Wallace, *5th Virginia Infantry*, p. 59; Colt, *Defend the Valley*, pp. 313, 314.

39. Doyle, "Memoir," LC; Caldwell, *Stonewall Jim*, pp. 109, 110; Colt, *Defend the Valley*, p. 314.

40. McCown, Memoirs, HL; Rhea, *Battles*, pp. 241, 242; *CV*, 36, p. 50; *OR*, 36, 1, p. 441; Description of Battleflag, 4th Virginia Infantry, ANB.

41. Rhea, *Battles*, Chapter 8, pp. 311–12.

42. Robertson, *Stonewall Brigade*, p. 226; Frye, *2nd Virginia Infantry*, p. 64; *OR*, 36, 2, p. 1001; Worsham, *One of Jackson's Foot Cavalry*, pp. 141, 142; Reidenbaugh, *27th Virginia Infantry*, p. 103.

43. *OR*, 36, 1, p. 813; Robertson, *Stonewall Brigade*, p. 228; Robertson, *4th Virginia Infantry*, p. 76.

44. Trudeau, *Bloody Roads South*, p. 211.

45. Rufus R. Dawes–My dear Wife, May 14, [1864], Dawes Papers, SHSW.

46. Ibid., May 14, 16, 1864; *OR*, 36, 1, p. 143; Dawes, *Service*, pp. 255, 257.

47. Rood, Memoir, pp. 110, 115, 117, 120, 125, 129, 130, 136, 138, SHSW; *Roster of Wisconsin Volunteers*, 1, p. 572.

48. Long, *Civil War*, pp. 507–20.

49. *OR*, 36, 1, pp. 158, 171, 203, 612; Cheek and Pointon, *History*, p. 107; *Roster of Wisconsin Volunteers*, 1, p. 597; Dawes, *Service*, p. 279; Gaff, *On Many a Bloody Field*, p. 350.

50. Henry F. Young–Delia, May 24, 1864, Father, June 8, 1864, Young Papers, SHSW; Dawes, *Service*, p. 284; Elmer Wallace–Parents, May 30, 1864, Wallace Papers, UM; Rufus R. Dawes–My dear Wife, June 1, 3, 4, 1864, Dawes Papers, SHSW.

51. Otis, *Second Wisconsin*, pp. 7–11, 99; Elmer Wallace–Parents, June 7, 1864, Wallace Papers, UM.

52. Second Wisconsin file, CR, NA; Otis, *Second Wisconsin*, p. 99; Reid-Green, *Letters Home*, p. 81; Curtis, *History*, p. 258; Henry F. Young–Father, June 27, 1864, Young Papers, SHSW; William Orr–My own Dearest Wife, June 20, 1864, Orr Papers, IU.

53. Long, *Civil War*, pp. 520–25.

54. Ibid., pp. 523–25.
55. Rufus R. Dawes–My dear Wife, June 19, 21, 1864, Dawes Papers, SHSW; William Orr–My own Dearest Wife, June 20, 1864, Orr Papers, IU; Gaff, *On Many a Bloody Field*, p. 363; Cheek and Pointon, *History*, pp. 114–16; Loring Winslow–Parents, June 19, 1864, Winslow Letters, SHSW.
56. Sixth Wisconsin file, CR, NA; Curtis, *History*, pp. 263–64; Henry F. Young–Father, June 27, 1864, Young Papers, SHSW; Cheek and Pointon, *History*, p. 127; *Roster of Wisconsin Volunteers*, 1, p. 499.
57. Rufus R. Dawes–My dear Father, June 23, July 2, 1864, Dawes Papers, SHSW; Elmer Wallace–Mother and Father, July 17, 1864, Wallace Papers, UM; Henry F. Young–Father, July 26, August 6, 1864, Young Papers, SHSW.
58. Jackson, Diary, IHS; William J. Ketner–Mother, July 20, 1864, Ketner Papers, SHSW; Special Orders, No. 183, July 27, 1864, Orr Papers, IU; Dawes, *Service*, p. 301; Dawes file, CSR, NA.
59. *OR*, 36, 1, p. 545; 42, 1, pp. 125, 534, 535; Cheek and Pointon, *History*, pp. 132, 135; Reid-Green, *Letters Home*, pp. 94, 95; Mark Tinnicum-Adjutant General, October 10, 1864, Adjutant General's Records, Series 1200, SHSW; Dawes, *Service*, pp. 307–10.
60. Chamberlin, *History*, pp. 278, 279; Perry Diary, Perry Papers, SHSW; Dawes, *Service*, p. 300; Smith, *Twenty-fourth Michigan*, p. 225; Warner, *Generals in Blue*, p. 42; Bragg file, CSR, NA.
61. Special Orders, No. 317, September 23, 1864, William Orr–Father, October 3, 1864, Orr Papers, IU; *OR*, 42, 1, p. 64; *ORS*, 48, p. 466; Perry Diary, Perry Papers, SHSW; Gaff, *On Many a Bloody Field*, p. 383.
62. Perry Diary, Perry Papers, SHSW; Elmer Wallace–Father, December 19, 1864, Wallace Papers, UM; Morrow, Diary, USAMHI; Peter Larsen–Wife, November 25, 1864, Larsen Papers, SHSW; Luther Hemingway-Edith, December 18, 1864, Hemingway Letter, UM; Cheek and Pointon, *History*, pp. 143, 144; Loring Winslow–Parents, November 9, December 18, 1864, Winslow Letters, SHSW; Sixth Wisconsin file, CR, NA; General Orders, No. 6, Gallup Papers, SHSW; Reid-Green, *Letters Home*, p. 98.
63. Morrow, Diary, USAMHI; Erwin H. Flagg–Sister, February 14, 1865, Flagg Letters, SHSW; Reid-Green, *Letters Home*, p. 107; Chamberlin, *History*, p. 293.
64. Curtis, *History*, p. 294; Morrow, Diary, USAMHI.
65. Curtis, *History*, pp. 294, 295; Morrow, Diary, USAMHI.
66. Curtis, *History*, pp. 295–297; Newspaper clipping, Green Papers, UM.
67. Curtis, *History*, pp. 312, 314, 317; Newspaper clipping, Green Papers, UM; Smith, *Twenty-fourth Michigan*, p. 254; Elmer Wallace–Parents, March 2, April 12, 1865, Wallace Papers, UM; *ORS*, 43, p. 461.
68. Loring Winslow–Brother, February 19, 1865, Winslow Letters, SHSW; Cheek and Pointon, *History*, p. 157; Reid-Green, *Letters Home*, p. 114; Nolan, *Iron Brigade*, pp. 279–81; Gaff, *On Many a Bloody Field*, pp. 412–18.
69. Nolan, *Iron Brigade*, p. 281.
70. Ibid., p. 281; Cheek and Pointon, *History*, p. 179; William H. Church–My Dearest Ella, May 14, 1865, Church Papers, SHSW; Curtis, *History*, p. 288; Morrow file, CSR, NA.

71. Gaff, *On Many a Bloody Field,* p. 463; Reid-Green, *Letters Home,* pp. 122–24.

72. Mooney, Memoir, VHS.

73. Wert, *From Winchester,* pp. 5–8.

74. Ibid., Chapters 1–3.

75. Ibid., Chapters 4–14.

76. Wallace, *5th Virginia Infantry,* p. 62; Colt, *Defend the Valley,* p. 296; Robertson, *Stonewall Brigade,* p. 234; Krick, *Lee's Colonels,* pp. 45, 266.

77. Krick, *Lee's Colonels,* p. 370; H. J. Williams–Jedediah Hotchkiss, January 30, 1897, Hotchkiss Papers, LC; Wallace, *5th Virginia Infantry,* pp. 63, 64.

78. Mooney, Memoir, p. 4, VHS.

79. E. W. Key–My Dear Companion, November 27, 1864, Key Family Papers, VT; Mooney, Memoir, p. 5, VHS.

80. Driver, *Lexington,* p. 83; Reidenbaugh, *27th Virginia Infantry,* p. 116; George W. Slifer–Uncle, [January 1865], Slifer Letters, FSNMP.

81. Wallace, *5th Virginia Infantry,* p. 66; Robertson, *4th Virginia Infantry,* p. 34; John P. Dull–Giney, March 24, 1865, Dull Letters, WL.

82. Robertson, *4th Virginia Infantry,* pp. 34, 64.

83. Brock, *Appomattox Roster,* pp. 85, 88, 89, 90, 91, 93; Reidenbaugh, *27th Virginia Infantry,* p. 120; Riedenbaugh, *33rd Virginia Infantry,* p. 100; Wallace, *5th Virginia Infantry,* p. 67.

CHAPTER 16: A BROTHERHOOD OF VALOR

1. Figures conflict as to the total number of members in each brigade. The figures used in the text reflect this disparity and are derived from Frye, *2nd Virginia Infantry,* pp. 80–142; Robertson, *4th Virginia Infantry,* pp. 37–84; Wallace, *5th Virginia Infantry,* pp. 89–173; Reidenbaugh, *27th Virginia Infantry,* pp. 127–85; Reidenbaugh, *33rd Virginia Infantry,* pp. 111–47; Nolan, *Iron Brigade,* p. 162; Otis, *Second Wisconsin,* p. 12; Historical Table of the 7th Wis. Vet. Vols., Perry Papers, SHSW; *Record of Service,* 24, p. 3; Fox, *Regimental Losses,* pp. 8, 14; the best analysis of Civil War soldiers' motivations is McPherson, *For Cause and Comrades, passim.*

2. Robertson, *Stonewall Brigade,* p. vii.

3. Ibid., p. 25; R. J. Hancock–John W. Daniel, May 10, 1904, Daniel Papers, UVA.

4. Total deaths in the Stonewall Brigade were tabulated from the rosters cited on the pages in footnote No. 1 above; Fox, *Regimental Losses,* pp. 556–58; McPherson, *For Cause and Comrades,* p. ix.

5. Reidenbaugh, *27th Virginia Infantry,* p. 156.

6. Frye, *2nd Virginia Infantry,* pp. 80–142; Robertson, *4th Virginia Infantry,* pp. 37–84; Wallace, *5th Virginia Infantry,* pp. 89–173; Reidenbaugh, *27th Virginia Infantry,* pp. 127–85; Reidenbaugh, *33rd Virginia Infantry,* pp. 111–47.

7. Permanent desertion figures were compiled from rosters in sources cited above in footnote No. 6; Gallagher, *Antietam,* p. 46.

8. R. J. Hancock–John W. Daniel, May 10, 1904, Daniel Papers, UVA.

9. Fox, *Regimental Losses,* pp. 117, 343, 390, 393, 396, 397, 501, 511, 512.

10. Ibid., pp. 8, 11, 14; McPherson, *For Cause and Comrades,* p. ix.

11. Fox, *Regimental Losses,* pp. 3, 512; Otis, *Second Wisconsin,* p. 101; Curtis, *History,* p. 381; Historical Table of the 7th Wis. Vet. Vols., Perry Papers, SHSW.
12. Smith, *Twenty-fourth Michigan,* pp. 237–38, 299n.
13. McPherson, *For Cause and Comrades,* pp. 5, 18, 23, 35, 82, 85, 86, 91, 94, 168; Cheek and Pointon, *History,* p. 184; Historical Table of the 7th Wis. Vet. Vols., Perry Papers, SHSW; Otis, *Second Wisconsin,* p. 101; Curtis, *History,* pp. 392–94.
14. *Official Army Register,* 7, pp. 59, 60, 163, 164, 170, 171, 172, 173, 332, 333.
15. Table of Casualties, Adjutant General's Reports, Series 1200, SHSW.
16. Beaudot and Herdegen, *Irishman,* p. 5; Zeitlin, "Flags," *WMH,* 69, 1, pp. 53, 54; Nolan, *Iron Brigade,* p. 167; Robertson, *Stonewall Brigade,* pp. 246–47; Reminiscences, Rollin Papers, SHSW.

Bibliography

Manuscripts

Adjutant General Reports, Series 1200, Iron Brigade. State Historical Society of Wisconsin, Madison, WI.

Anderson, Eugene. Papers. Typescript. Sixth Wisconsin Infantry File. Library, Antietam National Battlefield, Sharpsburg, MD.

Andrews, A. D. Papers. Davee Library, University of Wisconsin—River Falls, River Falls, WI.

Arndt, P. J. Letter. Typescript. State Historical Society of Wisconsin, Madison, WI.

Atkinson, Archibald, Jr. Memoirs. Typescript. Special Collections, University Libraries, Virginia Tech University, Blacksburg, VA.

Bachman, A. O. Papers. Nineteenth Indiana Infantry File. Library, Antietam National Battlefield, Sharpsburg, MD.

Banks, Nathaniel. Intelligence Reports, Records Group 393, Entry 2223. National Archives, Washington, D.C.

Bard, David. Correspondence. Typescript. Archives, Handley Library, Winchester, VA.

Barnett, Thomas. Letter. State Historical Society of Wisconsin, Madison, WI.

Barton, Robert E. Recollections. Typescript. Virginia Historical Society, Richmond, VA.

Baylor, William S. H. Excerpt of letter to John Peyton Clark. Typescript. John Peyton Clark Journal. Louisa Crawford Collection. Archives, Handley Library, Winchester, VA.

Baylor, William Smith Hanger. Correspondence. Special Collections, University Libraries, Virginia Tech University, Blacksburg, VA.

Beard, James E. Diary. Typescript. Library, Fredericksburg-Spotsylvania National Military Park, Fredericksburg, VA.

Bedinger, George R. Letters. Caroline D. Dandridge Papers. Special Collections, William R. Perkins Library, Duke University, Durham, NC.

Beecham, Henry W. Letters. State Historical Society of Wisconsin, Madison, WI.

Benton, Thomas H. Civil War Letters. Indiana Historical Society, Indianapolis, IN.

Bird, Robert B. V. Family Papers. State Historical Society of Wisconsin, Madison, WI.

Blackford Family. Manuscripts, No. 5088. Alderman Library, University of Virginia, Charlottesville, VA.

Botts, Lawson. Collection. Preston Library, Virginia Military Institute, Lexington, VA.

Bragg, Edward S. Letter. Sixth Wisconsin Infantry File. Library, Antietam National Battlefield, Sharpsburg, MD.

Bragg, Edward S. Papers. State Historical Society of Wisconsin, Madison, WI.

Brake, Robert L. Collection. United States Army Military History Institute, Carlisle Barracks, PA.

Briggs, Edward L. "Personal History of Edward L. Briggs' Services in the War of the Rebellion, 1861–1865." Typescript copy in possession of Larry Briggs, Tillamook, OR.

Brindle, Asa. Letters. Ward Family Papers. Burton Historical Collection, Detroit Public Library, MI.

Brown, Edwin A. Letters. Typescript. State Historical Society of Wisconsin, Madison, WI.

Brown, Elon F. Daily Journal. *Civil War Times Illustrated* Collection. Archives, United States Army Military History Institute, Carlisle Barracks, PA.

Brown, W. Morton. Papers. Bowman-Howard-Domingos Collection. Middle Georgia Archives, Washington Library, Macon, GA.

Buckles, A. J. "Battle of Wilderness: Personal Recollections of A. J. Buckles." Typescript. Henry C. Marsh Collection. Indiana State Library, Indianapolis, IN.

Burdick, Jeremiah Greenman. Papers. Typescript. Library, Fredericksburg-Spotsylvania National Military Park, Fredericksburg, VA.

Campbell, Robert Henry. Letters. Campbell-Varner Papers. Preston Library, Virginia Military Institute, Lexington, VA.

Carman, Ezra. Papers. Library, Antietam National Battlefield, Sharpsburg, MD.

Carpenter, John C. Letter. Typescript Copy. Library, Manassas National Battlefield Park, Manassas, VA.

Carson, Robert P. Memoirs. Typescript. Virginia Historical Society, Richmond, VA.

Casler, John O. Letter. Bidgood Papers. Archives, Virginia State Library, Richmond.

Charlton Family. Papers. Special Collections, University Libraries, Virginia Tech University, Blacksburg, VA.

Chase, Julia. "War Time Diary of Miss Julia Chase, Winchester, Virginia, 1861–1864." Archives, Handley Library, Winchester, VA.

Chesson, Frederick W. Collection. *Civil War Times Illustrated* Collection. Archives, United States Army Military History Institute, Carlisle Barracks, PA.

Church, William Henry. Papers. State Historical Society of Wisconsin, Madison, WI.

Clark, Caleb Beal. Letters. State Historical Society of Wisconsin, Madison, WI.

Codwise, George A. Letters. Vreeland-Warden Papers. Archives, United States Army Military History Institute, Carlisle Barracks, PA.

Coffman, B. H. Letters. Civil War Miscellaneous Collection. Archives, United States Army Military History Institute, Carlisle Barracks, PA.

Coleman, Clayton. Papers. Confederate Soldiers and Units Collection. Eleanor S. Brockenbrough Library, Museum of the Confederacy, Richmond, VA.

Colston, Raleigh E. Papers. Southern Historical Collection. Wilson Library, University of North Carolina, Chapel Hill, NC.

Compiled Records Showing Service of Military Units in Volunteer Union Organizations. M594. National Archives, Washington, D.C.

Compiled Service Records. Records Group 94. National Archives, Washington, D.C.

Confederate States Army Casualties: Lists and Narrative Reports 1861–1865. Records Group 109. National Archives, Washington, D.C.

Converse, James L. Letters. Chicago Historical Society, IL.

Cook, John H. Memoir. State Historical Society of Wisconsin, Madison, WI.

Currier, Horace. Papers. Typescript. State Historical Society of Wisconsin, Madison, WI.

Daniel, John Warwick. Papers, No. 158, 5383, A-E. Alderman Library, University of Virginia, Charlottesville, VA.

Davis, William G. Letters. Second Wisconsin Infantry File. Library, Manassas National Battlefield Park, Manassas, VA.

Dawes, Rufus R. Papers. State Historical Society of Wisconsin, Madison, WI.

Dean, Elisha A. Diary. Typescript. Carl Parcher Russell Papers. State Historical Society of Wisconsin, Madison, WI.

Description of Battleflag, Fourth Virginia Infantry. Fourth Virginia Infantry File. Library, Antietam National Battlefield, Sharpsburg, MD.

Douglas, Henry Kyd. Papers. Special Collections. William R. Perkins Library, Duke University, Durham, N.C.

Doyle, Thomas S. "Memoir of Thomas S. Doyle, Lt., Co. E, 33rd Virginia Infantry." Library of Congress, Washington, D.C.

Dull, John P. Letters. Special Collections, Leyburn Library, Washington and Lee University, Lexington, VA.

Dunlap, Ferdinand J. Letters. Civil War Miscellaneous Collection. Archives, United States Army Military History Institute, Carlisle Barracks, PA.

Dunlop, Samuel. Letters. Roger Stavis Collection. *Civil War Times Illustrated* Collection. Archives, United States Army Military History Institute, Carlisle Barracks, PA.

Eleventh North Carolina Infantry File. Library, Gettysburg National Military Park, Gettysburg, PA.

Emerson, Horace. Letters. William L. Clements Library, University of Michigan, Ann Arbor, MI.

Ewell, Richard S. Papers, "War 1861–65 Box 3: E#62." The New-York Historical Society, New York.

Fairfax, Randolph. Letters. Typescript. Eleanor S. Brockenbrough Library, Museum of the Confederacy, Richmond, VA.

Fairfield, George. Papers. State Historical Society of Wisconsin, Madison, WI.

Fishburne, Clement D. Memoirs, No. 3569. Alderman Library, University of Virginia, Charlottesville, VA.

Flagg, Erwin H. Letters. State Historical Society of Wisconsin, Madison, WI.

Flanigan, Mark. Diary. Burton Historical Collection. Detroit Public Library, Detroit, MI.

Fuller, Caleb F. Papers. State Historical Society of Wisconsin, Madison, WI.

Fuller, Charles W. Letter. Archives, United States Army Military History Institute, Carlisle Barracks, PA.

Gallup, Andrew. Papers. State Historical Society of Wisconsin, Madison, WI.

Garibaldi, John. Letters. Typescript. Archives, Preston Library, Virginia Military Institute, Lexington, VA.

Garnett, Richard B. Papers. Eleanor S. Brockenbrough Library, Museum of the Confederacy, Richmond, VA.

Gettysburg Newspaper Clippings. Library, Gettysburg National Military Park, Gettysburg, PA.

Gibbon, John. Papers. Historical Society of Pennsylvania, Philadelphia, PA.

Giles, Emerson F. Papers. State Historical Society of Wisconsin, Madison, WI.

Gordon, George C. Papers. State Archives of Michigan, Lansing, MI.

Grabill, John H. "Diary of a Soldier of the Stonewall Brigade," *Shenandoah Herald,* January 8–15, 1922. Typescript copy in author's possession.

Gratton, Charles. "Some Reminiscences of Camp Life with Stonewall Jackson." *Civil War Times Illustrated* Collection. Archives, United States Army Military History Institute, Carlisle Barracks, PA.

Green, Sullivan D. Papers. Bentley Historical Library, University of Michigan, Ann Arbor, MI.

Green, Sullivan D. Camp Sketches. Bentley Historical Library, University of Michigan, Ann Arbor, MI.

Hanger, Michael Reid. Diary. Typescript. Fourth Virginia Infantry File. Library, Manassas National Battlefield Park, Manassas, VA.

Handy, Haywood, and Handy, W. D. Papers. Special Collections. William R. Perkins Library, Duke University, Durham, NC.

Harlow, George K. Letters. Virginia Historical Society, Richmond, VA.

Harman, John A. "Extracts from Letters of Major John A. Harman; Quarter Master of Jackson's Division, Valley District, Army of Northern Virginia." Typescript. Library, Fredericksburg-Spotsylvania National Military Park, Fredericksburg, VA.

Harman, William H. Letters. Augusta County Historical Society, Staunton, VA.

Harper, Kenton. Papers. Southern Historical Collection. Wilson Library, University of North Carolina, Chapel Hill, NC.

Haskell, Frank A. Letters. Typescript. Wisconsin History Commission Papers. State Historical Society of Wisconsin, Madison, WI.

Hemingway, Luther. Letter. Typescript. Bentley Historical Library, University of Michigan, Ann Arbor, MI.

Hileman, Daniel. Civil War Letters, 1861–64. Rockbridge Historical Society Collection. Special Collections, Leyburn Library, Washington and Lee University, Lexington, VA.

Hite, Ambrose. Papers. Earl Gregg Swem Library, The College of William and Mary, Williamsburg, VA.

Hite, John P. Diary. Handley Library, Winchester, VA.

Holford, Lyman C. Diary. Library of Congress, Washington, D.C.

Holliday, F. W. M. Papers. Special Collections. William R. Perkins Library, Duke University, Durham, NC.

Holloway, William R. Collection. Indiana Historical Society, Indianapolis, IN.

Hotchkiss, Jedediah. Papers. Library of Congress, Washington, D.C.

Howe, Albion Pratt. Papers. Typescript. Library, Fredericksburg-Spotsylvania National Military Park, Fredericksburg, VA.

Hubler, Simon. "Narrative of Simon Hubler, First Sergeant, late of Co. 'I' 143 Reg. Pa. Vol. Inf." Civil War Miscellaneous Collection. Archives, United States Army Military History Institute, Carlisle Barracks, PA.

Hughes, Robert H. "Report of Movements of the 2nd Wisconsin." State Historical Society of Wisconsin, Madison, WI.

Hull, John N. Letter. Special Collections. University Libraries, Virginia Tech University, Blacksburg, VA.

Huntley, Reuben. Papers. State Historical Society of Wisconsin, Madison, WI.

Jackson, Thomas J. Letter. Copy in Robert K. Krick Collection, Fredericksburg, VA.

Jackson, William N. Diary. Typescript. Indiana Historical Society, Indianapolis, IN.

Jessup, John C. Letters. Indiana Historical Society, Indianapolis, IN.

Jones, Francis B. Family Collection. Archives, Handley Library, Winchester, VA.

Jones, Frank B. "A Short Diary." Archives, Handley Library, Winchester, VA.

Jones, John Henry Boswell. "Liberty Hall Volunteers at 1st Manassas." Rockbridge Historical Society Manuscripts. Special Collections, Leyburn Library, Washington and Lee University, Lexington, VA.

July 1st: Railroad Cut Action File. Library, Gettysburg National Military Park, Gettysburg, PA.

Kearns, Watkins. Diary. Virginia Historical Society, Richmond, VA.

Kelly, Dennis P. "Location and Significance of the Action at Brawner's Farm, August 28, 1862." Library, Manassas National Battlefield Park, Manassas, VA.

Kerr, Mary Beirne Jones. Letter. Fifth Virginia Infantry File. Library, Manassas National Battlefield Park, Manassas, VA.

Ketner, William J. Papers. State Historical Society of Wisconsin, Madison, WI.

Key Family. Papers. Special Collections. University Libraries, Virginia Tech University, Blacksburg, VA.

Kinzer, William T. Diary. Typescript. Virginia Historical Society, Richmond, VA.

Kiracofe, John H. Papers. Special Collections. William R. Perkins Library, Duke University, Durham, NC.

Kite, Oliver Hazard Perry. Diary. Handley Library, Winchester, VA.

Krick, Robert K. Thirty-third Virginia Infantry File. Library, Fredericksburg-Spotsylvania National Military Park, Fredericksburg, VA.

Kurtz, George W. Papers. Southern Historical Collection. Wilson Library, University of North Carolina, Chapel Hill, NC.

Langhorne, James H. Letters and Diary. Virginia Historical Society, Richmond, VA.

Langworthy, Andrew J. "Reminiscences." State Historical Society of Wisconsin, Madison, WI.

Larke, Alured. Letters. State Historical Society of Wisconsin, Madison, WI.

Larsen, Peter. Papers. State Historical Society of Wisconsin, Madison, WI.

Lee, Edwin Gray. Papers. Virginia Historical Society, Richmond, VA.

Legate, George H. Letter. Typescript. Library, Fredericksburg-Spotsylvania National Military Park, Fredericksburg, VA.

Longhenry, Ludolph. "A Yankee Piper in Dixie." Seventh Wisconsin Infantry File. Library, Antietam National Battlefield, Sharpsburg, MD.

Lyle, John Newton. "Stonewall Jackson's Guard: The Washington College Company." Special Collections, Leyburn Library, Washington and Lee University, Lexington, VA.

MacIntosh, L. L. Letters. Typescript. Second Wisconsin Infantry File. Library, Antietam National Battlefield, Sharpsburg, MD.

Marsh, Henry C. Letters and Diary. Henry C. Marsh Collection. Indiana State Library, Indianapolis, IN.

McAllister, William Miller. Papers. Special Collections. William R. Perkins Library, Duke University, Durham, NC.

McCown, James L. Memoirs. Typescript. Ben Ritter Collection. Archives, Handley Library, Winchester, VA.

McCutchan, James B. Correspondence, 1860–1863. Rockbridge Historical Society Collection. Special Collections, Leyburn Library, Washington and Lee University, Lexington, VA.

McDowell, William George. Correspondence and Short Biographies. Special Collections, Leyburn Library, Washington and Lee University, Lexington, VA.

McFarland, Francis. Letter. Rockbridge Historical Society Collection. Special Collections, Leyburn Library, Washington and Lee University, Lexington, VA.

McGuffin Family Papers. No. 6732. Alderman Library, University of Virginia, Charlottesville.

McGuire, Hunter Holmes. Papers. Virginia Historical Society, Richmond, VA.

Mead, Sydney B. "A Journal of the Marches, Reconnaissances, Skirmishes and Battles of the Second Regiment of Wisconsin Volunteer Infantry, June 11, 1861–March 29, 1864." State Historical Society of Wisconsin, Madison, WI.

Meredith, Solomon. Letter to Oliver P. Morton, August 31, 1862. Frank C. Darlington Collection. Indiana Historical Society, Indianapolis, IN.

Meredith, Solomon. Papers. Archives, Indiana Historical Society, Indianapolis, IN.

Mitchell, George. Papers. Murphy Library, University of Wisconsin—La Crosse, La Crosse, WI.

Monteith, Andrew. Papers. State Historical Society of Wisconsin, Madison, WI.

Monteith, Robert. Papers. State Historical Society of Wisconsin, Madison, WI.

Mooney, George McCulloch. Memoir. Virginia Historical Society, Richmond, VA.

Moore, Amos. "Civil War Experiences." Library, Fredericksburg-Spotsylvania National Military Park, Fredericksburg, VA.

Moore, Samuel J. C. Papers. Southern Historical Collection. Wilson Library, University of North Carolina, Chapel Hill, NC.

Moore, William Roby. Civil War Letters and Reminiscences. Indiana Historical Society, Indianapolis, IN.

Morrison, Henry Ruffner. Papers. *Civil War Times Illustrated* Collection. Archives, United States Army Military History Institute, Carlisle Barracks, PA.

Morrow, Henry A. Diary, November 11, 1864–March 3, 1865. Morrow-Boniface Family Papers. Archives, United States Army Military History Institute, Carlisle Barracks, PA.

Murray, Julius A. Family Papers. State Historical Society of Wisconsin, Madison, WI.

Musser, John. Civil War Letters. Typescript. Ronald D. Boyer Collection. Archives, United States Army Military History Institute, Carlisle Barracks, PA.

Nadenbousch, John Quincy Adams. Papers. Special Collections. William R. Perkins Library, Duke University, Durham, NC.

Nasmith, Samuel J. Letters. State Historical Society of Wisconsin, Madison, WI.

Neff, John F. Papers. *Civil War Times Illustrated* Collection. Archives, United States Army Military History Institute, Carlisle Barracks, PA.

Nihiser, James M. Letter. Typescript. Library, Fredericksburg-Spotsylvania National Military Park, Fredericksburg, VA.

Nineteenth Indiana Infantry File. Library, Gettysburg National Military Park, Gettysburg, PA.

Nineteenth Indiana Regimental Correspondence. Indiana State Library, Indianapolis, IN.

Noble, Alfred. "A 'G.I.' View of the Civil War: *The Diary of Alfred Noble.*" Alfred Noble Papers. Bentley Historical Library, University of Michigan, Ann Arbor, MI.

Noble, William. Diary. Davee Library, University of Wisconsin—River Falls, River Falls, WI.

O'Brien, Michael. Papers. Typescript. Burton Historical Collection. Detroit Public Library, MI.

Odle, Elisha B. Papers. Typescript. Nineteenth Indiana Infantry File. Library, Antietam National Battlefield, Sharpsburg, MD.

Orders and Circulars Issued by the Army of the Potomac and the Army and Department of Northern Virginia, C.S.A. M921. National Archives, Washington, D.C.

Ordway, Benjamin P. Letter. State Historical Society of Wisconsin, Madison, WI.

Orr, William. Papers. Lilly Library, Indiana University, Bloomington, IN.

Parker, Orson. Letters. State Historical Society of Wisconsin, Madison, WI.

Patterson, Robert. "Personal Recollections of the Scenes and Incidents of the Battle of Antietam." Typescript. Henry C. Marsh Collection. Indiana State Library, Indianapolis, IN.

Paxton Family. Papers, No. 38-328-a. Alderman Library, University of Virginia, Charlottesville, VA.

Peck, Abel G. Letter. Typescript. Library, Fredericksburg-Spotsylvania National Military Park, Fredericksburg, VA.

Peck, Abel G. Letters. University Archives and Historical Collections. Main Library, Michigan State University, Lansing, MI.

Pendleton, William Nelson. Papers. Southern Historical Collection. Wilson Library, University of North Carolina, Chapel Hill, NC.

Perry, James M. Papers. State Historical Society of Wisconsin, Madison, WI.

Pohanka, Brian C. "Notes on Charles Sidney Winder (1829–1862)." Typescript. Private Collection, Brian C. Pohanka, Alexandria, VA.

Pollock, Thomas Gordon. Papers, 1838–1910, No. 8458. Alderman Library, University of Virginia, Charlottesville, VA.

Preston, James F. Letter. Library, Fredericksburg-Spotsylvania National Military Park, Fredericksburg, VA.

Quarles, Narcissus F. Papers. Fifth Virginia Infantry File. Library, Manassas National Battlefield Park, Manassas, VA.

Quiner, E. B. Correspondence of the Wisconsin Volunteers, 1861–1865. State Historical Society of Wisconsin, Madison, WI.

Racine *Advocate,* undated newspaper clippings. Second Wisconsin Infantry File. Library, Manassas National Battlefield Park, Manassas, VA.

Ramseur, Stephen D. Papers. North Carolina State Archives, Raleigh, NC.

"Regimental Flag of 33rd Virginia Inf." Library, Fredericksburg-Spotsylvania National Military Park, Fredericksburg, VA.

Ritter, Ben. "Battle Flag with Record." Library, Fredericksburg-Spotsylvania National Military Park, Fredericksburg, VA.

Robbie, Member of the Stonewall Brigade. Letter. Thirty-third Virginia Infantry File. Library, Antietam National Battlefield, Sharpsburg, MD.

Roberts, Jesse M. Letters. Typescript. State Historical Society of Wisconsin, Madison, WI.

Robinson, David Tobias. Confederate Company List. Special Collections. University Libraries, Virginia Tech University, Blacksburg, VA.

Rollins, Nathaniel. Papers. State Historical Society of Wisconsin, Madison, WI.

Rood, Amos D. Memoir. Typescript. State Historical Society of Wisconsin, Madison, WI.

Root, Roswell L. Letter, August 23, 1863. Gregory A. Coco Collection, Harrisburg Civil War Round Table Collection. Archives, United States Army Military History Institute, Carlisle Barracks, PA.

Ryder, John E. Letters. Ryder Family Papers. Bentley Historical Library, University of Michigan, Ann Arbor, MI.

Saunders, Ainsworth. Letter. Davee Library, University of Wisconsin—River Falls, River Falls, WI.

Second Virginia Infantry File. Library, Gettysburg National Military Park, Gettysburg, PA.

Seventh Wisconsin Infantry File. Library, Gettysburg National Military Park, Gettysburg, PA.

Shaner, Joseph F. Correspondence, 1861–1865. Special Collections, Leyburn Library, Washington and Lee University, Lexington, VA.

Shanklin, Henry S. Letters. Virginia State Library, Richmond, VA.

Shattuck, Lucius L. Letters. Typescript. Bentley Historical Library, University of Michigan, Ann Arbor, MI.

Shuler, Michael. Diary. Library of Congress, Washington, D.C.

Slagle, Jacob F. Letter. Civil War Miscellaneous Collection. Archives, United States Army Military History Institute, Carlisle Barracks, PA.

Slifer, George W. Letters. Typescript. Library, Fredericksburg-Spotsylvania National Military Park, Fredericksburg, VA.

Smiley, Thomas M. Correspondence. Smiley Family Papers, No. 1807. Alderman Library, University of Virginia, Charlottesville, VA.

Smith, Edward B. Papers, No. 6722. Alderman Library, University of Virginia, Charlottesville, VA.

Smith, James Power. Correspondence. Eleanor S. Brockenbrough Library, Museum of the Confederacy, Richmond, VA.

Smith, Mary Kelly. Papers. North Carolina State Archives, Raleigh, NC.

Speed, William, and Speed, Frederick. Papers, 1857–1874. Schoff Civil War Collection: Soldiers' Letters. William L. Clements Library, University of Michigan, Ann Arbor, MI.

Sperry, Kate S., Jr. "'Surrender! Never Surrender!': The Diary of a Confederate Girl." Archives, Handley Library, Winchester, VA.

St. Clair, John Weslie. Papers. State Historical Society of Wisconsin, Madison, WI.

Starbuck, Julietta. Civil War Letters. Indiana Historical Society, Indianapolis, IN.

Strickler, G. B., and Jones, J. H. B. Diary and Record Book of Co. I, 4th Va. Infantry, Stonewall Brigade ("Liberty Hall Volunteers" unit), 1862–1864. Alderman Library, University of Virginia, Charlottesville, VA.

Strong, William E. Papers. State Historical Society of Wisconsin, Madison, WI.

Twenty-fourth Michigan Infantry File. Library, Gettysburg National Military Park, Gettysburg, PA.

Varner, Andrew W. "Journal." Alderman Library, University of Virginia, Charlottesville, VA.

Wadsworth, James W. Papers. Library of Congress, Washington, D.C.

Walker, James A. Papers. Southern Historical Collection. Wilson Library, University of North Carolina, Chapel Hill, NC.

Wallace, Elmer D. Papers. Bentley Historical Library, University of Michigan, Ann Arbor, MI.

Walton, David H. Letter. Typescript copy. Library, Manassas National Battlefield Park, Manassas, VA.

Ward, E. B. Papers. Detroit Public Library, MI.

Watrous, Jerome. Papers. State Historical Society of Wisconsin, Madison, WI.

Weirman, B. B. Letters. Typescript. Library, Fredericksburg-Spotsylvania National Military Park, Fredericksburg, VA.

Welsh Family Papers, 1817–1886. Special Collections, Leyburn Library, Washington and Lee University, Lexington, VA.

Welsh, John P. Letters. Virginia State Library, Richmond, VA.

White, Hugh A. Correspondence. Eleanor S. Brockenbrough Library, Museum of the Confederacy, Richmond, Va.

White, James Jones. Letters. Southern Historical Collection. Wilson Library, University of North Carolina, Chapel Hill, NC.

Whitman, William R. Letters. Alice Ellsworth Collection. Bentley Historical Library, University of Michigan, Ann Arbor, MI.

Wight, Charles Copland. Memoir. Wight Family Papers. Virginia Historical Society, Richmond, VA.

Winder, Charles S. Diary. Maryland Historical Society, Baltimore, MD.

Winfield, John Q. Papers. Southern Historical Collection. Wilson Library, University of North Carolina, Chapel Hill, NC.

Winslow, Loring B. F. Letters. State Historical Society of Wisconsin, Madison, WI.

Winston, Francis D. Papers. North Carolina State Archives, Raleigh, NC.

Young, Henry F. Papers. State Historical Society of Wisconsin, Madison, WI.

NEWSPAPERS

Detroit *Advertiser and Tribune*
Detroit *Free Press*
Lexington *Gazette*
Lexington *Gazette and Citizen*
Loudoun *Times Mirror*

Milwaukee *Sentinel*
Milwaukee *Sunday Telegraph*
Milwaukee *Telegraph*
Muncie *Press*
National Tribune
Racine *Advocate*
Richmond *Dispatch*
Richmond *Enquirer*
Richmond *Sentinel*
Richmond *Times-Dispatch*
Rockbridge County News
Shenandoah Herald
Staunton *Spectator*
Staunton *Spectator and Vindicator*
Staunton *Vindicator*
Winchester *Evening Star*

PUBLISHED SOURCES

Albaugh, William A. III, and Simmons, Edward N. *Confederate Arms.* Reprint, Wilmington, NC: Broadfoot Publishing Company, 1993.

Allan, William. *History of the Campaign of Gen. T. J. (Stonewall) Jackson in the Shenandoah Valley of Virginia from November 4, 1861, to June 17, 1862.* Reprint, Dayton, OH: Morningside House, 1987.

Bandy, Ken, and Freeland, Florence, eds. *The Gettysburg Papers.* Two volumes. Dayton, OH: Press of Morningside Bookshop, 1978.

Baylor, George. *Bull Run to Bull Run: Or, Four Years in the Army of Northern Virginia.* Richmond: B. F. Johnson Publishing Company, 1900.

Bean, W. G. "A House Divided: The Civil War Letters of a Virginia Family." *Virginia Magazine of History and Biography,* Vol. 59, No. 4 (October 1951).

———. *The Liberty Hall Volunteers: Stonewall's College Boys.* Charlottesville: University Press of Virginia, 1964.

———. *Stonewall's Man: Sandie Pendleton.* Reprint, Wilmington, NC: Broadfoot Publishing Company, 1987.

Bean, W. G., ed. "The Valley Campaign of 1862 as Revealed in Letters of Sandie Pendleton." *Virginia Magazine of History and Biography,* Vol. 78, No. 3 (July 1970).

Beaudot, William J. K. "Francis Asbury Wallar: A Medal of Honor at Gettysburg." *The Gettysburg Magazine,* No. 4 (January 1991).

Beaudot, William J. K., and Herdegen, Lance J., eds. *An Irishman in the Iron Brigade: The Civil War Memoirs of James P. Sullivan, Sergt., Company K, 6th Wisconsin Volunteers.* New York: Fordham University Press, 1993.

Beecham, R. K. *Gettysburg: The Pivotal Battle of the Civil War.* Chicago: A. C. McClurg, 1911.

Blackford, W. W. *War Years with Jeb Stuart.* New York: Charles Scribner's Sons, 1946.

Bosang, James N. *Memoirs of a Pulaski Veteran.* Berryville, VA: Virginia Book Co., 1930.

Brock, R. A., ed. *The Appomattox Roster*. New York: Antiquarian Press, Ltd., 1962.

Buell, Augustus. *The Cannoneer: Recollections of Service in the Army of the Potomac*. Washington, D.C.: The National Tribune, 1897.

Busey, John W., and Martin, David G. *Regimental Strengths at Gettysburg*. Baltimore: Gateway Press, 1982.

Byrne, Frank L., and Weaver, Andrew T. *Haskell of Gettysburg: His Life and Civil War Papers*. Madison: State Historical Society of Wisconsin, 1970.

Caldwell, Willie Walker. *Stonewall Jim: A Biography of General James A. Walker, C.S.A.* Elliston, VA: Northcross House, 1990.

Cartmell, T. K. *Shenandoah Valley Pioneers and Their Descendants: A History of Frederick County, Virginia*. Reprint, Berryville, VA: Chesapeake Book Company, 1963.

Casler, John O. *Four Years in the Stonewall Brigade*. Reprint, Dayton, OH: Press of Morningside Bookshop, 1971.

Chamberlin, Thomas. *History of the One Hundred and Fiftieth Regiment Pennsylvania Volunteers, Second Regiment, Bucktail Brigade*. Reprint, Baltimore: Butternut and Blue, 1986.

Cheek, Philip, and Pointon, Mair. *History of the Sauk County Riflemen*. Reprint, Gaithersburg, MD: Butternut Press, 1984.

Chew, Roger P. *Military Operations in Jefferson County Virginia (and West VA)*. Charlestown, WV: Farmers Advocate Print, 1911.

Clark, Walter. *Histories of the Several Regiments and Battalions from North Carolina in the Great War 1861–'65*. Five volumes. Reprint, Wendell, NC: Broadfoot's Bookmark, 1982.

Clemens, Tom. "'Black Hats' Off to the Original 'Iron Brigade.'" *Columbiad*, Vol. 1, No. 1 (Spring 1997).

Cockrell, Monroe F., ed. *Gunner with Stonewall: Reminiscences of William Thomas Poague*. Jackson, TN: McCowat-Mercer Press, 1957.

Coco, Gregory A. *The Civil War Infantryman in Camp, on the March, and in Battle*. Gettysburg, PA: Thomas Publications, 1996.

Coddington, Edwin B. *The Gettysburg Campaign: A Study in Command*. New York: Charles Scribner's Sons, 1968.

Colt, Margaretta Barton. *Defend the Valley: A Shenandoah Family in the Civil War*. New York: Orion Books, 1994.

The Confederate Veteran Magazine. Forty Volumes. Reprint, Wilmington, NC: Broadfoot Publishing Company, 1987–1988.

Cooling, Benjamin Franklin. *Symbol, Sword, and Shield: Defending Washington During the Civil War*. Shippensburg, PA: White Mane Publishing Company, 1991.

Crites, Susan. *Glimpses of the Civil War in the Lower Shenandoah Valley, 1861–1862*. Martinsburg, WV: Butternut Publications, 1996.

Curtis, O. B. *History of the Twenty-fourth Michigan of the Iron Brigade*. Reprint, Gaithersburg, MD: Butternut Press, 1984.

Davis, William C., ed. *The Confederate General*. Six volumes. Gettysburg, PA: The National Historical Society, 1991.

Dawes, Rufus R. *Service with the Sixth Wisconsin Volunteers*. Reprint, Dayton, OH: Press of Morningside Bookshop, 1991.

Douglas, Henry Kyd. *I Rode with Stonewall*. Chapel Hill: University of North Carolina Press, 1940.

Driver, Robert J., Jr. *The 1st and 2nd Rockbridge Artillery*. Lynchburg, VA: H. E. Howard, 1987.

———. *Lexington and Rockbridge County in the Civil War*. Lynchburg, VA: H. E. Howard, 1989.

Dunn, Craig L. *Iron Men, Iron Will: The Nineteenth Indiana Regiment of the Iron Brigade*. Indianapolis: Guild Press of Indiana, 1995.

Ecelbarger, Gary L. *"We Are in for It!": The First Battle of Kernstown, March 23, 1862*. Shippensburg, PA: White Mane Publishing Company, 1997.

Echoes from the Marches of the Famous Iron Brigade. Reprint, Gaithersburg, MD: Ron R. Van Sickle Military Books, 1988.

Felton, Silas. "The Iron Brigade Battery at Gettysburg." *The Gettysburg Magazine*, No. 11 (July 1994).

Fonerden, C. A. *A Brief History of the Military Career of Carpenter's Battery*. New Market, VA: Henkel & Company, Printers, 1911.

Fox, William F. *Regimental Losses in the American Civil War, 1861–1865*. Reprint, Dayton, OH: Press of Morningside Bookshop, 1985.

Frye, Dennis E. *2nd Virginia Infantry*. Lynchburg, VA: H. E. Howard, 1984.

Gaff, Alan D. *Brave Men's Tears: The Iron Brigade at Brawner Farm*. Dayton, OH: Morningside House, 1988.

———. "'Here Was Made Out Our Last and Hopeless Stand': The 'Lost' Gettysburg Reports of the Nineteenth Indiana." *The Gettysburg Magazine*, No. 2 (January 1990).

———. *If This Is War: A History of the Campaign of Bull's Run by the Wisconsin Regiment Thereafter Known as the Ragged Ass Second*. Dayton, OH: Morningside House, 1991.

———. *On Many a Bloody Field: Four Years in the Iron Brigade*. Bloomington and Indianapolis: Indiana University Press, 1996.

Gallagher, Gary W., ed. *Antietam: Essays on the 1862 Maryland Campaign*. Kent, Ohio, and London, England: Kent State University Press, 1989.

———. *The Third Day at Gettysburg and Beyond*. Chapel Hill and London: University of North Carolina Press, 1994.

Gibbon, John. *Personal Recollections of the Civil War*. Reprint, Dayton, OH: Press of Morningside Bookshop, 1978.

Gladstone, William. "A Flag for the Iron Brigade," *Military Images*, Vol. 9, No. 1 (July/August 1987).

Grimsley, Mark. *The Hard Hand of War: Union Military Policy Toward Southern Civilians, 1861–1865*. New York: Cambridge University Press, 1995.

Grunder, Charles S., and Beck, Brandon H. *The Second Battle of Winchester, June 12–15, 1863*. Lynchburg, VA: H. E. Howard, 1989.

Hadden, R. Lee. "The Deadly Embrace: The Meeting of the Twenty-fourth Regiment, Michigan Infantry and the Twenty-sixth Regiment of North Carolina Troops at McPherson's Woods, Gettysburg, Pennsylvania, July 1, 1863." *The Gettysburg Magazine*, No. 5 (July 1991).

Harden, Samuel. *Those I Have Met, or Boys in Blue*. Reprint, Evansville, IN: Unigraphic, 1970.

Harney, Richard J. *History of Winnebago County Wisconsin, and Early History of the Northwest*. Oshkosh, WI: Allen & Hicks, Book Printers, 1880.

Hartwig, D. Scott. "The Defense of McPherson's Ridge." *Gettysburg: Historical Articles of Lasting Interest*, No. 1 (July 1989).

———. "Guts and Good Leadership: The Action at the Railroad Cut, July 1, 1863." *Gettysburg: Historical Articles of Lasting Interest*, No. 1 (July 1989).

Hawkins, Norma Fuller. "Sergeant-Major Blanchard at Gettysburg." *Indiana Magazine of History*, Vol. 34, No. 2 (June 1938).

Hennessy, John. *The First Battle of Manassas: An End to Innocence, July 18–21, 1861*. Lynchburg, VA: H. E. Howard, 1989.

———. *Return to Bull Run: The Campaign and Battle of Second Manassas*. New York: Simon & Schuster, 1993.

Herdegen, Lance J. "The Lieutenant Who Arrested a General." *The Gettysburg Magazine*, No. 4 (January 1991).

———. *The Men Stood Like Iron: How the Iron Brigade Won Its Name*. Bloomington and Indianapolis: Indiana University Press, 1997.

Herdegen, Lance J., and Beaudot, William J. K. *In the Bloody Railroad Cut at Gettysburg*. Dayton, OH: Morningside House, 1990.

Herdegen, Lance J., and Beaudot, William J. K., eds. "With the Iron Brigade Guard at Gettysburg." *Gettysburg: Historical Articles of Lasting Interest*. No. 1 (July 1989).

Holsworth, Jerry W. "Uncommon Valor: Hood's Texas Brigade in the Maryland Campaign." *Blue & Gray Magazine*, Vol. 13, No. 6 (August 1996).

Howard, McHenry. *Recollections of a Maryland Confederate Soldier and Staff Officer Under Johnston, Jackson and Lee*. Reprint, Dayton, OH: Press of Morningside Bookshop, 1975.

Jackson, Mary Anna. *Memoirs of Stonewall Jackson*. Reprint, Dayton, OH: Press of Morningside Bookshop, 1976.

Johnson, John Lipscomb. *The University Memorial: Biographical Sketches of Alumni of the University of Virginia Who Fell in the Confederate War*. Baltimore: Turnbull Brothers, 1871.

Johnson, Robert Underwood, and Buel, Clarence Clough, eds. *Battles and Leaders of the Civil War*. Four volumes. Reprint, New York and London: Thomas Yoseloff, 1956.

Kleese, Richard B. *Shenandoah County in the Civil War: The Turbulent Years*. Lynchburg, VA: H. E. Howard, 1992.

Krick, Robert K. *Conquering the Valley: Stonewall Jackson at Port Republic*. New York: William Morrow, 1996.

———. *Lee's Colonels: A Biographical Register of the Field Officers of the Army of Northern Virginia*. Dayton, OH: Press of Morningside Bookshop, 1979.

———. *Stonewall Jackson at Cedar Mountain*. Chapel Hill and London: University of North Carolina Press, 1990.

Kurtz, Lucy Fitzhugh, and Ritter, Benny. *A Roster of Confederate Soldiers Buried in Stonewall Cemetery Winchester, Virginia*. Winchester, VA: Farmers and Merchants National Bank, 1984.

Ladd, David L., and Audrey J., eds. *The Bachelder Papers: Gettysburg in Their Own Words*. Three volumes. Dayton, OH: Morningside House, 1994–1995.

Lavery, Dennis S., and Jordon, Mark H. *Iron Brigade General: John Gibbon, A Rebel in Blue.* Westport, CT, and London, England: Greenwood Press, 1993.

Levin, Alexandra Lee. *"This Awful Drama": General Edwin Gray Lee, C.S.A., and His Family.* New York: Vantage Press, 1987.

Long, Andrew Davidson. *Stonewall's "Foot Cavalryman."* Austin, TX: Walter E. Long, 1965.

Long, E. B. *The Civil War Day by Day: An Almanac, 1861–1865.* Garden City: Doubleday, 1971.

Long, Roger. "A Mississippian in the Railroad Cut." *The Gettysburg Magazine,* No. 4 (January 1991).

Lord, Walter, ed. *The Fremantle Diary: Being the Journal of Lieutenant Colonel James Arthur Lyon Fremantle, Coldstream Guards, on his Three Months in the Southern States.* Boston: Little, Brown, 1954.

Love, William DeLoss. *Wisconsin in the War of the Rebellion: A History of All Regiments and Batteries.* Chicago: Church and Goodman, Publishers, 1866.

Madaus, Howard Michael. "Into the Fray: The Flags of the Iron Brigade, 1861–1865." *Wisconsin Magazine of History,* Vol. 69, No. 1 (Autumn 1985).

Mann, B. David. *They Were Heard From: VMI Alumni in the Civil War.* Lexington, VA: News-Gazette Custom Printing Department, 1986.

Martin, David G. *Gettysburg July 1.* Conshohocken, PA: Combined Books, 1995.

Matter, William D. *If It Takes All Summer: The Battle of Spotsylvania.* Chapel Hill and London: University of North Carolina Press, 1988.

McAllister, J. Gray. *Sketch of Captain Thompson McAllister, Co. A, 27th Virginia Regiment.* Petersburg, VA: Penn & Owen, Printers and Binders, 1896.

McDonald, Archie P., ed. *Make Me a Map of the Valley: The Civil War Journal of Stonewall Jackson's Topographer.* Dallas: Southern Methodist University Press, 1973.

McDonald, Cornelia Peake. *A Woman's Civil War: A Diary, with Reminiscences of the War, from March 1862.* Edited by Minrose C. Gwin. Madison: University of Wisconsin Press, 1992.

McKim, Randolph H. *A Soldier's Recollections: Leaves from the Diary of a Young Confederate.* Alexandria, VA: Time-Life Books, 1984.

McLean, James L., Jr. *Cutler's Brigade at Gettysburg.* Baltimore: Butternut and Blue, 1994.

McMullen, Glenn L., ed. *A Surgeon with Stonewall Jackson: The Civil War Letters of Dr. Harvey Black.* Baltimore: Butternut and Blue, 1995.

McPherson, James M. *For Cause and Comrades: Why Men Fought in the Civil War.* New York and Oxford: Oxford University Press, 1997.

Merrill, Catherine. *The Soldier of Indiana in the War for the Union.* Two volumes. Indianapolis: Merrill and Company, 1866–1869.

Miller, J. Michael. "Perrin's Brigade on July 1, 1863." *The Gettysburg Magazine,* No. 13 (July 1995).

Moore, Edward A. *The Story of a Cannoneer Under Stonewall Jackson.* Reprint, Freeport, NY: Books for Libraries Press, 1971.

Murfin, James V. *The Gleam of Bayonets: The Battle of Antietam and the Maryland Campaign of 1862.* New York and London: Thomas Yoseloff, 1968.

Nevins, Allan, ed. *A Diary of Battle: The Personal Journals of Colonel Charles S.*

Wainwright, 1861–1865. Reprint, Gettysburg, PA: Stan Clark Military Books, n.d.

Nolan, Alan T. *The Iron Brigade: A Military History*. New York: Macmillan, 1961.

Official Army Register of the Volunteer Force of the United States Army for the Years 1861, '62, '63, '64, '65. Washington, D.C.: Adjutant General's Office, 1867.

Opie, John N. *A Rebel Cavalryman with Lee Stuart and Jackson*. Dayton, OH: Press of Morningside Bookshop, 1972.

Otis, George H. *The Second Wisconsin Infantry*. Reprint, Dayton, OH: Press of Morningside Bookshop, 1984.

Paxton, John Gallatin, ed. *The Civil War Letters of General Frank "Bull" Paxton, CSA, a Lieutenant of Lee and Jackson*. Hillsboro, TX: Hill Junior College Press, 1978.

Pfanz, Harry W. *Gettysburg: Culp's Hill and Cemetery Hill*. Chapel Hill and London: University of North Carolina Press, 1993.

Phillips, Edward H. *The Lower Shenandoah Valley in the Civil War: The Impact of War Upon the Civilian Population and Upon Civil Institutions*. Lynchburg, VA: H. E. Howard, 1993.

Quarles, Garland R. *Occupied Winchester, 1861–1865*. Winchester, VA: Farmers & Merchants National Bank, 1976.

Rankin, Thomas M. *Stonewall Jackson's Romney Campaign January 1–February 20, 1862*. Lynchburg, VA: H. E. Howard, 1994.

Record of Service of Michigan Volunteers in the Civil War, 1861–1865: Twenty-fourth Michigan, Volume 24. Reprint, Detroit: Detroit Book Press, 1996.

Reidenbaugh, Lowell. *33rd Virginia Infantry*. Lynchburg, VA: H. E. Howard, 1987.

———. *27th Virginia Infantry*. Lynchburg, VA: H. E. Howard, 1993.

Reid-Green, Marcia, ed. *Letters Home: Henry Matrau of the Iron Brigade*. Lincoln and London: University of Nebraska Press, 1993.

Report of the Adjutant General of the State of Indiana. Four volumes. Indianapolis: W. R. Holloway, State Printer, 1865.

Rhea, Gordon C. *The Battle of the Wilderness, May 5–6, 1864*. Baton Rouge and London: Louisiana State University Press, 1994.

———. *The Battles for Spotsylvania Court House and the Road to Yellow Tavern, May 7–12, 1864*. Baton Rouge and London: Louisiana State University Press, 1997.

Robertson, James I. Jr., ed. *The Civil War Letters of General Robert McAllister*. New Brunswick, NJ: Rutgers University Press, 1965.

———. *4th Virginia Infantry*. Lynchburg, VA: H. E. Howard, 1982.

———. *The Stonewall Brigade*. Baton Rouge: Louisiana State University Press, 1963.

———. *Stonewall Jackson: The Man, the Soldier, the Legend*. New York: Macmillan, 1997.

Robson, John S. *How a One-Legged Rebel Lives: Reminiscences of the Civil War*. Reprint, Gaithersburg, MD: Butternut Press, 1984.

Rosentreter, Roger L. "Those Damned Black Hats: The Twenty-fourth Michigan at Gettysburg." *Michigan History Magazine,* July/August 1991.

Ross, Sam. *The Empty Sleeve: A Biography of Lucius Fairchild.* Madison: State Historical Society of Wisconsin, 1964.

Roster of Wisconsin Volunteers, War of the Rebellion, 1861–1865. Two volumes. Madison: Democrat Printing Company, State Printers, 1886.

Sawyer, Franklin. *A Military History of the 8th Regiment Ohio Vol. Inf'y: Its Battles, Marches and Army Movements.* Cleveland, OH: Fairbanks & Co. Printers, 1881.

Sears, Stephen W. *Chancellorsville.* Boston and New York: Houghton Mifflin, 1996.

———. *Landscape Turned Red: The Battle of Antietam.* New Haven and New York: Ticknor & Fields, 1983.

Shields, Randolph Tucker, Jr. "Recollections of a Liberty Hall Volunteer." *Rockbridge Historical Society Proceedings,* Vol. 9. (1975).

Shue, Richard S. *Morning at Willoughby Run, July 1, 1863.* Gettysburg, PA: Thomas Publications, 1995.

Sketches of War History, 1861–1865: Papers Prepared for the Ohio Commandery of the Military Order of the Loyal Legion of the United States. Nine volumes. Reprint, Wilmington, NC: Broadfoot Publishing Company, 1991–93.

Slaughter, Philip. *A Sketch of the Life of Randolph Fairfax.* Reprint, Falls Church, VA: Confederate Printers, 1984.

Smith, Donald L. *The Twenty-fourth Michigan of the Iron Brigade.* Harrisburg, PA: Stackpole Company, 1962.

Smith, James Power. *With Stonewall Jackson in the Army of Northern Virginia.* Reprint, Gaithersburg, MD: Zullo and Van Sickle Books, 1982.

Southern Historical Society Papers. Fifty-two volumes. Reprint, Wilmington, NC: Broadfoot Publishing Company—Morningside Bookshop, 1990–1992.

Stevenson, David. *Indiana's Roll of Honor.* Indianapolis: David Stevenson, 1864.

Storch, Marc, and Storch, Beth. "'What a Deadly Trap We Were In': Archer's Brigade on July 1, 1863." *The Gettysburg Magazine,* No. 6 (January 1992).

Supplement to the Official Records of the Union and Confederate Armies. Fifty-eight volumes. Wilmington, NC: Broadfoot Publishing Company, 1994–1997.

Sword, Wiley. "An Iron Brigade Captain's Revolver in the Fight on McPherson's Ridge." *The Gettysburg Magazine,* No. 7 (July 1992).

Tanner, Robert G. *Stonewall in the Valley: Thomas J. "Stonewall" Jackson's Shenandoah Valley Campaign, Spring 1862.* Mechanicsburg, PA: Stackpole Books, 1996.

Taylor, Richard. *Destruction and Reconstruction: Personal Experiences of the Late War.* Reprint, New York: Longmans, Green and Co., 1955.

Thomas, Henry W. *History of the Doles-Cook Brigade Army of Northern Virginia, C.S.A.* Reprint, Dayton, OH: Press of Morningside Bookshop, 1981.

Trudeau, Noah Andre. *Bloody Roads South: The Wilderness to Cold Harbor, May–June 1864.* Boston: Little, Brown, 1989.

Turner, Ann, ed. *A Chronology of Indiana in the Civil War.* Indianapolis: Indiana Civil War Centennial Commission, 1965.

Turner, Charles W., ed. *My Dear Emma: (War Letters of Col. James K. Edmondson, 1861–1865).* Verona, VA: McClure Printing Company, 1978.

———. *Old Zeus: Life and Letters (1860–'62) of James J. White*. Verona, VA: McClure Printing Company, 1983.

———. *Ted Barclay, Liberty Hall Volunteers: Letters from the Stonewall Brigade (1861–1864)*. Natural Bridge Station, VA: Rockbridge Publishing Company, 1992.

Waddell, J. A. *Annals of Augusta County, Virginia, from 1726 to 1871*. Staunton, VA: C. Russell Caldwell, Publisher, 1902.

Wallace, Lee A., Jr. *5th Virginia Infantry*. Lynchburg, VA: H. E. Howard, 1988.

———. *A Guide to Virginia Military Organizations, 1861–1865*. Lynchburg, VA: H. E. Howard, 1986.

Warner, Ezra J. *Generals in Blue: Lives of the Union Commanders*. Baton Rouge and London: Louisiana State University Press, 1981.

———. *Generals in Gray: Lives of the Confederate Commanders*. Baton Rouge: Louisiana State University Press, 1970.

The War of the Rebellion: A Compilation of the Official Records of the Union and Confederate Armies. 128 volumes. Washington, D.C.: Government Printing office, 1880–1902.

War Papers: Being Papers Read Before the Commandery of the State of Wisconsin, Military Order of the Loyal Legion of the United States. Four volumes. Reprint, Wilmington, NC: Broadfoot Publishing Company, 1993.

Wayland, John W. *A History of Rockingham County, Virginia*. Dayton, VA: Ruebush-Elkins Company, 1912.

———. *A History of Shenandoah County, Virginia*. Strasburg, VA: Shenandoah Publishing House, 1927.

———. *Stonewall Jackson's Way: Route, Method, Achievement*. Reprint, Dayton, OH: Press of Morningside Bookshop, 1984.

Wert, Jeffry D. *From Winchester to Cedar Creek: The Shenandoah Campaign of 1864*. Carlisle, PA: South Mountain Press, 1987.

———. *General James Longstreet: The Confederacy's Most Controversial Soldier*. New York: Simon & Schuster, 1993.

———. "The Valley Campaign of 1862." Two parts, *Virginia Cavalcade*, Vol. 34, No. 4/Vol. 35, No. 1 (Spring/Summer 1985).

White, William S. *Sketches of the Life of Captain Hugh A. White of the Stonewall Brigade*. Columbia, SC: South Carolinian Steam Press, 1864.

Whitehouse, Hugh L., ed. *Letters from the Iron Brigade: George Washington Patridge, Jr., 1839–1863, Civil War Letters to His Sister*. Indianapolis: Guild Press of Indiana, 1994.

Wiley, Bell Irvin. *The Life of Billy Yank: The Common Soldier of the Union*. Indianapolis and New York: Bobbs-Merrill, 1952.

———. *The Life of Johnny Reb: The Common Soldier of the Confederacy*. Indianapolis and New York: Bobbs-Merrill, 1943.

Williams, Edward B., ed. *Rebel Brothers: The Civil War Letters of the Truehearts*. College Station: Texas A & M University Press, 1995.

Wilson, Mindwell Crampton, ed. *Indiana Battle Flags*. Indianapolis: Indiana Battle Flag Commission, 1929.

Woodhead, Henry, ed. *Echoes of Glory: Arms and Equipment of the Confederacy*. Alexandria, VA: Time-Life Books, 1991.

————. *Echoes of Glory: Arms and Equipment of the Union.* Alexandria, VA: Time-Life Books, 1991.

Worsham, John H. *One of Jackson's Foot Cavalry.* Edited by James I. Robertson, Jr. Reprint, Jackson, TN: McCowat-Mercer Press, 1964.

Zeitlin, Richard H. "The Flags of the Iron Brigade, 1863–1918." *Wisconsin Magazine of History,* Vol. 69, No. 1 (Autumn 1985).

INDEX